The State and the Stork

The State and the Stork

The Population Debate and Policy Making in US History

DEREK S. HOFF

THE UNIVERSITY OF CHICAGO PRESS   CHICAGO AND LONDON

DEREK S. HOFF is an associate professor of history at Kansas State University. He is also coauthor, with John Fliter, of *Fighting Foreclosure: The* Blaisdell *Decision, the Contract Clause, and the Great Depression.*

The University of Chicago Press, Chicago 60637
The University of Chicago Press, Ltd., London

Printed in the United States of America
21 20 19 18 17 16 15 14 13 12   1 2 3 4 5

ISBN-13: 978-0-226-34762-2 (cloth)
ISBN-13: 978-0-226-34765-3 (e-book)
ISBN-10: 0-226-34762-1 (cloth)
ISBN-10: 0-226-34765-6 (e-book)

Portions of chapter 7 appeared in an earlier version as "'Kick That Population Commission in the Ass': Richard Nixon, the Commission on Population Growth and the American Future, and the Defusing of the Population Bomb," *Journal of Policy History* 22 (January 2010): 23–63.

Library of Congress Cataloging-in-Publication Data

Hoff, Derek S.
The state and the stork : the population debate and policy making in US history / Derek S. Hoff.
pages. cm.
Includes bibliographical references and index.
ISBN-13: 978-0-226-34762-2 (cloth: alkaline paper)
ISBN-10: 0-226-34762-1 (cloth: alkaline paper)
ISBN-13: 978-0-226-34765-3 (e-book)
ISBN-10: 0-226-34765-6 (e-book)
1. United States—Population policy. I. Title
HB3505.H64 2012
363.90973—dc23

2012001903

♾ This paper meets the requirements of ANSI/NISO Z39.48-1992 (Permanence of Paper).

TO THE MEMORY OF ISAAC STARR, AND TO JEANINE

Contents

Acknowledgments

This book would not exist had my mom not had a friend in graduate school in the early 1960s who was interested in American population issues long before the zero population movement rose to prominence at the end of that decade. A Yale biologist who teaches a class on population, Bob Wyman became a friend of mine as well, and I arrived at college in the early 1990s curious about why population growth seemed off the table for serious national discussion when, just a generation earlier, millions of Americans had cared passionately about its perceived social, economic, and environmental hazards. I began graduate school with the inchoate idea of researching this question, and I am grateful that Donald Critchlow (who had just published his fine history of family planning policy) struck up a correspondence with a new Ph.D. student and encouraged me to write a broad study of American population debates rather than another book on eugenics. A couple of my chapter titles come directly from an ancient e-mail from Don.

I had no idea what I was getting myself into, but luckily my advisor in the Corcoran Department of History at the University of Virginia, Olivier Zunz, stresses a "big tent" approach to the study of history, and luckily I had magnificent mentors to guide me through a sprawling topic. John James patiently brought me to up to speed on modern economic theory, and our meetings in the Colonnade Club were some of my favorite moments in graduate school. Charles McCurdy provided me ample access to his encyclopedic mind and pushed me to turn a jumbled mess into a coherent study. Brian Balogh is a tough but charitable critic who taught me that historians should gladly participate in public debates. Professor Zunz provided indefatigable support. His contributions to this project and to my career are too numerous to fully describe, but I thank him for the countless hours that he spent rereading and discussing grant applications and chapters, for providing me with frequent and interesting employment, and for instilling in me a refusal to accept mediocrity, an attention to detail, and a taste for scotch. My frequent visits to Chez Zunz were always a welcome and calming respite, and Christine Zunz provided not only friendship but also the best meals in Charlottesville.

It takes a small city to raise a book. At Carleton College, Diethelm Prowe first ignited my passion for history, and, after I passed the test of ignoring three warnings from him about the job market, encouraged me to make a living doing what I love most. I could not have asked for a better M.A. advisor than James Mohr, who trained me thoroughly in modern US history, introduced me to the burgeoning subfield of policy history, and first mentioned the possibility of moving on to Mr. Jefferson's University. Also at the University of Oregon, Daniel Pope showed me that studying the history of economic ideas holds the key to unlocking the mysteries of American civilization. I thank Jim and Daniel for their many years of support and friendship—and for commenting on chapter drafts up to the bitter end. Indeed, given the many flaws still present in this study, it is almost comic how many scholars from far and wide contributed meaningfully to it over the years, offering ideas that I subsequently borrowed, suggesting fruitful research paths, and reading and commenting on successive portions of endless drafts. That the book is not better is my fault alone. I especially wish to thank Daniel Aksamit, Louise Breen, Ham Cravens, John Fliter, Michael Hemesath, Shelly Hurt, Jim Huston, Alethia Jones, Richard John, Tom Maloney, Jim Reed, Ed Ramsden, Charles Sanders, and David Shreve, who first noted that I was onto something linking Keynesian and demographic debates. Many years removed from his obligatory duties, Michael Bernstein retains the title belt as the champion Miller Center mentor for his unstinting professional backing, indispensable intellectual guidance, and record-breaking e-mail response time. I am deeply appreciative that Robert Devens at the University of Chicago Press reached out to me based on a mere book review that I had written. Every author should be so lucky as to work with Robert. My copy editor, Richard Allen, well versed in Enlightenment philosophers and Indiana congressmen and everything in between, indulged my dash obsessions, was an absolute pleasure to work with, and kept me dreaming of little teahouses in the Scottish countryside. Finally, when Tom Robertson and I discovered that we were working on similar projects, headed toward similar publication dates, he proved himself to be the model scholar. I thank Tom for sharing his ideas and exchanging drafts and, in general, for making lemonade out of what I first thought was sour apples. Please read his book, too.

The history departments at the Universities of Oregon and Virginia provided fellowships, teaching positions, and surprisingly generous travel funds. The economics department at the University of Virginia awarded me a Bankard Dissertation Fellowship in Public Policy. The Miller Center of Public Affairs provided a munificent year-long fellowship (with office space!) that afforded me the truly thrilling experience of collaborating with a small community of fellows across disciplines. At Kansas State University, the Institute for Military History and 20th Century Studies, the Office of Research and Sponsored Programs, and my home department all provided research funds. I also thank my colleagues for enabling me to spend a semester away from campus in the spring of 2010 so I could write a new chapter and place the finish line in sight. Archivists across the country went above and beyond the call of duty and always miraculously seemed to know which generically titled correspondence folders contained significant population musings. David Vail was an invaluable research assistant (with whom it was very fun to suffer through the first year as a professor and a Ph.D. student, respectively). Elliot Creem enthusiastically checked hundreds of footnotes and demonstrated that undergraduate history education is alive and well. At the frantic eleventh hour—two frantic eleventh hours—Amy Cantone skillfully researched several important loose ends and heroically tracked down numerous obscure sources.

I hope my friends know that I often tell Jeanine I have the best friends in the world. Whether in Eugene, Charlottesville, or Manhattan, my friends have provided not only top-shelf ironic banter but also fantastic intellectual stimulation. For slogging through—and improving—*The State and the Stork* over the years, I owe special thanks to Gillian Glaes, Daniel Holt, Sean Kissane, Chris Loomis, Andy Morris, and Cedar Riener. Chris Nichols read the most versions over the years and was a wonderful companion in the trenches of graduate school. Chris Loss was there from the first day of the graduate survey in modern US history, and he intrepidly read each chapter thoughtfully as my deadline neared despite having his own book to finish. My book, at least, is much better as a result of our chapter swaps. I never would have survived my first year at Kansas State had Bonnie Lynn-Sherow and Jim Sherow not showed me the ropes. Ever since, Bonnie and Jim have provided me with an open door and an open fridge—and an office with a window. And I never would have finished the book had Tara, Sam, Aaron, Rob, Brent, Gerry, Janine, and everyone else in Thursday Beer Club not put up with my gripes about commuter marriages and listened to me drone on about running. Given the topic of this book, I cannot resist counting visits from the stork: beginning with my sister, Lydia, and Gary, at least a dozen couples close to me have had babies since I began this project, and I have enjoyed getting to know all of them (but of course none more than my now shockingly old and always ridiculously brilliant nephews, Owen and Milo).

My family has always acted as a backstop to my wild pitches. I am glad to have become a part of the lives of my in-laws, Pat and Bill, and I thank Bill for adding the real-world perspective of a banker to the draft. My enjoyable time with Jeanine's father, Gene, always reminds me that historians know little about how the world—and machines—work. My ongoing debates with my father (patiently refereed by Laura) sharpened my thinking and improved the book. I wish that his mother had survived to see the book in print—at age 98 she was still commenting critically on my ideas.

What I wrote a few years ago still stands: I am very much the product of my mom's unfailing assistance and generosity. A history teacher herself, she read my school essays, demanded that I write a better college-admission application, kept me afloat in graduate school, clipped articles for me to use in lectures, and, above all, insists (even in these poisonous times) that American politics can be a force for good. She often laments that I am more interested in the politics of the past than the present; Mom, I hope that this book contributes just a little bit to an important national discussion.

Finally, it's hard to put into words what my remarkable wife Jeanine means to me. She has waited far too long and far too patiently for The Book to stop hovering over our lives like a storm cloud, costing us the pleasures of untold movies, weekend trips, and simply quiet moments at the end of the day. The funniest person I know, Jeanine always cheers me up when I forget that writing history is fun. She has tolerated my reading drafts out loud in the car, made peace with my perfectionism, learned to love economic theory, and taught me to think like a scientist. And somehow she continues to believe that I can become a best-selling public intellectual and regular on *The Daily Show* despite all evidence to the contrary. Thanks, Jeanine, for taking a chance.

Introduction

Senator Daniel Patrick Moynihan once remarked, "There is simply nothing so important to a people and its government as how many of them there are."[1] But how many is too many? At any given moment throughout American history, the prevailing answer to this question—and to many others surrounding demography's influence on the nation's economy, social fabric, and natural environment—has primarily reflected the interplay of expertise and politics. Although the United States has enjoyed ample natural resources and nearly uninterrupted expansion of its population and wealth, a surprisingly large and varied number of Americans have perceived population trends as snakes in the garden. Population concerns, in turn, have remade American political development and the American political economy.

Sustained population growth has been a defining feature of the American experiment. The first census in 1790 recorded 4 million people, and, even as birthrates began coming down in response to modernization (a process demographers call the "demographic transition"), the population had risen to 31 million by the Civil War. In 1900, 76 million citizens inhabited the United States; in 2000, 281 million. After crossing the 300-million milestone in the fall of 2006, the population when this book came out was about 315 million. The US is the third most populous nation in the world, trailing only China and India.

Sheer size aside, the United States is a demographic outlier. Today, the global population of 7 billion increases by about 83 million, or 1.2 percent, per year.[2] Less developed nations account for 95 percent of this growth—and the US accounts for most of the remaining 5 percent. Put another way, many developed nations will see their populations stagnate or decline in the coming decades, but all indications suggest that the number of Americans will continue to soar. The Census Bureau projects a population of 439 million in 2050 and 570 million in 2100.[3] The current fertility rate in the United States is 2.06 births per woman, having recently reached 2.1, the highest level since 1971, and is higher than the rate in such low- and middle-income nations as Iran, Chile, Brazil, and Vietnam.[4] By additional comparison, the United Kingdom's fertility rate is 1.9, Spain's is 1.5, and Germany's is 1.4.[5] Higher fertility among Hispanics and immigrants partially accounts for American demographic exceptionalism. Yet largely because of the nation's atypical religiosity, "fertility is high even for white non-Hispanics, for states with the lowest fertility, and for college graduates," observe demographers Samuel Preston and Caroline Hartnett.[6] Rhode Island, the state with the lowest fertility, would rank among the highest fertility nations in Europe if it broke off from the US and joined the EU.[7]

Historically, Americans have used three overarching approaches when thinking about population. The first, the "limits to growth" perspective, insists that people eventually and disastrously outstrip the supply of natural resources. When twenty-first-century Americans hear the words "population debate," most think of—but do not agree with—the limits-to-growth principles set forth by British pastor Thomas Malthus (1766–1834). In his *Essay on the Principle of Population*, first published in 1798 but updated in a more widely read 1803 edition, Malthus concluded that overpopulation and misery were inevitable. "Population, when unchecked, increases in a geometrical ratio," he observed. "Subsistence [the food supply] increases only in an arithmetical ratio. A slight acquaintance with numbers will shew the immensity of the first power in comparison to the second."[8] However, Malthus failed to predict the future widespread use of birth control, women's movements, and dramatic gains in agricultural productivity, or that industrialization and economic growth would lower fertility. As he saw it, the only potential checks on population growth were a skyrocketing death rate induced by war and misery and the "moral restraint" of delayed marriage. European "classical economists" of the late eighteenth and early nineteenth centuries, who established many of the principles of modern economics, incorporated Malthusianism into their theory of "diminishing returns." They suggested that population expansion forces less fertile land into production and thus produces lower yields, and drives down wages by producing a glut of workers. This book will show that Malthusian ideas have waxed and waned throughout American history.

The second main approach to population emphasizes that its growth harms the "quality of life." Although there is no doubt that material comfort often has been a prerequisite to this argument, it is not a frivolous one, rather one that speaks directly to the essence of what it means to be human and to share the planet with other living things. Renowned classical economist John Stuart Mill launched this aesthetic approach when he wrote in his *Principles of Political Economy* (1848), "If the earth must lose that great portion of its pleasantness which it owes to things that the unlimited increase of wealth and population would extirpate from it, for the mere purpose of enabling it to support a larger, but not a better or a happier population, I sincerely hope, for the sake of posterity, that they will be content to be stationary, long before necessity compels them to it."[9] Quality-of-life concerns were relatively unimportant to the population discussion until the middle of the twentieth century, but they rose in significance as prosperity and the search for amenities spread across American society.

The third overarching position in the population debate welcomes expansion. William Godwin, Malthus's intellectual adversary, believed in the perfectibility of humans and that a radical restructuring of economic relationships, not fewer people, would eliminate poverty. Although most nineteenth-century classical economists looked forward to the cessation of population growth—what they called the "stationary state"—today's neoliberal (conservative) economists—who look to the classical school in so many other areas—ironically embrace population growth.[10] These conservatives argue that pessimists since Malthus have underestimated humans' technological and organizational ingenuity, and they stress that population growth creates economies of scale and drives innovation. They also believe that the market will determine the optimal number of children in a society, as well as minimize natural-resource scarcities by inducing substitutions. Its roots may lie with Godwin, but this ideological framework has come into prominence only since the 1970s.

Actually proving that population growth harms ecosystems, diminishes happiness, or promotes prosperity is another matter altogether from these sweeping theories. Economists and demographers struggle to make sense of nearly infinite combinations of demographic variables (e.g., birthrate, total population size, expected future growth rate, mortality, geographic distribution, and average age) and economic conditions (e.g., aggregate economic growth, average income, employment, and the extent of inequality). Further complicating these matters are questions of scale, location, and time. At the micro level, a family may find a fourth or fifth baby a pure joy and an investment in old-age security. At the intermediate level, many residents of Charlottesville, Virginia, and Manhattan, Kansas (the small college cities where I wrote this study), have welcomed explosive growth in their communities during the past few decades in part because housing values have soared. Conversely, a barber in the stagnant upstate New York city of Gloversville, where my mother grew up, lamented to me that post–World War II population loss meant "ten thousand fewer haircuts every year." Many individuals who write about environmental problems prefer to live in growing cities teeming with people and ideas. But at the macro level, global population growth makes it difficult to address climate change, species extinction, and lack of availability to clean water.

Viewed through a wide-angle lens, the curve of human population growth since the birth of our species remained practically flat for tens of thousands of years but, after 1860, spiked dramatically upwards in a nearly vertical line, prompting some on Wall Street to refer to human population growth as the "ultimate bubble." Given that environmental damage and the "momentum" of population expansion can persist for generations, it is impossible to consider population without thinking about intergenerational dynamics. Finally, economists and demographers must untangle not only the economic *consequences* of demographic trends but also the economic *causes* of them.

Not surprisingly, then, social scientists often disagree about population and the economy. Obviously a larger population increases an economy's total pie, so the important question has always been whether it also increases per capita wealth and happiness. The takeoff of European agriculture and economic growth around 1650 coincided with a dramatic increase in population, leading many economists to postulate that population growth drives economic growth. The oscillating Malthusian model of stagnation—higher incomes produce a population surge, but the excess of people drives incomes down, stunting population until incomes rise and the process starts all over—says little about most economies since 1800.[11] When examining the American experience, enthusiasts of population growth point to the coincidence of a sluggish birthrate with a sluggish economy in the 1930s and 1970s, and the coincidence of the Baby Boom with a healthy economy in the 1950s. John Maynard Keynes, one of the most important economists of all time and a major focus of this book, articulated perhaps the strongest argument that population growth aids the economy, and his stance was psychological: businesspeople tend to think that a bumper crop of babies is beneficial in the long run, and therefore they may invest accordingly. Yet history provides many counterexamples, in which sluggish population growth combined with vigorous economic expansion. In short, the multiplicity of variables related to demographic and economic change, and their overlapping nature, prevents the formulation of firm conclusions across time and space.[12]

Just as few ironclad laws apply to population and the economy, there is no consistent political economy of population. Population politics are always embedded in myriad overlapping narratives about not only the market and the state but also about individual liberty, national identity, and the meaning of the Good Life. Demographic concerns make for strange bedfellows. In contemporary America, for instance, some left-wing environmentalists and right-wing cultural conservatives have formed an anti-immigration alliance. Not surprisingly, neither of the two grand political traditions has ever made up its mind on whether or not population growth is beneficial. Karl Marx believed that capitalism necessarily creates a surplus population, and, well before him, theorists pointed out that "proletarian" and "prolific" share the same Latin root—*proles*, which means "offspring." Yet Marx rejected Malthus, and, ever since, some American socialists and left-liberals have concluded that the inequitable distribution of economic resources causes the problems incorrectly attributed to overpopulation. In contrast, nineteenth-century American workers, concerned about the pressure of population growth on wages, erected what has been called a "working-class neo-Malthusianism."[13] And during much of the twentieth century, American liberalism incorporated the position that a smaller population would improve per capita incomes and reduce inequality.

The Right has also divided on population matters. "Classical Manchester Liberalism [today's anti-statist conservative economics] is founded on the Malthusian population doctrine," observed Nobel laureate economist Gunnar Myrdal.[14] Some conservatives have used Malthusian precepts to argue that charity is counterproductive because it merely exacerbates population growth. Meanwhile, the Left has accused conservative supporters of population control of fearing the masses. Business interests, however, often value the cheap labor that they assume follows steady population increase. And today, many conservative theorists who otherwise espouse classical liberalism have dropped its aversion to population growth. Additionally, some contemporary conservatives argue that birth control threatens the family, which they see as the bedrock of an ordered society.

Americans are generally leery about direct state intervention to influence population trends. Law professor Marc Linder argues that liberal democracies tend to adopt a laissez-faire approach to procreation—even though an unregulated supply of labor creates economic difficulties—because the alternative would undermine capitalism's libertarian tenets.[15] Yet even though the US has never adopted explicit population targets, like some European states, it has used a variety of population policies to influence demographic trends, from immigration laws to family planning programs to tax credits for children. In the end, the population question in America historically has taken on a chameleon-like quality, colored not only by shifting population expertise but also by changing political and cultural anxieties.

At present, a decisive majority of American social scientists, policy makers, and public intellectuals favor domestic population growth. True, a few individuals—some the shipwrecked survivors of an environmental movement that sailed in the 1960s and 1970s—insist that the United States and the planet have too many people and so face ruined economies and ecosystems. Opponents of immigration dip into these arguments when convenient. Some popular authors worry about population, as well. Thomas Friedman's recent bestseller *Hot, Flat, and Crowded*, for example, argues that population growth and the worldwide expansion of a mass-consumption, middle-class lifestyle threatens to overwhelm policy makers' efforts to address global climate change.[16] On the whole, though, economists and policy makers in twenty-first-century America celebrate the nation's growth, reserving any unease about population increase for distant lands.[17] (The UN now projects a global population of ten billion in the year 2100, having recently revised upward its projection of a peak of 9 billion in 2050. But growth is concentrated in the poorest areas of the world, so one hears of population "cluster bombs" in places like sub-Saharan Africa rather than the generalized "population explosion" of decades past.)[18] Leading media outlets across the political spectrum have adopted this pro–population growth position (which I will call "pronatalist" or "populationist"). The *Economist* often runs cover stories with titles such as "How to Deal with a Shrinking Population."[19] In 2003, a *Washington Post* editorial argued, "If future generations are to carry on the American vibrancy and dynamism, the country must be prepared to embrace more babies, and more babies from around the world."[20] Perhaps the greatest demographic fear today, seen in a slew of books with ominous titles such as *The Coming Generational Storm* and *Shock of Gray*, is that

Americans are not having enough babies (future workers) to pay the imminent Social Security bill of the Baby Boom generation, born between 1946 and 1964.[21] This fear has been reinforced by the spiraling deficits of the Great Recession and media coverage of Europe's and Japan's very different demographics. Democrats and Republicans may fight viciously about US funding for overseas birth control programs, but the politics of abortion govern that discussion, not the steady rise of the earth's population.

Meanwhile, environmental concerns about population growth, whether in the US or abroad, have been marginalized and discredited.[22] Television programs routinely celebrate large families, and the tabloids feature celebrities' babies.[23] Conservative politicians dismiss environmentalists as the "'people are pollution' crowd."[24] Recently, Utah State Representative Mike Noel claimed that the idea of climate change is part of a "conspiracy to limit population not only in this country but across the globe."[25] A fundamentalist high-school textbook, *America's Providential History*, reports, "While many secularists view the world as over-populated, Christians know that God has made the earth sufficiently large, with plenty of resources to accommodate all of the people."[26]

Instead of challenging such views, many liberals observe a taboo against discussing population. Environmental organizations are still sympathetic to the idea that America is overpopulated, but they tend to avoid the issue because it is fraught with political risk. According to the US Census Bureau, immigration accounts for around 45 percent of annual US population growth,[27] and the Pew Hispanic Center estimates that immigrants and their children will account for 82 percent of population increase in the United States between 2005 and 2050.[28] Many individuals sense that talking about aggregate growth will brand them as anti-immigrant—or at least damage a liberal coalition that relies heavily on minority and immigrant votes. On at least two occasions within the past fifteen years, the Sierra Club has nearly splintered over whether to call for limits to immigration to promote population stabilization. A generation ago, reproductive-rights and feminist groups suggested that their reforms would have the added benefit of lowering population growth rates. They now stay clear of such positions, however, in part because they do not wish to provide conservative religious interests and the "pro-life" movement—both of which consider the idea that humans should limit their numbers an anathema—with the opportunity to score points in the ongoing "culture wars" by reminding Americans of the long and unfortunate history of coercive population control. As a result of the Left's refusal to engage population issues, as well as the prevailing celebration of the economic effects of population growth, the American media today, unlike a generation ago, largely avoids entertaining the possible connections between population increase and environmental and economic welfare.[29] Social scientists in a variety of fields have adopted the same strategy of benign neglect.

Current inattention aside, Americans took part in a robust discussion about the prospect of overpopulation since before the creation of the United States. And indeed, historians have long studied the influence of America's unique demography—and anxieties about it—on the American fabric. Most famously, University of Wisconsin historian Frederick Jackson Turner argued in 1893 that the recent "closing" of the frontier threatened American democracy; recourse to the cheap lands in the lightly populated West had provided an egalitarian safety valve to the teeming populations of the growing nation. But the approach by modern historians has been more piecemeal, with a tendency to address population ideas only to the extent that they intersect with obvious topics of demographic importance, such as immigration.

Recent studies fall into three broad categories. Environmental histories, led by Tom Robertson's new and vital *The Malthusian Moment: Global Population Growth and the Birth of American Environmentalism*, emphasize how Malthusianism—the movement to arrest and reverse population growth—has occupied a more central place in American conservation than previously recognized.[30] The second category comprises cultural historians studying the American family and the 1950s Baby Boom, who draw attention to ebullient celebration of population growth.[31]

Finally, some historians have concentrated narrowly on eugenics, which is the racist movement to engineer a "better" population by promoting births among the genetically "fit" and discouraging them among undesirables. Scholarship examining the development of the American demography profession in the early twentieth century, the same era during which eugenics peaked, reveals how eugenics haunts demography's past. Also, many scholars have examined—and often exaggerated—the resilience of eugenic ideas after World War II, even as the organized eugenics movement declined due to its associations with Nazi racial ideology.[32] Matthew Connelly's *Fatal Misconception: The Struggle to Control World Population*, for instance, locates neocolonial and eugenic motives behind the philanthropic campaigns in the Western nations to lower global population growth rates in the 1950s and 1960s. Connelly, along with many other scholars, claims that the domestic family planning programs developed in the United States in this era were designed primarily to combat the perceived threat of an out-of-control birthrate among unwed African Americans.[33] Similarly, many studies argue that the Malthusian campaign for "zero population growth" in the late 1960s was merely the old wine of eugenics in new bottles.[34]

Race is central to how Americans have made sense of their numbers. Moreover, it is sometimes hard to separate racial and nonracial concerns. For example, at the turn of the twentieth century, the American labor movement claimed justifiably that stepped-up immigration stunted wage growth, but this economic argument gained reinforcement from racist disdain for immigrant groups. Nonetheless, the emphasis on the survival of eugenics, natural resources, and America's persistent cultural emphasis on family and babies neglects how population attitudes developed in tandem with and helped shape a variety of mainstream economic theories.

While acknowledging the importance of studies about Americans who have asked if we are too many of the wrong ethnic kind? (eugenics) or if we are too many for the supply of natural resources? (Malthusianism), this book considers population history from a different perspective, using a different set of questions posed by social scientists, interest groups, and policy makers: Are we too many or too few to maximize economic growth? Are we too many for the best quality of life? Where should we live? And are we too old or too young? Given America's unique position as a demographic outlier—to say little of the current global energy, food, climate, and pension crises, which are bringing demography to the forefront once again—a thorough retelling of the American population debate is needed.

This book's argument proceeds along two distinct but overlapping tracks. The first concerns the population debate as a historical development in its own right. Trepidation of demographic change has been deeper, wider, and more persistent in the United States than we have assumed. The current celebration of growth is surprisingly novel. But beyond a simple and unadulterated Malthusianism that assumes humans will exhaust natural resources, historical disquiet over population has assumed many forms.

The second track focuses on the population debate's wide-ranging significance, examining its underappreciated influence on America's broader political development, policy making, and political economy. Existing studies fail to convey how demographic discussions shaped not only the development of mainstream political-economic philosophies but also state action. It is impossible to understand the evolution of population issues in the United States without considering how population attitudes were embedded in and shaped broader economic ideas. A major goal of this study, therefore, is to trace how population concerns have influenced not only policy areas with obvious demographic links (such as immigration and birth control) but also additional and more surprising arenas, from the extension of slavery into the territories to the promotion of mass consumption and employment to wilderness preservation.

At several key moments in the history of American politics, the population question was a political flash point that divided liberal and conservative theorists and politicians into coherent camps. Yet the fault lines continually shifted and did not follow consistent ideological lines. A fuller understanding of the links between demographic, economic, and policy debates throughout US history allows better comprehension of how the current pro–population growth climate emerged, even as America's growth has rocketed ahead of its fellow wealthy nations.

Before proceeding, it is worth mentioning what this study is not. It is not a demographic history of the United States.[35] Although it reviews shifts in the birthrate, immigration patterns, age distribution, etc., it is more concerned with how experts treated these shifts than with demographic fundamentals themselves. In addition, this book focuses on the population debate in and pertaining to the United States. Because the US provides aid to overseas family planning programs, and because most of today's population growth takes place in the developing world, many nonspecialists tend to think about population issues in international terms. The history of America's overseas population policies is important, but it appears in these pages only when it intersects with the domestic debate. Finally, this is not a study of popular opinion; it emphasizes the social scientists, policy makers, and interest groups that ultimately drove ideas and policies.

The book's narrative begins in the colonial era, when Americans generally celebrated their prodigious expansion. As conflict with England emerged, they believed that population growth portended future American power. The population policies of the new United States were indirect but powerful: the federal government subsidized the numerical and geographical expansion of the citizenry by acquiring new territories and removing Indians from them, providing cheap land to settlers and railroads, and welcoming the nearly unlimited immigration of people not of "African descent." But the founders' "republican" theory of democracy, sprung from the Enlightenment, valued an agrarian society with room to expand and fostered population anxieties among the elite well before Thomas Malthus published his *Essay on the Principle of Population* in 1798. In the Early Republic, Thomas Jefferson's Democratic-Republican Party worried that population growth threatened the agrarian republic, whereas the Federalist Party embraced rising numbers, believing they accelerated commerce and spurred beneficial manufacturing. Population concerns remained robust and intimately connected to foundational policy questions surrounding slavery and westward expansion in the decades before the Civil War.

Apprehension of enlargement did not, as is often supposed, develop merely in response to the "closing of the frontier" at the end of the nineteenth century. True, the closing of the frontier led many white Americans to worry that their nation had "filled up"—and, given the era's mass immigration from Southern and Eastern Europe, filled up with the wrong kinds of people. It also fueled the popular culture's nostalgia for an imagined untamed West. Among economists, however, Malthusians were on the defensive at the turn of the twentieth century. Conservatives theorists, following the classical economists (and breaking with their Federalist forbearers), suggested that steady population expansion threatened the economy and supply of natural resources. Liberals, including many in the reformist cohort who founded the American Economic Association, argued that conservatives relied on supposedly "natural" laws of social development, such as the Malthusian population law, to paper over inequalities produced by society. Liberals also argued that conservatives failed to appreciate the dynamism of a developing industrial economy. By the 1920s, however, newly professionalized American demographers, economists, and natural-resource experts had reached a consensus that America's "optimum population" was lower than its current one.

This consensus did not disappear, as the prevailing wisdom suggests, only reemerging briefly in the late 1960s in the form of the Malthusian "zero population growth" movement. Rather, unease about population growth incorporated the innovative liberal economic ideas that prevailed at midcentury, particularly British economist John Maynard Keynes's stress on government-sponsored mass consumption. During the Great Depression of the 1930s, the birthrate declined meaningfully, and demographers projected an eventual drop in the total population. Historians widely but incorrectly assume that the falling birthrate, given its concurrence with the Great Depression, led to a universal advocacy of population growth as an economic virtue. True, popular magazines and some economists argued that more babies were needed to grow the economy. Also, Keynes and his American disciples believed, as part of their theory that the industrialized nations had reached "economic maturity," that population growth was essential for economic recovery. Population experts and many New Dealers, however, rewrote Keynesianism to advance the idea that reaching and maintaining a stable population was desirable and entirely compatible with a prosperous economy. Indeed, they claimed that the former might actually promote the latter, especially if the federal government engaged in Keynesian management of the economy to increase personal consumption. The state, not the stork, would sustain economic growth. I call this fusion of Malthusianism and Keynesianism "Stable Population Keynesianism."

From the 1930s to the 1960s, prevailing American economic thought held that a smaller population would have macro- as well as microeconomic benefits; it would enhance the overall American economy as well as individual welfare. After World War II, swelling population growth overseas and the unexpected population surge of the Baby Boom at home nullified the prewar stress on investing in a stable population. Although faith in technological progress tempered Malthusian suspicions, Americans worried that plenty of people threatened their status as a "People of Plenty," as historian David Potter dubbed them.[36] Economists, natural scientists, demographers, and policy makers feared that population growth endangered the new abundance, mass consumption, and high quality of life. They suggested that the economy would have to run faster just to stand still. In addition, they launched an aesthetic critique of population growth focused not on matters of survival but on the threat to the "quality of life" in the United States, the high standard of living that provided noneconomic amenities previously considered luxuries.

Meanwhile, policy makers tried to reconcile the United States to its ongoing expansion. The economic and quality-of-life critiques of population growth underlay not only the establishment of federal birth control programs (usually depicted by scholars as racially motivated) but also several other reforms of the Lyndon Johnson years. Fear of unregulated population increase also helped trigger the expansive environmental policy making of the 1960s, long before Stanford biologist Paul Ehrlich's Malthusian treatise, *The Population Bomb* (1968), launched the ecologically oriented zero population growth movement.

For a brief moment, the American Establishment, including President Richard Nixon, embraced the 1960s Malthusianism, which, if more drastic than anything that preceded it, was more a culmination than a break. But the zero population growth movement quickly fizzled. Historians have attributed its demise primarily to the new abortion battles in the United States (the Supreme Court's *Roe v. Wade* decision came in 1973), which created a reproductive politics that eroded bipartisan support for family planning and population control. Liberals and conservatives, however, had already diverged on population matters in the 1960s, when a revival of laissez-faire economics on the Right incorporated a celebration of population growth, and many liberals, especially environmentalists, had come to reject the pursuit of economic growth.

In the 1970s, the crumbling of Keynesian economics and the turn against economic growth led to the disappearance of the argument that the state and not the stork could propel prosperity. It is thus another major goal of this study to show that the population debate provides a new and unexpected window into the rise and fall of Keynesianism from the 1930s to the 1970s and into the triumph of conservative economics thereafter. By the end of the 1970s, the politics had changed once again. The economic malaise and lower birthrates caused many on the Left to rethink their anti–economic growth position, and they now joined conservatives in arguing that population growth could sustain economic recovery. Meanwhile, the emergence of an "aging crisis" called for more babies to fund the future retirement of the Baby Boomers and cemented the widespread celebration of population growth that has persisted to this day.

For two hundred years, anxiety about population growth fitted squarely within America's mainstream economic thinking, including the Keynesian quest for constant economic growth. Malthus and markets mixed. And the aesthetic critique of growth impeding the quality of life resonated deeply with many Americans. Beginning in the late 1960s, however, the fracturing of American society and economic expertise completely upended the traditional political economy of population.

Swedish demographer Göran Ohlin once suggested that demography has three things in common with popular novels and espionage: travel, sex, and death. This book is not a spy novel, but it does touch on all three as it traces the surprising intersections between population issues and American political development and seeks to unravel the strange mysteries of the American population debate.

CHAPTER ONE

Foundations

"Thus in the beginning all the World was America," wrote Enlightenment philosopher John Locke in the *Second Treatise of Government* (1690).[1] To be an American in the seventeenth century was to live unfettered by tradition in sparse settlements amid a vast and foreboding wilderness. Emerging from a near barbarous condition, the first European settlers in America saw a steadily rising number of inhabitants as a cause for celebration, a hallmark of security and progress toward a higher stage of civilization. A century later, French adventurer turned New York farmer J. Hector St. John Crèvecoeur echoed Locke's depiction of America as a latter-day Eden. "The American is a new man," he pronounced in *Letters from an American Farmer* (1782), one free from the stifling social hierarchies of Europe who could advance from roughly mannered immigrant to prosperous and virtuous yeoman farmer in a mere generation.[2] Crèvecoeur believed that it was America's natural bounty that drove this rapid social, material, and demographic progress. He proposed that in the US, "nature opens her broad lap to receive the perpetual accession of new comers, and to supply them food."[3] And when Europeans traveled to America, he remarked, their imaginations, "instead of submitting to the painful and useless retrospect of revolutions, desolations, and plagues . . . wisely spring forward to the anticipated fields of future cultivation and improvement, to the future extent of those generations which are to replenish and embellish this boundless continent."[4]

Crèvecoeur had witnessed remarkable demographic changes in America. The colonial population, after a sluggish first few decades, was doubling every twenty-five years by the middle of the seventeenth century.[5] Colonial birthrates were exceptionally high, even by the worldwide standards of the era, and far exceeded those of Europe. In 1700, the

European-American population was still just 250,000, but as remarkable growth continued through the eighteenth century, the population swelled to 2.8 million in 1780.[6] In sharp contrast, Native Americans were decimated by diseases that European Americans introduced, and their numbers east of the Mississippi River shrank from perhaps two million in 1492 to 250,000 in 1750.[7]

Different views on these demographic changes informed the intellectual and political debates in the young United States. From colonial times to the Civil War, millions of European Americans celebrated the dramatic expansion of the white population and associated it with the colonies' and then young nation's remarkable economic progress. These celebrants included the common farmers who moved westward and the railroad boosters who recruited them and promoted new towns in the name of democratic settlement. Some American intellectuals, too, looked favorably upon population growth. Drawing on the "classical liberalism" of Enlightenment theorists John Locke and Adam Smith, these optimists assumed that maximizing human freedom and choice, especially in the realm of the market, would unleash societal changes and technological innovations that would outpace resource pressures stemming from demographic expansion.

Yet many learned Americans harbored deep reservations about growth. Another strain of Enlightenment thought permeating Early America, what scholars today call "republicanism" or sometimes "civic humanism," theorized that democracy demanded virtuous and public-oriented citizens. Its followers feared that a rising population was fraught with peril and heralded the kind of fully settled, commercial- and manufacturing-based, deeply inegalitarian, and morally decrepit European society from which the colonists had fled.[8] Ideas about population were not a perfect proxy for party affiliation, but whereas Jefferson's Democratic-Republicans tended to imbibe republicanism's aversion to population growth, John Adams's Federalists and later the Whig Party tended to embrace liberalism's celebration of it—and hoped to keep it confined to America's great cities rather than seeing it disperse across the West.

Thus Americans had engaged in substantial population debates long before the Rev. Thomas Malthus argued in *An Essay on the Principle of Population as it Affects the Future Improvement of Society* (1798) that population growth doomed human societies by overwhelming natural resources. (Although Malthus published the first edition anonymously, and it was little read, he made no attempt to hide his authorship. The revised

1803 edition with Malthus's official imprimatur enjoyed a much greater readership.) The *Essay*, as important as it is to the intellectual history of the nineteenth century and to the development of modern demography, did not usher in an intellectual sea change. Nonetheless, an examination of Americans' reactions to Malthus offers an illuminating window into pre–Civil War politics. Malthus initially had more detractors than supporters in the US, but many of the former agreed with his basic assumptions even as they questioned their applicability to American circumstances. In the Early Republic, nationalistic pride in a swelling population continued to mix with unease that such growth would lead the young nation to turn its back on the low-population-density agrarianism at the core of its identity and instead embrace manufacturing and "luxury," which would produce corruption and vice. During the middle of the nineteenth century, foundational questions surrounding slavery dominated politics and became the primary prism through which Americans thought about population. Northern and southern elites both hoped for population growth in their respective regions but also used Malthusian premises to claim the superiority of their civilization and labor systems. By the 1840s, many white Americans believed in their "Manifest Destiny" to spread "Anglo-Saxon" Christian civilization across the entire North American continent. As it drove American territorial expansion, the doctrine of Manifest Destiny superficially celebrated population growth but also revealed dread of what unending increase might produce without the social safety valve of geographic expansion.

In contrast to the prevailing scholarly assumption that Americans almost universally celebrated population growth before the Civil War, this chapter shows how debates about democracy, slavery, and westward expansion revealed deep-seated ambivalence about the nation's seemingly endless growth. And it highlights the surprising breadth and continuity of population concerns from the colonial era to the Civil War. This chapter also introduces two topics important for the rest of the study. First, it introduces the apprehension of population-induced natural-resource scarcity—and the competing technological optimism—that would animate the American population debate long after Revolutionary-era ideologies faded. Second, it reviews the theories of Malthus and the other leading classical economists of the late eighteenth and early nineteenth centuries, whose ideas, two centuries later, remain the starting point for serious discussion of population, resources, and the economy.

Population in Colonial and Revolutionary America

After suffering through an initial high-mortality deathtrap, many colonists celebrated the demographic paradise that whites enjoyed in the New World. Colonial promotional literature portrayed a biblical land of milk and honey with high fertility, low mortality, and rapid population growth.[9] Historian Susan Klepp writes in her study of fertility in Early America that, before the Revolution, men and women alike "were exuberant about the 'teeming,' 'flourishing,' or 'big' pregnant body. Large families were part of a bountiful natural order that celebrated abundance, especially of sons. Women's essence was found in their productivity."[10] In the eighteenth century, population ideas also reflected the spread of science, as theorists anticipated modern demography by envisioning a natural science of human numbers. The Reverend Ezra Stiles, a Yale College president who believed that colonial population expansion augured national greatness, declared, "the laws of human increase and degeneracy are as properly a subject of systematical Science, as botany, the theory of agriculture, or raising and improving stock."[11]

Demographic discourse during the eighteenth and early nineteenth centuries overlapped with the republicanism that sprang from the Enlightenment and swept across British America. The product of an era when representative democracy was a radical and tenuous experiment, republican ideology harked back to ancient Greece and Rome and claimed that a republic's survival demanded a virtuous citizenry dominated by independent yeoman farmers. Virtue, however, was continually threatened by human avarice and corruption; early republicans believed that commerce and especially manufacturing, while beneficial to a point, brought out the worst traits in people and ultimately led to the production and consumption of virtue-sapping "luxuries."[12] Therefore, many elite British North Americans wished to delay manufacturing in the New World for as long as possible. They argued that their mobile and predominantly agricultural social order was infinitely preferable to Europe's stagnant and "settled" societies, where the industrial revolution had created surplus pools of labor doomed to toil in debauched factories and cities. In short, republicans worried about population growth because manufacturing naturally followed it. Thomas Jefferson and other republican proponents of an agricultural economy did promote the small-scale manufacturing of "coarse" household goods such as chairs and tables, but they wished to prevent a pell-mell rush into the domestic production and consumption of nonessential luxuries. Only later, when the size and geographic scope of markets exploded in the second quarter of the nineteenth century, would an active citizenry and the "spirit of commerce" replace Spartan simplicity and virtue as republican ideals.

Widespread rejection of mercantilism, a nationalistic and pro-population growth economic philosophy in vogue among the European powers, further reinforced skepticism of population increase. Mercantilism sought to maximize exports, minimize imports, and hoard silver and gold. Its proponents not only viewed people as the building blocks of national power and wealth but also assumed that an export-driven economy could thrive only by preserving a pool of surplus (and hence poorly paid) workers, so as to keep production costs low.[13]

Republican ideology postulated that societies pass through several phases, progressing from the primitive to the commercialized, usually the four stages envisioned by Scottish theorist Adam Smith: hunting, pasturage, agriculture, and commerce.[14] Population growth propels progress from one stage to the next because the need to increase food production necessitates social changes. Smith and classical liberals writing in his tradition welcomed the final stage because they believed that market-based societies enhance individual freedom and social peace. Republicans conceded that societies get richer as they progress but worried that the end point comes with significant costs: populous societies are forced to develop manufacturing to employ their human surpluses, resulting in excessive inequality and cultural decay. "Manufacturers are founded in poverty," Benjamin Franklin wrote.[15]

American intellectuals, then, needed to reconcile pride in their swelling numbers with the republican fear of surging toward the final, crowded, and depraved stage of social development. Population dispersal offered a potential solution to this dilemma. Well before the creation of the nation, Thomas Jefferson and James Madison articulated one of the most crucial elements of the budding American political economy: internal migration westward would alleviate the threat that population increase posed to the democratic experiment. Republicans maintained that North America was sufficiently vast and underpopulated to remain agricultural for generations to come, especially if free trade allowed farmers to export crop surpluses. (Colonists believed that Native Americans lived at such an early stage of development that contact and competition with Europeans could produce only two possible outcomes: assimilation or extinction.) As historian Drew McCoy observes in his classic study of republican political economy, the essence of Jeffersonianism was the promotion of development across space rather than time; westward expansion would stall the progression through the social stages that ended in corruption and decay.[16]

British Americans who thought about population in geopolitical terms, though, tended to celebrate their rising numbers. As early as the mid-seventeenth century, writes historian Patricia Cohen, "colonial promoters recognized that a reputedly large and growing population signified the vitality of a colony and made it less vulnerable to attack."[17] In his 1751 essay "Observations Concerning the Increase of Mankind," Benjamin Franklin correctly estimated that the colonial population was doubling every twenty years, even more rapidly than widely assumed.[18] "People increase faster by Generation in those Colonies, where all can have full Employ, and there is Room and Business for Millions yet unborn," Franklin observed.[19] He predicted that in another century, more English people would live in the colonies than in England, even if immigration came to a halt.[20] Franklin admired the English and loved the empire, but he attributed many of England's problems to its supposed "fully settled" maturity.[21] He gloomily suggested that the mixture of prodigious population growth in the colonies and slower growth in England augured conflict unless American commerce enjoyed free rein.

In fact, the population of England and Wales declined from 1720 to 1750 and then increased 15 percent from 1750 to 1770, whereas the colonial American population doubled between 1720 and 1750 and then nearly doubled again from 1750 to 1770.[22] (The mother country, however, still enjoyed a large lead in absolute numbers in 1770: 7.5 million to America's 2.3 million.)[23] Colonial American population growth was unimaginable to most Europeans,[24] and indeed Franklin's estimates feature prominently in Malthus's *Essay on the Principle of Population.* One of Franklin's goals, therefore, was to convert fear of colonial expansion into rejoicing that such expansion would further augment England's imperial power.[25] Edmund Morgan, one of Franklin's leading biographers, writes that Franklin "took it as a given that the wealth of any country lay in the numbers of its people, and proceeded to show (before Malthus was born) that the growth of population was governed by economic opportunity, that economic opportunity in America would for a long time be almost unlimited because of the unique abundance of land, that population in America increased accordingly, by natural propagation, far more rapidly than population in England and more rapidly than English manufacturers would be able to supply. It was therefore unnecessary and unwise to restrain American manufacturing, unwise to do anything to discourage economic opportunity and growth within the empire."[26]

Franklin is also well known for anticipating scientific racism and eugenics. He desired the preservation not only of the British Empire but also of an empire of Englishmen, a reactionary goal given the ethnic diversity of the colonies.[27] Franklin disliked the immigration to the colonies of African slaves and also Germans (the latter with their "swarthy Complexion").[28] "This will in a few Years become a German Colony," he lamented in 1749 after observing several thousand German immigrants arrive at Philadelphia's docks.[29] Like many in this era, Franklin assumed that human population growth followed the same biological laws as plants and animals. In a line Malthus echoed, Franklin wrote, "There is in short, no Bound to the prolific Nature of Plants or Animals, but what is made by their crowding and interfering with each others Means of Subsistence."[30] This model of ceaseless competition drove his zero-sum racial thinking. Morgan calls Franklin the "first spokesman for a lily-white America."[31]

As Franklin predicted, conflict rooted in a shared belief that people equals power contributed to the onset of the American Revolution. After the global Seven Years' War (1756–63), the British government's alarm at the demographic gap between mother country and colony helped solidify the crown's developing hard-line policies.[32] "And how are we to rule them?" an English official asked in 1766 as he predicted another quick doubling of the colonial population.[33] England's effort to restrain colonists' expansion beyond the Appalachian Mountains and preserve peace with Native Americans through the Proclamation of 1763 and additional treaties was a major irritant to the colonists because it limited the opportunities many saw as the core attraction of the colonies.[34] Early plans for a political union among the colonies pointed to population growth and the resulting gains in power for America as a reason such a union would work.[35] Subsequently, Samuel Adams and other revolutionaries justified their campaign on the grounds that the colonists' increasing numbers would allow them to withstand a long war and made their long-term dominance inevitable.[36] Just before the Revolution, colonists even revised Franklin's projection of when the British in American would outnumber the British in England, moving the date up by a quarter century to 1825.[37] In 1776, the Declaration of Independence immortalized Americans' pride in their rising numbers and also emphasized the necessity of geographic dispersal. The Second Continental Congress listed among its grievances against King George III: "He has endeavored to prevent the Population of these States; for that Purpose obstructing the Laws for Naturalization of Foreigners; refusing to pass others to encourage their Migrations hither; and raising the Conditions of new Appropriations of Lands."

After the creation of the United States, the population ideas of the nascent political parties diverged as they competed to define a unique American political economy. Jeffersonians, who coalesced into the Democratic-Republican Party, embraced the demographic doctrine of classical republicanism. Stanley Elkins and Eric McKitrick note in their study of America's first decade that for Jeffersonians, "The problem for political economy was that of prolonging the stage of youthful vigor and making the onset of decay as remote as possible. A master variable, moreover, was assumed to be the pressure of population growth, well before Thomas Malthus produced his celebrated essay on that subject toward the close of the century."[38] Leading Americans began to suggest that Franklin and others had overoptimistically estimated how long the United States could remain young and underpopulated. While grounded in republican theory, their concerns reflected wariness about the dramatic population expansion of the 1780s, likely the decade with the most rapid growth of any in US history.[39] According to historian Drew McCoy, "the pressure of population growth on a limited supply of land in some eastern areas of the United States, especially in New England, seems actually to have created by the 1780s a situation of 'crowding,' with an increase in social stratification, a growing concentration of wealth, and the development of a more visible and mobile class of poor people."[40]

Federalists, however, tended to view population growth more sympathetically, both for the commercial benefits that they assumed it produced and because they did not fear its perceived concomitants of luxury and private acquisitiveness. Federalists increasingly claimed in republican terms that manufacturing and commerce in fact promoted virtuous citizens. Federalist John Adams went so far as to call population expansion "the surest indication of national happiness."[41] Because they welcomed cities intellectually and found their political support in them, Federalists were less enamored with westward expansion than Democratic-Republicans. Renowned historian Gordon Wood writes, "The Federalists had thought that America's rapid multiplication of people would force the country to develop the same sorts of civilized urban institutions, the same kinds of integrated social hierarchies and industrial centers, the same types of balanced economies in which manufacturing was as important as farming, the same sorts of bureaucratic governments that made the states of Europe, at least before the accursed French Revolution erupted, so impressive, so powerful, and so civilized."[42]

Still, the partisan chasm was not vast. For example, Jeffersonian Tench Coxe, an assistant secretary of the treasury who helped Secretary Alexander Hamilton write his famous *Report on Manufactures* (1791), believed that America's natural abundance and the dawning machine age promised unimaginable wealth and that population growth naturally reflected a society's progression through the stages of development.[43] Separately, Federalists claimed allegiance to republican values as much as Jeffersonians. While they sought to update them for a modern economy, they did not completely abandon core principles such as the anxiety about crowding. Even Hamilton, who advocated government-subsidized manufacturing, suggested that England had turned to manufacturing and exports because it was a ripened and overpopulated nation. He proposed that US manufacturing should occur only in areas where population had become dense and agriculture was no longer viable.[44]

Few comprehended the subtleties in Early American population theory better than James Madison. The future fourth president primarily thought about demographic change in terms of human welfare, believing that migration—both between and within nations—enhanced it.[45] He also thought that a steadily increasing population would help preserve American independence.[46] Madison's most famous statements of political philosophy, his essays in *The Federalist* supporting the not-yet-ratified US Constitution, reveal the proclivity in Early America to embrace the virtues of bigness, particularly when thinking about democracy, while still rejecting dense European-style populations.

In *Federalist 10*, Madison seems to advocate population growth by observing that large societies are better equipped to withstand the ravages of special interests or "factions" better than small ones. But this seminal essay is primarily a defense of the proposed political "consolidation" of the individual states, and Madison defines "large" republics in geographic and political rather than demographic terms. Madison considered a large republic one that centralizes power in the national government, rather than diffuses it among the states, and grows across space rather than time. "Extend the sphere," he writes, "and you take in a greater variety of interests; you make it less probable that a majority of the whole will have a common motive to invade the rights of other citizens."[47] True, Madison was countering an anti-ratification argument, derived from French theorist Montesquieu, that large republics thwart liberty. And Montesquieu had defined size in demographic as well as territorial terms, concluding that "a free republic cannot succeed over a country of such immense extent, containing such a number of inhabitants, and these increasing in such rapid progression as that of the whole United States."[48] Further, with regard to the question of the ideal number of representatives for congressional districts, Madison does support the idea that more populous districts enable better leaders to emerge.[49] Even so, *Federalist 10* does not address population growth directly, and elsewhere Madison stipulates that he cannot predict its effects. In *Federalist* 55, he calls the proposed number of members for the House of Representatives sufficient to protect liberty but then adds, "What change of circumstances, time, and a fuller population of our country may produce, requires a prophetic spirit to declare, which makes no part of my pretensions."[50]

Revealingly, Madison consistently asserted throughout his career that westward expansion, combined with easy access to export markets, would delay the onset of widespread manufacturing and thus the ills of population concentration. Although he supported immigration to the US, he never abandoned the premise that population growth was dangerous, and he emphasized that the country needed population distribution not only to prevent the tyranny of a faction but also to provide breathing room for what he anticipated would be "redundant members of a populous society."[51] Anticipating Malthus, Madison wrote Jefferson in 1786, "Our limited population has probably as large a share in producing [high living standards] as the political advantages which distinguish us. A certain degree of misery seems inseparable from a high degree of populousness."[52] Disturbed that the Constitution might encourage a "leveling" spirit among the masses, Madison said at the Constitutional Convention, "In framing a system which we wish to last for ages, we shd. not lose sight of the changes which ages will produce. An increase of population will of necessity increase the proportion of those who will labor under all of the hardships of life, and secretly sigh for a more equal distribution of its blessings."[53] Madison thus supported a more powerful central government in part because he hoped that it would have the capacity to manage westward expansion and promote the commercial and foreign policies necessary to stave off the final stage of social development. Although he secured most of what he wanted in the Constitution, he still worried about the moment, just around the corner, when "population becomes so great as to compel us to recur to manufacturers."[54]

Public land policy in the new nation revealed politically divergent views on population. The Federalist Land Act of 1796 authorized the sale of

640-acre-minimum parcels, as established in the Land Ordinance of 1785, but doubled the minimum price to $2 an acre. This high price reflected Federalists' preference for keeping the population from moving west, as these parcels were too big and expensive for the average would-be buyer. In contrast, the Land Act of 1800, backed by the Democratic-Republicans, dropped the minimum parcel to 320 acres and allowed payments to be spread out over a longer period, making it easier for citizens to strike out for the western territories. The Land Act of 1804 reduced the parcels further to 160 acres.[55]

The Democratic-Republican emphasis on distributing the population also fostered the goal of free trade. Although the young nation's trade politics were determined as much by practical interests as by ideas (northern industrialists tended to support protective tariffs, whereas southern planters wanted unimpeded trade with British manufacturers), Jeffersonians especially sought the freest trade possible to preserve ample markets for agricultural surpluses and stave off urban population conglomerations and intensive manufacturing.[56] But the British forced the Americans' hand. They frustrated US efforts to construct an international trading order and refused to enter into reciprocal trade agreements, which led many Jeffersonians to call for commercial "retaliation." These trade tensions eventually led the Jefferson administration to impose a trade embargo in 1807, and then helped cause the War of 1812, a war that undercut many of Jefferson's goals by freezing trade and accordingly spurring domestic manufacturing. Nonetheless, dispersal to the West coupled with free trade remained the preferred antidote to population growth.

Population debates, in sum, were lively in the US before Malthus wrote his *Essay* at the turn of the nineteenth century, with republicanism anticipating Malthusianism's skepticism of population growth (albeit from a very different premise). Subsequently, Americans integrated their responses to Malthus's *Essay* into their population thinking, often toward political as much as intellectual ends. Before detailing Americans' reactions to the *Essay*, however, a brief review of Malthus's place in the history of economic thought is in order.

Malthus and the Classical Tradition

The sixth of seven children, the Rev. Thomas Robert Malthus was a mild-mannered, married, Anglican minster with three children. He was also a professor of history and political economy at the East India College, a new school in England's West Midlands created to train agents of the East India Company. Helping to found several leading intellectual and professional societies, he emerged as one of the earliest "classical" economists, a group of mostly British theorists in the first half of the nineteenth century who promulgated the body of ideas that evolved into modern economics.

Malthus wrote his seminal 1798 *Essay on the Principle of Population* to challenge the utopian ideas of the radical political philosopher William Godwin, author of *An Enquiry Concerning Political Justice*, who, inspired by the revolutionary epoch of the late eighteenth century, believed that paradise, plenty, and human perfectibility were within the grasp of the people of his age. (Godwin was the husband of feminist Mary Wollstonecraft and the father of *Frankenstein* author Mary Shelley.) As historian Steven Stoll puts it, "Malthus dropped the red velvet curtain on the pageant of plenty."[57] Starting from the postulates that "the passion between the sexes" is irrepressible and that fertility rises with the standard of living,[58] Malthus grimy concluded that "the power of population is indefinitely greater than the power in the earth to provide subsistence for man."[59] According to his vicious Catch-22, human beings cannot avert poverty, as Godwin and other optimistic theorists of social improvement insisted; momentary abundance only encourages more births, which in turn produce a subsistence crisis. In the long run, the standard of living does not improve. Malthus did allow that the "preventive check" of delayed marriage and childbearing was already in operation in English society.[60] But more likely to significantly limit fertility was the "positive" check of death, brought about by poor people's "want of proper and sufficient food," war, and, in sum, "misery."[61] In the second, 1803 edition—practically a new book—Malthus, in his own words, "endeavored to soften some of the harshest conclusions of the first Essay."[62] Here he afforded more power to his preventive checks. He also concluded that wages might not plummet to their starting point each time population surged ahead. For the remainder of his career, Malthus continued to chip away at his original notion that population is an endogenous factor; that is, he allowed that external forces such as business depressions, culture, and technology all influence demographic patterns. "Malthus was at the end a somewhat dubious Malthusian," economist Mark Perlman noted a century and a half later.[63]

Malthus's name has become nearly synonymous with "population theory," but several Enlightenment theorists anticipated his ideas. Scottish philosopher David Hume believed that population levels depend on the standard of living and identified many of the same checks on growth, e.g., war, plague, and unjust government.[64] Adam Smith also articulated several insights about the relationship between fertility and the economy that presaged Malthus, but he was optimistic about population growth (in part because he significantly underestimated it in England), and, as mentioned earlier, welcomed the social advancement presumed to accompany it.[65] He wrote, "The progressive state is in reality the cheerful and the hearty state to all the different orders of the society. The stationary is dull; the declining melancholy."[66] Smith's contention that populousness induces a munificent division of labor and economies of scale remains central to pro–population growth theories today. But even if Malthus's *Essay on Population* detoured from the prevailing optimism of the Enlightenment, it was born of immediate political and intellectual circumstances. It reflected the burgeoning of biological science. It also was part of a broader attack by the classical economists on the doctrine of mercantilism.[67] Insisting that all societies progress toward overpopulation and misery, Malthus conformed to Enlightenment stages theory. Above all, Malthus was a theorist of economic growth; his emphasis on population dynamics reflected his larger project of demystifying and promoting capitalist development.

Because Malthusian ideas create such strange political configurations and because Malthus did not leave behind a significant correspondence, scholars have long debated the political intent and implications of his writings. Malthus opposed the English system of poor relief on the grounds it provided an artificial boost to population; he contended that charity eliminated the individual incentive for responsible procreation and promoted early marriage and sexual imprudence. A man who marries without the means to provide for his children, Malthus wrote in the second edition, "should be taught to know that the laws of nature, which are the laws of God, had doomed him and his family to suffer for disobeying their repeated admonitions; that he had no claim of *right* on society for the smallest portion of food."[68] Accordingly, some opponents of government intervention and charity have praised Malthus for his anti-collectivism and emphasis on the sexual habits of the poor. Others have used his model to claim that unemployment is immutable. Karl Marx bitterly suggested that the essence of Malthusian doctrine is the belief that "charity . . . fostered social evils."[69] Malthus's fellow classical economist Nassau Senior, the first professor of political economy at Oxford, wrote that the Malthusian principle was "the stalking-horse of negligence and injustice, the favourite objection to every project for making the resources of the country more productive."[70] Yet others have made Malthus out to be a friend of the working class who genuinely wished to reduce poverty and realized that workers were ultimately not responsible for their plight. Like other famous and almost-never-read-in-the-original theorists, Malthus has been twisted both by his enemies and his allies. Since the late nineteenth century, for example, proponents of population limitation have been called Malthusian or neo-Malthusian, but they have often advocated artificial birth control, which Malthus opposed for theological reasons.

Less ambiguously, the Malthusian framework was a pillar of classic economics.[71] Indeed, economist Ralph Hess was correct when he wrote nearly a century ago, "A combination of the Malthusian doctrine of population and the Ricardian theory of rent [the economic return to land] constitutes the foundation of modern theories of economic welfare and wealth distribution."[72] Moreover, conservative presumptions about the limited efficacy of social reform are rooted in Malthusian population doctrine. Englishman David Ricardo, the towering figure in classical economics most famous for developing the theory that nations ought to specialize in exports in which they have a "comparative advantage," challenged Malthus's late-career work on economic value but extended his basic model of demographically induced scarcity. Ricardo refined the Malthusian formula that workers are doomed to perpetual poverty into an "iron law of wages": the cost of labor is that which allows workers to survive without either an increase or decrease in their numbers. (Whenever wages rise, population growth rises in tandem, which forces wages back down. If wages decrease below the level of subsistence, population contracts accordingly.) Ricardo also formally developed the theory of diminishing returns to production suggested by Malthusian doctrine: because newer lands brought under cultivation are less fertile than those already cultivated, they yield increasingly less per unit of input.[73]

John Stuart Mill, the most renowned classical economist after Adam Smith, also began his population analysis from Malthus's basic model. Like Smith, Mill acknowledged that wage levels could rise permanently, especially if population could be reduced, and he allowed for technological progress in harnessing natural resources. But he affirmed the premise that population growth ultimately engulfs resources. Mill envisioned a much happier final stage than Malthusian misery, however; as investment opportunities wane and population levels off, civilization will reach a "stationary state," a pleasant end-point that frees people to pursue the finer aspects of life.[74]

Some later classical economists, such as Nassau Senior, cast a skeptical eye on Malthus's and Ricardo's grim conclusions, emphasizing that technological innovation could stave off diminishing returns. They also argued that the desire to improve one's station in life by limiting family size counteracted the proclivity to procreate.[75] But on the whole, economic historian D. P. O'Brien writes, the Malthusian theory of population "remained a continuing thread in Classical economics."[76] In 1875, economist J. E. Cairnes noted that although the Malthusian doctrine was periodically challenged, it remained "quite fundamental in the science of Political Economy."[77] The next chapter discusses how this Malthusian legacy would become an important point of contestation for the first generation of professional American economists in the late nineteenth century. More immediately, Malthusian ideas also played a role in the greatest political crisis in American history.

From the *Essay* to the Sectional Crisis

Historians generally conclude that nineteenth-century Americans paid Malthus little heed.[78] "In the United States," writes Laura Lovett in her study of pronatalism, "Malthus's warnings concerning unchecked reproduction did not have the same force [as in England]. The United States in the mid-nineteenth century still imagined that it had free land with seemingly unlimited resources and was a destination for European immigrants as a result."[79] In this vein, the nation was providing its mushrooming population with cheap and fertile land, abundant export markets for its surplus, and a steadily rising standard of living.[80] Americans were predisposed to find distasteful the pastor's comment that anyone who believed that the US could retain "perpetual youth" and the "happy state of the lower classes of people . . . by preventing the introduction of manufactures and luxury . . . might as reasonably expect to prevent a wife or mistress from growing old by never exposing her to the sun or air."[81] Moreover, Malthus's rejection of progress and his presumption of intractable social inequality ran counter to the democratic spirit of the Revolution, which continued to animate national identity well into the nineteenth century. Perhaps some theorists recognized the ultimate logic of Malthus's model, the argument goes, but they assumed that a high standard of living would eventually induce Americans to limit their numbers. Or, they simply stressed the uniqueness and providential grace of the American experiment.

Although a sense of unbridled optimism ran through nineteenth-century American society, with some antebellum political economists giving it a theoretical and ebulliently nationalistic imprimatur, other theorists retained the republican aversion to the final, populous stage of societal development, even after explosive growth in manufacturing rendered anti-commercialism obsolete. These thinkers also embraced the anti–population growth posture of the European classical economists. By the 1830s and 1840s, Malthusian ideas had become especially salient as they were increasingly linked to—and distorted by—the two great interrelated policy issues of the day: slavery and westward expansion. Although northern and southern partisans both used Malthusian precepts, it was southern intellectuals especially who constructed a distinct Malthusianism, one meant to reinforce the region's maturing proslavery ideology.

Malthus's *Essay* initially garnered mixed reviews. Few Americans read the anonymously published 1798 edition, and those who did, including Thomas Jefferson, generally disliked it.[82] McCoy notes that the second, 1803 edition was better received than the first because it dropped claims of biologically inevitable poverty and emphasized the insidious economic harms of mercantilism. Praising Malthus's anti-mercantilism, Jefferson labeled the second edition "one of the ablest I have ever seen."[83] But the third president, much more optimistic than Malthus about the fate of the masses, was also a high-profile critic. In response to the axiom that population grows exponentially whereas food supplies increase merely arithmetically, Jefferson opined that America, because of its "immensity of land,"[84] could enlarge its harvest exponentially, thus staving off European-style manufacturing.[85] Anticipating future land acquisitions, Jefferson assured his compatriots in his First Inaugural Address that their "chosen country" contained "room enough for our descendants to the thousandth and thousandth generation."[86] American harvests grew "geometrically with our labors," he wrote in 1804 to French theorist J. B. Say, allowing Americans to "nourish the now perishing births of Europe."[87] The Virginian also faulted Malthus for not recognizing that emigration could alleviate population problems.[88]

Disparate other Americans doubted the Reverend's wisdom. Americans working in the nascent field of statistics supported Jefferson's assumptions and rejected Malthus's mathematics. Crunching the numbers on the American land-to-person ratio after the Louisiana Purchase of 1803, these early statisticians concluded that ease of emigration to the western frontier would allow the states to enjoy the benefits of increased population density in older areas without the social drawbacks Europe endured.[89] Diplomat Alexander Everett criticized Malthus for failing to see that every additional person is a producer as well as a consumer,[90] and Ralph Waldo Emerson noted that ancient philosophers "saw before them no sinister political economy; no ominous Malthus."[91] Antebellum writers who claimed that the Malthusian model was inapplicable to their wide-open, thinly populated, and democratic land often espoused an early version of American "exceptionalism," the conviction that America is the apple of God's eye.[92] A determination to develop a political economy shaped by America's unique climate, high birthrate, and huge land mass rather than by European experiences reinforced this exceptionalism. Nathaniel Ware, a southern planter, banker, and political economist, conceded the fact of eventual world overpopulation but placed faith in the fantastic bounty of America's land and the unique ingenuity of its citizens.[93] He felt certain that science and technology would dramatically increase crop yields, and that a higher standard of living would lower the birthrate because Americans took "pride" in their appearance and possessions.[94] He also opposed further extension of American territory because "population must have a certain density to accomplish any great object."[95] German émigré Friedrich List captured exceptionalist sentiments perfectly when he wrote of his adopted country, "The condition of this nation cannot be compared with the condition of any other nation. The same kind of government and same structure of society were never seen before; not such general and equal distribution of property, of instruction, of industry, of power and wealth; nor similar accomplishments in the gifts of nature, bestowing upon this people natural riches and advantages of the north, of the south, and of the temperate climates, all the advantages of vast sea shores and of an immense unsettled continent."[96] List predicted that high fertility would ensure future American domination of the world economy.[97]

List, Ware, and other political economists in the Federalist tradition—Whigs by the 1830s—argued that America's unique position demanded significant federal intervention in the economy. Sometimes called the "American School," this camp promoted a nationalist (and optimistic) political economy that broke with the classical economists' laissez-faire (and pessimistic) ideology. Whereas many classical economists promoted free trade (that is, low tariff barriers), nationalist economists supported the "American System" of protective tariffs on manufactured goods, support for infant industries, stimulation of immigration, and state-sponsored internal improvements. Members of the American School tended to frown upon Malthus's and most other classical economists' supposition that economic relations are the inevitable outcome of "natural" laws of population, and they had no qualms with population and manufacturing rising in tandem.

Perhaps the most important member of the American School was Henry Carey, an insurance executive and famous political economist who, in several pro-tariff texts written from the 1820s to the 1840s, argued that advanced societies successfully regulate the size of their populations and that wise government policy and technology trump population-induced scarcity.[98] Carey's protectionism and anti-Malthusianism were closely linked; he maintained that Americans' wages were high not because of ample lands but because industrialization enhanced workers skills and productivity and spurred investment in education.[99] Moreover, writes historian James Huston, protectionists simply did not like the pessimistic theories of Malthus and Ricardo because they made republican notions of rough equality "utterly untenable."[100]

Although they stressed the uniqueness of the American project, optimists borrowed from disparate European intellectual traditions, including Deism, Rationalism, and Jacobean Radicalism, to denounce Malthusianism.[101] Some theorists maintained that the US was immune from Malthus's iron law because it had skipped various stages of development.[102] Francis Wayland, president of Brown University and author of a leading antebellum political economy textbook, doubted that the Creator would make the world as Malthus described it and argued that capital formation in the United States outpaced population growth.[103] Others contended that Malthus minimized the benefits of international trade. Jedidiah Morse, a well-known geographer and demographer of Indian tribes, claimed that economic development and population were mutually and positively reinforcing as he worried New England was losing the battle of population growth to the other regions.[104] Still others anticipated the modern anti-Malthusian position that population growth spurs innovation and thus creates more wealth for more people.[105] In keeping with List's reference to America's beneficent climate, however, most antebellum population optimists were content to sing the praises of America's natural bounty. Erasmus Peshine Smith, a mathematician and federal official, published a refutation of Malthus in 1853. He wrote, "It is impossible to conjecture a limit to the increase of population if man will but conform to the law which Nature exemplifies in all her processes, by which the soil regains whatever material of nutrient it has lent for the support of vegetable and animal life."[106] Daniel Raymond, author of one of the earliest American treatises on political economy (1820), wrote that "the earth is capable of being made to yield an indefinite and almost unlimited quantity of food."[107]

This rejection of limits reflected a transformative intellectual development nurtured in the US. During the first few decades of the nineteenth century, remarkable advancements in transportation and technology and a more fully integrated national market combined to bring consumerism to the middle classes. Public-oriented republicanism gradually yielded to individual- and property rights–oriented liberalism. These developments helped give birth to a novel idea that human societies could enjoy perpetual economic progress—growth—beyond mere expansion across geographic space. Put another way, societies need not stagnate or decline after reaching the final stage of development, as republican theory maintained. Steven Stoll argues that the new concept of economic growth, advanced between the 1820s and the 1850s, was nothing less than a radical utopian project that assumed human ingenuity would discover, unleash, and create from scratch unlimited natural resources. Furthermore, growth would solve myriad social problems but produce none. At the center of Stoll's *Great Delusion* is John Adulphus Etzler, a utopian German engineer who emigrated to the US in 1831 and then died in Venezuela trying to perfect his bizarre farm machinery and utopian social arrangements. Etzler believed that the earth could support a population of one trillion.[108]

One more development encouraged population optimism. Antebellum Americans recognized that population growth rates, although certain to remain high, were decreasing from those Franklin and Malthus used in their projections. Fecundity lost its revered status as a civic virtue at the turn of the nineteenth century. As women increasingly participated in civic affairs and the market, and egalitarian notions of the household took root, average family size began to decline.[109] (During the nineteenth century, each generation would have fewer children than the one before it, and the birthrate decreased from about eight babies per woman in 1800 to four in 1900.)[110] White Americans underwent the "demographic transition" to lower birthrates well in advance of women in every European nation except France. The immediate causes of the transition were later marriages and planned and spaced procreation (more so than increased use of contraception). Historians debate potential deeper causes, such as the rise of companionate marriage, a more sentimental view of childbearing, the higher cost of raising children, consumerism, urbanization and industrialization, the spread of the wage system, and, for women, the leveling spirit of the American Revolution.[111]

Yet even as families had fewer children, many older elite Americans weaned on Revolutionary-era republicanism still feared the limits described by Malthus. In his retirement, James Madison complained about English writer William Godwin's continued attacks on Malthus.[112] Although Madison thought that America's beneficent institutions would allow it to grow for some time to come, and suggested that a true crisis of subsistence lay only in the remote future, he argued, as he had in the prior century, that population growth engenders poverty and myriad social problems. For instance, Madison doubted the wisdom of manufacturer-turned-socialist Robert Owen's vision of a utopian community in New Harmony, Indiana. Hosting Owen at his home in Virginia, Madison asked him what he planned to do when his experimental community outgrew its food supply—and was not satisfied with Owen's anti-Malthusian reply.[113]

To a new generation of pro-Malthus political economists writing in the 1820s and 1830s, such as Columbia University's John McVickar, older republican anxieties about population expansion were less important than the ideas of the classical economists.[114] In addition, theorists influenced by Calvinism's harsh theology tended to view Malthusianism more favorably than those influenced by Unitarianism, which rejected the idea that humans are doomed at birth.[115] By the 1840s, however, sectional politics had become paramount to the American population debate. As the "great tariff debate" engulfed England, American proponents of free trade (that is, those who wanted low tariff barriers) were more likely to accept Malthusian precepts than protectionists. Free traders agreed with Malthus's assumption that government ultimately has little control over the direction of the economy and his forgiveness of large levels of inequality, even if many still argued that the open lands of the West would retard the development of a European-style society.[116] Importantly, Southerners were significantly more prone to support free trade than Northerners; they had fewer industries to protect and desired open markets for their cotton and other raw materials. This geographic divide added another layer through which demographic anxieties contributed to the intensifying division between the North and the South, known as the sectional crisis.

Already by the second quarter of the nineteenth century, sectional bias and positions in the slavery debate increasingly had affected analysis of population trends, including the crucial facts that population was increasing faster in the free states than in the slaves states and that, after

1830, the fertility rate among slaves surpassed that of whites and would remain higher until the Civil War.[117] (American slaves enjoyed relatively good health and high birthrates compared with slaves in most of the world and indeed constituted one of the only slave populations that reproduced itself.) A smattering of southern antislavery writers did suggest that slavery kept the southern population dangerously weighted in favor of blacks and retarded white immigration to the region, but the ranks of these southern opponents of slavery declined precipitously after 1830. More prominently, a swath of southern theorists drew on Malthusian ideas, especially the inexorable downward pressure of wages, because they could twist them to promote a proslavery agenda. Joseph Spengler, a leading twentieth-century population economist whom we will encounter throughout this book, noted that by the 1830s, when southern elites developed a more assertive proslavery doctrine in response to several slave insurrections, elements of Malthusian theory were "virtually the most important, though not always explicitly recognized, basis of the proslavery argument."[118]

That the South became a hotbed of Malthusian economics prior to the Civil War reflected an ironic reversal. The Southerners who helped create the United States had believed that the demographic cards favored their region and celebrated its anticipated growth.[119] Anticipating heavy migration and immigration to the southern backcountry, Northerners generally agreed that southern growth would outpace northern.[120] Many Revolutionary-era elites also considered the North demographically mature and fully settled—perhaps even headed toward depopulation—and underestimated the coming settlement in the territories that became the Old Northwest.[121] "If there be any event, on which we may calculate with certainty, I take it that the centre of population will continually advance in a south-western direction," James Madison wrote in 1789 as he lobbied to place the new national government in what became Washington, D.C., and not in a more northern city.[122]

These assumptions of pending regional demographic divergence encouraged southern acceptance of the compromises at the Constitutional Convention that based congressional representation on population and considered a slave to be three-fifths of a person. But after the 1810 and 1820 censuses diminished southern power in Congress, many Southerners realized that their region was not the demographic juggernaut imagined in Philadelphia.[123] A sense of impending demographic decline was already present during the congressional debates in 1820 about whether to admit Missouri as a slave state. (The Missouri Compromise banned slavery north of 36° 30′, except in the territory that became Missouri.) Thereafter, demographic projections became even more politically charged as sectional relations deteriorated and the South's share of the national population decreased steadily.[124]

Proslavery Southerners such as well-known propagandist George Fitzhugh turned to Malthus to condemn northern "free labor" society.[125] Emerging in the 1830s, free labor discourse updated republican emphasis on the land-owning farmer by lionizing all independent entrepreneurs, including shopkeepers and even small factory owners.[126] Its emphasis on the necessity of owning the fruits of one's own labor also explicitly critiqued the un-free labor of slavery. In Abraham Lincoln's words, "the word liberty may mean for each man to do as he pleases with himself, and the product of his labor."[127] Southern Malthusians, however, equated the free labor system with unemployment and low wages, which, they believed, inevitably accompanied population pressure. More specifically, following the Malthusian-Ricardian iron law of wages, which predicted the immiseration of the earth's masses, they claimed that slavery, in contrast to the northern wage system, protected a surplus labor pool from the ravages of excessive competition and population pressure. In addition, they argued that slavery helped keep population and natural resources in balance because it retarded population increase among whites. Poor whites could not compete with slave labor, so immigration to the region was checked. Finally, slavery fostered efficient land use by preserving an agricultural economy, which, in classic republican terms, prevented manufacturing-induced population concentrations.

A few Southerners denied that slavery put pressure on white population growth, but the majority admitted a demographic drag, and, in Malthusian terms, identified social advantages arising from it. According to a classic study of proslavery ideology, "the slaveholder concluded that slavery was the best answer to the gloomy speculation advanced under the Malthusian law."[128] In this vein, the South's languid demographics and slow pace of life compared favorably to the rapid population growth in northern industrial cities, which pauperized workers and created a permanent class of urban wage slaves. One contributor to the widely read southern journal *De Bow's Review* declared, "Great cities are beginning to be plague-centers in the social system."[129] (Editor James De Bow was a prominent Malthusian.) Southern theorists in this camp usually opposed white immigration as well, and, in a further rebuke of free labor doctrine, branded European immigrants "white slaves" who could not be assimilated into American society.[130]

Although some proslavery voices suggested that the slave system would eventually triumph over free labor because it retarded Malthusian pressure on wages and kept society harmonious, others used Malthusian arguments to predict the eventual demise of slavery! Another leading proslavery Malthusian was George Tucker, a political economist and US Representative from Virginia. Initially anti-Malthus, Tucker reversed course in the 1840s, claiming that the procreative impulse would depress wages and identifying "natural limits, which cannot be exceeded" to the food supply.[131] He also suggested that rising numbers of people would eventually eradicate slavery organically because population pressure would reduce the cost of free labor—thereby eliminating the advantage for slave labor over free. This insistence on the future unprofitability of slavery was an important component of the prevailing southern argument that the slave system required no forceful intervention—it would die on its own. Among many others, political economist Thomas R. Dew, president of the College of William and Mary, also predicted that population growth would doom slavery's economic advantage (and, therefore, that it was unwise for the state to sponsor the emigration of slaves from Virginia).[132] More specifically, Dew contended that, at present, slavery was a superior system to free labor but, as the South gained in wealth and numbers, a process he hoped to accelerate through internal improvements, more cities and higher population densities would "render the division of labor more complete, break down the large farms into small ones, and substitute, in a great measure, the garden for the plantation cultivation; consequently, less slave, and more free labor will be requisite, and in due time the abolitionists will find this most lucrative system working to their heart's content."[133] Other Southerners indirectly used Malthusian foundations to argue against social welfare spending. For instance, they argued that public education encouraged pauperism by providing the offspring of the idle poor with an undeserved boon.[134]

To be sure, the South also nurtured a strain of Malthusian unrelated to the slavery question, in part because the region's agrarianism—and the exhaustion of much of its soil—fit with Malthus's land-based model better than the North's industrial society. For example, chemist and political economist Thomas Cooper, president of what became the University of South Carolina, maintained in simple Malthusian terms that rising numbers of people would overwhelm agricultural innovation and technological progress.[135] Cooper considered the Malthusian wage position "manifest truth,"[136] and he proposed that only people who could afford a family be allowed to marry![137] But Cooper's wage theory was also connected to the free-trade doctrine that prevailed in the region, a doctrine, like the Malthusian-Ricardian theory of diminishing returns, central to classical economics. Whereas protectionists in both regions dismissed Malthusian-Ricardian economics and were optimists about improving the lot of mankind—they in fact anticipated the modern rejection of Malthus based on the expectation of the rational limiting of births—advocates of free trade such as Cooper, in line with the classical tradition, were optimistic only as long as abundant land existed and believed that wages eventually shrank to subsistence level.[138] Thus in the South, it was generally the small minority of protectionists who comprised the ranks of the anti-Malthusians.[139]

In the South, both protectionists and free traders believed that slavery would eventually die on its own. But the assumed paths toward disappearance were entirely different. As mentioned, free traders/Malthusians such as Tucker believed that population growth would depress wages to the point that free labor would be cheaper than slave labor, thus ending the economic viability of the latter. Protectionists, however, believed that over time free labor would become much more productive than slavery. Accordingly, capitalists would willingly pay higher wages for the output gains and higher profits free labor realized over slavery. And slaveholders would convert their slaves to free labor to enjoy the higher returns of productivity.[140] This idea, incidentally, was part of a theory most famously espoused by Henry Carey that a Harmony of Interests existed between laborers and capitalists—both groups could earn more over time, which directly rebutted the Ricardian insistence on a conflict between wages and profits. Southerners with disparate views on economic policy thus united to the extent that they all advanced the self-serving position that sectional strife was not worth the trouble; their region could and should maintain slavery as long as it was profitable, but abolitionists could take solace in the future elimination of the peculiar institution.

Abolitionists, for their part, did not often advance population theories of their own to counter proslavery Malthusianism, instead stressing a basic human-rights argument against slavery and insisting that it stunted the southern economy.[141] Still, some theorists in the North did argue against slavery because, in their view, it lowered the overall growth of the US population by driving down wages and thus reducing the desire of whites to have children, while also lessening the incentive for foreigners to emigrate. Northerners would increasingly dip into these Malthusian themes when the territorial expansion of slavery came to dominate the national discussion.[142]

The demographic-slavery debate came to a head when America expanded to the Pacific Ocean, annexing Texas in 1845 and, after the resulting Mexican-American War of 1846–48, acquiring all of what became California, Nevada, and Utah and parts of four additional states. Expansionists also threatened war with Great Britain in 1846 over the borders of the Oregon Territory before reaching a compromise. In 1846, Rep. David Wilmot (Whig-Pa.) unsuccessfully introduced a proviso that would have barred slavery from any territory captured during the imminent war with Mexico. Thereafter, until the Civil War resolved it, the question of whether to extend slavery into the territories was the central policy question in the United States. Now, demographic theories were complicated not only by different readings of Malthusian theory and projections of future population patterns but also by the contest between pro- and antislavery forces for political power. The debate reflected the lingering tendency to think about economic growth in geographic terms rather than as an indigenous and potentially perennial process.

Many Southerners supposed that efforts to block slavery in the territories represented a power grab by the North and was akin to abolitionism. They argued that expansion of slavery would prevent a dangerous increase in slave densities where the institution currently existed. Conversely, they stipulated, in Malthusian terms, that limiting the reach of slavery would overpopulate the eastern states and drive down overall wage levels. In turn, poverty would diminish the white population. Moreover, an increase in slaves and a decrease in whites would produce slave rebellions and race war.[143] Southerners in favor of the US's 1845 annexation of the Republic of Texas also borrowed from Jefferson to argue that territorial expansion would beneficently "diffuse" the slave population into the West.[144] If slaves were dispersed into the territories, small farms would replace large plantations, humanizing relations between master and slave and putting the institution on the path toward extinction. Or perhaps eventually slaves would exhaust the soil of the southwestern United States and would cease to be profitable.[145]

The northern parties opposed to the extension of slavery—Free Soil, Liberty, and eventually Republican—also articulated Malthusian themes. They held that if slavery were permitted to expand onto new lands, the number of slaves would grow exponentially.[146] But if slavery could be restricted to its present locations, it would eventually die a natural death after rapid population growth among slaves exhausted the soil and generated a Malthusian crisis. The actual assumed implications here were quite grim. Abraham Lincoln suggested during his famous 1858 Illinois senatorial debates with Stephen A. Douglas that containing slavery in its present locations would eventually cause slaves to die of starvation, an argument that Douglas mocked as "the humane and Christian remedy that he proposes for the great crime of slavery."[147] Northern opponents of slavery's extension also argued in republican and Malthusian terms that the very point of the territories was that they provided a bastion for free labor that helped stave off the ills associated with dense populations.

In the end, James Huston concludes, "Malthusian population theory misled everyone in the antebellum period and it may be proposed that it only made the sectional dispute worse. It led northerners to believe that slavery could be ended by a restriction policy and convinced southerners that if slavery were to be restricted from westward expansion the apocalypse would not be long in coming."[148]

Malthusian Destiny

Apart from different demographic readings, basic attitudes toward slavery were, of course, a key variable in the debate about expanding the borders of the United States. Some Southerners promoted territorial expansion—and especially war with Mexico—because they believed that it would advance the cause of securing additional slave states, and some Northerners opposed expansion because they feared the spread of slavery.[149] Yet many Americans in both regions, regardless of their position on slavery, thought that territorial growth would continue to keep America "young" and free from the excessive manufacturing, class conflict, and corruption of "old" nations. This older republican line of thought merged with the newer doctrine of "Manifest Destiny," a racialized ideology claiming that the American people possessed not only the wherewithal and the right but indeed the duty to expand the boundaries of the United States and spread the trappings of their nearly perfect democracy across the entire continent. Notions of American exceptionalism and the superiority of America were as old as the first colonies, but Manifest Destiny expanded these ideas, emerging in the second quarter of the nineteenth century as the product of several factors: scientific racism and the social construction of a unique and superior "Anglo-Saxon race"; the development of an American Romantic movement; confidence resulting from astonishing technological and economic progress; and an impulse to rationalize slavery and the brutal treatment of Native Americans.

Pro-population dogma, especially the assumption America's population growth was a sign of God's favorable treatment, ran through Manifest Destiny. In December 1830, the year his Indian Removal bill passed Congress, President Andrew Jackson, the first president from the new Democratic Party (which followed the Democratic-Republican Party) said in his annual message, "What good man would prefer a country covered with forests and ranged by a few thousand savages to our extensive Republic, studded with cities, towns, and prosperous farms, embellished with all the improvements which art can devise or industry execute, occupied by more than 12,000,000 happy people, and filled with all the blessings of liberty, civilization, and religion?"[150] Editor and Democratic politician John O' Sullivan coined the term "Manifest Destiny" in 1845 while defending Congress's and President Tyler's recent decision to annex Texas. O'Sullivan complained that other countries were interfering with the inevitable American domination of the continent, "thwarting our policy and hampering our power, limiting our greatness and checking the fulfillment of our manifest destiny to overspread the continent allotted by Providence for the free development of our yearly multiplying millions."[151] He asserted that other countries were interfering with the inevitable American domination of the continent. During the crisis with England over the Oregon Territory, *Merchants' Magazine and Commercial Review* asserted, "No power on earth, nor all the powers of the earth, can check the swelling tide of the American population.... Every portion of this continent, from the sunny south to the frozen north, will be, in a very few years, filled with industrious and thriving Anglo-Saxons."[152] Sen. Thomas Hart Benton (D-Mich.) said, "It would seem that the White race alone received the divine command, to subdue and replenish the earth; for it is the only race that has obeyed it—the only race that hunts out new and distant lands, and even a New World, to subdue and replenish."[153]

Underneath its imperialist and racist rhetoric, however, Manifest Destiny extended the republican tradition of seeking to diffuse social tensions through geographic growth, revealing continued anxieties about population increase without new lands to offset its concomitant effects. According to the zero-sum thinking of many proponents of westward expansion, the alternatives to territorial domination were stagnation and decline. In the 1840s and 1850s, such sentiments became central to the Democratic Party's promotion of not only territorial expansion but also population redistribution to the West to settle homesteads carved from the public domain. Encouraging the westward dispersal of the population of workers would keep wages high in the East and maintain egalitarian economic opportunity. Horace Greeley, the editor of the *New York Tribune* who famously urged the poor to strike out for the West, wrote in 1854, "The public lands are the great regulator of the relations of Labor and Capital, the safety valve of our industrial and social engine."[154] O'Sullivan boasted of the nation's population growth, but he stressed the virtues of sparsely settled lands and called the remaining public domain America's "safety valve."[155] Promoting resettlement in the West for economic reasons was not precisely the same as providence- and race-based Manifest Destiny, but both offered solutions to perceived dilemmas of demographic maturity. Expansionists, in sum, agreed with Jefferson that the solution to population growth was westward expansion, but they did not share his vision of there being "room enough for our descendants to the thousandth and thousandth generation." In their view, it was the task, and opportunity, of present generations to settle the large but limited lands of the West.

Northern Democrats used population-pressure arguments to defend westward expansion, but they were not so Malthusian as to oppose immigration to the United States; indeed, during the 1830s and 1840s, the Democratic Party forged an alliance with immigrants that has persisted to the present day. Whigs became more favorable to the suppression of immigration, but this position reflected simple racism, and fears that immigrant voting would corrupt republican institutions, rather than Malthusian logic.[156] It was attitudes towards geographic expansion that illuminated the key difference between the parties' population thinking. Democrats insisted that new lands were needed to stave off social problems, poverty, and demographic maturity. "Our population has become comparatively dense; our new lands are exhausted," read the Democratic *Quarterly Review* in 1844.[157] Expansion was thus needed to stave off the creation of permanent and hostile classes. More mundanely, westward expansion would reduce tensions between native-born and immigrant workers within the Democratic Party.[158] According to historian Thomas Hietala, Democrats' recourse to Manifest Destiny reflected a "crisis of confidence" more than it did the rise of scientific racism—and central to the anxieties prompting western adventures were fears of population growth and modernization.[159] Many Democrats, especially in the South, supported several Jeffersonian policies designed to slow down modernization, such as keeping the public lands cheap and trade as free as possible—which would ensure that factories remained in Europe—but territorial expansion was absolutely essential. A desire to produce enough cotton to control world markets additionally boosted expansionist sentiment.

Some antislavery Whigs advocated expansion because they believed that it would reduce the number of slaves in the border states and that diffusing slavery would put it on the road to elimination.[160] Most Whigs, however, opposed expansion and dismissed or even disputed the population-pressure argument. "To Whigs," writes historian Daniel Howe in his study of the antebellum period, "westward expansion seemed a recipe for continuing an undue reliance on agriculture and an inefficiently thin dispersion of population, perpetuating America's neocolonial dependence on foreign manufacturers and capital."[161] They also opposed expansion because they were fearful of the extension of slavery into new territories and did not want white Americans amalgamating with Mexicans. Whigs supported modernizing the American economy rather than merely increasing its geographic scope. Like the Federalists before them, they welcomed population growth—so long as the industrial centers it produced remained in the East, where they enjoyed their political base.

Such were the terms of the debate when US politicians decided the fate of Oregon and northern Mexico. The prelude to the Mexican War pitted President James Polk and most of his fellow Democrats, who supported expansion and specifically the invasion of Mexico, against the Whigs, who either opposed expansion for the reasons just discussed or, in limited cases, were morally opposed to war. Polk unabashedly linked American "greatness" to rapid population growth and territorial expansion,[162] and suggested that the expected doubling of the population every twenty-three years necessitated the acquisition of additional western lands.[163] Senator Lewis Cass, formerly Andrew Jackson's secretary of war, predicted that the US would one day be as populous as China and, pointing to the evils lurking in Europe's crowded cities, identified Mexico as America's "safety valve."[164] In turn, these ultimately successful calls for expansionism suggested the endurance of the same demographic contradictions embodied in the founders' republicanism. Simultaneous to his argument that expansion was essential to thwart population pressure, Polk also crowed that "as our population has expanded, the union has been cemented and strengthened."[165] Population growth remained a double-edged sword; Americans celebrated it while simultaneously fearing the consequences of it in the absence of territorial expansion.

The Civil War seemed to confirm Alexis de Tocqueville's nervous observation after his visit to the rapidly growing United States: "For a society of nations as for a society of individuals, there are three principal chances for longevity: the wisdom of the members, their individual weakness, and their small number."[166] Drew Gilpin Faust writes in *This Republic of Suffering*, "more than 2 percent of the nation's inhabitants were dead as a direct result of the war—the approximate equivalent of the population in 1860 of the state of Maine, more than the entire population of Arkansas or Connecticut, twice the population of Vermont, more than the whole male population of Georgia or Alabama."[167] Even after this carnage, however, and even after Americans disproved Tocqueville's observation by rebuilding their nation and numbers, pouring into the West, and rushing headlong into the hurly-burly of industrial capitalism, republican anxieties about population growth remained. Indeed, the "closing of the frontier" in the late nineteenth century seemed to confirm the old fear that America lived on borrowed demographic time. Yet in these same years, the birth of modern economic theory threw the old classical certainties regarding population into disarray, and a fresh optimism about the consequences of population growth emanated from the first generation of professionally trained American economists.

CHAPTER TWO

The Birth of the Modern Population Debate

The specter of an expanding populace prematurely aging the young republic and ushering in manufacturing, luxury, and corruption permeated the Early American political economy and animated the sectional crisis. Yet many scholars date the arrival of widespread population anxiety to the end of the nineteenth century. They suggest that the "closing" of the frontier (after the Census of 1890, the Census Bureau noted the absence of a clear geographic line of westward settlement), economic depression in the 1890s, accelerating immigration, the maturation of a European-style urban industrial proletariat, and, finally, the emergence of the American eugenics movement, which in turn boosted the movement to restrict immigration, all facilitated the widespread belief that the United States had "filled up"—that its natural resource base and social fabric could no longer absorb population growth.[1]

Although this narrative exaggerates population optimism in the nineteenth century, it holds some validity. As David Wrobel chronicles in *The End of American Exceptionalism*, the closing of the frontier provided intellectual undercurrents that buttressed American Malthusianism. Hence Richard T. Ely, arguably America's most famous economist at the turn of the century and one of the liberal founders of the American Economic Association, argued in 1893, "All countries tend to fullness, and newness always disappears in time."[2] Unless the US tamed its population growth, Ely warned, "in a comparatively short period there would not be standing room on the surface of the earth for all the people."[3] Ely wrote the same year that his friend historian Frederick Jackson Turner proffered his famous "frontier thesis," which posits that American democracy and individualism were forged through the steady recourse to "free land" in the West.[4] Summarizing the history of American population thought a half century later, Duke University economist Joseph Spengler, a leading actor in population policy debates from the 1920s to 1970s, wrote: "In the closing period covered by our study, 1890–1910, Malthusianism was defended by almost every [American] economist of note."[5]

This chapter shows, however, that Malthusianism was actually on shaky ground in fin de siècle America. To be sure, business and town boosters, who always make the best populationists, continued to articulate a vision of America as the land of unlimited growth and natural wealth. Yet a closer look at the era's political-economic expertise reveals that economists disagreed fervently on population matters—in short, many seemed to have missed the closing-of-the-frontier memo. By the turn of the twentieth century, economists divided into pro- and anti-Malthusian camps largely along political lines, with conservatives generally expressing reservations about population growth and liberals embracing it. And the great theoretical development in economics at the end of the nineteenth century—the "marginalist revolution"—had done little to alter this bifurcated state of affairs because population theory occupied an ambiguous place in it.

As students of American history know well, during the first three decades of the twentieth century, the American eugenics movement played a significant role in increasing anxiety about population change. It helped pass spurious laws that sterilized thousands of institutionalized women deemed genetically inferior, aided in the cause of immigration restriction, and, more generally, contributed to the reactionary politics of the interwar years. But eugenics and Malthusianism were often at odds. By the 1920s, Malthusian sentiment was ascendant in the broader culture, and economists and demographers had formed a moderate Malthusian consensus, but this consensus resulted from the professionalization of population social science as much as from eugenics.

Marginal Concerns

After 1870, British, Continental, and to a lesser degree American economists erected the doctrine of marginalism, a new stress on the individual preferences of consumers and producers which, according to leading economic historian Thomas McCraw, "began to shake the very foundations of economics" and launched modern (or "neoclassical") economics.[6] Marginal doctrine was ambiguous regarding the relationship between population growth and the economy; this ambiguity contributed to the lack of consensus regarding population at the turn of the century and, more broadly, revealed that modern economic theory mandates no particular set of ideas regarding population.

Starting from the observation that human beings are essentially self-interested, marginalists emphasized the individual choices consumers and producers make to maximize happiness and economic performance. They overturned the classical economists' labor theory of value, which claimed that price is determined by the costs of inputs to the product plus profit, and even older notions of a "just" price set by the community, and erected a new definition of value based on individualistic behavioral propositions. More specifically, the "marginal utility theory of value" posited that the utility (value) of a commodity is subjective, based solely on what the market can bear at a particular moment given consumers' tastes and income. (The related theory of marginal productivity stressed producers' current and anticipated expenses and revenue.) The value of each additional unit of something produced—that is, the unit produced at the margin—decreases or increases depending upon the situational preferences of the consumer. For example, a meal is worth more to someone when he or she has been fasting than when he or she has just eaten. Hotel minibars vividly demonstrate the theory of marginal utility. A guest may balk at a $9 jar of cashews at 6 p.m. but devour it at 2 a.m., when no other options exist! And marginal utility characteristically diminishes—that first bunch of cashews is worth more than the second and so forth. The marginalists anticipated the mathematical emphasis of today's economics by devising new quantitative methods of analyzing the subjective and psychological variables surrounding human decision-making.[7]

As we have seen, a theory of diminishing returns, espoused most starkly by Malthus and best by his contemporary David Ricardo, was central to classical economics.[8] Examining their predominantly nonindustrial world through an agricultural lens, the classical economists observed that newer land brought under cultivation yields less than older and better land—diminishing returns to a factor of production, often shortened to simply diminishing returns. From this land-based observation, they extrapolated a more general principle that ramping up any economic activity leads to increasingly smaller gains in production—diminishing returns to scale.[9]

The economists who launched marginalism, however, were of mixed minds on the theories of diminishing returns and diminishing returns to scale. Some seamlessly incorporated them into the neoclassical revolution; and indeed the idea of diminishing returns remains an important element of mainstream economic theory today. Other marginalists rejected the classicalists' skeptical posture. These optimistic individuals did not disavow the theoretical principle of diminishing returns—few economists then or now have ever done so—but they insisted on the real-world presence of *increasing* returns to scale. As it pertained to the population question, this optimists' camp helped develop the idea that the more people, the more wealth: assuming technological improvements and multiple inputs, population growth increases production and happily engenders economies of scale that permit more people to live well.[10] On the whole, probably a slight majority of economists who shaped the development of neoclassical theory was sympathetic to Malthusian tenets. These theorists were more likely to pessimistically emphasize diminishing returns than to optimistically emphasize increasing returns to scale. But nothing theoretically intrinsic to the rise of modern economics demanded a particular perspective on the population-resources question.

The three most important European pioneers of marginal utility theory interpreted Malthus variously. Englishman W. Stanley Jevons agreed with the Malthusian resource-depletion paradigm and today is considered one of the pioneers of ecological economics, a branch of economics that emerged after World War II.[11] In *The Coal Question* (1865), which, the *New Yorker* reported, "made him a minor celebrity," Jevons argued—erroneously—that the gradual depletion of British coal mines, the backbone of the nation's geopolitical dominance, would eventually generate population-resources collapse and economic stagnation.[12] Neither substitutions nor technological advance could reverse the trend, he concluded. "*We cannot long continue our present rate of progress*. . . . Emigration may relive it [population pressure], and by exciting increased trade tend to keep up our progress, but after a time we must either sink down into poverty, adopting wholly new habits, or else witness a constant annual exodus of the youth of the country."[13] Still, Jevons did not develop a rigorous theory of population. His foundational 1871 statement of neoclassicism was all but silent on population dynamics, labeling them exogenous variables to economic development.[14] Galician-born Carl Menger, considered the founder of the conservative "Austrian" (or "Vienna") School of economic theory, worked out several elements of the theory of marginal utility at nearly the same time as Jevons.[15] Menger, too, failed to integrate population dynamics into this theory.[16] French-Swiss Léon Walras, professor at the University of Lausanne and the father of general equilibrium theory, staked out a middle ground between population optimism and pessimism, or perhaps simply contradicted himself. In 1874, Walras allowed that economic progress was possible despite ongoing population growth and a lack of new lands, assuming a society "takes care to expand its capital."[17] But in the same work he also suggested that, while Malthus may have overreached in denying any room for innovation to chase away scarcity, population growth still proceeds more rapidly than technical progress.[18] Walras wrote, "The late Jules Duval exclaimed one day at the Société d'Économie Politique in Paris: 'What! You rejoice at the birth of a calf and not at the birth of a man!' As I pointed out to him, these two cases are very different, since one represents more food on the table and the other an extra mouth to feed."[19]

Another significant continental neoclassicist, radical Swedish social reformer Knut Wicksell, was an ardent Malthusianism and birth control proponent who, according to one scholar, "believed that the population problem was the most important social question."[20] In a pamphlet he wrote in 1909 while in jail for blaspheming Christ's virgin birth, Wicksell linked population growth to Sweden's poverty and a host of other social ills.[21] More importantly, Wicksell was once of the first to propose that we can determine a society's "optimum" population size, measured in terms of the general welfare.

Englishman Alfred Marshall, a crucial synthesizer of marginal utility theory and perhaps the best-known economist at the turn of the twentieth century,[22] further revealed the ambiguous place that population dynamics occupied in the formation of modern neoclassical economics. Learned opinion on the nation's population growth was mixed in Great Britain as the nineteenth century drew to a close, though optimism may have been on the rise due to increased emigration from England, a decreasing birthrate, and the technological optimism that accompanied the new machine age.[23] Marshall's work captured the lack of consensus. The dean of conservative (or, more accurately, non-reformist) economists at this time, he argued in his enormously influential *Principles of Economics* (1890) that the agriculturally rooted theory of diminishing returns applied to modern industries, which could expect to see rising costs and diminishing returns to scale once they expanded past their most efficient inputs and locations for manufacturing.[24] The crucial question, however, as it would be for subsequent generations of economists, was to what extent do efficiencies and innovations derived from larger markets, and the geographic clustering of enterprises, offset diminishing returns. After conceding that "the part which Nature plays in production conforms to the Law of Diminishing Returns," Marshall observed that "the part which man plays conforms to the Law of Increasing Return."[25] His conclusions are worth citing at length because they express the Smithean notion, central to today's population optimists, that bigness drives economies of scale:

> It remains true that the collective efficiency of a people with a given average of individual strength and energy increases more than in proportion to their numbers. If they can import as much food as they want on easy terms, and, by this or other means, escape from the pressure of the Law of Diminishing Return so far as raw produce goes; if, as may be reasonably supposed, their wealth increases at least as fast as their numbers . . . then every increase in their numbers is likely to bring a more than proportionate increase in their power of obtaining material goods. For it enables them to secure the many various economies of specialized skill and specialized machinery, of localized industries and production on a large scale: it enables them to have increased facilities of communication of all kinds; while the very closeness of their neighborhood diminishes the expense of time and effort involved in every sort of traffic between them, and gives them new opportunities of getting social enjoyments and the comforts and luxuries of culture in every form.[26]

Marshall noted that the property-less did not gain from the wealth created by population growth, and he warned that his optimistic findings were dependent upon favorable trade conditions that eventually could deteriorate.[27] But he did not foresee an immediate problem for his nation in securing external resources. Anticipating a mid-twentieth-century, quality-of-life critique, Marshall also lamented that population growth makes for "the growing difficulty of finding solitude and quiet and even fresh air."[28] But even here the end result was a "balance of good."[29]

Population thus occupied an ambiguous place in the marginalist revolution. Some key figures espoused Malthusian tenets, while others believed that a rising large population induces technological innovation and, broadening the market, captures the benefits of specialization. Nothing in the novel theory that individual preferences determine prices demanded a particular posture on demographic theory. Between the 1870s and the 1920s, American economists continued and deepened these debates.

Openly participating in the era's fractious struggle between capital and labor—and lacking guidance from marginal doctrine—their divisions were rooted in political persuasion rather than in economic theory.

Politicizing Population

During the 1870s and 1880s, a cadre of liberal and reform-minded social scientists trained in Europe established the American Economic Association (AEA) and helped transplant marginalism from the Continent, albeit slowly and incompletely.[30] This first generation of professional American economists embarked on an explicitly political project: they sought to counter the prevailing laissez-faire orthodoxy espoused, in most reactionary form, by the school of social theory known as Social Darwinism. Articulated most famously by English philosopher Herbert Spencer and Yale polymath William Graham Sumner, one of the founders of American sociology, Social Darwinism rejected charity and the activist state on the grounds that only "natural selection" produces beneficent social change.[31] American liberals, in contrast, adopted an "institutionalist" approach to economics that highlighted the contingency and fragility of capitalist arrangements and demanded state intervention in economic activities in the service of progressive reform.

Social Darwinism was rooted in Malthusianism. In the mid nineteenth century, demographer Dennis Hodgson has observed, Charles Darwin "used Malthus's idea of excess reproduction fueling a fight for survival to develop an explanation of biological change."[32] In turn, the Social Darwinists refitted Darwin to the social sphere and relied upon a crude form of Malthusianism to rail against government intervention.[33] Well before Frederick Jackson Turner's frontier thesis, for example, Sumner suggested that Americans enjoyed a high standard of living and freedom because they were relatively few. "Inferences as to the law of population drawn from the status of an under-populated country," he noted, "are sure to be fallacious."[34] Indeed, Sumner considered the twin laws of population and diminishing returns the driving forces of human progress, "the iron spur which has driven the race on to all which it has ever achieved."[35] Fewer people meant a less brutal struggle for survival and less true progress.[36] The liberal institutionalists, however, generally embraced the possibilities of population growth. This optimistic posture reflected not only distaste for the laissez-faire orthodoxy of the apologists, an orthodoxy rooted in the alleged iron-clad certainty of the laws of classical economics, but also the longer tradition of American population optimism.

It is true that conservative political economy contained some room for anti-Malthusianism. In particular, a providential emphasis eschewed population pessimism. For example, Edward Atkinson, an American businessman who followed the dictates of the nineteenth century's conservative (classical liberal), pro–free trade and pre-professional economic tradition, supposed that God rules the world well. He wrote of a "law of life that the power of mankind to consume the means of subsistence is limited, while on the other hand, the power of mankind to produce and distribute the means of subsistence is practically unlimited."[37] Atkinson nimbly rejected the theory of diminishing returns with this analogy: "Land itself may be exhausted when treated as a mine; it may be maintained when worked as laboratory."[38] The Rev. Arthur Latham Perry, like Atkinson, author of a leading economics textbook, similarly excoriated Malthus for dismissing God's ameliorative powers and rejected the Malthusian theory of declining wages.[39]

Especially during the tumultuous 1890s, however, Malthusianism—because it assumes that artificially increasing incomes merely produces more babies and then a subsequent return to unemployment and misery—offered conservatives an attractive starting point from which to reject state intervention on behalf of workers. In the main, conservative apologists accepted Malthus's views, if not as coarsely as the Social Darwinists. For instance, J. Laurence Laughlin, the old-guard head professor of political economy at the University of Chicago, called the law of diminishing returns to land "simply a physical fact . . . which Nature has disclosed to us, just as we say it is a fact that water runs down hill."[40] Suggesting that population growth among the "undesirable classes" reinforced their poverty, Laughlin wrote that "those who advise moral restraint on the growth of this class of persons . . . can not be called 'hard-hearted,' or 'un-Christian,' or 'dismal Malthusians.' They are rather the true friends of the unfortunate people, who need real, not sentimental and misdirected, kindness and help."[41] Frank Taussig, who taught at Harvard for over fifty years (his preeminent colleague Joseph Schumpeter called him the "American [Alfred] Marshall"),[42] wrote in his economics textbook that the "Malthusian position is impregnable" and welcomed the eventual stationary state envisioned by John Stuart Mill.[43] "A limitation of numbers is not a *cause* of higher wages," Taussig observed, "but it is a *condition* of the maintenance of high wages."[44] Yale's future president Arthur Hadley scoffed at the young maverick opponents of laissez-faire for trying to wish away the iron laws of economics—including the law that too many children led to starvation wages.[45] Frank Fetter, a Cornell and Princeton professor closely associated with the Austrian School of political economy, had critiqued Malthusian theory in his 1894 doctoral dissertation from the University of Halle.[46] But in his 1913 presidential address to the AEA, "Population or Prosperity," Fetter declared, "It is high time to revise the optimistic American doctrine of population."[47] Due to population growth, "popular welfare in America is already threatened," he asserted. "To preserve the favorable relation of population to resources and to control in some measure the fate and fortunes of the children of this and future generations the most important means possible are: conservation of national resources, and retarding the rate of increase of population."[48]

One is hard-pressed to identify a clear trend among the conservatives either toward or away from Malthusianism, although if anything their population concerns moderated at the turn of the century.[49] True, Fetter's evolution suggests a larger drift toward the dismal conclusions of the classical economists, especially as the first generation of liberal optimists who built the AEA gave way to Taussig and Hadley's more conservative generation at the turn of the century. Yet one can just as easily argue the opposite—that like the curmudgeonly classical economics in which it was embedded, traditional Malthusianism dissipated with the nineteenth century. As historian Michael Bernstein notes, economic theorists had long "located their primary analytical categories in the natural realm—in the sphere of subsistence."[50] The marginalist revolution, however, replaced the emphasis on the natural world of the classical economists with the emphasis on the market-based preferences of consumers and producers. It thus makes sense that many American economists who wrote within the marginalist framework—and after the pitched battles of the Gilded Age between labor and capital had faded—deemphasized the land-based Malthusianism of their classical forbearers. Moreover, Fetter's desire in 1913 to overturn the "optimistic American doctrine of population," while obviously underestimating the strength of the pessimists, suggests something of a turn away from the Malthusian camp in the early twentieth century.

Indeed, at the turn of the century, some moderate conservatives distanced themselves from the Malthusian, Social Darwinist position even as they affirmed laissez-faire principles. John Bates Clark, a leading American neoclassicalist and the first vice-president of the AEA, was a member of the youthful cohort sympathetic to moderate socialism. But after the labor upheavals of the 1880s, he became a conservative apologist and gradually discarded Malthusianism.[51] Clark's work was crucial in advancing what came to be called the "marginal productivity theory of distribution,"[52] which holds that wages reflect workers' contribution to the final product, assuming competitive markets.[53] This theory overturned the classical doctrine of wages, which postulated a fixed "wages fund" based on the ratio of capital to the labor supply and denied that wages could permanently increase. Clark's marginal productivity theory, nevertheless, remained rooted in the Malthus-Ricardo theory of diminishing returns—a fixed plot of land suffers from diminishing marginal productivity. As Clark put it, "Put one man on only a square mile of prairie, and he will get a rich return. Two laborers on the same ground will get less per man; and, if you enlarge the force to ten, the last man will perhaps get wages only."[54] Yet as he adhered to the basic principle of diminishing returns, and allowed that "a retarding of the rate of increase of population is an ultimate necessity if humanity is to fully enjoy the earth, and to perfect itself,"[55] Clark suggested that technological improvements produce increasing returns to scale. Regardless, modern economies were increasingly less dependent upon natural resources. Clark wrote:

> That which produces [economic development] is not the creative power of nature, but the transforming power of men; and this power becomes progressively efficient as production enlarges. New motive powers, machines, and processes are multiplying, and promise to increase, beyond any discernible limit, the capacity of man to transform what nature places in his hand. . . . We may, then, admit the law of diminishing returns in agriculture, and fear nothing for the future of humanity. The basis of economic welfare is broadening, and if this tendency is ever reversed, it will be at a time too far in the future to be a subject of present consideration.[56]

Finally, Clark proposed that "desire for personal esteem"—the impulse at the heart of marginal analysis—acted as a check on overpopulation because the poor would rather have money to promote their prestige than breed themselves back into misery.[57]

Francis Walker, a prominent anti-socialist and immigration restrictionist who was superintendant of the 1870 and 1880 US censuses, president of the Massachusetts Institute of Technology, and inaugural president of the AEA, also rejected significant portions of Malthusian economics, even though he accepted the basic premise that a society eventually reaches diminishing returns. (Walker echoed the views of his father, Amasa Walker, a professor of political economy who argued in his 1872 economics textbook that "all this [Malthusian] British philosophy of population is perverted and diseased from its root.")[58] More specifically, Francis Walker argued that the desire to consume more and more goods, and the steady process by which access to luxuries moved down the income ladder to become common "decencies," served as the ultimate check on population expansion.[59] Walker also emphasized that technological progress and improvements in human capital would enhance living standards and permit demographic expansion.[60] Well-known conservative economic writer David Wells claimed that America's ample land created a "barrier against want" that shielded the nation from the Malthusian calculus.[61] Wells also argued that subscribing to Malthusianism was akin to assuming God had improperly designed the earth.[62]

If some apologists of the new industrial order were moving toward dismissal of Malthusian precepts, many of their critics had long occupied this perch. After the Civil War, it was ironically left-leaning theorists who extended the population optimism of the Federalists and Whigs. Henry George, an illustrious anti-monopolist and proponent of a "single tax" on what he saw as unearned profits from speculative land ownership, added a Marxist twist to anti-Malthusianism. In *Progress and Poverty* (1879), which devoted multiple chapters to disproving the Malthusian theory, George alleged that economic inequality and the "injustice of society" caused the problems incorrectly associated with overpopulation, not population growth itself or the "niggardliness of nature."[63] He argued that rising populations spur production, that dietary plants and animals reproduce more rapidly than humans, and that underpopulation in new countries produces misery. Rejecting the classical law that wages drift toward subsistence, George proposed that wages and population rise in tandem, assuming the rich do not monopolize wealth.[64] Malthusian theory "has no real support either in fact or analogy," *Progress and Poverty* concluded, and "when brought to a decisive test it is utterly disproved."[65]

Simon Patten, a Wharton School of Business professor who helped point America toward an economics of mass consumption, further rejected the dismal economics of scarcity. As Patten "discovered abundance," to borrow his biographer's phrase,[66] he insisted that productivity gains trump population growth and that modern societies, which tend toward an ever-increasing standard of living, generate multiple checks to population growth not envisioned by Malthus.[67] According to historian Arthur Ekirch, Patten lamented that "the old era of economic individualism had led to ruthless exploitation of the nation's resources" but believed that "these resources were still abundant enough to stamp out poverty and make possible further progress, if only they were subject to adequate social controls."[68] In his economics textbook, Patten complained that Malthus only looked at population growth in the colonies, "where the tendency [toward rapid growth] has the fewest checks."[69] "By the same method of reasoning," Patten scoffed, "we could prove that all men are natural drunkards, cannibals, adulterers, and murderers, since we find communities in various parts of the world where drunkenness, cannibalism, etc., are common."[70] Patten evoked British India to suggest that the classical economists had failed to observe how improving agricultural and colonial practices promised to eliminate scarcity. "The lives of the weakest in crowded towns [in India] seem still ordered by the Law of Diminishing Returns," he wrote in *The New Basis of Civilization* (1907). "But here the new players intervene and promise that millions of the weak shall be added to industrial civilization without the tragic climax of starvation, disease, and despair."[71] Challenging theorists who equated Darwin and Malthus, Patten pointed out an important contradiction between the two: Malthus assumed that humans have immutable tendencies whereas Darwin assumed that humans bend their behavior according to circumstance.[72] Patten, like Fetter (but from the opposite side of the spectrum), was all too happy to exaggerate the windmills he tilted against. "Teachers Lay down the Law of Diminishing Returns as emphatically as ever, and expound afresh the sweeping Malthusian doctrine of population," Patten wrote.[73]

The majority of other reformist leaders in the first generation of professional American economists (from the 1880s onward) echoed Patten and wrote optimistically about population, a position that made perfect sense given their worldview. Whereas conservative proponents of laissez-faire tended to agree with Malthus that fixed natural laws inexorably shape human society, liberal reformers believed that human organization and progress trump biology. And the triumph of marginal analysis did not alter this basic posture.[74] E. R. A. Seligman, co-organizer of the AEA, claimed that prosperity and population expand in tandem. Distinguishing his critique of Malthus from that of the socialists, and highlighting productivity gains and slowing population growth in the industrialized world, Seligman wrote, "The doctrine of over-population has therefore lost its terrors for modern society."[75] In his view, demography had become simply another variable related to distribution and production in a modern economy. Regarding the overall population–resources question, he concluded, "The stress has been shifted from food to wealth and efficiency."[76]

And what of Richard Ely, the preeminent liberal economist who, in 1893, had fretted about the future possibility of "standing room only" for the earth's inhabitants? It turns out that Ely's Malthusianism was ephemeral; over the course of his long career, he reversed course. By World War I, as his research shifted away from labor and tax and toward land economics and he grew more conservative politically, Ely's fear of overpopulation had moderated to a mundane support for the conservation of natural resources largely detached from demographic variables.[77] Ely still considered Malthusian tenets foundational to modern economics, but he rejected the paradigm of permanent scarcity and argued that market mechanisms ameliorate temporary scarcities and induce innovation. During the prosperous 1920s, Ely published an essay in a popular agricultural magazine entitled "The Population Bugaboo," which warned farmers not to hastily expand production based on predictions of future population increase. Since the time of Malthus's *Essay*, he wrote, "it has become constantly easier to produce subsistence from the earth."[78] In a 1931 address titled "The Changing Mind in the Changing World," Ely declared, "The productive power increases far more rapidly than the population," a conclusion he later reiterated in his memoirs.[79]

During the first decades of the twentieth century, then, the US economics profession failed to achieve a consensus on the supposed virtues or pitfalls of population growth. The waning of the first generation's liberalism muted pro–population growth ideas, but at the same time, conservatives moved away from a strident Malthusian, Social Darwinist position.

The broader progressive movement that swirled around these debates also contained both pro– and anti–population growth thought. Progressive intellectuals such as Walter Weyl, one of the founders of the *New Republic*, were captivated by the metaphor of the closing of the frontier and utilized Malthusian arguments to call for new frontiers of social democracy.[80] Further, postfrontier concerns with the possible exhaustion of America's natural resources animated the turn-of-the-century conservation movement. Yet, progressive conservation was driven not by Malthusianism but by a desire to scientifically manage natural resources in the name of economic efficiency.[81] Samuel Hays notes in his classic study of the progressives that although conservationists "expressed some fear that diminishing resources would create critical shortages in the future . . . they were not Malthusian prophets of despair and gloom."[82]

In addition, even though poverty had been linked to demography since Malthus, progressives did not assume that overpopulation played much of a role in the ills of the city. Granted, progressive-era poverty discourse occasionally resorted to a simple, more-people-pauperizes perspective. Robert Kelso, a president of the leading American charity organization, the National Conference of Social Work, labeled poverty "the outward symptom of overpopulation."[83] But on the whole, progressive reformers adopted a structural analysis of poverty that downplayed simple "natural" explanations such as the people-land ratio.[84] Most poverty experts found population-based explanations woefully inadequate to explain the inequalities of a sprawling modern and industrialized society. Seligman, for instance, suggested that overpopulation could be one of many causes of poverty but was an inadequate explanation on its own given the multifaceted nature of poverty.[85] Rejecting the Malthusian assumptions of classical economists, Amos Warner, later the superintendent of charities for Washington, D.C., complained in a study of charity, "It has been a fundamental thought in the writing of many economists that poverty exists mainly, if not entirely, because population tends to increase faster than food supply. . . . A rise of wages will promote early marriages and rapid increase among laborers, until population is again checked by over-crowding and consequent misery and death. So wise a man as John Stuart Mill allowed his economic philosophy to be overshadowed by this idea."[86] Warner conceded that there was something to the theory of overpopulation-induced poverty, just as there was something to Marx's insistence on capitalists' appropriation of surplus, Henry George's theory of land monopoly, and the conservative position that personal vice causes poverty. Yet no single theory could explicate the poverty that accompanied modern industrialization; according to Warner, "the causes of destitution must be indefinitely numerous and complicated."[87]

Many American economists and poverty experts did assume (correctly) that mass immigration to the United States, which picked up steam in the 1880s, stunted the wages of the working class.[88] As the anti-immigrant movement strengthened in the early twentieth century, however, it was guided less by pure Malthusianism and more by a new idea used to explain poverty and justify harsh treatment of the poor: genetic deficiency. An American eugenics movement, which sought to breed a "better" population by promoting procreation among the genetically "fit" and discouraging it among the "unfit," rose to prominence and reinforced currents of garden-variety racism and nativism that had long plagued the nation.

Professing Malthus

Today, scholars commonly but erroneously equate eugenics and Malthusianism, especially when disparaging the post–World War II campaign to lower birthrates in the developing world. Yet the two phenomena are distinct; and in the first decades of the twentieth century, eugenics overlapped only selectively with, and did not foster, orthodox Malthusianism. The popular culture had expressed Malthusian anxieties, such as the trope of the heroic untamed cowboy, since the "closing of the frontier,"[89] but the eugenics movement, which peaked in the 1910s and 1920s, worried more about population quality than quantity and integrated various opinions of Malthus. True, some reactionary writers mixed a racist Malthusianism with eugenics. But as population studies split off from economics at the turn of the twentieth century to become the separate field of demography, it simultaneously embraced Malthusianism and sought to distance the study of population from the scientific flaws and normative excesses of eugenics. Promoting the ideal of objectivity, newly professionalized population social scientists forged a social science–based network I call the "population-policy community." The demographic-economic research emanating from the population-policy community, including new investigations into the environmental damage wrought by the nation's pell-mell development and a maturing theory of "optimum population," solidified a Malthusian consensus—but not a dire one—among learned Americans on the eve of the Great Depression.

The turn-of-the-century population debate was biological as well as economic. In the final third of the nineteenth century, proto–social scientists such as John Fiske, a historian and lecturer who helped popularize the theory of evolution in the United States, built on Social Darwinist assumptions to postulate a new science of "race" based on the competition between "higher" and "lower" racial groups.[90] Social radicals on both sides of the Atlantic invoked the prospect of better human breeding to promote their goal of sexual liberty.[91] In the 1880s, British aristocrat and scientist Francis Galton, a cousin of Charles Darwin, coined the term eugenics and launched a trans-Atlantic eugenics movement, which sought to "improve" the human population through the application of hereditary science. Karl Pearson, a socialist Cambridge statistician, championed the cause in the new century. Captivated by new (as well as older but rediscovered) research into the immutability of genes and their consistent transmission,[92] eugenicists posited a close relationship between social class/ethnicity and genetic quality: the biologically superior rose in the class structure, and the inferior sank. The eugenics movement sought to curtail the birthrate among the unfit—"negative" eugenics—and to stimulate the birthrate among the fit—"positive" eugenics. The ultimate goal was a genetically superior (white) population.

The American eugenics movement had close ties to its counterpart in the United Kingdom but maintained a distinct slant. For example, racism animated the American eugenics movement far more than the British one, which primarily reflected class anxieties.[93] The unofficial leader of the American movement (the American Eugenics Society was not created until 1923) was biologist Charles Davenport, the first director of the Carnegie Institution–funded Station for Experimental Evolution at Cold Spring Harbor on Long Island, which soon spawned the Eugenics Record Office. Here researchers set out to map the genetic basis of physical and mental capabilities (or, more often than not, deficiencies). Eugenic ideas enjoyed significant reach in the first third of the twentieth century among American intellectuals and professionals across the political spectrum.

Although it encouraged identification of population "problems," eugenics did not in and of itself engender a revival of pure Malthusianism. To use historical demographer Dennis Hodgson's term, eugenics was "biological Malthusianism" that concerned itself more with the biological quality of the population rather than with aggregate population levels or the relationship between population and the standard of living.[94] In fact, Galton had rejected Malthus's calls for self-limiting procreation because he believed that only better groups of people would practice it.[95] American eugenicists feared the declining fertility of the white middle and upper classes, both in real terms and compared to the higher fertility of immigrants, African Americans, and lower-class whites. Eugenicists exaggerated the class and ethnic disparities in fertility, as illustrated by Theodore Roosevelt's lament that prosperous whites were practicing "race suicide," but these disparities did exist.[96]

The movement to limit immigration to the United States encompassed a Malthusian strand, but its primary goal was to exclude certain peoples, not shrink aggregate growth. Exclusionists sought to reduce the number of "new immigrants" from Southern and Eastern Europe, whom they deemed racially inferior, the cause of social ills, exploitive of native-born workers, and above all corrosive to the "white race." Malthusian arguments were present in the debates that culminated with passage of the 1921 and 1924 immigration acts, which essentially closed the nation to non-Northern Europeans, but racial concerns were paramount.[97] Many elites who opposed immigration on eugenic grounds actually insisted that immigration stunted the birthrate of the native-born population. Francis Walker had long hypothesized that immigration was a zero-sum game for the aggregate total of people because it retarded enlargement of the native-born population.[98] He also believed that immigrants from Southern Europe were "vast masses of peasantry, degraded below our utmost conceptions."[99] Put another way, for eugenicists, immigration raised the specter not of Malthusian aggregate overpopulation and resource scarcity but of the "annihilation of Native American stock," as the charity reformer Robert Hunter argued in *Poverty* (1905).[100]

Several reformist, progressive-era economists echoed these eugenic views. Well-known labor economist John Commons, for example, concluded that immigration (which he opposed on unabashedly racist grounds) stunted wages, but he also insisted that it dragged down the domestic-born birthrate. Commons wrote that after immigration surged in the nineteenth century, "Americans shrank alike from the social contract and the economic competition thus created. They became increasingly unwilling to bring forth sons and daughters who should be obliged to compete in the market for labor and in the walks of life with those whom they did not recognize as of their own grade and condition."[101] Others promoted liberal reforms on eugenic grounds—for example, a minimum wage would lead to job losses and thus weed out the undesirable and unemployable.[102]

Certainly some eugenicists were avowed Malthusians. For instance, Henry Fairfield Osborn, director of the American Museum of Natural History, was a major early-century Malthusian and immigration restrictionist who promoted the slogan "Not more but better Americans."[103] Madison Grant, a leading conservationist and author of the one of the nastiest eugenic polemics that masqueraded as history, *The Passing of the Great Race* (1916), also was an avowed Malthusian.[104] But the eugenics movement as a whole was more concerned with differential fertility among social classes—and with repopulating the upper classes—than fearful of the relationship between aggregate numbers and natural resources.

In addition to the economists, anti-immigrationists, and eugenicists, birth control advocates were leading participants in early twentieth-century population debates. They contributed significantly to the expansion of Malthusianism. In 1914, before opening her first birth control clinic in New York City, Margaret Sanger consulted on population issues with the prophets of overpopulation who headed England's Neo-Malthusian League.[105] (The movement for contraceptive rights was often referred to as "neo-Malthusianism.") Early leaders of the birth control movement frequently asserted that birth control would help check overpopulation and prevent war.[106] Historians debate whether we should consider Sanger a eugenicist, but they agree that she remained attached to her Malthusianism moorings even in the 1930s, when depopulation rather than overpopulation emerged as the prevailing concern.[107]

Eugenic thought was found across the political spectrum and permeated American culture during the 1910s and 1920s, as seen in everything from the rise of IQ tests to "Fitter Family" contests at state fairs.[108] Tragically, the eugenics movement facilitated the development of the racist and exclusive national immigration system that prevailed until the 1960s and secured laws in more than half the states that ultimately led to the involuntary sterilization of over sixty thousand institutionalized Americans deemed mentally, sexually, or racially "unfit."[109] These laws were upheld by the Supreme Court in its famous 1927 *Buck v. Bell* decision. After these significant successes, however, the movement failed to secure more explicit population policies. Moreover, its elitist and undemocratic perspective checked its popular influence. Even many influential white Americans sympathetic to eugenic racial ideas opposed the organized movement on the grounds that it was undemocratic. Opposition to compulsory sterilization, advances in genetics, and recognition of flawed IQ testing methodology further eroded support. As Daniel Kevles reminds us in his still-unsurpassed history of eugenics, "long before the Nazis came to power a growing, influential coalition had turned against the mainline movement."[110] And African-American leaders such as W. E. B. Du Bois vehemently opposed eugenics.[111]

As we will see in more depth in the next chapter, in the 1930s, a small group of eugenicists responded to their movement's decline by promoting a "reform eugenics" that would sever the American movement from its racist past and replace the stress on hereditary factors with a newfound recognition of the importance of the environment. Here it is important simply to note that social scientists were a crucial part of the anti-eugenics coalition, along with biologists, geneticists, religious critics, and humanists.[112] Since the turn of the century, population researchers had increasingly argued that social as well as biological factors shaped population dynamics. By 1930, social science population expertise had largely trumped eugenic discourse. As the remainder of this chapter shows, the professionalization of American demography involved developing an ideology that demographers should privilege "neutral" scientific inquiry over social action, in the process creating institutions dedicated to population research and forming professional organizations.[113] Modern demography was also born of a Malthusian consensus that fused natural and economic science: societies could identify their "optimum" level of population.

We may date demography's emergence as an independent social science (if one still wed to eugenic assumptions) to A. M. Carr-Saunders's *The Population Problem: A Study in Evolution* (1922).[114] A British biologist and arctic explorer turned sociologist who later headed the London School of Economics, Carr-Saunders rejected Malthus's biological determinism and argued that human efforts to adjust their numbers and composition to their environment were influenced by a mixture of heredity and, more importantly, social adjustment. Every society, in other words, has an optimum level of population. With population now a social question, demographers faced a quandary that captivated the American social sciences in the 1920s: What role in society should social scientists and their research play? That research should be modeled on the natural sciences was not in dispute, though there were hints of today's debate about whether bias-free research is ever truly possible. The larger question was whether social science research is an end in itself or a means towards social change, and, if the latter, who is responsible for turning research into practical application? In short, who controls the knowledge? Scholars have chronicled the triumph in the 1920s of the ideal that research and researchers should retreat from social action.[115] Demographers have received less attention, but they too demanded that their field be "objective." Most American demographers spurned not merely the science of activist population groups, especially the eugenics movement, but also activists' assumption that they knew how to best apply their research. Instead, demographers subscribed to what historian Mark Smith calls the "service intellectual" ideal: population scientists would accumulate data but not prescribe solutions.[116] American demographers were undoubtedly following the path toward scientific neutrality chosen by colleagues in more traditional fields. But they also had field-specific reasons for promoting objectivity: most considered earlier-century population studies, rooted in eugenics, scientifically faulty and socially reactionary, and some wished to avoid association with the birth control movement.

All of this is not to claim that by 1930 American demography had entirely distanced itself from its eugenic origins; eugenic ideals, now sanitized under the rubric of social science, continued to find a home in respectable trans-Atlantic thought. Despite the new scientific and environmentalist approach to "quality" and the objectivist posture, demographers were unable to discard the old eugenic assumption that class and ethnicity were reliable stand-ins for genetic "quality," defined by the norms of the white upper class. The very persistence of research into differential fertility among social groups revealed the strength of eugenic frameworks.[117] By the late 1920s, however, most demographers—even those sympathetic to eugenic precepts—did assume that eugenics was at odds with hard science. And as they built their field's institutions, demographers generally insisted that members of their guild divorce issue activism from research.[118]

Although the Census Bureau became a permanent agency in 1903, private and nonprofit sites were as essential as the state to the professionalization of American demography. In 1909, the Metropolitan Life Insurance Company established a Welfare Division, motivated by a genuine desire to advance corporate participation in social reform as well as the bottom-line-driven goal of increasing life expectancy. The key figure in the Welfare Division was demographer Louis I. Dublin, later president of the American Statistical Association, the American Public Health Association, and the Population Association of America (more on this last group in a moment). Often cited in the mainstream press, Dublin was born in Lithuania and grew up in New York's East Side, where he saw firsthand the sad state of urban public health.[119] In the course of running the Metropolitan's health campaigns and related research, Dublin did much to advance the technical science of demography.[120]

To create research centers, demographers tapped the large American foundations created with the Gilded Age's vast fortunes. The foundations reinforced the objectivist stance of American demography; skittish of eugenics and birth control, they demanded that their funds be spent on empirical research rather than issue agitation. In 1922, Edward W. Scripps, the newspaper magnate, established the Scripps Foundation for Research in Population Problems at Miami University, Ohio. Scripps's interest in Asian population issues brought him to the Columbia University library, where he unearthed a doctoral dissertation influenced by Malthusian theory by Warren Thompson. Scripps invited Thompson on a tour of the supposedly overpopulated Far East and made him the foundation's first director. Thompson subsequently hired as his assistant P. K. Whelpton, an agricultural economist. Thompson came to the field as a sociologist, and Whelpton was a technically minded statistician; together they collaborated on demographic studies until the mid 1960s. Thompson wrote a leading American textbook on population, and Whelpton eventually became head of the Population Division at the United Nations. Nurtured in a foundation born of Malthusian fears, their estimates of future population trends would ironically help raise the specter of depopulation in the United States by the 1930s.[121]

The Great Depression depleted the Scripps Foundation, but Thompson and Whelpton successfully tapped the philanthropic sector. In 1923, the Laura Spelman Rockefeller Memorial, established by John D. Rockefeller to honor his wife, decided to concentrate on funding the social sciences. The Spelman Memorial's first director, Beardsley Ruml, was a young statistician and economist who gained experience working at the National Research Council and the Carnegie Corporation.[122] Ruml worshipped at the altar of objectivist social science; earlier, as director of the General Education Fund of the Rockefeller Foundation, he wrote a well-known memo recommending that the foundation divorce itself from any social reforms and only support empirical research because it more easily avoided controversy.[123] In the late 1920s and 1930s, Spelman supported population science during the formative period in its development, albeit modestly. A more generous supporter was the Milbank Memorial Fund (MMF). Like the Metropolitan Life Insurance Company, the MMF approached population issues from a public health perspective. Created in 1905 by an heiress to the Borden milk fortune, it emphasized public health projects such as clinics in poor neighborhoods. Albert Milbank, a corporate liberal who ran Borden and wrote magazine articles promoting national health insurance, presided over the fund, and several members of the MMF's Advisory Council were leading population scientists.[124] The MMF trustee who most pushed it toward population research was Thomas Cochran, a life insurance executive and J.P. Morgan and Co. board member. A devotee of Margaret Sanger, Cochran wed Malthusian and public health perspectives. He convinced the fund to pursue population research, threatening to use his influence to choke support for other projects unless the MMF made forays into population and birth control.[125]

The MMF's Division of Research, created in 1928 in "realization of the need of applying scientific procedures in the study of the factors affecting the health of human populations," contributed significantly to the maturation of American demography.[126] The division's director, economist Edgar Sydenstricker, served on the early-century federal Commissions on Industrial Relations and Immigration, became the first Public Health Statistician in the United States Public Health Service in 1915, and set up an epidemiological service at the League of Nations in Geneva.[127] The MMF researched contraception, public health, and the psychological causes of fertility, and was best known for a project examining the causes of differential fertility by social class, overseen by Frank Notestein. Subsequently the head of the Office for Population Research at Princeton when the MMF helped create it in 1936, Notestein became, after the war, the head of the UN's Population Division and a leader in the demographers' campaign to educate leaders about world overpopulation. Importantly, the MMF fertility studies demonstrated the path that researchers had traveled from the early-century eugenics movement; they began with assumptions of biological determinism but strove to scientifically document fertility regimes rather than make normative assertions about the need to alter them.

American demographers also lent a hand in building international organizations. Raymond Pearl, who studied biology and zoology in England and Germany before becoming director of the Institute for Biological Research at Johns Hopkins, joined Margaret Sanger in helping to create the International Union for the Scientific Investigation of Population Problems (IUSIPP).[128] The IUSIPP grew out of the 1927 World Population Conference in Geneva, which Margaret Sanger organized and which brought together demographers from twenty-eight nations.[129] Sanger turned to for Pearl for two reasons. First, he sat on the executive board of the National Research Council, an organization formed during World War I to promote both the natural and social sciences. In 1926, he wrested from it a tentative promise to support an international body of population scientists, if additional funds could be obtained elsewhere. Pearl turned to Beardsley Ruml at the Laura Spelman Rockefeller Memorial for a $10,000 grant.[130] Second, as the leader of a contentious social movement, Sanger needed to demonstrate the rigorous scientism of the conference and new organization; and Pearl insisted that population scientists conduct only pure research, which would ultimately translate into beneficent public policy.[131] (Pearl had turned against the mainstream eugenics movement, and MMF research later prompted him to abandon his earlier assumption that biology accounted for group differences in fertility.) Pearl was allowed to determine the agenda in Geneva due to his access to funds,[132] and the IUSIPP's bylaws stated the organization's intention to remain a strictly a scientific organization that "refuses either to enter upon religious, moral, or political discussion, or as a Union to support a policy regarding population, of any sort whatever, particularly in the direction either of increased or of diminished birth rates."[133]

The Population Association of America (PAA), to this day the main organization of American demographers, emerged from efforts in 1931 to reorganize the stalled American National Committee of the IUSIPP, headed by Louis Dublin. (The IUSIPP's structure called for affiliated committees in the member nations.) Pearl had secured funding for the IUSIPP from the Milbank Memorial Fund, which provided $10,000 annually from 1929 to 1931.[134] But money promised by the Social Science Research Council and the National Research Council to launch the US committee did not materialize because of a conflict between Pearl and mathematician Edwin Wilson, president of the SSRC.[135] In June 1931, Pearl resigned as president of the IUSIPP, and several demographers involved with the languishing US committee, again spurred on by Margaret Sanger (and again funded by Milbank), created the PAA as a virtually parallel organization. At this juncture, the debate over scientific inquiry versus social action came to a head once again, as the various factions of population discourse at the time (population scientists, eugenicists, Malthusians, and birth controllers) competed to chart the path of the new group. NYU sociologist Henry Pratt Fairchild, the organization's first president, nominated Margaret Sanger to be vice-president, but this bid failed because Dublin and others did not consider her a rigorous scientist. In the end, the neutral-social-science camp prevailed.[136] "We went to organizational lengths beyond all lengths to keep out all but the purest of the academically pure," Frank Notestein recalled years later.[137]

Then again, Notestein painted this moment in very generous terms, as Fairchild was recently president of the American Eugenics Society. In other words, the rhetoric and even methods of scientism were genuine, but eugenic ideas did not necessarily disqualify one as a scientist. The PAA sought to combine reform-eugenics assumptions with the service-intellectual goal of severing scientific inquiry from social action. As its Committee on Publications and Policy stated, the organization should "disseminate scientific information and create interest in population problems among the public at large."[138] But the waters remained muddy. Pearl and many service intellectuals in the PAA were vague about which body would arbitrate the transition from research to public policy—and fell into the trap of viewing the prescriptive conclusions based on their research as somehow non-normative. Hence the PAA responded favorably to a request from the American Birth Control League to conduct a "scientific examination to determine what effect instruction in the best contraceptive method technique has upon the fecundity of the socially inadequate classes."[139]

In his speech as the departing president of the IUSIPP, Pearl said, "It requires no expert to perceive that the growing hordes of people on the face of the earth are constantly and increasingly adding to the economic and social difficulties of an already sufficiently harassed world."[140] The danger of overpopulation was objective truth to Pearl, who had reformulated the "logistic" law of population growth developed in the 1840s by a French mathematician studying fruit flies. Pearl's law assumed that populations followed nearly inexorable natural laws (which actually caused him to believe that populations would eventually stabilize), leaving little room for the role of social conditions and changing mores.

Pearl's vision of developing the field of demography as a natural science did not prevail; after the initial skirmishes surrounding the creation of the PAA, leading practitioners such as Frank Notestein would successfully define demography as a social science dedicated to the statistical study of human populations.[141] But Pearl's anti-eugenic Malthusianism would prevail. In H. L. Menken's *American Mercury* magazine, Pearl called eugenics "a mingled mess of ill-grounded and uncritical sociology, economics, anthropology, and politics, full of emotional appeals to class and race prejudices, solemnly put forth as science, and unfortunately accepted as such by the general public."[142] And he wrote editorials such as "World Overcrowding: Saturation Point for Earth's Population Soon Will Be in Sight."[143] Pearl's alarmism waned in the late 1920s, but in its wake he espoused a novel and moderate variation of Malthusian theory: the idea that somewhere between a too-high population (which presses on resources and is too large for efficient production) and a too-low population (which retards economies of scale) resides an "optimum population."[144] During the 1920s, American demographers and economists forged a rough consensus that the earth—and the United States—were rapidly approaching a state of overpopulation—that their optimal populations were lower.

European thinkers were slower than Americans in sounding Malthusian alarms because the human carnage of World War I engendered widespread worries about population decline, especially in Britain and France, but they were at the forefront of optimum theory. Swede Knut Wicksell (whom we last saw in jail) may have been the first to use the term "optimum population."[145] In the 1920s, several well-known British economists centered in London pursued optimum theory, including Edwin Cannan and Lionel Robbins; the latter would emerge as a leading figure in modern, post–World War II economic growth theory.[146] A more traditional Malthusianism emanated from economists associated with Cambridge University, led by Harold Wright and John Maynard Keynes. As we will see, Keynes would break away from Malthusianism in the 1930s.[147]

The leading American theorist of the optimum population was Ohio State's A. B. Wolfe.[148] In scholarly collections such as Louis Dublin's *Population Problems* (1926) as well as in more popular forums, Wolfe demanded that public policy seek the optimum population, rather than merely prevent "absolute overpopulation," through measures "which will secure such adjustment between population and natural resources as will enable us to live as well as possible."[149] Operating from the Malthusian scarcity perspective, Wolfe rejected the assumptions of those he deemed "anti-Malthusian optimists" that migration and invention held the dual keys to avoiding the Malthusian squeeze.[150] On the question of migration, Wolfe joined the end-of-frontier chorus and suggested, "Only inferior lands, limited in extent, remain for settlement."[151] Much more original, during a decade of unbridled optimism about the benefits of technology, was Wolfe's insistence on the limits of technical innovation. He wrote, "Progress itself involves a paradox, for . . . it is inconceivable that technical advance can maintain the pace it set in what [naturalist Alfred Russel] Wallace called 'the wonderful century' and which [John Maynard] Keynes thinks may prove to have been 'a magnificent episode' in history. In the main, future improvements are to be 'looked for in the fourth decimal place.' There was a 'pace that killed Athens.'"[152]

In assuming that a rising population produces economic benefits to a certain point, and that this point varies across societies and may shift with social and technological advancement, optimum theory rejected dire Malthusianism. In the early 1920s, Richard Ely described a consensus among American statisticians and economists "that so far as the immediate future is concerned there is no reason for alarm."[153] Optimum theory also moved the population debate past the simple Malthusian food-supply calculus by identifying the tipping point as the level of population when output per head decreases.[154] Nonetheless, it implied sympathy for Malthusian assumptions, and its theorists generally applauded the steadily decreasing birthrates in the industrialized nations. Indeed, the new theory received criticism as a "mere rationalization for the cause of population stability or decline."[155] This complaint was unfair to those theorists who valued objectivity, but it is true that some population activists, including racist eugenicists, profited from optimum theory. A few academics in the 1920s fused optimum theory, eugenics, and Malthusianism, as did Harvard geographer Edward East in *Mankind at the Crossroads* (1923).[156] Beyond racists borrowing from it, optimum theory's larger problems were that its definitions of the social and economic conditions constituting the ideal were entirely subjective, and that it treated population and resources as static variables.[157]

Other social scientists arrived at a more dynamic analysis of the optimum. The global food supply had become an important issue in the wake of World War I, and investigation of natural resources in the United States quickened during the 1920s.[158] Conservationists developed the theory of the "carrying capacity" of a particular natural area.[159] Agricultural and resource economists turned their attention to the relationship between resources and the geographical location of people—the search for optimums on a smaller scale. Economist Ralph Hess suggested in *The Foundations of National Prosperity*, a 1917 collection of essays edited by Richard Ely, "Settlement and industries should be so located as to secure the fullest possible benefits from the natural resources of the country, as well as the benefits of mechanical development and scientific discoveries."[160] Meanwhile, the spread of electrification in the 1920s enhanced the locational flexibility of American firms—and thus supported calls for the state to engineer new economic geographies.[161] Resource economists focused on *localized* pockets of overpopulation where resources had become exhausted but people remained—for example in Appalachia and in the "cut-over" lands of northern Wisconsin and Minnesota, where the timber industry left depleted forests and an economically redundant surplus population in its wake.[162] Within the federal government, a Department of Labor study called *Employment and Natural Resources*, penned by Benton MacKaye, subsequently a co-founder of the Wilderness Society and a leading midcentury conservationist, called for new government-sponsored communities on public lands to combat inefficient land use (and the deceasing real wages of the American worker).[163] US Department of Agriculture economists also promoted the idea of engineering population movements. The key figures here were Lewis Gray, whose work on intergenerational equity and the renewability rates of natural resources pointed the way toward today's economic analysis of environments,[164] and Oliver E. Baker, Gray's colleague in the Bureau of Agricultural Economics. They argued for more comprehensive federal policies expanding the agricultural lands of the nation so as to feed a growing population.[165]

Concern with industrial decline in certain regions is not identical to classic Malthusianism; in some cases, resource economists assumed that the solution to exhausted resources in one location was to pick up and find new virgin areas to exploit. And as we have seen, Richard Ely among others diverged from the growing Malthusian consensus. On the whole, however, economists believed that pockets of overpopulation were part of a broader national pattern of population pressing on resources. Hess, for example, advocated more efficient population and industrial location within a broader context of the US population becoming "superabundant" with people.[166] Baker in particular espoused Malthusian ideas, writing, "Our nation is probably near, possibly past, the crest of average income per capita; and every increment in population is likely to increase the complaint of the high cost of living."[167] Baker, notes historian David Wrobel, was one whose Malthusianism was entirely divorced from any racism.[168]

In the end, optimum theory and a desire among social scientists to distance themselves from polemicists fostered a moderate Malthusianism. Examining the history of America's resource exploitation, University of Wisconsin economist Ralph Hess captured the prevailing view when he wrote:

> Over-population and over-consumption constantly menace the economic prosperity which should accompany industrial maturity. Prosperity in itself is a stimulus to the growth of population, and the physical limits which nature has placed upon industrial opportunity undoubtedly validate the principle theme of the much abused Malthusian doctrine that *population tends to over-run the means of subsistence*. We are not yet seriously facing this problem in the United States. Nevertheless, the experiences of other nations are prophetic of our possible future.[169]

Hess's mention of "over-consumption" and "limits" sounds to us today like an ecological indictment of the double whammy of population growth and ever-greater consumption. But his criticism of consumption did not primarily concern the use of natural resources; rather, it reflected an older stream of American economic thinking that valued production above all and treated consumption as the amoral stepchild of production. In explaining the potential causes of economic decline, Hess identified not only overpopulation but also "over-consumption, due to an inequitable distribution of wealth and income, resulting in impoverishment of society through a sapping of economic vitality and reduction of productive capacity by the indolence and luxury of the rich and the non-productivity of the coterie which surround them."[170]

Given how the Great Depression soon would alter the population debate, these were ironic comments. In the 1930s, many demographers and economists would retain sympathy for Malthusian principles, but they would not identify overconsumption as an economic (or environmental) problem. Instead, they would argue that *under*-consumption caused the economic malaise. And they would combine new praise for consumption with an older faith in the virtues of a smaller population. The end result would be a novel doctrine holding that a declining or steady population would be better poised than a growing one to harness the economic power of mass consumption.

CHAPTER THREE

Population Depressed

By the late 1920s, most American economists and demographers believed that the US needed fewer people to achieve an "optimum population." Economic and perceived demographic crises during the 1930s reshaped, but did not fundamentally alter, this consensus. Population experts updated Malthusianism by grafting it onto a revolutionary new set of economic ideas expounded by preeminent British economist John Maynard Keynes.

In the 1930s, Keynes explained the depth and seeming permanence of the Great Depression by overturning the classical economists' assumption that markets self-correct. He concluded that wealthy and "mature" economies can arrive at an unfortunate "high unemployment equilibrium." Put in less technical terms, economies can get stuck in quicksand. More happily, according to Keynes, because mass consumption would henceforth hold the key to prosperity in the industrialized nations, governments can cure "secular stagnation" (secular here means long-term) by increasing their direct spending in the economy, thereby propping up demand for goods and services and maintaining a floor on wages and prices. Although we remember Keynes less today for his demographic ideas than for his advocacy of government deficits to stimulate prosperity, he believed that the sluggish birthrates of the 1930s contributed to the Depression by lowering the number of consumers and hence aggregate demand and by squashing the business community's expectations of the size of future markets.

The scholarly tendency has been to assume that, in 1930s America, lower birthrates (which dipped below the replacement level of 2.1) and a stagnant economy—and the causal linking of the two by Keynes and popular observers alike—engendered a widespread celebration of domestic population growth that prevailed until an ecologically based apprehension of population growth picked up steam in the 1960s. In fact, during the 1930s, the population-policy community—the informal cadre of demographers, economists, sociologists, birth control advocates, reform eugenicists, and a smattering of urban planners which had come together in universities and independent population institutions in the 1920s—retooled and reinvigorated anti–population growth thought in response to the new demographic, intellectual, and economic realities of the day. In short, the community promoted the virtues of a smaller and stable population. This support for a stable population defined the Depression-era population debate, and it also reveals that antipathy to population growth prevailed for longer periods of the twentieth century, and with more breadth, than we normally recognize.

The retooling of anti–population growth thought among social scientists influenced the broader American political economy. More specifically, demographic concerns helped shape the diffusion of Keynesian ideas in Depression-era America. Keynesian ideas proved pliable enough to simultaneously promote population growth and energize arguments in favor of a smaller population. The central Keynesianism concept that can be bent either way in regard to demographic matters is that mass consumption drives prosperity. In the 1930s, Keynes shook off his earlier Malthusianism and now claimed that population growth is virtuous because it creates more consumers.[1] Many population experts sympathetic to the overall Keynesian paradigm, however, maintained that the sheer size of the population was increasingly irrelevant in a modern, mass-consumption economy. What mattered were innovation and savings and consumption patterns. A smaller population is consistent with or might even contribute to per capita economic growth, they argued, if the power of increased consumption can be harnessed, in part through state-led redistributive policies. The state, not the stork, would maintain aggregate demand.

I label this reconfigured Keynesianism "Stable Population Keynesianism" (SPK). The term captures the affinities with the Keynesian stress on consumption and government intervention but incorporates the divergence from the pro–population growth position that Keynes himself held by the 1930s. SPK ironically provided much of the intellectual apparatus for the late-1930s dismantling of Keynes's theory that the Western economies had entered a phase of long-term economic stagnation.

The new thinking about population produced shifts in public policy as well as economic thought. Policy makers and social scientists debated possible public initiatives to address the perceived demographic problems in 1930s America—primarily the declining birthrate. A campaign arose for various policies designed to influence the size, location, and "quality" of the US population. Although birthrates would rebound during the war, this campaign was a short-term failure; no state policies emerged with the specific goal of altering the birthrate (e.g., paying mothers for every baby). Several factors contributed to this policy inaction, but one overlooked factor is that support for population expansion was lukewarm and contingent at most. While many population experts supported moderate population growth in the short term—to prevent aggregate population decline in the long-term—resistance to steady population growth continued to hold sway. The National Resources Committee's *The Problems of a Changing Population* (1938) put an official government stamp on the pro-stable population position.[2]

The New Deal did embark on one tangible population policy: the geographic relocation of thousands of Americans, most often from "marginal" farmlands to New Deal–sponsored communities on the suburban fringe. Historians have not integrated this population redistribution into the broader 1930s population debate, usually discussing it solely in the context of New Deal efforts to forge solidarity and community. Yet population redistribution also implemented SPK. This demographic policy operated under the assumption that the United States needed not a numerical increase of people but a populace with higher incomes and greater consumption.

The Prospect of Population Decline

Three developments exerted the greatest influence on Depression-era demographic discussion. The first was the prospect of future population decline. The birthrate in the United States had been decreasing since 1800, but throughout the nineteenth century it remained high by the standards of the industrialized world.[3] In the early twentieth century, eugenicists, politicians, and some professional demographers bemoaned the declining fertility of the "white" and native-born middle and upper classes. After the 1930 census, however, the prediction that decreasing birthrates would cause *absolute* population decline in the US and Western European nations gained acceptance in mainstream public policy circles.[4] A typical estimate was that from 123 million in 1930, the American population would peak at about 150 million in 1970 and thereafter stabilize at about 140 million by 2000.[5] (The actual number in 2000 was 281 million.) The long-term causes of the slowdown in growth were modernization and urbanization and accompanying changes in social mores. The more immediate causes were the closing of the immigration gates in the 1920s and the Great Depression.[6] Between 1930 and 1940, the American population increased to 132 million from 123 million, a gain of just over 7 percent, to this day the smallest percentage gain of any decade in US history.

Economic disruption was the second development that fundamentally altered the population debate. Assessing the future of a nation with one-third of its inhabitants "ill-housed, ill-clad [and] ill-nourished," as Franklin D. Roosevelt noted in his Second Inaugural Address, many thoughtful Americans feared permanent scarcity.[7] On the one hand, these fears extended the land-based sense of scarcity that matured after the "closing of the frontier" in the 1890s, animated progressive-era debates over the nation's stock of natural resources, and reappeared in the 1920s discussion about the need to balance people and resources. To some agricultural economists, for example, the recurring drought in the western United States in the 1930s augured environmental collapse. In traditional Malthusian terms, they suggested that the "exhausted" farmland in many parts of the US revealed the ironclad law of diminishing returns. Some demographers continued to theorize crudely that population growth rates were pegged to the amount of fertile land available. On the other hand, the man-to-land paradigm seemed inadequate to explain what many saw as a deeper failure of American capitalism. And most agricultural experts believed that the farm sector's major problem was overproduction, not scarcity. (This argument prevailed and led to the modern agricultural welfare state, which pays farmers not to produce.) Given the crushing economic misery of the 1930s, the population question boiled down to a debate not only about abuse of the land but also about the relationship between demographic trends and macroeconomic performance.

Finally, the maturation of consumption-oriented and specifically Keynesian economics remade the population debate. Keynesian theory encouraged new formulations of both the case for population augmentation and the case against it, and hence the debates about Keynesianism and about demography became intertwined. Keynesianism interjected a major new set of ideas into the American population debate, while demographers helped to redefine Keynesianism.

The prospect of population decline provoked rejoicing in some circles but alarm in others. In the first camp, a few leftists and labor leaders saw in the decade's massive unemployment ample argument against even short-term population growth. To the other camp, dwindling birthrates raised the specter of a reverse-Malthusian crisis, a baby shortage that might lead to dangerous socioeconomic consequences, including the permanent stunting of economic growth. These pronatalists argued that population and economic growth had always reinforced each other in the United States and in the rest of the developed world. They maintained that 1930s America faced the problem of overabundance, not scarcity—too many consumer goods and crops and too few people to consume them. The business community urged repopulation, though in a muted and fractured manner. Passionate support for population growth also came from Catholics who tried to fend off the rising birth control movement.[8]

Economists provided the primary momentum for repopulation. As we have seen, classical economic theory held that a smaller population produces a higher standard of living, and some liberals in the 1930s were happy to abandon that proposition and welcome population growth as part of their broader rejection of classical economics.[9] When historians discuss 1930s population debates, they tend to focus on this pronatalist thread. In particular, they highlight the mid-1930s development of "secular stagnation" or "mature economy" doctrine.[10] Proponents of stagnation theory, led by John Maynard Keynes and Harvard's Alvin Hansen,[11] claimed that a triumvirate of factors in Western economies augured dwindling capital accumulation, continued high unemployment, and perhaps even a permanent economic plateau: (a) the cessation of population growth; (b) a lack of new lands to develop; and (c) a paucity of new technologies. After hinting at the importance of population growth in his seminal work, *The General Theory of Employment, Interest and Money* (1936),[12] Keynes argued in an enormously influential 1937 essay, "Some Economic Consequences of a Declining Population," that the Malthusian devil had been locked in chains and replaced with the new devil of mass unemployment.[13] In his 1938 presidential address to the American Economic Association (AEA), "Economic Progress and Declining Population," Hansen confirmed the triumvirate of perceived causes of stagnation. "The constituent elements of economic progress are (a) inventions, (b) the discovery and development of new territory and new resources, and (c) the growth of population," he said.[14] In this speech, wrote Mark Perlman, the founding editor of the *Journal of Economic Literature*, Hansen "abandoned his earlier hope that a cessation of population growth would result in greater per capita allocation of resources."[15] To counteract stagnation, Keynes and Hansen emphasized activist fiscal policy to stimulate consumption more than direct policies to increase the birthrate. Hansen declared, "Let us now turn to a high-consumption economy and develop that as the great frontier of the future."[16] Still, they believed that a rising population, chiefly derived from an increase in the birthrate, would aid economic recovery by enlarging the market and improving the psychological outlook of investors. Conversely, according to Keynes, "the first result to prosperity of a change-over from an increasing to a declining population may be very disastrous."[17]

Stagnation theory and the desire for population growth were powerful currents in 1930s political economy. What I want to highlight is a competing and overlooked camp. In between the extremes of pronatalism and working-class Malthusianism, many population experts embraced the smaller and stabilized population expected to arrive in a few decades (they did not go so far as to welcome the prospect of perpetual population decline). Individuals in this camp did not claim that the decade's high unemployment resulted primarily from ongoing population growth. They did argue, however, that a stable population would either directly contribute to the return of abundance or at least necessitate new public policies and socioeconomic arrangements that would, in turn, foster prosperity. In short, this camp retained Hansen's hope that a smaller population would broaden wealth. The divergence from the Keynes-Hansen thesis, though profound, was subtle.[18] Like the stagnationists, proponents of a stable population sought population increase *in the short term*. But preventing population decline was distinguished from seeking never-ending population growth. Moreover, although many population experts agreed with the basic *premise* of the Keynes-Hansen thesis that the economy had matured, and even believed that lower birthrates had exacerbated the Depression, they did not agree with the Keynes-Hansen *prescription* of population growth. All told, slowing population growth, the Depression, and ascendant Keynesian theories did not neutralize Malthusianism but, in fact, left a retooled and reenergized Malthusianism in their wake.

Pro–stable population ideas unified a diverse set of actors, from proponents of the new consumptionist economics to demographers and veteran population policy advocates. Historians pay scant attention to calls for population stabilization because they were partially embedded in "reform eugenics" discourse, which, though operating within a less bluntly deterministic framework than early-century eugenics, nonetheless still sought to increase the birthrate among Americans with supposedly "better" genetic qualities. (Promoting births among the supposedly superior segments of society was known as "positive eugenics.") Accordingly, scholars have neglected the intersection of eugenics and economic debates. Positive eugenics contributed a pronatalist thread to the 1930s discussion in the sense that it called for more babies among favored groups, but most eugenicists, population scientists, and birth control advocates continued to support an overall lower and stabilized population.

The Campaign for a Comprehensive American Population Policy

During the 1930s, the population-policy community and sympathetic social reformers proposed social and economic measures designed to tackle the perceived demographic dilemmas of the time: the declining birthrate and the prospect of aggregate population decline; the continued differential fertility between social classes; the persistent pockets of poverty in certain geographic regions; and ecological degradation. A "comprehensive population policy" did not materialize, nor did any significant individual policies explicitly designed to alter the birthrate. Disparate factors contributed to this failure, but, crucially, long-term repopulation was never the primary emphasis of the public policy campaign. The main thrust of the proposals was to create economic arrangements conducive to a smooth transition to a stable population. The ultimate significance of the proposed population policies resides not in their failed efforts to address the prospect of depopulation but in their overlooked contribution to the growing consumptionist and redistributionist ideas of the day. In short, they helped to diffuse SPK.

In tune with the New Deal's economic philosophy, the American population-policy community endorsed proposals designed to increase incomes and boost purchasing power; it eschewed explicitly pronatalist proposals—e.g., cash "baby bonuses" or "family allowances" rewarding the mother or household for each birth. Beyond stressing the right of voluntary parenthood, which masked a fierce debate between proponents and opponents of birth control, experts called for the conservation of natural resources, subsidies to relocate industry to bring people and jobs into geographic equilibrium, direct aid to poor geographic regions that tended to be "overpopulated," and a new social discourse and policies favoring what today we might refer to as "family values." Above all, they advocated public investment to socialize the cost of raising children and to redistribute income from the wealthy to the middle class, from bachelors to families, and from small families to large families. Proposed measures along these lines included state spending on maternity care and recreation, more progressive taxation, child tax credits, educational subsidies, and even wage regulations designed to lessen the effect of seniority on wages, that is, to redistribute wages from older to younger workers. A majority believed in protecting a woman's right to combine work and family, though some reactionaries claimed that reversing the trend of more women entering the labor force was necessary to increase the birthrate. Most population experts promoted a norm of "medium-sized" families with two to four children.

The campaign for population policies was part of two larger and interrelated intellectual projects during the 1930s: the maturation of reform eugenics and a new "social demography." By the 1930s, continued scientific advances in the field of genetics, such as those that revealed the fallacy of racial determinism, had caused most social scientists to recognize that mainline eugenics was a farce.[19] A small group of reformers within the American Eugenics Society hoped to save eugenics from irrelevancy by moving it away from its draconian and purely hereditarian assumptions toward an acceptance of environmental as well as genetic differences.[20] The key figure here was Frederick Osborn. Born into the New York City financial elite, and the nephew of prominent Malthusian Henry Fairfield Osborn, Frederick made his own fortunes in railroads and banking and retired as a young man in the 1920s to pursue his interest in population. Through the efforts of Osborn and other reformers, "positive eugenics" resonated widely in the 1930s, even as the broader eugenics movement declined. Eugenics was not a dirty word in learned circles. The word had been so sanitized that Louis Dublin, the demographer of Lithuanian Jewish origins highlighted in the previous chapter, could call himself a eugenicist despite the movement's racist and anti-Semitic heritage. Although genetic implications remained, and the number of states with compulsory sterilization programs continued to expand, eugenics became largely associated with a broad array of mundane programs designed to "improve" the population, such as public health initiatives.

As we have seen, the American demography profession was not built upon a clean break with its eugenic heritage. Now, during the policy crises of the 1930s, a softened reform eugenics discourse remained part of an increasingly public service–oriented demography sometimes referred to by practitioners as "social demography." The term "social demography" encompassed several meanings: it recognized the social, as opposed to the biological, differences among individuals and groups; it sought to uncover the social causes of different fertility patterns; it operated within a social science tradition; and it offered expertise in the service of social reform.[21] There should be no doubt that eugenic goals, however sanitized from their early-century incarnation, did partially motivate the community of social scientists who lobbied for American population policies in the 1930s; the goal remained of improving the genetic "quality" of the American population. As Osborn and Frank Lorimer, a leading demographer, wrote in *Dynamics of Population* (1934), a range of social spending was needed to counteract population trends causing "an apparent very gradual but by no means negligible drift toward undermining our most precious inheritance, the capacity for high intelligence."[22] But Osborn and Lorimer's book, like many similar to it in these years, was far removed from the eugenic rubbish of the 1910s and 1920s. Methodologically, Milbank Memorial Fund demographer Clyde Kiser wrote in a review, "*Dynamics of Population* reflects in every detail the bent of mind of the true scientist."[23] And in terms of policy goals, most of what the population-policy community sought was indistinguishable from that sought by mainstream advocates of increased social spending.

Population policy prescriptions were found in any number of scholarly studies as well as in more popular forums.[24] A public relations campaign (complete with radio appearances) by Osborn and the reform eugenics movement also supported the drive to manage the nation's demographic regime. In 1935, the Population Association of America (PAA) sponsored the "Conference on Population Studies in Relation to Social Planning." The conference brought together several New Deal figures and the leading population social scientists of the day.[25] Frank Lorimer, the PAA's secretary beginning in 1934, told Eleanor Roosevelt that the conference sprang from the belief that demographic research was a "neglected phase of science that is fundamental to the establishment of a more rational social order."[26] The First Lady attended the conference and also hosted a tea at the White House for its leaders. Also in 1935, the PAA, the American Eugenics Society, and leading birth control organizations joined forces to form the Council on Population Policy, an ad hoc committee that served as a clearinghouse for population information and reform efforts.[27]

The American campaign to enact population policies was part of a trans-Atlantic effort to build more robust and pro-family welfare states, a new progressive way of thinking about state policy filtered through the prism of demography. In 1937, the Carnegie Corporation invited the Swedish population experts Alva and Gunnar Myrdal to the United States, primarily to study race relations.[28] Gunnar's famous resultant book, *An America Dilemma* (1944), helped spur the civil rights movement.[29] But he also took the time to write *Population: A Problem for Democracy* (1940), based on lectures at Harvard. Gunnar, who would eventually win the Nobel Prize in Economics (Alva would win the Nobel Peace Prize) stressed the need to rejuvenate birthrates in the industrialized world, but he welcomed a stable population in the long term. As he saw it, the dynamics of population change—the friction of moving from one demographic regime to the next—shape the economy more than "the quantities at any particular point."[30] Current population problems should be used as a "crowbar for social reforms," he wrote.[31]

Similarly, in *Nation and Family* (1941), which compared demographic issues in the US and Sweden (the latter had one of the lowest birthrates in the world), Alva Myrdal proposed policies that were pronatalist—but only tepidly so and even then only directed toward the short term. These proposed policies were geared more toward reforming social relations than altering the birthrate in a heavy-handed manner. *Nation and Family* assumed that depopulation was a serious problem, but its larger argument was that industrialized nations pursue a laissez-faire approach to demographic and family matters at their peril. Moreover, population policy entails far more than specific measures to influence the birthrate. "It is a general thesis of this book," Myrdal wrote, "that a population policy can be nothing less than a social policy at large."[32] She then lamented, "The very phrase 'population policy' connotes to the lay mind—and, alas, sometimes also to the population expert—nothing more than one contrivance or another for controlling migration or for encouraging childbearing. To avoid this political short circuit there must be wide realization of the inadequacy of such an approach."[33] Unlike Swedish conservatives, who supported anti-contraception laws, Social Democrats like the Myrdals opposed such explicitly pronatalist policies on libertarian grounds.[34] A quarter century later, Myrdal suggested in a new preface to *Nation and Family* that commentators had exaggerated the pronatalism of the 1930s campaign for population policies. She wrote, "Perhaps, however, I should, if writing the book anew today, have slightly re-emphasized certain aspects of the 'message.' For one, I should now reduce any semblance I might have to a 'pronatalist' approach; the fact that population trends in Sweden during the 1920's and 1930's *if unchecked* pointed in the direction of depopulation was a temporary thing, serving to dramatize the message of our work on formulating a social family policy but not in reality directing that policy to any greater inclination to breed children."[35]

What resulted from the quest for population policy? The new stress on "positive" efforts to induce the "fit" to have more babies by emphasizing the joys of large families and promoting child-friendly public policies produced little effect besides launching a vogue for college courses on marriage and the family.[36] Certainly no explicitly pronatalist measures emerged in the United States. In 1940, legislation was introduced in Congress offering cash payments to mothers, but it quietly disappeared.[37] Subtler proposals geared toward socializing the costs of children did not fare any better. The 1935 Social Security Act included programs to aid single mothers and their children but did not seek to influence demographic patterns. The lack of specific population policies contrasted with the experience of Great Britain and Western Europe, where social democratic parties stressed the prospect of population decline, advocated broadening the welfare state to reverse it, and secured passage of pronatalist measures.[38] American policy inaction contrasted most of all with Nazi Germany, which embarked on a heavy-handed but barely successful population-growth effort. One essence of Nazism was the quest to depopulate Eastern Europe so as to creating more living space for a growing population of supposedly racially pure Germans.[39]

Several causes doomed the quest for American population policy. Even as experts debated demographic trends, the more immediate problem of unemployment often dominated. With millions of Americans unemployed, it was an uphill challenge to argue that the economy, in fact, needed more Americans—even as the populationist Keynes-Hansen doctrine made inroads among economists. Alva Myrdal put it this way in 1941: "Any concern for replenishing the population [in the US] has seemed gratuitous to the ordinary mind during the prolonged depression of the 1930's, while millions were unemployed and it was doubtful whether the productive apparatus ever would be able to make use of them."[40]

The Depression, however, cannot have been solely responsible for the American failure to formulate population policy. European nations suffered through the economic calamity but enacted baby bonuses and family allowances. Hence a puzzle remains: if so many feared the prospect of population decline, why did the United States not pass explicitly pronatalist measures?[41] I offer a few speculative explanations. Consistent with traditional explanations of the comparative weakness of the American welfare state, the first is anti-statism. As Alvin Hansen noted, population policy in a democratic society runs up against a basic contradiction: it asks that individuals trained to be self-governing, acquisitive, and atomistic consider children a public good.[42] In the US especially, opposition to a larger nanny state was reinforced by a late-developing central government with limited capacity and perhaps by a puritanical aversion to discussing matters of sex.[43] (Major victories for birth control advocates were only just beginning in the 1930s.) The American state had historically pursued implicitly pronatalist policies such as westward expansion but eschewed explicit demographic policies, adhering to the position that in a liberal democracy, reproduction ultimately falls under the individual's purview.[44]

Second, different understandings of eugenics may help explain the divergent outcomes. European eugenics coupled easily with pronatalism. Due to high levels of ethno-racial homogeneity, the European discussion was primarily about "degenerates," class, and fear of declining military power. In addition, the European eugenics movement contained a robust left-wing strand. Radicals and some social democrats maintained that capitalism itself was responsible for the low birthrate because the average member of the proletariat could never achieve a sufficient surplus to provide for a large family. In the US, however, fears of the racial "other" having excess children were paramount (though reform eugenicists usually couched such anxieties in racially neutral terms). The American eugenics movement had always incorporated both liberal and reactionary strands,[45] but the latter produced a language of fiscal austerity that constructed population increase as a public burden. For example, Margaret Sanger noted that the birthrate was high among those on public relief. "We have increased that strata of our population that we do not need," she suggested in 1937.[46] Such attitudes were hardly conducive to programs to increase the American population at large. Eugenicists struggled with the tension between the prospect of depopulation and the fear that efforts to increase the population would lead to a higher birthrate among the "dysgenic" groups in society.[47]

The third possible explanation for the absence of population policy in the United States is timing. Fertility had been declining in both Europe and the United States for more than a century, but the trend had recently accelerated in Europe. Moreover, heavy European losses in World

War I fostered pronatalist sentiment. In the US, however, widespread debate about the declining birthrate emerged only in the mid 1930s, just as the reformist mood of the nation was waning, and then the onset of World War II froze all reform efforts in their tracks. During the war, the American effort to plan for the postwar years included some calls for population policy (as did Great Britain's "Beveridge Report," the blueprint of that nation's postwar welfare state).[48] In a brochure written for the National Resources Planning Board, the New Deal's primary planning organization, Alvin Hansen suggested that family allowances would be an important component of the postwar high-consumption economy.[49] But the movement for population policy fizzled along with support for planning in the United States, epitomized by the wartime collapse of the National Resources Planning Board.[50]

In the end, however, the most important difference between the US and Europe was that reformers in the former operated within the dominant anti–population growth framework of the first decades of the twentieth century and were ambivalent about advocating pronatalist policies. Scholars have noted that 1930s reform eugenicists sought to link population policies to broader reformist and left-leaning goals, but they have exaggerated the populationism of this campaign, failing to distinguish between the short-term goal of a higher population and the long-term goal of a stable one.[51] Reform eugenicists, adhering to traditional Malthusian views, generally welcomed the anticipated population decline. Their main goal was to ensure quality as quantity waned; they hoped that net population decline would result from lower birthrates among the poorer classes and higher birthrates among the well-off.[52]

Beyond the longstanding motivation of improving the "quality" of the population, the campaign for a comprehensive population policy amalgamated three newer goals: a stable population, an expanded welfare state, and a rise in average personal consumption.[53] Historians of social policy, then, might benefit from devoting more attention to the ways in which population thinking helped account for the relative stinginess of the American welfare state compared to those in Europe.[54] Finally, populationist Europeans adhered to the Keynes-Hansen stagnation thesis. Myrdal, for example, suggested that "the expansionist capitalistic system of private enterprise had as one of its prerequisites a progressive population."[55] American economists and policy makers interested in population, however, saw in the declining birthrate and coming stable population an opportunity to retool the economy. Stable Population Keynesianism's confidence that the state can sustain aggregate demand in the absence of demographic expansion tempered the pronatalism of the campaign for a comprehensive population policy. More broadly, SPK provided the common vocabulary of the 1930s population debate.

Stable Population Keynesianism

Given its sympathy to state action, the campaign for comprehensive population policy easily accommodated an interventionist approach to the economy. In promoting downward income redistribution as a way to manage the predicted stable population, the campaign helped develop and diffuse two seminal and related economic ideas—both of which are central to Keynesian economics—and at the same time add an important twist to them. The first idea was that consumption rather than production, the old bellwether, is the linchpin of industrialized economies. The 1930s population debate was thus a bridge and mediator between an older discourse of scarcity and a newer discourse of abundance in the United States. The second was that a more equitable distribution of income, which in turn increases average personal consumption, is not merely humane, or good politics, but actually an engine of economic growth.

From the 1880s to the 1920s, American liberalism had partially discarded the antipathy to consumption central to classical political economy and moved toward admiration for consumption and the consumer. The primacy of consumption to modern economies seems obvious today, but this recognition—and the subsequent deployment of state policy to promote purchasing power—represented a seismic intellectual shift.[56] During the 1930s, academic theorists and popular writers continued to build the case for a high-consumption and more equitable society, usually one that included a heavy dose of state economic planning.[57] Consumptionist liberalism incorporated the argument that "underconsumption," the purported tendency of capitalist societies to produce more goods than people can afford to purchase, had caused or at least prolonged the Great Depression. Underconsumption was also attributed to income inequality, which, assuming the wealthy save more than the poor, generates excess savings.[58] Keynes's *General Theory of Employment, Interest and Money* formally theorized a "consumption function"—the controversial proposition that, as an individual's income rises, he or she saves an increasing percentage of income and devotes proportionally less to consumption.[59]

Although the aristocratic Keynes was not personally passionate about reducing inequality, the policy prescription logically derived from Keynes's analysis was that getting more money into the hands of the lower and middle classes relative to the upper classes spurs economic growth more than the converse. (In other words, the premise is the opposite of "trickle-down" economics.) In the following decades, the American political economy embraced a watered-down version of Keynesian economics.[60] Nonetheless, a general stress on the virtues of mass consumption among policy makers, economists, and intellectuals muted class conflict, redefined American liberalism, and fostered the state-sponsored widening of the middle class after World War II.[61]

How did the drive for population policy advance yet also reformulate these ideas? Proponents of a stable population incorporated the Keynesian emphasis on consumption and redistribution but diverged from Keynes's insistence on population growth. According to Keynes, a declining population would exacerbate the problem of excess savings in mature economies. In his view, the smaller families resulting from slowing or no population growth, as well as the older average population, would reduce the average propensity to consume.[62] To the modifiers of Keynes's demographic theory, however, macroeconomic benefits from reduced inequality, especially when combined with higher consumption, were sufficient to combat any negative effects of a smaller population. They espoused Stable Population Keynesianism (SPK), which, to reiterate, contends that a stable population is consistent with a healthy or even growing economy, assuming a more equitable distribution of income and higher levels of personal consumption, most likely engineered through federal economic policy making.

Well before Keynes and Hansen codified the doctrine of secular stagnation in the mid-1930s, a few theorists had articulated themes of economic exhaustion and debated the relative importance of slowing population growth. Importantly, they also challenged the notion that pronatalism was the necessary response. For example, Stuart Chase, a progressive journalist and popular author, articulated a nascent version of SPK as he promoted a planned economy that would produce, in historian Robert Westbrook's words, "the greatest abundance of the highest quality of goods in the most efficient manner."[63] In *A New Deal* (1932), Chase argued that the cessation of population increase need not pose a problem for the economy—and might even contribute to abundance—assuming transformations in economic arrangements. In part, he came to this position through a traditional people–resources calculus. With the coming population plateau, in his words, "The Malthusian formula has been knocked galley-west. Militarists may deplore it, the economic system will have to make heroic adjustments to it . . . but in the long run the slackening of the pressure of population on the food supply is one of the best things which can happen to us."[64] Primarily, however, Chase focused on shifts in production, consumption, and the distribution of income. In his view, a static population has less need to save than a growing one, meaning "a static population is in a position to produce more consumers' goods, relatively, than a growing one, and the chances of *really raising living standards* for the mass of the people, become, theoretically, far better."[65] Chase wrote "theoretically" because he felt that such an improvement could come about only with a more egalitarian distribution of wealth. "In a functional society living standards would impressively increase," he continued. "If we maintain our present hodgepodge, complete with all . . . the inequities in the distribution of national income, the chances dim."[66]

Stable Population Keynesians hovered between the view that a state-sponsored rise in consumption could compensate for slowing population growth and the bolder argument that population decrease would in fact increase the propensity to consume. According to the first strand of thought—and here was a specific link to proposed population policies—governments would be forced to respond to dwindling birthrates with increased spending on welfare policies, especially those that socialized the costs of children. According to the second strand, a stable population would increase the marginal productivity and hence the wages of labor. Moreover, the changed age distribution of the economy—i.e., one with a smaller percentage of workers—would favor higher consumption. (In an era before the teen market came to dominate the consumer economy, economists took it for granted that more money was spent on adults than on children!) And finally, private firms, no longer able to assume a steady increase in the raw size of their markets, would have to develop new products—and sell them to a greater proportion of the populace—to generate profits. Indeed, this camp assumed that the business community did not demand steady population growth because, although businesspeople might eye the size of the overall market when deciding whether to make a long-term investment, real incomes and purchasing power have more significance. A stationary population would stabilize entrepreneurial expectations because firms value predictability over all.

One immersed in the 1930s population debate was Joseph Spengler, a professor at Duke University and arguably the most important American population economist of the twentieth century.[67] Spengler's long career was a microcosm of the twentieth-century population debate. As a graduate student in the 1920s, he supported the American Eugenics Society; in the 1930s, he helped articulate SPK; and as an emeritus professor in the 1970s, he studied the aging of the American population. Although after World War II Spengler inched closer to an optimistic orientation regarding the consequences of population growth, he never shook his basic Malthusian worldview.[68] In the 1930s, Spengler adhered to the views of his graduate adviser, A. B. Wolfe, who, as we saw, was a leading theorist of a stable population. Spengler conceded Keynes and Hansen's point that slower population growth produces a shortage of investment outlets. Capitalist democracies would suffer several problems from depopulation, Spengler suggested, and might lack the state capacity to confront them. Hence he called for several pro–population growth policies, especially higher wages, to close the gap between the micro costs of children at the household level and their macro benefits to society. Like his fellow SPK adherents, however, Spengler did not consider calls for short-term repopulation as inconsistent with his basic Malthusianism. As he saw it, the demographic source of economic disequilibrium was not population decrease *per se* but irregular, sudden spurts of growth or decline in the total population, as well as disparate rates of change in the various segments of the population—e.g., by age, ethnicity, occupational class, or geographic region.[69] Demographic frictions aside, the American economy could adjust to the predicted long-term, aggregate population decline with minimal stress.

The key to recovery and preventing future depressions was conversion to a high-consumption economy. More specifically, Spengler advocated a switch in production from durable goods (more sensitive to demographic trends) to mass-consumption goods.[70] Such a switch was likely because, he contended, "A decline in population will probably be accompanied by several changes conducive to an increase in the propensity to consume."[71] Increased marginal productivity of labor (and thus wages), state subsidies designed to increase the birthrate (that is, population policies), and an older society would all foster higher consumption. In Spengler's view, Keynes had exaggerated the extent to which depopulation reduces the marginal productivity of capital as well as the entrepreneurial incentive to invest. Moreover, the pro–population growth side too crudely assumed that consumer demand is driven by the sheer number of bodies. "Business men are interested in the effective demand for particular goods," the Duke economist argued in Keynesian terms, "not in the demand for goods in general."[72] Further, the tendency toward unemployment is no greater in a stationary than in a growing population. Unlike many in the population community, Spengler did not look to the government to change consumption patterns. True to his faith in free enterprise, he insisted that "given intelligent entrepreneurial policy, the rapid cessation of population growth entails no difficulties, no pronounced tendencies toward specific overproduction, no profitlessness."[73] Spengler was a eugenicist early in his career, and after World War II he would continue to think in terms of improving the genetic quality of the population while rejecting racial determinism.[74] Therefore, part of his desire to reduce inequality and promote consumption was guided by the hope that such measures would reduce the disparity in the birthrate between low- and high-income households. Yet he defended the stable population, beyond its desired qualitative effects, on much broader macroeconomic grounds.

Among demographers whose work reached more popular audiences, Pascal Whelpton at the Scripps Foundation for Population Research argued for a stabilized, "optimal" population.[75] Whelpton summarized his support for a stable population this way: "If this nation could choose between having a stationary population of 131,000,000 (our present size) or 150,000,000 or 100,000,000, it can be shown quite conclusively that the smaller number would be best from an economic standpoint."[76] Inverting the claim that creating a higher standard of living required an increasing flow of long-term investment, in turn dependent upon a burgeoning population, he wrote: "The more rapidly a population is increasing, the larger the share of its productive effort which should be directed toward expanding capacity for the future, and the smaller the share left to produce for present day needs. A stationary population thus has the advantage over a growing population that it can put more emphasis on producing for itself and less on producing for the future, which should mean more consumption goods per capita and higher living standards."[77] Whelpton acknowledged that a larger population created economies of scale in manufacturing, but he averred that these gains were outweighed by the loss from lower returns and productivity in agriculture.[78] Speaking to a reporter at the 1937 World Population Congress in Paris about slowing US population growth, he said, "Most of us agree it is a good thing, leading to a higher standard of living."[79]

Whelpton downplayed any link between overpopulation and the decade's unprecedented unemployment, but some supporters of a lower population tapped into a broader debate about technologically induced unemployment.[80] Shrugging off a discourse from the prosperous 1920s heralding the onset of a technology-based utopia, labor leaders, economists, and producers of popular culture lamented the machine's alleged displacement of the worker.[81] The prospect of reduced technological unemployment thus provided another point in favor of the stable population. Guy Irving Burch, founder of the Population Reference Bureau, a clearinghouse for demographic information as well as a Malthusian, pro–birth control pressure group, concluded, "We don't need a lot of unskilled labors [*sic*], because already the invention of labor saving devices is throwing millions out of employment."[82] At times, this argument spilled over into the critique that capitalism demands (or at least capitalist elites insist upon) a surplus of labor to keep wages low. More often, though, this camp assuaged capitalists by suggesting that a smaller labor pool would force firms to adopt more capital-intensive methods, in the long run making them more profitable and labor more productive.

Sociologist Henry Pratt Fairchild, president of the PAA during its first four years, also identified advantages of a stable and smaller population. Fairchild wrote mass-market books extolling "limited socialism" and consumptionist economics, and he illuminates the links between the population-policy community, mainstream economic debates, and middlebrow economic discussion.[83] He argued in *People* (1939), "Overpopulation has been the chronic and virtually universal state of human societies from time immemorial."[84] Fairchild also articulated a vision of a new economy freed from the outdated populationist doctrine of "industrial barons and overlords," as he wrote in *Survey Graphic* magazine.[85] Fairchild continued:

> First there was the assumption [among industrialists] that prosperity depended on large production, and that this in turn required an abundant labor force. A more realistic economics within the last few years has demonstrated that true prosperity is a matter of consumption, rather than production, and for a time the economic argument took the form of advocating a large population in order that there might be no deficiency of consumers. Now, at last, the conviction is rapidly winning ground that prosperity is not necessarily a matter of numbers at all, but of social and economic organization, and an equitable and rational distribution of the social product.[86]

In the 1930s, proponents of a smaller, stable population injected distributional concerns into the concept of the "optimal" population. Whereas

A. B. Wolfe had maintained in the 1920s that the concept of the optimal population was divorced from matters of distribution, Fairchild, Whelpton, and Chase based their definition of the optimum in part on whether such a level would reduce inequality, and they insisted that the slowing of population growth then taking place would produce the positive distributional effect of increasing equity.

Several European economists contributed to the development of SPK. Polish-born Michal Kalecki was an important theorist who operated largely within the Keynesian framework. Indeed, he claimed to have beaten Keynes to press (in Polish) with many of the ideas in the *General Theory*, an assertion still debated today.[87] Yet Kalecki had little use for Keynes's promotion of population growth. More specifically, he asserted that a population's spending habits were much more economically significant than its sheer size. "It is sometimes maintained that the increase in population encourages investment because the entrepreneurs anticipate a broadening market," Kalecki wrote in 1943. "What is important, however . . . is not the increase in population but in purchasing power. The increase in the number of paupers does not broaden the market."[88]

The British economist Brian Reddaway, a former student of Keynes, offered one of the fullest statements of SPK in *The Economic Consequences of a Declining Population* (1939).[89] Reddaway shared his mentor's anxiety about the possibility of a sudden decline in the British population but was ultimately upbeat about a moderate pullback. Reddaway acknowledged short-term drawbacks of depopulation. Because anticipated demand governs risk-taking, entrepreneurs would be more reluctant to take risks and existing firms less likely to make long-term capital investments. As a result, the normal turnover inherent in a market economy would no longer be absorbed by growth elsewhere, making the economy less adaptable and exacerbating downturns.[90] And the coming increase in the number of elderly might engender a pension crisis.[91] In the end, however, Reddaway concluded that the "economic outlook [of a slightly declining population] must be regarded as at least potentially favorable. Provided we can learn how to take advantage of it, the new situation should enable us to raise our standard of living at least as rapidly as in the past."[92] The "overriding proviso" to this "optimistic conclusion" was that the British (or any other) government must solve the unemployment problem, which, in his view, a declining population could possibly exacerbate.[93]

Herein lay the rub of SPK: population decline need not be a significant problem, provided states assumed more of the burden of maintaining aggregate demand. Reddaway worried that a smaller population would reduce capital formation, and that relying upon a rise in the average level of consumption carried with it certain risks because the demand for semi-luxury goods was more fickle than that for consumer staples.[94] But good public policies could trump demography. Spending on public works, using monetary policy to keep interest rates low, directly subsidizing new investment, and more robustly checking monopolies would encourage capital outlay. Plus governments could address the reduced adaptability of the economy that might result from a smaller population through additional public policies, for example by aiding labor mobility.[95] Reddaway also advocated an enhanced welfare state to reduce the costs of childrearing for middle-income families. In doing so, he offered a clear example of how the population debate promoted the idea that downward wealth redistribution promoted higher consumption and drove economic growth. Echoing Keynes's language, Reddaway wrote that, independent of any possible effect on the birthrate, "A system of family allowances will redistribute income in favor of people who are extremely likely to spend it. . . . It will, therefore, undoubtedly raise the propensity to consume."[96] Today, Reddaway's prescriptions serve as a reminder of the remarkable extent to which advocates of a smaller population placed their faith in the ability of states to fine-tune the economy. Such an approach became increasingly hard to sustain in the final decades of the twentieth century as the entire Keynesian paradigm came under attack, robbing the anti–population growth camp of an important weapon in its arsenal.

Still, SPK had staying power and would remain a dominant demographic-economic paradigm for the next three decades. Even more importantly, it spilled over from the confines of the population debate to influence the broader American political economy. By contending that the size of the population means little to the economy compared to spending and saving habits, it contributed to the rise of consumerist liberalism in the United States. And in doing so, it provided a significant and direct challenge to the Keynes-Hansen doctrine of economic maturity. Generally, historians examining the decline of stagnation theory simply suggest that postwar prosperity and the Baby Boom rendered theories of secular stagnation moot.[97] Or they emphasize conservative opposition to it, which was certainly important.[98] For instance, financier Alexander Sachs, one of FDR's economic advisers, believed that the nation was suffering from excessive taxation and an "under-investment" depression rather than a permanent economic plateau.[99] Yet leading conservatives, including Austrian-born Harvard economist Joseph Schumpeter and former President Herbert Hoover, tended to reject the end-of-innovation pillar of stagnation more than the end-of-population-growth pillar.[100] Population experts themselves offered an important and original revolt against 1930s stagnationist thought.[101] And mainstream anti-stagnationists included SPK in their intellectual tool kit.

As we have seen, Alvin Hansen's 1938 AEA presidential address spotlighted stagnation doctrine, and the topic saturated economic journals thereafter.[102] New York University's Willford King, for instance, used Malthusian precepts to reject mature-economy theory's populationism. Since the 1910s, King had argued that a reduction in the population would improve the lot of the average American.[103] In the late 1930s, he rejected Keynes-Hansen doctrine on the grounds a stable population would engender innovation. He did so, curiously enough, by imagining the manager of George Washington's Mount Vernon plantation informing the first president that all necessary work had been completed and that the slaves were having fewer children than ever before. "Tell everyone on the estate to gather tomorrow for a grand holiday to celebrate the completion of our major improvements—our arrival at a mature economy," King imagined the manager telling Washington. "This is the day . . . for which I have long been waiting. Now we can begin on the really worth-while things."[104] King wrote more directly, "Complete cessation of population growth would tend to enhance the economic welfare of the nation; in other words, it would aid in accelerating rather than retarding the upward movement of per capita income."[105] King's logic incorporated the traditional Malthusian obsession with the food supply, but it also included the consumptionist core of SPK. Whereas rapidly growing societies spend to meet the basic needs of all the new people, he suggested, demographically flat societies would spend to enhance the lives of the existing population, resulting in a "marked increase in production of consumable goods and hence in average income per capita."[106]

King's sepia portrait of plantation life also shows how some individuals believed that population leveling would usher in the Good Life, one defined by the pursuit of goals loftier than material gain. No population watcher prioritized this noneconomic, aesthetic argument, traceable to John Stuart Mill and Alfred Marshall,[107] but many deployed it from time to time, suggesting that if economic growth could not be preserved in the coming stable-population era, then more humane values and ample leisure were second-best outcomes. Louis Dublin frequently highlighted both the economic benefits of a reduced population as well as quality-of-life considerations.[108] Warren Thompson, author of *Population Problems* (and the other original researcher at the Scripps Foundation along with Whelpton), put it this way:

> The criticism so often made of us by Europeans, that we have become the slaves of machines, is more or less true of all Western peoples and is in part a consequence of our efforts to supply the demands of a rapidly growing population. . . . A slowing up of population growth, or even its complete cessation, may be a prerequisite for the development of a civilization in which the art of living will receive a larger share of attention . . . [and] will make us pause to consider whether we can make such adaptations to these new conditions that life will be more worthwhile and living will be more joyous than formerly.[109]

In the 1930s, the quality-of-life argument reflected the high social status of population scientists, and it revealed the rather lofty rhetoric into which adherents of social and economic planning often drifted. This aesthetic critique was only modestly important to a 1930s discussion shaped by the Great Depression, but it would become crucial after World War II.

Even theorists with little expertise in population matters utilized SPK ideas during the stagnationist debate. One of the most vocal opponents of mature-economy theory was George Terborgh, an economist at the Brookings Institution and the Federal Reserve Board.[110] In front of a temporary congressional committee investigating the American economy in 1938,[111] and in works such as *The Bogey of Economic Maturity*, Terborgh scoffed at all three pillars of mature-economy doctrine: he rejected the premise that the frontier had been a particularly important factor in economic development;[112] celebrated the promise of automation and technological advancement;[113] and, on the basis of historical investigation, denied any connection between population growth rates and economic progress. "Changes in demographic growth rates are glacial in movement," he wrote. "Why should a trend that has proceeded harmlessly for three quarters of a century suddenly turn malignant in 1929?"[114] Other anti-stagnationists who doubted that procreation promoted prosperity included Howard Ellis, who exclaimed in the *American Economic Review*: "Growth of population! Do we propose to cure unemployment by encouraging the birthrate?"[115] Like Terborgh, Harold Moulton, a consumption-oriented economist and president of the Brookings Institution for a quarter century, rejected the population strand of mature-economy thought on the grounds the birthrate long had been decreasing. "If the rate of population increase had been of controlling importance," he wrote, "we should have had a sharply declining rate of increase in production as early as 1870, with a continuing downward trend to the present time." Moulton concluded, "The conception of population growth as a controlling factor in economic expansion involves an elementary fallacy . . . that the only impetus to economic growth is that which comes from increased numbers of people."[116]

Keynes-Hansen demographic doctrine came under attack from economists both to the political left and right of Keynes. Paul Sweezy, whom the famous economist John Kenneth Galbraith called "the most noted American Marxist scholar,"[117] claimed that slowing population growth exacerbated unemployment and underconsumption because it drove capitalists to accelerate the substitution of capital for labor.[118] However, ambivalence about the boon from population growth also mixed with conservative support for balanced budgets and limited government. Moulton, for one, opposed the New Deal. A 1939 *Fortune* magazine roundtable on government spending set up a dichotomy between an unwise "government-spending school" that fretted about the decline in population growth and a "budget-balancing school" that assumed ample investment opportunities existed without either demographic or fiscal stimulus.[119] *Fortune* noted that the second camp believed that smaller families would "increase the demand for better housing and luxury goods. In the future a smaller proportion of investment may go into capital goods, such as railroads or steel plant, in favor of greater production of consumers' goods."[120]

Inside the New Deal

As the cadre of prominent population experts floated between academia and government, the Roosevelt administration also helped disseminate SPK. Many policy makers did accept the notion that the American economy had reached economic maturity, but existing histories of the New Deal incorrectly extrapolate from this acceptance a full-blown embrace of Keynes-Hansen pronatalism. The New Deal did not usher in a new celebration of an expanding populace. The ideas of its leaders, its official publications, and its population relocation efforts contributed to a centrist argument that would subsequently reign for three decades: the United States did not need more people to enjoy economic growth.

Policy makers frequently used the metaphor of the closed frontier during the 1930s. Even if they did not understand the details of Keynes-Hansen theory, they latched onto the idea that the US had entered a new economic era in which the ill effects of the closing of the frontier required unprecedented levels of state intervention.[121] Sen. Hugo Black (D-Ala.) put it this way in 1937 in support of minimum-wage and maximum-hour legislation: "Having conquered and overcome our geographic frontiers, we must extend the frontiers of social progress."[122] The impression that rugged individualism only worked in an open-frontier society, in other words, fostered some of the intellectual attacks on laissez-faire thought during the 1930s. In 1934, the US Supreme Court upheld a temporary mortgage-foreclosure moratorium enacted by Minnesota in response to the Great Depression. *Home Building and Loan Association v. Blaisdell* focused on—and substantially weakened—the Contract Clause of the US Constitution, which stipulates that no state shall make any law "impairing the Obligation of Contracts." In supporting increased economic regulation, Chief Justice Charles Evans Hughes wrote for the Court, "The settlement and consequent contraction of the public domain, the pressure of a constantly increasing density of population, the interrelation of the activities of our people and the complexity of our economic interests, have inevitably led to an increased use of the organization of society in order to protect the very bases of individual opportunity."[123]

Many New Dealers also adhered to the view the American economy suffered from "underconsumption." In trying to find order in the New Deal's mélange of economic ideas and policies, many historians identify a unifying goal of trying to bolster mass consumption.[124] As Harry Hopkins, FDR's relief administrator, told Congress in 1938, "The measures with which this administration chose to fight depression were mainly directed toward one central . . . purpose. That was to fortify consumer purchasing power."[125] Consumptionist reasoning became particularly salient in Roosevelt's second term.[126] The underconsumptionist analysis (and the concomitant prescription of increasing purchasing power) did not necessarily correlate to any particular demographic analysis. Indeed, early statements of underconsumptionist doctrine in the 1920s largely ignored demography.[127] As recognition of the decreasing birthrate spread, however, the underconsumption and mature-economy theses fused. Five years before Keynes and Hansen formally constructed the theory of secular stagnation, FDR wed underconsumption and mature-economy ideas in a 1932 campaign speech:

> As long as we had free land; as long as population was growing by leaps and bounds; as long as our industrial plants were insufficient to supply our own needs, society chose to give the ambitious man free play and unlimited reward provided only that he produced the economic plant so much desired. . . . Our industrial plant is built; the problem just now is whether under existing conditions it is not overbuilt. Our last frontier has long since been reached, and there is practically no more free land. . . . We are not able to invite the immigration from Europe to share our endless plenty. . . . Our task now is not discovery or exploitation of natural resources, or necessarily producing more goods. It is the soberer, less dramatic business of administrating resources and plants already in hand, of seeking to reestablish foreign markets for our surplus production, of meeting the problem of underconsumption, of adjusting production to consumption, of distributing wealth and products more equitably.[128]

Many New Dealers subscribed to this basic assumption that the economy had matured, and they assumed that the slowdown in population growth played some part in it.[129] Moreover, some explicitly pro–population growth sentiment was present within the National Resources Planning Board. As mentioned earlier, Alvin Hansen served as a consultant to the NRPB, and his wartime pamphlets on the employment problem written for the agency praised population growth.[130] Given the particular difficulties faced by American agriculture during the 1930s—too much production and too few consumers able to pay for it—agricultural experts often noted the Malthusian devil had been temporarily locked in its chains. Liberal economist and planning enthusiast Rexford Tugwell, Roosevelt's undersecretary of agriculture, argued in *The Battle for Democracy* (1935), "The Malthusian thesis of a population pressing upon the food supply has become, for the time being, at least, a food supply pressing upon the population. The Malthusians feared scarcity, for they could not visualize its conquest. Yet in our generation we have seen scarcity vanquished, and our ever-present fear, so far as agriculture is concerned, is a fear of overabundance."[131]

Nonetheless, support for the basic assumptions of the Keynes-Hansen thesis did not necessarily—or often—translate into calls for a ceaselessly rising population. Disparate New Dealers claimed that the new era demanded wise management or even celebration of the expected cessation of growth, not repopulation. The nexus of support for the stable population was located in the New Deal's various natural resources planning agencies. The National Resources Committee (the immediate precursor of the more famous National Resources Planning Board) established a Science Committee in 1935, which in turn created a Committee on Population Problems, partially due to pressure from the PAA.[132] Members of this committee included Warren Thompson of the Scripps Foundation and well-known sociologist William Ogburn. Frank Lorimer, president of the PAA, headed the technical staff. The committee's work resulted in the publication of *The Problems of a Changing Population* (1938). Starting from the familiar premise that the nation's population was headed toward decline and then stabilization, *Problems* offered the era's most comprehensive compendium of demographic analysis and would remain the most significant government document on population matters until the report of Richard Nixon's population commission over three decades later.

Problems was sanguine about the economic consequences of a stable population.[133] "The change from an expanding to a stabilized or slowly decreasing national population entails new economic and social problems," the Committee on Population Problems observed in the introduction, "but it also opens up new possibilities of orderly progress."[134] Foremost among these anticipated problems were cultural and economic frictions caused by a rising average age of the population, which resulted from both increases in longevity and the slowdown in the birthrate. But the report concluded that the new demographic regime "may on the whole be beneficial to the life of the Nation."[135] In addition to the traditional people-to-natural-resources calculus,[136] the committee based this assertion on the Stable Population Keynesian outlook that the per capita consumption of a population matters much more than the sheer size of it. "It follows from an analysis of the trend of the Nation's population," *Problems* suggested, "that continued expansion of the domestic market for American goods and services must be sought through the increase of effective consumer demand, through increased productivity and broadened distribution of income, rather than in the numerical increase of population. . . . There is certainly ample opportunity for the improvement of levels of living among large population groups in the United States."[137] The report also rejected the thesis that declining birthrates helped cause the Great Depression.

Problems also examined microeconomic topics, identifying maladjustments among the geographic distribution of the population, the location of natural resources, and the location of industry.[138] These purported problems were being addressed by the most tangible New Deal population policy: the geographic relocation of Americans, especially those who lived on "marginal lands," to state-subsidized farms and suburbs. Historians have examined these relocation efforts as environmental conservation measures and examples of the New Deal's romantic esteem for the countryside, and they have traced the intellectual and institutional links between New Deal community-building efforts and trans-Atlantic intellectual currents, such as the Garden City and Arts and Crafts movements. But they overlook how New Deal population redistribution also reinforced the prevailing idea that the United States was already sufficiently populated as a whole.[139] Relocation policy was SPK in practice.

The dream of large-scale relocation was first and foremost antipoverty policy, but it built upon Jeffersonian agrarianism as well as more recent efforts to halt migration to the cities. In the first two decades of the twentieth century, a "back to the land" campaign known as the country life movement had tried to slow the inexorable urbanization of America by encouraging migration to rural areas. In the 1920s and 1930s, a regionalist movement embracing local traditions in response to the centralizing, industrializing, and allegedly homogenizing effects of American capitalism and culture provided additional intellectual impetus for the goal of slowing migration to the cities.[140] American economists had fretted since the First World War about the supposed disequilibrium between the locations of people and industry, for example, in the cut-over lands in the northern Great Lakes states.

Three Depression-specific developments reinforced momentum for population redistribution. The first was a modest migration of Americans from the cities to the countryside.[141] This seemed at first glance a welcome development because it reversed the decades-old trend of movement from the farms to the cities. Yet at the same time, experts bemoaned the fact that this "depression migration" was often to poor areas with even poorer soil; one scholar called 1930s migration patterns a "back-to-the-worst-land movement."[142] The second development was the modest "decentralization" of industry from city centers to the surrounding counties—today's "exurbs"—which seemed to demand that populations move in tandem.[143] Finally, New Dealers often thought about the population issue in regional terms and were especially concerned about poor populations in economically depressed regions, such as in Appalachia and much of the South. Anxiety about regional imbalance encompassed eugenic fears that the poorest regions had higher birthrates, and produced more inferior babies, than did the cities.[144] But the regional bent also reflected genuine interest in reducing poverty where it was most concentrated.[145]

Population experts, Roosevelt, and New Deal planners argued that redistribution policies would bring population and industry into equilibrium and maximize both human and natural resources.[146] Though the New Deal made a few modest gestures toward inducing businesses to relocate,[147] New Dealers generally assumed that, as Mordecai Ezekiel, a USDA economist and consumptionist author, declared, "under industrial conditions which prevail in this country it is easier to move populations than to move industry."[148] They also knew that despite the efforts mustered to encourage migration to farm areas, all signs pointed to further population losses in both city centers and the countryside and gains in the suburbs.[149]

Relocation policies emerged soon after Roosevelt's election. Using language lifted directly from Roosevelt's First Inaugural Address, the National Industrial Recovery Act (1933) authorized $25 million for the president to "provide for aiding the redistribution of the overbalance of population in industrial centers."[150] Roosevelt launched federal programs that purchased and retired marginal lands, built government-owned "subsistence homestead" communities, and provided loans for families to relocate.[151] In 1935, Roosevelt created the Resettlement Administration to consolidate a mishmash of programs, installing Rexford Tugwell as its administrator.[152] Given Roosevelt's longstanding interest in community programs, it would be an exaggeration to suggest that the population community was the driving force behind these policies. Still, population experts beat the drums in the press and lobbied policy makers. And several New Deal officials maintained intellectual connections to the population community. Most notably, Rexford Tugwell had links to the birth control movement.[153] Several New Dealers, including Secretary of Agriculture Henry A. Wallace and Mordecai Ezekiel, attended the 1935 Conference on Population Studies in Relation to Social Planning, organized by the PAA, where members of the population-policy community situated population redistribution as an important component of the New Deal's broader assault on laissez-faire.[154] Louis Dublin, for example, observed that individual settlement decisions produced negative externalities. "There is no phase of governmental interest which is more important than this very one, namely of concern in population increase, population movement, population distribution," Dublin said. "Individuals can hardly be expected to use wisdom in their movement."[155]

The tangible results of the New Deal's campaign to influence internal migration were more modest than planned.[156] By the late 1930s, various programs had relocated about ten thousand families (about half to rural areas) and built about one hundred new communities, including three suburbs from scratch, most famously Greenbelt, Maryland.[157] Several government-run communities, such as a frequently criticized one in Arthurdale, West Virginia, closely connected with Eleanor Roosevelt, were wasteful failures, and efforts to decentralize industry by attracting it to these projects proved especially fruitless.[158] With a substantial surplus of unemployed, American business was little concerned with disequilibrium between place and people. The New Deal's crop-reduction programs, which induced farm labor to move to urban areas, nullified the effects of the population distribution from the cities to the farms engineered by the resettlement efforts. And what rural migration did occur was often to already poor areas. Finally, interest groups, especially builders, quickly turned against the resettlement programs.

By 1936, the Resettlement Administration and Tugwell had become political liabilities for the administration, and Tugwell resigned after Roosevelt's reelection that fall. In 1937 a new agency, the Farm Security Administration, assumed some of the responsibilities of the Resettlement Administration. The New Deal did end up remaking the map of the United States in dramatic fashion by subsidizing flight to the suburbs and pumping money into the South and West. Its large-scale public works programs also shaped migration patterns.[159] The specific and targeted efforts to alter population trends, however, succumbed to the general conservative attack on the New Deal as well as to the growing preference among liberals to fight the Depression through fiscal policy rather than through planning.

Despite their modest outcomes, New Deal locational policies, and the discussion surrounding them, revealed deep support for a stable population. To be sure, migration policies have an ambiguous relationship to questions of aggregate population size. Malthusianism can be localized—there is nothing intellectually inconsistent in identifying "surplus populations" in certain scattered local areas while simultaneously supporting a larger aggregate population more efficiently arranged.[160] Moreover, some policy makers hoped that population redistribution programs would help arrest the declining national birthrate.[161] Yet demands for redistribution mixed smoothly with support for the cessation of aggregate population growth. To begin with, population experts and New Dealers thought about migration in terms of the closing of the frontier. Malthusian fears subsided somewhat during the 1930s, given the prospect of population decline, but the sense of having arrived at a new era of diminishing returns prevailed. The difference was simply that instead of fretting about the dangers of overpopulation, population theorists now hailed the coming stable population. And the very idea of moving people around the map of the United States like a chessboard exposed a sense of national maturity. If the closing of the frontier had signaled the end of supposed rugged economic individualism, population redistribution was state action designed to replace the Turnerian safety valve afforded by the frontier.

In addition, the traditional population–resources nexus promoted affinities between the goal of population redistribution and acceptance of the stable population. Resource experts felt that preexisting population growth (and industry's slash-and-burn mentality) had put excessive pressure on the landscape and exacerbated the inefficient location of the population, and they linked this misdistribution to the broader problem of overpopulation. In addition, proponents of state-sponsored migration assumed that pockets of rural overpopulation reflected the onset of diminishing returns as a whole for America's natural resources.[162] Despite his assertion that Malthusian precepts had flipped on their head during the Depression due to agricultural overproduction, for example, Rexford Tugwell still saw population growth pressing on natural resources, especially soil. He wanted his Resettlement Administration to conserve natural as well as human resources, to prevent soil erosion from "riotous farming" as well as "human erosion."[163] Tugwell not only noted the unfortunate aggregation of Americans in areas unable to support them. He also suggested that population growth ironically depopulated rural areas as they became exhausted. In an essay entitled "No More Frontiers" he wrote, "It is a matter of record with us that some of the most fertile land of early America is now waste, covered with scrubby second growth, dotted with abandoned farms, inhabited by a dwindling population which supports life by exploiting the tourist trade and selling antiques to 'summer people.'"[164] Tugwell identified widespread disequilibrium between natural resources and people, and his insistence on conservation included support for a diminution in population.[165]

Social science on migration during this era also mixed distress over overpopulation in depressed areas with a sense that the nation had exceeded its optimum aggregate size. In 1936, the Wharton Business School's Study of Population Redistribution published *Migration and Economic Opportunity*, "to consider what movements of population within the United States might be necessary and desirable, and what part, if any, the Government should take in encouraging or guiding them."[166] The authors, led by economic historian Carter Goodrich, supported out-migration from each of the four problem regions they studied. Regarding Appalachia, for example, they noted, "The fundamental cause of the low level of living is excessive pressure of population on available resources."[167] The situation in the Cotton Belt was somewhat more complicated, as the optimum population there depended on the world cotton market, but the authors suggested that an out-migration of six or seven million would be necessary if the market dried up.[168] To be sure, *Migration and Economic Opportunity* focused on perceived overpopulation in trouble spots. Yet in addition to the fact that their reference to "population pressure" seemed to preclude a favorable opinion of population growth, the authors concluded that the anticipated arrival of a stable population would be less relevant to per capita production and consumption than the necessity of "provid[ing] the machinery for making use of what can easily be produced."[169] Not sheer numbers but "social organization" determined per capita national income.[170] While the arrival of a stable population would entail transitional costs, "there is certainly no proof that the resulting [stationary] level would be any further from the economic optimum," *Migration and Economic Opportunity* concluded.[171]

The New Deal's foray into population redistribution sought to counteract the perceived harms of aggregate population growth in one final way. Although it targeted rural Americans and emphasized relocation to the urban-rural fringe, it was ultimately urban-development policy with the goal of stemming population growth in and migration to the cities. As Eleanor Roosevelt suggested in a magazine article on the subsistence homesteads program, the relocation of people and factories to new rural locations would make possible "the decentralization of crowded populations" in the cities.[172] Given that US population growth in the twentieth century was primarily urban growth—a trend that few at any point thought was reversible—the pursuit of population dispersal away from the cities almost demanded the concomitant goal of a smaller total population.

During the 1930s, the prevailing wisdom presumed that the state should act to stave off population *decline*, which generated interest in building a more generous welfare state that might reduce the cost of children. But the population-policy community and New Dealers continued to advocate an ultimately smaller and stable population. In attaching concern over declining birthrates to larger discourses on consumption and the distribution of wealth, the population community bequeathed to the American political economy the crucial idea that economic growth could still be achieved with—or even enhanced by—a stable or declining population, given higher levels of consumption. Cessation of population growth, combined with a more equitable distribution of wealth, would help transform scarcity into abundance. The development of Stable Population Keynesianism grafted support for population limitation onto the reigning economic-policy paradigm from the 1930s to the 1970s.

World War II—during which the global population grew substantially despite the unprecedented carnage—brought the 1930s population debate to a screeching halt. Some concerns carried over into the war—for example, the manpower needs of industry focused a great deal of attention on migration issues—but the prosperity and higher birthrates that began during the war and extended well beyond it completely altered population politics and theory.[173] Still, anti–population growth ideas did not wither in the postwar era. They metamorphosed once again as the economics of scarcity gave way to the economics of abundance.

CHAPTER FOUR

Population Unbound

Prior to World War II, the premise of scarcity guided all sides of the demographic debate. First, traditional Malthusians insisted that natural resources are finite and that pressure exerted upon them by population growth produces diminishing economic returns that trump economies of scale. Second, amid the sluggish birthrates and Depression of the 1930s, populationists, now echoing John Maynard Keynes and his American disciple Alvin Hansen, claimed that demographic growth was essential to economic recovery—that is, to the elimination of material scarcity. A third, majority camp espoused Stable Population Keynesianism (SPK). This theory, simultaneously an offshoot from Keynesianism and a challenge to Keynes's specific demographic ideas, suggests that a stable population, if combined with appropriate fiscal policies, produces a rise in average consumption and economic welfare and reduces inequality. SPK holds that the number of a nation's inhabitants is of much less importance to its economy than income and consumption patterns.

The prosperous—and populous—postwar period shifted the debate once again. These were the peak years of the Baby Boom, the unexpected near doubling of the American birthrate between 1946 and 1964 that led to predictions of an American population of 600 million in 2050.[1] The Boom took place against a backdrop of real prosperity and, perhaps more importantly, the backdrop of expected future prosperity. Americans of all political stripes celebrated a new secular religion of never-ending economic growth. According to many politicians, economists, and intellectuals, recurrent prosperity would finance victory in the Cold War, smooth over class conflict, and usher in an age of permanent abundance. The pursuit of economic growth became official government policy, and leading economists and historians wrote books with titles such as *The Affluent Society* and *People of Plenty*.[2]

Those who thought closely about the population question, then, had to grapple with the meaning of population growth in a society newly enjoying mass abundance. Those enthusiastic about the Baby Boom credited it for spurring aggregate demand and creating abundance, and also latched onto a new optimism emanating from the natural sciences about the long-term supply of natural resources. At the same time, widespread skepticism about population growth remained not only among the population-policy community but also among a wider swath of economists and conservationists. The skepticism shifted from the prewar years, however. Although many still predicted that an excess people would exhaust raw materials, or, along Stable Population Keynesian lines, harm individual economic welfare, the aesthetic or quality-of-life critique of population growth rose in prominence. This critique reflected the massive social and economic changes of postwar America, epitomized by a shift in emphasis from production to consumption. It was also in step with a liberal critique of American mass society, materialism, and conformity then in vogue among intellectuals. Historians have described how mounting wealth—and the assumption that American society had conquered the task of meeting the basic necessities of life—spurred greater interest in the pursuit of the Good Life. But they have missed the importance of the population debate to this new "postmaterial" mindset.

The triumph of the quality-of-life perspective occurred against the backdrop of a Cold War–fueled discussion about the massive increase in population in the "developing world" (or "Third World") that threatened to keep African and Asian nations mired in poverty.[3] This discussion about international growth remained firmly moored to the language of scarcity. During the interwar years, some theorists had suggested that population growth in the developing world, which then did not exceed growth in the industrialized nations, endangered global security and natural resources.[4] After World War II, a widespread sense that a lack of resources and living space had helped cause the conflict—coupled with the new rampant growth—increased the ranks of these "neo-Malthusians," as some observers labeled them. (I call them Malthusians for simplicity's sake.)[5] Postwar Malthusians ranged in outlook; demographers and foundation officials preferred the sober language of science and placed faith in the gradual amelioration of population problems, while radical activists demanded immediate and draconian measures to arrest growth. Notwithstanding disagreement over urgency, American Malthusians embarked on a mission to publicize the perceived dilemma of overpopulation. They greatly expanded the policy community at universities and large foundations and eventually lobbied the federal government to sponsor overseas birth control programs.

The debates about overseas and domestic population growth were intimately linked, and many economists, demographers, and policy makers participated in both simultaneously. To radical Malthusians, the only difference between the two geographic spheres was a modest difference of time scale; although America's prosperity and large land mass would buy it time, sooner or later the nation would follow the developing countries and descend into overpopulation-induced social and environmental catastrophe. After all, the postwar American population growth rate exceeded India's![6] Historians have devoted the most attention to this Malthusian camp.[7] Yet many in the population-policy community, as well as a growing number of journalists and opinion makers, rejected the applicability of the overseas paradigm to the domestic one, or at least would do so until the late 1960s. Instead, these experts focused on quality-of-life and social concerns and developed a uniquely American aesthetic critique of the Baby Boom.

The Global Population Surge

The population conversation in 1950s America continued the two-hundred-year-old debate on the applicability of Malthus's model to the nation, but new demographic realities, new theories regarding the relationship between demographic change and the economy, a new geopolitical landscape, and new population interest groups shifted the discussion. In part, the postwar dialogue reflected an unprecedented expansion of population in the developing world made all the more urgent by the Cold War. Primarily due to decreased mortality resulting from improvements in sanitation and public health, global population quadrupled during the twentieth century, and grew most dramatically from 1950 to 1985.[8] During these years the world's population increased from 2.5 billion to 4.8 billion.[9] (Today over seven billion people live on earth.) To strident Malthusians, overseas population growth constituted a "population bomb" primed to explode in waves of resource scarcity, economic misery, and starvation.[10] These radical views enjoyed a burst of popular attention in the late 1940s with the publication of two widely discussed books: Fairfield Osborn's *Our Plundered Planet* and William Vogt's *Road to Survival*.[11]

Most social scientists and policy makers were not doomsayers, but they bought into population concerns nonetheless. To begin with, rapid overseas population growth was the defining topic in postwar demography via the maturation of "demographic transition theory."[12] First sketched by Scripps demographer Warren Thompson in 1929, and greatly refined at midcentury, transition theory holds that industrialization and economic development in underdeveloped regions initially drive population increase: medical and sanitary improvements lower mortality before cultural norms of copious childbearing shift. In the next stage, birthrates drop in response to new gender and economic arrangements that accompany modernization, such as more freedom and education for women and an increase in wage labor outside the home. Eventually, population stabilizes. Midcentury transition theory used the nineteenth-century experience of Western Europe and the United States as a baseline and was influenced by the development of "modernization theory," which theorizes invariable development from agriculturally based societies to modern, industrial nations.[13] Immediately after World War II, a majority of demographers, treating birthrates as dependent variables, concluded that the problem of excessive population growth would solve itself in the Third World—modernization, perhaps given a jump start via Western economic aid, would work its magic and lower birthrates. In the 1950s, however, a consensus emerged that high fertility itself (along with structural legacies of European imperialism) kept poor nations poor and blocked modernization. Hence birthrates, now seen as independent variables, should and could be reduced more immediately through the direct intervention of family planning programs.[14]

Why, according to so many, did high fertility pauperize nations and stunt economic development? The consensus regarding the negative effects of population growth was rooted in the basic Malthusian formula that population increase outpaces natural resources. It was also infused with economic concepts of more recent lineage, especially a notion that high fertility creates a large pool of dependent children and thus a high "burden of dependency."[15] When lots of babies are born in a community or society, the argument went, income that might otherwise be saved and eventually converted into investment is spent instead on the immediate needs of dependent children (e.g., food, shelter, education, and healthcare). The capstone work in this vein was *Population Growth and Economic Development in Low-Income Countries: A Case Study of India's Prospects* (1958), by Ansley Coale and Edgar Hoover.[16] Coale, one of the giants of postwar American demography, headed the Office of Population Research at Princeton. Hoover was an academic economist who had worked in several government agencies after a stint with the New Deal's National Resources Planning Board. Imagining India's future economy based on various fertility projections, the authors determined that lower fertility would significantly increase incomes. This conclusion enveloped two important assumptions: (1) the more children a family has, the less it saves and the more it consumes, and (2) investments to satisfy the more immediate needs of children are less productive than (or can even be detached from) investments in factories, new technology, etc. Although later these two points would be fiercely contested, the pro–population growth economics that crystallized in opposition to the Coale-Hoover paradigm was just a blip on the horizon in the late 1950s.

Cold War exigencies also fostered unease in the United States about global population intensification. As historians Tom Robertson and Björn-Ola Linnér have documented, Malthusianism informed US agricultural and security policies; presuming that communism and desperate masses went hand in hand, policy makers feared that burgeoning populations in the Third World would create breeding grounds for Stalinism.[17] They also imagined that population-induced natural resource shortages might destabilize the world system, sparking communist revolutions and violent conflicts over raw materials. In the foreword to Linnér's *The Return of Malthus*, leading environmental historian Donald Worster writes, "Conservation became part of the programme to 'modernise' the more backward regions, which meant making them more like us in all ways. They too must see the dangers in runaway population growth, the impossibility of growing enough food to satisfy an infinite number of people."[18] The new Central Intelligence Agency in particular linked population, natural resources, and national security through what Linnér calls "resource-security theory"—the supposition that overpopulation would generate a domino effect of destruction beginning with resource exhaustion, continuing with social unrest and the destabilization of states, and ending with Soviet expansion.

Federal policy makers also maintained that international resource conservation would help bind together a peaceful world order in which the US would exercise power through multinational organizations. Toward this end, President Truman helped organize the 1949 United Nations Scientific Conference on the Conservation and Utilization of Resources. Truman linked this conference to his "Point Four" program for US aid to the developing world, so named because he called for it in the fourth plank of his Inaugural Address.[19] Although resource conservation was central to the policy of containing communism, US policy makers did not devote much energy to the population side of the population–resources equation, and Truman did not mention population in his Inaugural Address. The UN conference largely avoided the topic because of the sensitivity of the birth control question.[20] Moreover, the thrust of the conference was that technological advances could solve the world's resource scarcity problems. Still, given the longstanding connection between resources and population (and the widely discussed Malthusian treatises that appeared around this time), population issues were woven into the national security debate, especially after the State Department blamed the fall of China to the Communists on the Nationalists' failure to feed a burgeoning population.[21]

The philanthropic sector rather than the state took the lead in using research and propaganda to combat the perceived population explosion. John D. Rockefeller III created the Population Council in 1952 with a private gift of $100,000 after he became frustrated with the Rockefeller Foundation's slow pace on the population issue. (In 1966, he wrote former President Eisenhower that he had told his father of his "interest in population" as early as 1934.)[22] Under Rockefeller's guidance, the Population Council helped expand the prewar population-policy community into a tight-knit issue network consisting of the Council, older population research centers and interest groups, big foundations (especially Ford and Rockefeller), and university demographers. The Population Council and the large foundations soon supporting it represented America's establishment, and they preferred sober research to issue activism. But during the 1950s, the population network laid the groundwork for the intellectual acceptance of the global overpopulation paradigm and the federal government's development of an active international population policy in the 1960s.[23]

Many impulses spurred the postwar rise of the organized movement to curb population growth, and certainly a residual eugenic concern with population "quality" was one of them. But scholars have exaggerated this impulse. It is true, for example, that the interdisciplinary conference of population experts held in Williamsburg, Virginia, in 1952, which Rockefeller convened and which gave birth to the Population Council, included a nasty discussion about whether family planning aid would artificially and dangerously inflate the population in nonwhite nations such as India and "engulf" the developed world.[24] Racism was widespread in American society at this time, and population experts were hardly exempt from it. Yet tellingly, as Oscar Harkavy, a longtime Ford Foundation official, recorded in his account of the population movement, the "brief discussion of whether population 'quality' would suffer as mortality falls and more 'weak' lives are saved . . . seems to have been dismissed" at the Williamsburg conference.[25] A genuine philanthropic impulse to improve the lives of rapidly growing populations in the developed world, together with concerns about natural resources, the food supply, and natural security, primarily drove the campaign to tame population growth. And as the 1950s progressed, the population movement increasingly worried about domestic growth as well.

The Baby Boom

The American population surge was more unexpected and no less dramatic than the global one. From the end of World War II to 1960, the US population increased from 140 million to 180 million. The 1950s saw the largest absolute increase in population of any decade in American history other than the 1990s. A then all-time high of 3.4 million babies were born in 1946. By 1954, total US births per annum reached four million, a level sustained throughout the 1950s. After dipping under the replacement level of 2.1 during the 1930s, the fertility rate in 1957 shot up to 3.6, a level not seen since 1898.[26]

In the first few years after the war, many population experts were unconvinced of the Baby Boom's staying power. They argued that the surge in births merely reflected pent-up demand stunted by World War II and that fertility would soon resume its long-term downward trend.[27] This assumption spread into the other social sciences. In *The Lonely Crowd* (1950), sociologist David Riesman asserted that the "other-directedness" of the American people—their constant need to win the approval of others and willingness to adjust their behavior according to norms—was rooted in the "incipient population decline" of modern industrialized societies, which encouraged rapid capital accumulation and an acquisitive material culture.[28] The editors of *Fortune* magazine, meanwhile, proposed that the expected return of relatively low birthrates, improvements in healthcare, and powerful unions, which were lowering the retirement age, augured future problems in funding Social Security.[29] After the 1950 census confirmed the scale of the post-peace Baby Boom, however, demographers dramatically ratcheted up their population projections.[30] The media soon noted the revolutionary nature of the Boom (it broke the downward trend in fertility ongoing since 1800), and social scientists debated the causes and consequences of persistent high fertility.

The Baby Boom resulted from mothers of the era marrying and having children earlier than the mothers before or after them. During the Boom, American women on average had their first child at the earliest age of the twentieth century (20.3 in 1956).[31] All ethnic groups and social classes participated, though the greatest birthrate increases came in the middle-to-upper income range.[32] Broadly speaking, scholars have proposed two ultimate causes of the Baby Boom. Combining psychological and socio-economic analysis, the "Great Expectations" theory postulates that the fertility increase was caused not by economic prosperity *per se* but by the optimistic expectations of young adults in the 1950s. The second explanation is cultural and theorizes that a "procreation ethic," reinforced by popular culture and even federal propaganda, inspired women to marry earlier and have more babies. Historians have thus situated the Baby Boom within the 1950s cult of domesticity. In *Homeward Bound*, for example, Elaine Tyler-May ties the Baby Boom to the Cold War–enhanced celebration of domestic femininity and "normalcy" and to a new legitimization of birth control as a tool in spacing (large) families. May writes, "The baby boom was accompanied and reinforced by a widespread ideology favoring large families, reflected in everything from media images and medical theories to public policies."[33] Similarly, economist Kenneth Boulding wrote in 1964 that the Baby Boom "may signify a retreat into the family as the one island of security in a world in which the state has become a monster incapable of providing security or of attracting true affection."[34]

Cultural explanations can be persuasive in accounting for the development of the Boom, since pro-family rhetoric unquestionably saturated America during the 1950s. These explanations are less persuasive, however, in accounting for the decline in the birthrate after its peak in 1957. That was a year of recession, which suggests a close relationship between the birthrate and the economy. The Cold War also accelerated in 1957 after the USSR beat the US in the race to launch the first successful satellite. Moreover, if the birthrate were so closely tied up with culture, it makes little sense that it would begin declining in the late 1950s, when the widespread rejection of gender norms forthcoming in the 1960s was only percolating beneath the surface in a few bohemian outposts. Finally, cultural and geopolitical explanations of the Baby Boom discount the extent to which population pessimism competed with pro-family images in the popular media. The cult of the family and the child-centered theories of parenting, most famously espoused by Dr. Spock, were not synonymous with a cult of the large family. Flipping through women's magazines of the era, for example, one is struck by the fact that most of the photographs of families, in both the features and the ads, portray a nuclear family with two children. Magazine editors saw nothing incongruous about singing the praises of the family and, in the same issue, highlighting the potential drawbacks of a burgeoning population.

Histories of postwar America generally provide descriptions of the Baby Boom that combine the two leading theories of causation (economic and cultural) and suggest that popular culture as well as social scientists universally celebrated the Boom.[35] These studies review how the Boom created a new youth culture in the United States, one eagerly reinforced by advertisers who discovered the joys of marketing to a bulging cohort of children with ample spending money.[36] But the analysis of broader economic debates surrounding the Boom is perfunctory, the evidence usually limited to one of several pro-population articles from popular magazines with titles such as "Kids: A Built-In Recession Cure."[37] This analysis is valid insofar as economists talked about the demand for products related to the formation of new (and larger) households. And a few economists were unabashed supporters of population growth. Yet many social scientists, policy makers, and intellectuals continued to voice reservations about the benefits of continued population increase; it was primarily business magazines that served as the Baby Boom's boosters.[38] Instead of focusing on a small band of radical Malthusians or on the population boosters, it is more telling to look at how population questions pervaded some of the most crucial mainstream economic and political discussions of the 1940s and 1950s.

Between the Cornucopianists and the Prophets of Doom: Population and Resources in Postwar America

Cultural histories emphasize celebration of the Baby Boom. Environmental histories note the burst of Malthusian writings in the late 1940s but put forward that the population issue subsequently disappeared from conservationists' radar screens until the late-1960s zero population growth movement.[39] Neither approach is satisfying. Population anxiety was more prevalent in postwar America than most scholars have supposed, even if unadulterated Malthusianism waned. Postwar fears of a population-resources crisis in the United States were checked not only by Americans' new faith in endless abundance but also by the rise of what might be termed "resource optimism"—the belief that technological innovation can stave off population-resources crises. After all, these were the early years of the "Green Revolution" in agriculture, the vast improvement in yields in developing nations due to new crop varieties and planting methods. Still, most population experts espoused a moderate position, continuing to insist that population growth yielded diminishing economic returns from the existing stock of raw materials but rejecting doomsday Malthusianism.

As we have seen, anxiety about resource depletion in America had waxed and waned since the colonial era. During World War II, recognition that America's bountiful natural resources were contributing to victory—and a belief that the Axis nations had pursued war in part because they lacked an adequate resources base—forged a new conservation-as-war-effort sentiment. The Roosevelt administration orchestrated a fragmented but nonetheless far-reaching program of domestic resource mobilization that conserved militarily essential materials (and created substitutions such as synthetic rubber) while still preventing prices from rising precipitously, as they had during World War I.[40] In the late 1940s, the escalating Cold War, an upsurge in mineral prices caused by relaxation of government controls and Soviet machinations, and the aforementioned Malthusian books escalated calls to conserve scarce raw materials, but policy moved forward in fits and starts.[41] The Korean War spurred passage of the Defense Production Act of 1950, which offered direct financial incentives and contract guarantees to firms in raw materials industries.[42]

In addition, President Truman created the President's Materials Policy Commission, chaired by William Paley, president of CBS, to investigate the total resource situation in the United States.[43] The commission's final report, *Resources for Freedom*, was the most pessimistic federal statement on natural resources until the 1970s but was still ultimately sanguine about the ability of the nation to meet its resource challenges.[44] *Resources for Freedom* did warn that the US's rising population, combined with its "Gargantuan" and "insatiable" appetite for resources, would create sporadic shortages requiring a Herculean response.[45] It predicted higher costs for fossil fuels and timber and water shortages in the American West. Noting that the US used half the natural resources as the communist nations with only 10 percent of the people, it also worried about increasing dependence upon foreign materials. Still, the specter was not of Malthusian depletion but of rising costs. "The problem is not that we will suddenly wake up to find the last barrel of oil exhausted or the last pound of lead gone, and that economic activity has suddenly collapsed," *Resources for Freedom* declared; rather, "We face instead the threat of having to devote constantly increasing efforts to win each pound of materials from resources which are dwindling both in quantity and quality."[46] Resource problems could be managed, even assuming a continued population surge, through the "Promise of Technology" and appropriate mixed-economy policies.[47]

During the 1950s, the resource optimism embedded in *Resources for Freedom* grew not only within the American bureaucracy but also among most resource economists. In 1952—the same year it made its first grant for population research—the Ford Foundation bankrolled the creation of Resources for the Future, a think tank that emphasized market-based solutions to resource problems.[48] Natural scientists and the philanthropists who funded them, dazzled by the Green Revolution and the prospect of atomic energy too cheap to meter, remained optimistic about the nation's ability to continually replenish its basic materials and feed a growing population.[49] In works such as *The Road to Abundance*, cornucopianists predicted a caloric paradise, especially from the sea.[50] Writing in *Foreign Affairs*, agricultural economist Joseph Davis argued, "Considering our present knowledge, I believe that expanding population will promote essential soil and water conservation rather than intensify depletion."[51] Likewise, predictions of peak oil production met with quick dismissal.[52] Henry Luce, the famous publisher of *Time* magazine, declared that "by 1980 all 'power' (electric, atomic, solar) is likely to be virtually costless."[53]

In 1958, Resources for the Future held a series of forums at the Cosmos Club in Washington, D.C., that addressed topics from "the A of aesthetics to the Z of zoology" and that led to the widely cited volume *Perspectives on Conservation: Essays on America's Natural Resources* (1958).[54] The resource optimism mantle fell to Thomas Nolan, director of the United States Geological Survey. Resource problems still existed, Nolan conceded, but they could be solved through the better application of the "inexhaustible resource of technology" and ultimately by the marketplace, which would induce efficient resource substitutions. To refute the Malthusian position, Nolan quoted renowned nuclear physicist Edward Teller, who contended, "Human fertility is undoubtedly great, but so far human ingenuity has proved greater. I suspect that ultimately the population of the earth will be limited not by any scarcity but rather by our ability to put up with each other."[55] Overall, the conservation of resources was the mundane purview of economists, not the stuff of mass movements.

A small cadre of Malthusians, however, argued that postwar abundance in the United States was fleeting. Hugh Moore, the wealthy founder of the Dixie Cup Corporation, was crucial in spreading the gospel of overpopulation, although his discussion of the United States seemed an afterthought to his obsession with lowering populations in the communist world. A decade later, Paul Ehrlich's *Population Bomb* would actually take its title from a pamphlet Moore sent to more than a million and a half people in the 1950s (the title of which obviously tapped into Cold War fears of the nuclear bomb).[56] Moore was such a strident prophet of doom that the Population Council tried to distance itself from him.[57] Other 1950s Malthusians were veterans of the 1920s and 1930s population-policy and reform-eugenics communities. For example, Robert Cook, director of the Population Reference Bureau and editor of the *Journal of Heredity*, remained a well-published figure. His calls for overseas family planning programs revealed a more international approach to population matters than prior to World War II. In *Perspectives on Conservation*, Cook also criticized the postwar faith in science and technology ("god Science"), which would become an increasingly important trope to Malthusians into the 1960s.[58] Further, Cook noted that the technological benefits touted by the optimists were enjoyed by a tiny percentage of the world's population and that fertility, poverty, and hunger in the Third World were all increasing. Due to rapid population growth—in some nations as high as 3 percent per annum—the economies of poor nations were required to grow by 4 or 5 percent a year to reduce poverty—in his view an impossible task since overpopulation and poverty prevented the capital accumulation necessary for economic growth.[59] Sounding more like today's environmental ethicists than any of his peers, Cook situated America's use of resources in a global context, excoriating the United States for consuming such a disproportionate slice of world resources. He wrote, "At the present moment in history, we, the incredibly fortunate 6 per cent, having pre-empted much of the earth's industrial bread . . . seem to be able to offer our less fortunate neighbors little more than a pious hope that they will be able to eat granite some fine day a century or so hence. . . . If this is the best we can offer the earth's people in this time of crisis, surely we will have nobody but ourselves to blame when the deluge engulfs us."[60] Perhaps the best-known Malthusian natural scientist in this period was Harrison Brown, a professor of geochemistry at the California Institute of Technology and the unofficial scientific adviser to the population movement. Brown argued that the potential for new resource-stretching technologies was vast indeed, but he also urged consideration of what would happen to resource consumption levels when the developing world caught up to the West. He predicted an uncomfortable future for the entire globe unless population could be stabilized.[61]

Among the economists, Joseph Spengler reigned as the leading Malthusian, though he now showed glimmers of optimism. He continued to argue that rising numbers of people would exert pressure against finite natural resources, ultimately reducing income per capita.[62] In the *Harvard Business Review*, Spengler announced that the United States was not immune from the resource problems endured by developed nations, and, in response to the optimists who looked to the wonders of science, asked whether a diet of plankton would really be satisfying.[63] He emphasized that water was no longer virtually free in the US,[64] and he warned of potential global shortages of copper, lead, zinc, tin, and chromite as consumption begat more consumption.[65]

Although resource utopianists and Malthusians wrote memorable copy, most social scientists' discussion of population and resources in the 1950s took place between those two extremes. The prevailing moderate stance tempered faith in science with the observation that adjusting to the resource needs of a growing population would incur heavy costs. In *Perspectives on Conservation*, for example, Byron Shaw, the administrator of the USDA's Agricultural Research Service, doubted that the market could magically solve environmental problems.[66] He suggested that higher resource costs might curtail gains in the standard of living because Americans would have less money to spend on consumer goods. Leading demographers also tended to occupy the middle ground. Though they generally fretted about global population trends, the assumption that technology could improve living standards was built into their dominant demographic transition theory, and they generally distrusted the Malthusians.[67]

The popular press, notwithstanding an occasional foray into headline-grabbing Malthusianism, also struck a balanced note, especially regarding domestic population issues.[68] Early in the decade, even alarmist articles on these topics, such as *Reader's Digest*'s "Danger! Population Explosion

Ahead," hardly mentioned domestic trends.[69] Later, the press contended that American growth would have unpleasant side effects, but it hardly sounded Malthusian alarms. In a 1955 *New York Times Sunday Magazine* article, demographer Kingsley Davis advocated a US population in the year 2000 of "not more than 220 million."[70] (At the time, experts anticipated between 275 and 300 million Americans in 2000.) Davis allowed that from a national security standpoint, the US needed a relatively large population, but, without a policy of population reduction, numbers would reach a level that left the nation dangerously dependent on energy imports. He also predicted that gains in farm productivity were unlikely to keep up with population growth, thus rejecting the "'cornucopian boys'" on the grounds that "science is not magic."[71] Speaking to the housewives of America, then greatly concerned about inflation, he concluded, "as our population grows but our agricultural resources do not, we may find steaks and lamb chops even dearer than they are today."[72] Applauding the founding of the Population Council, the *New York Times* insisted, "There is no question that the world must prepare itself to face a crisis in another fifty years. How far science can go in satisfying the world's needs is largely a question of romantic speculation."[73]

Although the traditional population–natural resources nexus remained important, it was not the only lens through which learned Americans thought about demographic change in the 1950s. The population debate was woven into new developments in mainstream postwar economic thinking, and, as a result, prewar SPK evolved in response to the decade's economic and baby booms.

The "Realm of the Red Queen": The Economic Case against the Baby Boom

Since Malthus, theorists had debated whether population growth enriches societies by broadening the market and fostering economies of scale, or pushes upon the limits of resources and creates a pool of excess labor.[74] Most of the 1950s economic-demographic discussion, however, engaged more recent paradigms established by Keynes, his detractors, and a new crop of theorists who developed the modern theory of economic growth. Advocates of depopulation, or even a slower rate of expansion, swam upstream against the American political economy's preference for rapid growth of all kinds, an intellectual strand buttressed by the postwar prosperity. Historically, "population stagnation got a bum rap," observed Walt Rostow, a leading theorist of economic growth and adviser to presidents Kennedy and Johnson.[75] Nonetheless, an economic case against population growth remained prominent in postwar America. Stable Population Keynesianism evolved in the face of economic prosperity and the maturation of economic growth theory. Just as the Red Queen in *Through the Looking-Glass* told Alice she would have to run fast just to stand still, now many population watchers in the 1950s claimed that the American economic machine, due to accelerating population growth, would have to ramp up just to avoid breaking down.

To recap: the Great Depression led to a reexamination of the classical argument that population growth lowers the standard of living. Keynes and the "stagnationists" believed that sluggish population growth had caused an investment gap, and they claimed that accelerated population growth would spur consumer demand, the engine of the modern economy, and stave off economic "maturity." In contrast, Stable Population Keynesians—including many who actively sought a "population policy" for the United States that would adjust to and welcome the coming era of meager population growth—were sympathetic to Keynes's broader model but broke with Keynes on the specific question of population. They maintained that population size is largely irrelevant to modern, industrialized economies; what determines per capita output levels and the growth rate are spending and saving habits. Hence, if aggregate demand can be maintained through government spending and if income inequality can be reduced so that each person consumes more, then a stable population is consistent with rising per capita and even aggregate output. The SPK camp hoped that the combination of declining birthrates and economic crisis would induce redistributive policies to engineer the transformation to a high-consumption and permanently prosperous economy. Just before and during World War II, SPK effectively challenged mature-economy theory and its stress on population growth.

With the postwar confluence of economic prosperity and a higher birthrate, mature-economy theory was not so much disproved as rendered moot, as the effects of a stable population on the economy remained untested. Stagnation theory's decline was not only a response to prosperity but also part of a postwar dismissal of explanations of economic change, in vogue during the Depression, that stressed "secular," that is long-term or "evolutionary," economic change.[76] A less ambitious Keynesianism (known by such terms as "bastard Keynesianism," "short-run Keynesianism," and the "neoclassical synthesis") emerged as the dominant economic paradigm but became—even in the hands of some of the leading prewar Keynesians—merely a tool with which the state might avoid cyclical instability and manage growth rather than a grand theory of the instability of market economies.[77] Keynes, in short, was stuffed back into classical economics.[78] Solving the mysteries of economic growth, rather than addressing the distributive issues at the core of Keynesian theory, became the order of the day in the 1940s and 1950s.[79]

Still, the main elements of SPK survived the watering down of Keynesianism and the maturation of economic growth theory. "Short-run Keynesianism" allowed ample room for anti–population growth ideas. It emphasized short-run demand (as opposed to long-term investment) more than the pure Keynesianism of the 1930s—and a central premise of SPK was that population growth was a poor way of maintaining aggregate demand. Moreover, growth theory minimized the role of population growth in the economic growth process.

True, some economists in the postwar years sounded like the population boosters from business magazines featured in histories of the era.[80] Alvin Hansen argued that mass consumption, population growth, and prosperity reinforced one another in the 1950s and vindicated his prewar stagnation theory.[81] Optimists also relied heavily upon historical analysis, pointing to the confluence of population growth and industrial development in the West. They embraced the observation of J. R. Hicks, a legendary Oxford economist and extender of Keynes's theories, who noted in 1946, "one cannot repress the thought that perhaps the whole Industrial Revolution of the last two hundred years has been nothing else but a vast secular boom, largely induced by the unparalleled rise in population."[82]

However, skepticism regarding the economic consequences of population growth thrived despite the economic and demographic booms. The aforementioned agricultural economist Joseph Davis indicated the burden of proof remained on him and his fellow optimists. "Aside from cyclical influences," he wrote, "economists here and in England have been disposed to argue that slow population growth, or none, is favorable to raising levels of consumption and living and that the necessity of devoting a sizable fraction of the national product to capital expansion tends to limit the advances in per capita consumption in a growing population."[83] Skeptics of population growth continued to draw on Stable Population Keynesian principles. Just after World War II, much of the economic-demographic debate still hinged on the slippery concept of an "optimal population," the hard-to-define level beyond which additional growth produces decreasing economic returns, scarcer natural resources, or unhappier societies. During the 1930s, Stable Population Keynesians added to optimum theory by arguing that higher levels of personal consumption would alleviate any investment-sapping effects of a transition to a smaller and stabilized population. Although a consensual definition of the optimal population remained elusive,[84] the concept remained alive and well in the 1950s, a fact that belies the characterization of the decade as a pronatalist barbecue.[85] For example, economist Manuel Gottlieb wrote, "Cessation of population growth objectively relieves society of the 'burden' of mere 'extensive' accumulation and makes it possible to increase consumption quotas or develop more efficient . . . production."[86]

A central debate in the postwar years concerned the workings of the Keynesian "consumption function," the multiplier effect through which consumption drives economic growth. Several theorists surmised that population growth offered a meager boost, if any, to the consumption function. An important example was Horace Belshaw, a New Zealander who taught at the University of California and worked for the United Nations Food and Agriculture Organization. Belshaw had studied under Keynes at Cambridge in the mid 1930s, but he diverged from his mentor's populationism. In *Population Growth and Levels of Consumption* (1956), Belshaw argued that the former generally hindered the latter. Perhaps demographic expansion offers poorly performing economies a meager boost, but any benefits while at full employment are the "exception rather than the rule."[87] "The case for population growth in terms of . . . [higher] consumption," he concluded, "rests on the failure to sustain full employment by other means."[88]

Minimization of the importance of population growth also emanated, ironically, from some theorists who, despite the obvious inaccuracy of 1930s secular-stagnation theory's predictions of the end of economic growth, continued to believe that modern capitalism had run its course. After the war, those who diagnosed secular stagnation in developed economies identified not a lack of exogenous variables necessary for economic growth (population growth, new lands, and new technologies) but endogenous, structural failings. They considered population growth a shibboleth compared to the factors of oligopoly and imperfect competition. Josef Steindl, a leader in the developing "Post-Keynesian" school, was an Austrian economist who fled to Oxford University before the war. Steindl believed that capitalism's long-term propensity was toward overproduction and stagnation. In *Maturity and Stagnation in American Capitalism* (1952), he rejected the contention that a rising population had spurred economic growth historically. Steindl claimed that Keynes and Hansen had missed the fact that the growth rates of capital and the working population had both been declining for fifty years. And he asserted the impossibility of establishing a long-term relationship between demography and production.[89]

Other pessimists troubled by the Baby Boom imported a concept from the debate about the developing world: the notion that population growth stunts capital formation. The prewar pioneers of modern growth theory, Oxford's Roy Harrod and MIT's Evsey Domar, did not make population central to their theories, though Harrod's maximum rate of economic growth was partially determined by the rate of population growth, and he allowed that the cessation of population growth worsened economic slumps.[90] Nonetheless, population pessimists latched onto what came to be called the Harrod-Domar model of savings and investment, which attempts to extend a model of short-term disequilibrium into a model for economic development in developing economies.[91] The model suggests that growth can be achieved in poor nations by increasing savings, thereby improving output per unit of capital; some economist-demographers used it to argue high birthrates deplete savings because large families have so many immediate needs. This was the basic contention behind Coale and Hoover's *Population Growth and Economic Development in Low-Income Countries*, the previously mentioned seminal work on population and development.[92]

In this vein, America's own population surge necessitated increased levels of spending just to maintain the existing capital stock and prevent declining productivity. The economy constantly had to play catch-up with a growing population—running and yet merely standing still—instead of adding to per capita wealth. This was not a radical view. Even the opposing camp of optimists, which held that population growth is a relatively neutral phenomenon so long as technological progress continues and the growth of the capital stock exceeds population growth, doubted whether the supposedly virtuous cycle of mutually reinforcing population and capital growth could continue indefinitely. Everett Hagen, for example, stated that the implications of his model were "more optimistic than those of the conventional model only [in that they suggest] in some cases a longer period of grace, before per capita income falls to the subsistence level, in which to attain technological progress."[93]

Joseph Spengler helped connect the population and economic growth debates, serving on the Social Science Research Council's Committee on Economic Growth for its entire two-decade existence. Spengler fused his Malthusianism and SPK to new ideas emanating from growth theory.[94] He insisted that population growth in the United States, as in the developing world, depleted savings that would otherwise convert into capital formation and put up a "major obstacle to economic betterment."[95] Rejecting the contention that population growth spurs economies of scale, Spengler estimated that every 1 percent increase in population reduced per capita income by roughly 1 percent.[96] Spengler qualified his concerns about capital formation by admitting one could not predict the benefits from continued technological progress. Nonetheless, the thrust of his thesis was simple. In a 1959 *U.S. News & World Report* interview, he predicted that by the end of the century, "Living standards could be better than they are now, not because of the growth of the population but in spite of it."[97] In Stable Population Keynesian terms, moreover, Spengler argued that the United States could surely find better means of propping up the economy than relying upon population. "Within the framework of an economy more or less like that we now have," he wrote, "we can have full and effective employment whether numbers be growing or not."[98] Finally, Spengler criticized the American business community for what he saw as its myopic support for population increase.

Earle Rauber, a widely cited population pessimist and vice president of the Atlanta Federal Reserve Bank, also argued that rapid population growth necessitated excessive expenditures to merely replace existing resources that otherwise would be used for true efficiency-enhancing investment. He framed the issue this way: "The baby boom that followed World War II and that upset the forecasts of the population experts—a boom that may repeat itself when the wartime crop of babies comes to marriageable age—is forcing us once more to consider the relation between population growth and our ability to expand production enough if we are to avoid a decline in the standard of living of which we are all so proud."[99] Rauber claimed that the large crop of nonproductive, dependent young was a drain on the economy, and he often used the *Through the Looking-Glass* metaphor of having to run faster just to stand still.[100] He concluded, "Sooner or later, if it persists at its present rate, the increase in population will encroach on all other elements in our standard of living which will then of necessity begin to decline."[101]

Rauber's concern about dependent youth reflected an increasing awareness of the new age distribution in the United States: an age pyramid both more top-heavy, as the percentage of old people continued to grow, and more bottom-heavy because of all the new births. (Perhaps a dumbbell is a better image than a pyramid.) Especially after the 1957–58 recession, economists turned their attention to the possible correlation between the bulging Baby Boom cohort and unemployment. The US Department of Labor's *Monthly Labor Review* concluded in 1959, "What then are among the most pressing problems which must be met in the future in terms of the labor force? The first and most obvious of these is the forthcoming flood of youth."[102] As we will see, these concerns about the youth bubble would become quite salient to policy makers in the 1960s.

Spengler and Rauber were specialists in population matters, but postwar pioneers of neoclassical economic growth theory not immersed in the population-policy community also remained skeptical about the virtues of larger populations.[103] For example, the midcentury Cobb-Douglas production function, central to neoclassical growth theory, assumes that population growth leads to diminishing returns when the savings rate is equal to the population growth rate.[104] Put in the simpler terms of Julian Simon, one of the late twentieth century's leading population economists, neoclassical growth theory "implies that faster population [growth] leads to a lower rate of economic growth . . . [and] a lower rate of growth of consumption."[105] Many postwar growth specialists did allow that population growth historically had spurred economic growth in the US, given that the young nation had enjoyed a relatively unpopulated continent with ample natural resources. Yet at the same time, they concluded that in modern economies, population growth was deleterious—or, at the least, merely tangential to—economic development. For example, Nicholas Kaldor, a leading refiner of the Keynesian tradition at Cambridge University, suggested that population growth reduces the level of per capita technological progress and stunts income growth.[106] Moses Abramovitz, who studied the growth process for half a century and was later president of the American Economic Association, summed up the matter this way: "It is now clear that rich countries can maintain high levels of average income without rapid [population] growth."[107] And in his *Theory of Economic Growth*, W. A. Lewis, who won the Nobel Prize for his development research, illuminated the traditional principle of diminishing returns and guessed that the United States was "neither over- nor under-populated."[108] Perhaps most importantly, a seminal 1956 statement on growth theory by

Nobel laureate Robert Solow assumed that a rising population reduces the level of capital per worker.[109]

The evolving strategy of the Population Council, the leading anti–population growth organization founded by John D. Rockefeller in 1952 and subsequently supported by the Ford Foundation, reflected the developing mainstream view that population problems could be found at home as well as overseas. Three years after its creation, the Population Council convened an ad hoc committee to discuss the state of the population movement and address ways to sharpen its message.[110] At the committee's first meeting in May 1955, Frederick Osborn, the Council's president, urged greater emphasis on population problems in the United States.[111] This emphasis was in part a tactic to show foreign governments that the US was taking its own population issues seriously. One internal memo argued, "The example of the US and of Europe is important [to the developing world]. . . . The US should have a population policy authoritative enough to be quotable."[112] Frank Notestein, director of the Princeton Office of Population Research, told Osborn, "It does seem wise to have meetings devoted to problems of the United States for their intrinsic merits and for the fact that it is wise from a public relations point of view."[113] But the largest factor in the Population Council's growing desire to address domestic issues was the Baby Boom; and the goal was to measure the applicability of the consequences of population growth in the developing world to the United States' own demographic expansion.

The committee members began with an anti–population growth bias.[114] But for the first meeting they fielded papers from several influential population experts with a wide range of views: Spengler; Arnold Harberger, a University of Chicago economist; Simon Kuznets, one of the giants of twentieth-century economics; geochemist Harrison Brown; Ansley Coale of Coale-Hoover fame; and Theodore Schultz, an agricultural economist about to relocate to the University of Chicago and emerge as a leading human capital theorist. Spengler, Brown, and Coale represented the pessimists. Coale was a couple of years away from publishing *Population Growth and Economic Development in Low-Income Countries*, and at the Population Council meeting he articulated the thesis of that forthcoming work while applying it to the United States. Rejecting what he called the "*Newsweek* etc." position that population growth beneficially increases demand, Coale argued that, in the US, it was inflationary, sucked savings away from productive uses of capital, and gradually reduced the rate of output growth.[115]

In contrast, Harberger was optimistic about the economic effects of population growth, estimating that current income levels could be maintained with a 5 percent annual population increase.[116] Schultz too was sanguine, predicting that the US, in the following century, was "more likely to have food still running out of our ears rather than any shortage."[117] Schultz also previewed the coming alliance between pronatalist thought and human capital theory. More specifically, Schultz presaged the pro-population theories of the 1960s when he argued that population growth reduces human inertia—that it forces stagnant societies to innovate and compensate for population growth or else face a deteriorating standard of living. Schultz further insisted that knowledge diffuses quickly throughout societies; in other words, the masses could become educated and skilled workers (who desire fewer children) with surprisingly alacrity.

Kuznets was ambivalent. He had long been impressed by historical connections between demographic and economic expansion, although he believed that the causal link between them was tenuous.[118] In the 1960s, Kuznets would move into the pro–population growth camp, but in the 1950s he was still sympathetic to the Coale-Hoover paradigm that rapid population growth—what he called "population swarming"—stunts capital formation and income growth.[119] At the 1954 Columbia University Conference on Economic Welfare, Kuznets doubted whether continual population growth is necessary to preserve full employment, noting the "elusive . . . indirect association between population growth patterns and economic growth."[120] At the Population Council meeting, Kuznets declared that neither Harberger nor Spengler had sufficient evidence to prove the forecast that continued population growth would stunt per capita income, and he retained his view that the relationship between population and economic growth was unresolved.[121] Overall, the meeting's participants seem to have debated to a draw, and Osborn captured the unresolved nature of the economic debate when he wrote in his summary: "Economists seem generally to agree that per capita production and per capita consumption are now handicapped rather than benefitted by further increase in numbers of people, though technical advances, new capital and other factors will for a long time to come more than offset this handicap."[122]

Though population anxiety remained widespread, several theoretical contradictions and barriers squeezed the economic case against population growth. First, population specialists did not fully utilize all of the ideas emanating from the economic growth debate. In particular, proponents of a smaller population might have stressed a simple conclusion of the growth theorists: regardless of whether population growth helped or hurt the economy at the margins, population was increasingly tangential to the growth process compared with many other factors. Primary among these factors were the application of science in the pursuit of economic growth, a more skilled workforce, and technology-induced gains in productivity.[123] With this surge in US productivity, economists were increasingly less concerned with analyzing sheer numbers of people than with analyzing the tools people had.

Attendant to the new stress on productivity was a de-emphasis on natural resources as a source of economic growth.[124] Walt Rostow and other growth theorists increasingly predicted that modern economies, moving toward services and information technology and away from extractive industries like oil and timber, would become less reliant upon natural resources and more reliant upon human ingenuity.[125] Historian David Potter conveyed this idea eloquently in *People of Plenty* (1954) when he described an American "society where the majority now work for others, where service bulks large in the economy, and where wealth is gained more readily by organizing and manipulating other men than by further raids upon nature."[126] But to population pessimists, the stress on technology and human ingenuity—and the concomitant de-emphasis of natural resources—represented a double-edged sword. On the one hand, these ideas implied that the sheer size of the population meant little to the economy and thus could have been used to reinforce the central logic of SPK. On the other hand, individuals accustomed to thinking in Malthusian terms were predisposed to reject any doctrine highlighting technological progress, the trump card of the anti-Malthusians during this era of technological optimism.

In addition to failing to capitalize on developments in growth theory, opponents of population growth suffered from the postwar watering down of Keynesianism. The development of short-run Keynesianism did not alter fundamentally the Stable Population Keynesian premise that government policy could stimulate the economy in lieu of population growth. Indeed, the new emphasis on short-term demand management actually jelled smoothly with SPK. Yet the overall emasculation of Keynesianism did limit the scope of the argument that the state was more efficient than the stork. Just after World War II, Horace Belshaw and other skeptics of population growth had promoted government-sponsored public works projects and other means besides demographic change to sustain full employment.[127] But with the return of general prosperity and the transformation of Keynesianism into a theory of short-term demand stimulation, such calls for public investment faded (at least until Harvard Keynesian John Kenneth Galbraith's vigorous defense of them late in the decade).[128] Hence, the population pessimists lost an opening through which to attack the argument that population growth was essential to propping up aggregate demand.

There was one final contradiction, albeit a muted one, endemic to the 1950s population conversation. Although most economists who voiced concern about population growth generally did so within the rubric of abundance, a few moved toward a rejection of economic growth itself. This development marked the emergence of the central conundrum in the postwar population debate: the tension between the argument that slower population increase would help per capita economic growth and welfare and the argument that both population and economic expansion had to be halted to prevent ecological (and hence social and economic) catastrophe. In 1948, William Vogt's *Road to Survival* had called for limiting not only population but also economic growth and professed that the profit motive was fundamentally incompatible with ecological health. Vogt called for a planned economy to manage resources and economic redistribution between the rich and poor nations.[129] However, his economic critique was largely ignored at the time, as other Malthusians stopped well short of advocating a planned economy.[130] According to historian Jeffrey Ellis, the political climate of the Cold War made conservationists much more likely to identify overpopulation rather than capitalism as the root cause of resource scarcity.[131] Hence, though postwar Malthusians expressed nascent limits-to-growth thought, they primarily articulated their message in simple ecological terms (e.g., "Is there enough water?") rather than in terms of imperative drastic changes to economic arrangements.

Malthusianism hovered at the fringes of environmental discourse until the mid 1960s. As important to the development of limits-to-growth thought as the dire Malthusian framework was the moderate idea that population enlargement was reducing the "quality of life" in the United States. Rather than predicting ruin or highlighting per capita output, many population experts, environmental organizations, and intellectuals proposed that population growth led to overcrowded cities, reduced the land available for conservation, and made Americans more conformist (to name just a few points). In the 1950s, this identification of aesthetic limits remained precariously within the framework of abundance, accepting the overall virtues of economic growth but insisting upon compensating for its deleterious side effects. Along with the doomsday prognostications that grabbed headlines, the aesthetic critique catapulted the population issue back to public prominence by 1960.

The "Precious Intangibles": The Aesthetic Critique of Baby Boom America

Demographers John Wilmoth and Patrick Ball canvassed hundreds of postwar magazine articles and concluded that quality-of-life arguments against population growth increased just as the population issue hit critical mass around 1960.[132] The bulk of these aesthetic arguments concerned the natural environment, but they primarily expressed what might be termed "soft" resource-related concerns (e.g., the loss of open spaces), not the "hard" resource-scarcity concerns of the Malthusians. Quality-of-life arguments had been part of the population discussion ever since John Stuart Mill extended the question of natural-resource scarcity to incorporate the need for people to enjoy beauty and solitude. And in some measure they were a legacy of the eugenics movement's cultural elitism and stress on population "quality." But postwar developments primarily propelled the analysis. Quality-of-life arguments may have come to the fore because, although SPK remained effervescent, its reach was limited by the narrowing of Keynesian economics.[133] Quality-of-life arguments also reflected wise strategy, as they were easier to convey to a broad audience than macroeconomic explanations. Above all, they tapped into broader developments in postwar American culture that included an antitotalitarian rejection of "mass society," soul-searching about the meaning of prosperity, and a "postmaterial" quest to redefine happiness and abundance in a consumer society. In short, the aesthetic critique reflected the expectations of abundance, not the economics of scarcity. The most important rhetorical development to emerge from the new stress on the quality of life was the concept of the "aesthetic optimum" level of population, essentially the level at which the most people could lead the Good Life. By its very definition, the aesthetic optimum incorporated the economic-welfare and resource-scarcity concerns embedded in traditional understandings of the optimum—and augured the radical identification of economic and ecological "limits" that crystallized at the end of the 1960s. But early in the decade, proponents of an aesthetic optimum primarily deemed population growth a postmaterial issue rather than a harbinger of scarcity.

Radical critics were essential to this discourse, but so too were Cold War liberals.[134] Historian Arthur Schlesinger Jr. called for a new "qualitative liberalism" distinct from the conventional economic liberalism of days gone by.[135] In *The Affluent Society* (1958), John Kenneth Galbraith argued that the fundamental paradox of postwar prosperity was that the unceasing drive for increased production was starving the public sector and hence ruining many of the amenities that made a society livable.[136] "We must explicitly assert the claims of beauty against those of economics," Galbraith wrote elsewhere.[137] Population experts tapped into this vein and were leading popularizers of it. Even intellectuals who did not specialize in population matters linked the Baby Boom to their unease about American society. As mentioned, sociologist David Riesman had argued in 1950, before the full extent of the Baby Boom was evident, that incipient population decline caused conformity. Later in the decade, this argument was turned on its head; as the suburbs, bulging with Baby Boomers, came under attack for their conformity and anti-intellectualism, theorists claimed that an increasing numeric mass of people exacerbated the stultifying conformity of consumer-driven "mass society." Lewis Mumford, a famous critic of the American city, even worried that population increase had driven cemeteries to the edges of the cities. He complained that without a dramatic change of course, "the demand for open spaces for the dead threatens to crowd the quarters of the living on a scale impossible to conceive in earlier urban cultures."[138]

Because many quality-of-life arguments concerned the landscape, they fell within the purview of mainstream conservationists. Environmental historians have begun to devote more attention to the link between the liberal critique of prosperity and the rise of modern American environmentalism.[139] Adam Rome, for example, has shown how midcentury intellectuals such as Arthur Schlesinger and John Kenneth Galbraith, although not personally immersed in conservation circles, grasped the ways in which conservation themes could animate liberalism's critique of the unregulated society.[140] But the quality-of-life critique in the mid to late 1950s deserves further exploration along two lines. First, aesthetic environmentalism pointed the way toward the limits-to-growth thought that would emerge in the mid-1960s.[141] In a now-famous passage from *The Affluent Society*, Galbraith described a family driving in an air-conditioned car through polluted air, blighted cities, and a commercialized countryside to picnic by a polluted stream.[142] More strikingly, however, in "How Much Should a Country Consume?," his essay in *Perspectives in Conservation*, Galbraith chided conservationists for their random value judgments and myopic selectiveness and, using Malthus's "geometric" phrase, came very close to espousing the stationary state, the end point of economic and population growth according to the classical economists. Galbraith wrote:

> If we are concerned about our great appetite for materials, it is plausible to seek to increase the supply, to decrease waste, to make better use of the stocks that are available, and to develop substitutes. But what of the appetite itself? Surely this is the ultimate source of the problem. If it continues its geometric course, will it not one day have to be restrained? Yet in the literature of the resource problem this is the forbidden question. Over it hangs a nearly total silence.[143]

Galbraith concluded that "restraint on consumption can no longer be excluded as a remedy."[144]

Second, the population debate was central to the emergence of the postwar quality-of-life perspective.[145] Although a wide range of 1950s intellectuals tapped into this perspective, population experts were among the earliest to use it. As they built a case that population growth creates negative externalities, they also were among the first to demand that economists try to capture a fuller range of costs and benefits from various transactions.[146] This position, too, promoted questioning the virtues of economic growth itself.

In his 1957 presidential address to the Population Association of America, "The Aesthetics of Population," Joseph Spengler said that population growth and the resultant use of natural resources imposed hidden costs on society and ultimately on the consumer. He called for a new aesthetically determined optimum level of population and concluded that "an overworked stork is the enemy of the beautiful."[147] Spengler's address reflected the prevalent ambiguity about whether aesthetic goods were ultimately economic or noneconomic. On the one hand, he asserted that economists should more accurately price the negative spillover effects of population growth. Previewing today's environmentally based criticisms of economic indexes such as Gross Domestic Product, he complained that measures of output failed to allow for aesthetic values.[148] On the other hand, Spengler insisted on a category of items that simply cannot be priced. "Aesthetics is concerned with aesthetic value, above all, with beauty, with the beautiful," he said. "Whether this value is autonomous, or whether it must somehow be harmonized with ethical and utilitarian considerations, is not my primary concern."[149]

Examples abound of 1950s population experts using quality-of-life arguments that simultaneously pointed the way toward the limits-to-growth paradigm. For example, Philip Hauser, a leading demographer, explicitly wed the quality-of-life and limits-to-growth concepts.[150] As he argued that the Baby Boom was eroding the Good Life, he remained moored to the Malthusian paradigm. Hauser essentially argued for a safety-first position; though he suggested technology might obviate the need for conservation, he warned of the looming depletion of natural resources. More strikingly, he called for overall economic retrenchment, albeit in a qualified and selective way. "For we have never as a nation seriously considered the alternatives to growth," Hauser wrote, "even though I suspect there is no one who would not be forced to admit that on a finite globe (or in a finite solar system shall we say now in the post-Sputnik era) there must be some limit to 'growth.'"[151] In the next decade, with much more fanfare, the economist Kenneth Boulding would echo Hauser's metaphor and propose that, given limited resources, humans should think of themselves as living on spaceship earth.[152]

Other experts drew on anticommunist sentiment—and surging interest in psychology in postwar America—to claim that population growth had deleterious political and psychological consequences. A common motif was that rising numbers of inhabitants would make America more like the Soviet Union. Robert Cook of the Population Reference Bureau wrote in *Parents'* magazine: "How long it will be possible to maintain the American tradition of liberty for the individual in an increasingly crowded economy is another basic question—one for all Americans to ponder. Some social scientists note an inverse relationship between crowding and liberty."[153] Spengler, too, remarked that human freedom decreased as population increased. A favorable reviewer of Friedrich Hayek's *The Road to Serfdom* (1945),[154] a foundational book of modern American libertarianism, Spengler averred that larger populations would induce greater centralization and planning. "When the business community puts so much stress on population growth," he told *U.S. News & World Report*, "it overlooks . . . that, when the United States numbers 600 million, as it well might 90 years from now, a heavily planned and quite regimented way of life will probably become necessary, and many of the values we presently prize will have to be given up."[155]

The Population Council championed the new aesthetic critique. At the ad hoc meeting on the economics of population discussed earlier, Frederick Osborn was not content to simply point out a population-induced "economic squeeze" was coming in the United States. "But how about the cultural side which we have discussed only briefly here today?" he wondered. "What effect will this doubling of the population have on our political institutions, on our recreation, on our freedom of movement, on the spiritual and moral growth of individuals? Our views on these matters cannot always be supported by statistical and factual analysis. . . . It would be a fair guess that . . . there is a strong cultural case against the present rapid rate of growth."[156] A subsequent meeting addressed these concerns. Here Dudley Kirk not only presented the familiar arguments about quality of life and "space per capita" but also latched onto the critique of mass society. He observed, "It seems to be a corollary of the pressures created by more people on space that it evokes frictions that must be resolved by formal rules and especially by government controls at all levels. Could it further [be] argued that the crowding of people in metropolitan areas has contributed to the mass market, to mass society, and to stereotypes that pervade our life and impose conformity?"[157]

John D. Rockefeller III, the public face of the population movement, neatly summarized the contours of the population debate as it entered the next decade. Speaking at a 1960 population conference co-sponsored by *Newsweek*, Rockefeller claimed that population growth harmed the standard of living. Yet he also revealed the increasing quality-of-life emphasis, stating:

> Man is more than animal. The needs of his life are more than bread alone. Man, highest of all the creatures, has mental, emotional, and spiritual needs that arise from the very fact of his humanness. They go far beyond the simple necessities, the creature comforts, the much-discussed standards of living. These other, higher needs are the third dimension—the overlooked dimension—of the population problem. They are the precious intangibles that make life worth the living. There is education, for one, and the satisfactions earned by well-used leisure time. There is the quiet joy of appreciation of art and beauty, and deep spiritual and aesthetic rewards. These should be every man's birthright.[158]

Population anxiety permeated Cold War America. Although a new optimism concerning the future availability of natural resources neutralized the era's braying Malthusianism, many economists and demographers remained moored to traditional assumptions that population growth squeezes natural resources and reduces per capita income. And the overseas population explosion promoted new concerns about the capital-absorbing tendencies of youthful and rapidly growing populations. Economic growth theories were ambiguous regarding the role of population growth, and SPK's tenet that population is tangential to economic development remained vital to expert discourse.

The maturation of an aesthetic critique of population growth was the most significant development in the postwar era. This critique emerged from a framework of abundance—a polity can worry about amenities only after it has conquered basic material needs—and it assumed that the unwelcome effects of population growth could be managed without a frontal attack on growth itself. At the same time, the quality-of-life perspective hastened the return of a new framework of scarcity and limits by suggesting that less is sometimes more. It thus presaged the idea that economic growth itself should be reined in, illuminating the central conundrum of the postwar population debate: a tension between (a) the idea that a smaller population would improve the economy and (b) the idea that affluence itself was the problem, in which case not only demographic expansion but also economic growth should be capped to prevent environmental and ultimately economic and social catastrophe.

At the end of the 1950s, population issues saw an uptick in media coverage.[159] In the winter of 1959–60, for example, the new CBS newsmagazine *CBS Reports* devoted two of its first five episodes to the "Population Crisis," focusing on population growth in India. In the short term, as the next chapter explores, the quality-of-life and Malthusian perspectives (although the latter was not yet the dire Malthusianism of the late 1960s) would help shape several Kennedy and Johnson reforms. In the long term, this combination eroded the Stable Population Keynesian center of population discourse—the notion that fewer people would enhance economic welfare—and thus helped set the stage for the triumph of a new conservative celebration of growth.

CHAPTER FIVE

Managing the Great Society's Population Growth

In the early 1960s, population growth accelerated overseas and at home. The all-time peak in the growth rate of global population, 2.1 per year, occurred from 1965 to 1970.[1] Though the American birthrate had peaked in 1957, the number of Americans was expanding by about 1.6 percent per year, and this growth seemed poised to accelerate as Baby Boomers reached reproductive age.[2] If the growth rates of the early 1960s were to continue unabated, the American population promised to grow from 179 million in 1960 to one billion a century later. Policy makers also faced more immediate age-distribution and employment dilemmas. President Kennedy pointed out, "The fact is that in 1960 we had 2,600,000 youths reach the age of 18. In 1965 it will be 3,800,000. This is a tremendous problem for us."[3]

Kennedy's was not an idle comment. This chapter demonstrates that policy makers' wariness of domestic population change, and their desire to manage the social, economic, and environmental consequences of it, contributed significantly to the shaping of the New Frontier and Great Society reforms of the Kennedy and Johnson administrations. As always, the demographic debate was about more than birthrates and sheer numbers of people; made manifest in diverse policy discussions, it encapsulated several interconnected issues related to the age, geographical location, and racial distribution of the population. Disparate population concerns left their mark not only on the development of federal contraception policy—the era's best-known "population policy"—but also on macroeconomic and employment policy, the "War on Poverty," and immigration reform. Nervousness about the economic fortunes of Baby Boomers—and the macroeconomic effects of the Baby Boom cohort—added momentum for the state to pursue a "high-pressure" economy managed along Keynesian lines, broadened the base of support for family planning programs, and ensured immigration reform was designed to not increase the total population.

As the population debate influenced a wide swath of public policies, and as economic liberalism reigned, Stable Population Keynesianism (SPK) remained vibrant. This partial challenge to pure late-1930s Keynesianism suggests that population growth is not a prerequisite for economic growth or enlarged prosperity given the leverage of fiscal (and, to a lesser degree, monetary) policy and the inherent power of redistribution. The leading economic policy makers of the early 1960s, especially the Keynesian advisers to Presidents Kennedy and Johnson, generally subscribed to SPK. In *The Stages of Economic Growth: A Non-Communist Manifesto* (1960), Walt Rostow, a leading modernization theorist and Cold War liberal who served under Presidents Kennedy and Johnson, asserted that the ultimate stage of economic development was "high mass-consumption" democratic capitalism, not communism.[4] *Stages* also provided a primer on demographic change. Regarding the developing world, Rostow echoed Ansley Coale and Edgar Hoover (whose seminal work on India was published just before *Stages*) and maintained that population growth stunts economic development.[5] Regarding the United States, Rostow believed that the cessation of population growth would promote the Good Life and that technological innovation (rather than raw numbers) was the engine of the modern economy. Conversely, population growth required the economy to continually run harder just to stay in place. Pondering what would come after the final stage of mass consumption, Rostow observed that "societies have it open to them, if they wish to continue the strenuous life, to follow the American lead and re-impose a Malthusian surge of population, when they get bored with gadgets."[6]

At the same time, however, the high tide of liberal economic policy making represented a lost opportunity for proponents of a smaller US population. Although SPK remained intact, much population discourse retreated from concerns traditionally at its core—especially those related to the interplay of demographic change, long-term macroeconomic performance, and the distribution of wealth. To some degree, this retreat reflected a deepening of the 1950s aesthetic critique of population growth, which stressed the ways in which the population surge harmed the quality of life. The rhetoric of the New Frontier and the Great Society reinforced this emphasis on amenities; 1960s reform was guided in part by the idea that the US had moved beyond the era of scarcity and entered an era of permanent abundance.[7] At the other end of the spectrum, doomsday "population bomb" rhetoric intensified in the early 1960s. Jeremiads about capitalism and population growth spiraling together toward eco-catastrophe had little use for the mundane economic concerns of SPK—indeed doomsday forecasts completely rejected the goals of economic growth and increases in personal consumption. Malthusian ideas gained ground in mainstream circles during the early and mid 1960s, en route to cresting around 1970.

Most importantly, the macroeconomic case against population growth narrowed because policy makers focused on the short-term effects of the Baby Boom, not on the expected long-term demographic expansion it fueled. Had the leading economic policy makers of the early 1960s situated prevailing anti–population growth views within their Keynesian "new economics"—and had population activists engaged the new economics—the economic case against population growth might have survived the collision with the two diametrically opposed forces that eventually overwhelmed it: (1) a pervasive fear of ecological destruction by a "population bomb," and (2) an ascendant adoration of population growth among economic conservatives.

The Demographic Bubble, Structural Unemployment, and the War on Poverty

Among domestic policy makers, the most pressing demographic topic was whether the large cohort of Americans born since World War II—the "demographic bubble"—posed a threat to the economy and high quality of life. Policy makers primarily thought about the bulging Baby Boom cohort in terms of its employment effects. The activist employment policies of the Kennedy and Johnson administrations and the War on Poverty's emphasis on youth were in large measure an effort to respond to the demographic bubble.

Demographers commonly label 1964 as the final year of the Baby Boom.[8] During the early 1960s, many demographers believed that birthrates would remain high, given prosperity and a continued celebration of the nuclear family rooted in the conservative cultural politics of the Cold War. Others assumed a return to the lower fertility levels of the prewar era. One demographic fact was ironclad: teenagers were now legion. Unease about this army of youth appeared in several forms—such as through revived fears of the "juvenile delinquent"—but was primarily related to employment. Under any circumstances, absorbing such a bloated cohort into the labor force would challenge the economy. Yet the population growth–employment issue resonated at an especially high frequency and amplitude because the sluggish economy was the primary domestic policy concern of the Kennedy administration. In 1960, as the nation endured a slowdown, unemployment stood at 5.6 percent, and candidate Kennedy often pointed to the "gap" in the American economy between actual production and the potential production that full employment would bring.[9] The 1960 Democratic platform stated that the growth rate of the American economy "must grow more swiftly"—by 5 percent annually—to keep pace with the massive influx of youth poised to enter the labor market.[10]

After he assumed the presidency, Kennedy's "concern over the recalcitrance of the unemployment rate," as a member of the Council of Economic Advisers (CEA) put it, was not enough to stem the tide.[11] Unemployment reached 6.9 percent in 1961.[12] "Unemployment remains very high," John Kenneth Galbraith joked to the president. "This in spite of the very large number of people currently employed in foretelling the economic future."[13] Rising youth unemployment rates were especially worrisome. In 1959, one-third of the unemployed were under the age of 25,[14] and in 1962, the teenage unemployment rate stood at 14 percent.[15] In short, the Baby Boomers seemed to be reaching adulthood at exactly the wrong moment. The CEA predicted that an already soft labor market would need to absorb 26 million young Americans during the 1960s, a third more than the 19 million who had entered the workforce during the 1950s.[16] Moreover, a rising percentage of women working outside the home further expanded the total labor force.

The question of how to manage the Baby Boomers' entrance into the workforce was woven into a broader quest to explain the era's nagging high unemployment. A debate raged between a minority camp, which stressed various systemic or structural explanations, and a majority camp, which, following the prevailing Keynesianism, focused on macroeconomic causes, in this case a simple lack of aggregate demand.[17] The Department of Health, Education, and Welfare (HEW) and the Department of Labor were structuralist strongholds. Federal Reserve Chairman William McChesney Martin was sympathetic,[18] and some congressional Republicans made good structuralists. These Republicans were skeptical of Keynesianism, which undergirded the opposing aggregate-demand thesis and offered a more fundamentally pessimistic explanation of the era's economic difficulties, and they also found in structural analysis a convenient way of excusing the creeping unemployment of the late Eisenhower years.[19]

The first central element of the structural thesis, reminiscent of the 1930s, was distress that increased automation in the workplace exacerbated unemployment.[20] The working class and its unions were natural constituents of the automation thesis, fearing such transformations in the workplace as the New York Transit Authority's 1962 experiment with driverless subway cars.[21] Agricultural interests also had decades of experience with the isolated negative effects of enhanced technological productivity on farms. The postwar popular culture even reflected a fear of robots and other symbols of automation.[22] Second, since World War II, labor economists had worried that American workers were failing to acquire the skills necessary to optimize economic growth and national security. In particular, some were apprehensive the US was producing too few scientists and engineers to compete with the Soviet Union, and this sense of a "manpower crisis" deepened after the Soviets launched the Sputnik satellite in 1957.[23] Third, structuralists pointed to the obdurate high unemployment in "depressed areas," such as the poor sections of West Virginia that candidate Kennedy famously visited in 1960 and vowed to aid.[24] Fourth, structuralists identified job discrimination, whether by age, ethnicity, or sex, as a cause of unemployment.

Structuralists pointed to the rising population, especially of young adults, as an additional deep explanation of the high unemployment of the early 1960s.[25] This position began with the simple premise that Baby Boomers faced a tough labor market because of their sheer numbers. One organization studying these issues, for example, concluded that misallocation of human resources had increased since World War II because of "the low birth rates of the 1930s and the population explosion which began in the following decade."[26] Whereas the Keynesian, aggregate-demand camp assumed that closing the gap between demand and output would dissolve unemployment across the board (an economic boom results in tight labor markets and hence the hiring of the elderly, the young, and other sometimes marginal workers, e.g., Wal-Mart greeters), structuralists promoted public policies to directly address youth unemployment, such as training programs, hiring incentives to firms, and increased access to higher education.

Unease with the Baby Boom cohort permeated all the structural explanations. Individuals who pointed to pockets of poverty in depressed areas often noted that these regions had especially high birthrates. And anxieties about the demographic bubble and automation fused. In 1963, the Senate Labor Committee's Subcommittee on Employment and Manpower held extensive hearings on unemployment and the "manpower revolution." The subcommittee's chair, Sen. Joseph Clark (D-Pa.), wondered whether "change, not only in the field of cybernation [automation], but in terms of population growth, perhaps in a good many other areas of human life, has not [*sic*] suddenly begun to shift into an almost geometric progression of speed and we are just not prepared to cope with it at all."[27] Leading economists also connected automation and unemployment. Nobel laureate Gunnar Myrdal, who warned that America's economy was nearly stagnant when population growth was taken into consideration,[28] believed that the combination of technological changes and the surging army of youth augured continued high unemployment and hence necessitated vigorous government economic policies.[29] The population lobby and the mainstream media also latched onto the purported link.[30]

The Kennedy administration and Congress launched several initiatives to smooth the entrance of the Baby Boomers into the workforce. Some were subsumed under measures to combat other perceived structural causes of unemployment. Federal aid to depressed areas, which began in the New Deal and continued on a small scale during the 1950s, expanded greatly with the passage of the Area Redevelopment Act of 1961, one of Kennedy's first legislative priorities.[31] The next year saw passage of the Accelerated Public Works Act, which funneled public works programs to areas of high unemployment.[32] (In this era, more than a few Keynesian lawmakers believed that public investment was good for macroeconomic as well as political reasons—and thought so even without the spur of a financial crisis!) Also in 1962, Kennedy signed the Manpower Development and Training Act (MDTA), which subsidized training programs for workers, especially in high-demand skills, and required the president to submit an annual Manpower Report. The MDTA reserved a portion of funds for youth programs.[33] The Elementary and Secondary Education and Higher Education Acts of 1965 reflected not only longstanding goals of democratizing access to education but also immediate concerns about youth unemployment.[34]

Youth unemployment policy followed its own distinct path. During the 1950s, Sen. Hubert Humphrey (D-Minn.) spearheaded efforts to create a Youth Conservation Corps modeled on the New Deal's Civilian Conservation Corps.[35] Humphrey's legislation passed the Senate but stalled in the House. After Kennedy became president, Humphrey and the White

House each offered youth employment legislation that included a new Youth Corps, but these attempts, as well as House measures, made little headway despite extensive hearings.[36] Nonetheless, early in his tenure Kennedy created a Committee on Youth Employment, consisting of various cabinet heads.[37] He and his secretaries of labor, Arthur Goldberg and Willard Wirtz, spoke frequently about the demographic contours of the unemployment problem.[38] In early 1963, Kennedy sent a special message on youth to Congress accompanied by another youth employment bill, which proposed a more ambitious Youth Conservation Corps. "We do not conceal the problems and imperfections which still confront our youth," Kennedy wrote, "but they are in large part a reflection of the growing number of youth in this country today."[39] Soon thereafter, his Committee on Youth Unemployment released *The Challenge of Jobless Youth*, which documented the ways in which the Baby Boom's arrival into the labor market would exacerbate unemployment problems for years to come.[40]

Like so much of Kennedy's legislative program, youth unemployment policy emerged in earnest only after his assassination. President Johnson's January 1964 economic message to Congress embraced the idea, warning of the combination of population increase and rising output per worker driven by automation.[41] Apprehension of the structural unemployment resulting from the Baby Boomers turning eighteen was thus important to the general zeitgeist surrounding Johnson's War on Poverty. More specifically, the Youth Corps reemerged in the 1964 Economic Opportunity Act, the legislative cornerstone of the Great Society.[42] The War on Poverty emphasized youth not only because, as historian Irwin Unger wrote, it was "the group among the poor who seemed most salvageable and most promising," but also because it was the group growing the fastest.[43] Yet while the stress on the Baby Boom cohort's employment prospects was easily translatable into public policies, it also conveyed the impression that the sum total of the "population problem" in the United States was managing the Baby Boom generation's entrance into adulthood. Hence, the focus on the Baby Boom partially pushed to the side the traditional economic issues surrounding long-run population growth.

The Council of Economic Advisers and the Realm of the Red Queen

Whereas the structuralists believed that certain types of unemployment were intractable and thus largely unaffected by aggregate economic growth, a second community of economists held that the primary cause of unemployment was a sluggish macroeconomy. Led by the Council of Economic Advisers (CEA), an executive branch advisory board created in 1946, this Keynesian, aggregate-demand camp favored federal intervention through fiscal and monetary policy but saw the structure of the American economy as sound and believed that labor and other markets generally work best when left alone. Accordingly, they believed that economic growth would be a panacea for all but the most recalcitrant pockets of unemployment.[44] Business advocates opposed to state spending often articulated the aggregate-demand thesis, as it allowed them to argue that economic growth should run its course without government intervention.

Theoretically, the aggregate-demand camp was in a better position than the structuralists to integrate demographic theory into its analysis. More specifically, the "new economics" of the early 1960s—the invigorated Keynesianism that sought to return the economy to full employment through activist fiscal policy and relatively loose monetary policy—easily accommodated SPK.[45] Ultimately, however, the new economics' accent on the short-term macroeconomic effects of the Baby Boom blocked the continued amalgamation of anti–population growth thought and economic growth theory.

From the start of the Kennedy administration, CEA economists pointed to the ominous combination of a growing labor force and increased productivity to underscore the need for "high-pressure" economic policy. Walter Heller, the chair of Kennedy's and then initially Johnson's CEA, often articulated the running-to-stand-still position. "Our labor force rises by 1.5 percent a year," he wrote. "In the normal course of things, output per man increases by 2 percent a year. Just to hold our own—let alone achieve some desired new goals—the nation's economic growth has to average 3.5 percent a year. Even on today's low base, and without further price increases, that means a rise of $17 billion a year in total output. Right now, we are not making it."[46] The idea of a demographically induced gap between current and necessary economic growth received the administration's stamp of approval in the 1962 *Economic Report of the President*, which CEA member James Tobin called one of the agency's two "economic manifestos" (the other came under Ronald Reagan).[47] The impression that the demographic bubble forced the economy to work harder just to stand still was thus an important weapon in the push for an aggressive full-employment policy, which culminated in major Keynesian-inspired tax cuts in 1964.

The aggregate-demand camp's emphasis on the sluggish macroeconomy did not run counter to SPK.[48] The community of economists surrounding the Kennedy and Johnson administrations maintained that, given the state's ability to spur prosperity and full employment, population growth was a neutral economic variable—and hence the regulation of population growth proposed from various quarters could proceed. On occasion, leading economists expressed SPK sentiments directly. In his 1961 macroeconomics textbook, H. Gardner Ackley, who joined Kennedy's CEA in 1962 and eventually chaired Johnson's, criticized Alvin Hansen's continued insistence that population growth was necessary for a healthy economy.[49] In a later edition, Ackley called for economists to better incorporate demographic variables into their studies of consumption.[50] John Kenneth Galbraith, too, argued in SPK terms that a managed population promotes prosperity. "In all well-to-do communities, there is a strong tendency to limit the number of children in order to protect the given standard of living," he wrote in the mid 1960s.[51] Galbraith also noted that the Industrial Revolution emerged in Great Britain and the United States when those nations had low populations, whereas modern developing nations suffered from large populations.[52] Individuals outside of the Kennedy and Johnson circles also argued that Keynesian fiscal policy, not population, was the key to maintaining consumer demand. In a 1961 article entitled "The Trojan Horse of Population Growth," the *Harvard Business Review* claimed that rising productivity is the true source of economic progress, not sheer numbers. Introducing this article, the editors stated, "The idea that more people mean more demand, more jobs, more prosperity may turn out to be hollow and dangerous."[53] At the 1960 National Bureau of Economic Research conference, "Demographic and Economic Change in Developed Countries," Ansley Coale exported the Coale-Hoover thesis to the developed world, arguing that, in the wealthy nations, high population growth rates only helped when the economy was poor; normally, lower population growth rates led to better forms of consumption and growth in the per capita stock of goods, assuming governments engaged in Keynesian demand management.[54]

Yet while they remained wary of population growth, the CEA primarily approached the demographic bubble as a one-time problem solvable through aggressive fiscal policies and economic growth. As a result, they worried little about either the long-term consequences of demographic change in the United States or the causal relationship between population and economic growth. And while CEA members promoted redistributive policies elsewhere, they did not ponder whether population growth exacerbates inequality. In the end, the CEA's treatment of demographic variables was not so much a conscious choice to exclude something (SPK) as it was a case of misplaced optimism that the emerging consensus around the "new economics" would encompass these ideas. Faced with enormous political challenges, the CEA, although sympathetic to population control abroad and a regulated population at home—and hopeful these views could be integrated into the new macroeconomic consensus they hoped to build—handed the population baton off to the economists and sociologists after the opening leg.

Meanwhile, concern over the short-term employment prospects of the Baby Boom produced a half-century's focus on the macroeconomic and fiscal effects of this cohort, which, however warranted, diverted attention from the traditional and broader questions surrounding demographic expansion. Ironically, *how* policy makers thought about age distribution put the matter of aggregate population growth on the backburner. The CEA ignored the then-nascent concept of the "dependency ratio"—the ratio between productive and unproductive workers—as it focused on the gap in production, perhaps because it tended not to worry about deficits and deemed a rising dependency ratio amenable to Keynesian fiscal treatment.[55] In the early 1960s, a focus on the problems of a youth-dominated high dependency ratio (e.g., diminished savings), would have supported calls to lower the birthrate. In contrast, today the perceived problem is too many elderly dependents—a situation that promotes calls for increasing the birthrate—and talk of the dependency ratio is everywhere.

The early 1960s was perhaps the last moment during which a robust integration of anti–population growth ideas into prevailing economic wisdom might have occurred. As subsequent chapters detail, beginning in the 1960s, market-oriented economists and their allies among population specialists would promote new ideas extolling the economic virtues of uninterrupted population growth. The entire Keynesian paradigm necessary for the broad economic case against population growth—one not exclusively dependent upon the premise of natural-resource scarcity—would crumble completely. A new populationist consensus would emerge from the Keynesian ashes. In the shorter term, economists in the early 1960s could not have anticipated that a powerful social critique—that encouraging broader access to birth control was racist—would remove the goal of regulating population from the consensus that they worked so hard to achieve.

The Emergence of Family Planning Policy

During the 1960s, the US government erected an intricate policy apparatus—involving federal and state agencies, foundations, private health-care providers, foreign states, and nongovernmental organizations—to make inexpensive contraception available overseas and at home. This apparatus emerged from four decades of research by the population-policy community into the causes and effects of high fertility.[56] Fears of overpopulation and resource exhaustion, filtered through Cold War imperatives, stirred by the relentless educational efforts of the Population Council and the Ford Foundation in particular, and increasingly poured out by the media, spurred the policy agreement behind new international family planning programs. Domestic family planning policy also sprang from a fear of overpopulation, as population experts and policy makers sold domestic birth control initiatives as a way to preserve natural resources and the quality of life and to boost the economy. In keeping with the ambitious health- and welfare-reform agenda of the Kennedy and Johnson administrations, they also promoted birth control as a palliative for America's social ills. For example, Sen. Joseph Tydings (D-Md.), a congressional leader on the family planning issue, argued, "Voluntary family-planning programs must be an important part of any realistic welfare reforms or campaigns to eliminate poverty in this country."[57] Many scholars have detected in the population–poverty connection a racist agenda to lower minority birthrates and reduce the tax bill for welfare,[58] but family planning reformers drew on a broad political economy that incorporated not only the genuine desire to reduce poverty but also the wide range of economic-demographic anxieties chronicled so far in this study.

The drive to reduce international and domestic birthrates through family planning programs took off around 1960.[59] During the next few years, the population lobby's effort to publicize the perceived dangers of Third World population growth led to the inclusion of family planning measures in US foreign aid programs and then, in fits and starts, in domestic social programs. Although Eisenhower told his National Security Council that he worried greatly about overseas population growth and the "menace" of five hundred million hungry people,[60] and although after his presidency he would emerge as a firm public supporter of US family planning aid, he said of birth control in 1959, "I cannot imagine anything more emphatically a subject that is not a proper political or governmental activity or function or responsibility."[61] The 1959 Draper Report, as the report of Eisenhower's Committee to Study the US Military Assistance Program was commonly called, was the Magna Carta of US population policy.[62] William Draper, the investment banker who chaired the committee, was not initially interested in population matters, but John D. Rockefeller III at the Population Council and Hugh Moore, the wealthy, ultra-Malthusian founder of the Dixie Cup Corporation, educated him.[63] The Draper Report echoed the Coale-Hoover thesis that slowing population growth in the developing world would promote economic growth and prevent the spread of communism. The report also advocated grafting family planning assistance onto existing US economic development aid. Eisenhower distanced himself from the Draper Report, but with its release the population issue landed on the agenda on Capitol Hill.

The population community lobbied the subsequent Kennedy administration for the development of governmental family planning programs and accelerated funding of private ones. Birth control advocates also reached out to liberal Catholic leaders (conservative ones had already condemned the Draper Report) and continued to educate the American public about what they saw as the problems of international and domestic overpopulation.[64] The development of meaningful domestic population policy became much more feasible after the Food and Drug Administration approved the "pill" in 1960. The pill—and a sexual revolution already under way by 1960[65]—made the American public less puritanical about discussing fertility issues. Kennedy, however, was initially chary of addressing the issue publicly, fearing a backlash from social conservatives. In 1961, his office turned down a request by a scientist to meet with the president to discuss the "population explosion," despite efforts by Eleanor Roosevelt on the individual's behalf.[66] Kennedy did not speak publicly about the prospect of overpopulation until 1963, when he answered noncommittally a reporter's question on whether "the Federal Government should participate actively in an attack on uncontrolled population growth."[67] At the 1963 World Food Congress, Kennedy spoke again in muted terms, declaring, "Population increases have become a matter of serious concern—not because world food production will be insufficient to keep pace with the two percent rate of increase—but because the population growth rate is too often the highest where hunger is already the most prevalent."[68] Nonetheless, Kennedy's Department of State took baby steps to promote a reduction in international population growth,[69] and administration officials were free to speak more forcefully. At the 1963 annual meeting of Planned Parenthood, the leading pro–birth control organization traceable to Margaret Sanger's World War I–era organizing, US Ambassador to the UN Adlai Stevenson placed population growth squarely in the pantheon of postwar crises. He said, "Sometime ago I came across a comment that the major problems confronting the world today could be summarized as bombs, babies, and bulldozers: Nuclear bombs and missiles which might destroy civilization overnight; an excess of babies which could frustrate efforts at economic development; and bulldozers which are well on their way to leveling the world's countryside to make way for a chaotic urban sprawl."[70]

In the months before Kennedy's November 1963 assassination, Congress and the bureaucracy moved ahead of the president and set the stage for what historian Donald Critchlow identifies as a quiet "policy revolution."[71] In August, Sen. Joseph Clark (D-Pa.) gave the first major speech in Congress identifying a need for population reduction at home and abroad.[72] Clark and Sen. Ernest Gruening (D-Alaska), whom *Life* magazine dubbed "Mr. Birth Control," introduced legislation encouraging the National Institutes of Health to research population issues and establishing a Presidential Commission on Population.[73] The bill did not emerge from committee, but, separately, "President Kennedy approved enlarging NIH activities to include reproductive research."[74] Hearings on the 1963 Foreign Assistance Act included extensive discussion of the world population issue, and Sen. William Fulbright (D-Ark.) successfully introduced an amendment authorizing the Agency for International Development (USAID) to support population research.[75]

When Lyndon Johnson became president, the policy process accelerated. Johnson initially refused to meet with the population community, but under intense lobbying he promised in his 1965 State of the Union address to "seek new ways to use our knowledge to help deal with the explosion in world population and the growing scarcity in world resources."[76] Population activists were thrilled, but Johnson kept his distance. Still, the president did speak about the need to control overseas population growth—"this most profound challenge to the future of all the world"—at ceremonies marking the twentieth anniversary of the United Nations.[77] He also wrote John D. Rockefeller III, "Realism and facts demand that all nations face up to the problem of population control."[78]

In early 1965, Sen. Gruening introduced ambitious legislation creating new population offices in the Department of State and HEW. The bill was referred to the newly created Subcommittee on Foreign Aid Expenditures of the Committee on Government Operations, which Gruening chaired.[79]

Also in 1965, the Supreme Court affirmed the right to sell birth control on privacy grounds in the landmark *Griswold v. Connecticut* decision.[80] Gruening's subcommittee began a series of thirty-two hearings, over three years, which included lengthy discussion of the potential role that population programs might play in foreign aid.[81] Gruening's legislation stalled, but the hearings provided significant publicity for the population issue. The *Washington Post* called them "the longest running show on Capitol Hill."[82] Meanwhile, the Office of Economic Opportunity issued regulations that allowed the Great Society's "Community Action" programs to participate in family planning activities.[83] To minimize turf battles, President Johnson established an informal White House task force on family planning with representatives from several agencies. In 1966, Congress authorized federal grants for health services programs that included family planning, and HEW issued new guidelines under which states received federal matching funds. The Foreign Assistance Act of 1966 authorized the use of foreign currencies generated through food sales for family planning programs. The administration encouraged USAID to provide "technical assistance" (though not contraceptives) to countries that requested it, and, most dramatically, made food aid to India dependent on progress on the population front.[84] Despite these actions, the federal role in family planning remained small and disorganized compared to the combined efforts of the philanthropic sector and the thirty states that, by 1966, provided some sort of family planning services.[85] USAID did little to convert President Johnson's exhortations and its statutory permission under foreign-aid laws into concrete measures to provide family planning.[86]

The watershed year for federal birth control policy was 1967, with Johnson setting the stage in his State of the Union address by identifying a "race between food supply and population."[87] That year Congress specifically earmarked $35 million for USAID family planning projects, a figure that would rise to $75 million in 1970.[88] Amendments to the Social Security Act mandated that state welfare agencies create family planning programs, permitted the federal government to provide grants to private organizations, and required that 6 percent of the HEW budget be put toward family planning.[89] This significant policy shift enjoyed bipartisan support, with George Bush (R-Tex.) and Hermann Schneebeli (R-Pa.) taking the lead among Republicans in the House.[90] The Social Security amendments, though, went largely unnoticed, in large measure because that summer's urban racial tensions focused the spotlight on other amendments (eventually dropped) that required welfare recipients to participate in work-training programs. HEW was slow to react, but under its new secretary, John Gardner, a former president of the Carnegie Foundation, it created a more formal bureaucracy for family planning programs and secured expanded appropriations for them. As Critchlow concludes, "Family planning became integral to [Johnson's] War on Poverty."[91]

The bipartisan—and international[92]—consensus in favor of stepped-up family planning programs held for the moment, but a backlash was already underway from Catholics and social conservatives. In addition, some African-American leaders saw in family planning policies an organized campaign to reduce the minority population.[93] However, this reaction tended to reflect a radical male perspective; many African-American women saw in birth control an opportunity to improve their lives, and many mainstream male African-American leaders, including Martin Luther King, supported greater access to family planning technologies.[94] In response to the simmering backlash, President Johnson exercised caution in the waning days of his presidency. He opposed legislation by Senators Gruening and Tydings that would have greatly increased family planning appropriations, choosing the safer route of letting his bureaucracy expand existing programs and appointing an Advisory Committee on Population and Family Planning.[95]

Rethinking Race and Family Planning Policy

As the Johnson administration's caution indicated, by the late 1960s contraception policy had moved beyond its historic roots in the women's movement and the campaign to combat overpopulation and had become embroiled with discussions surrounding America's social pathologies. According to Critchlow, "Family planning policy offered a means of solving a social problem through technique without directly confronting the underlying structural issues of income inequality, race, or the breakdown of traditional values and culture, as evidenced by a growing divorce rate and out-of-wedlock births that began to skyrocket in the mid 1960s. If the federal government could prevail upon the poor to have fewer children, it followed, the rate of poverty could be reduced. The key was to make family planning accessible to the estimated 5.2 million poor women in need of birth control."[96] Critchlow also notes that underneath the era's antipoverty push "lay a deep anxiety about the breakdown of the American family, especially among African-Americans."[97]

Some scholars, including Matthew Connelly in his recent *Fatal Misconception*, have pushed this racial analysis much further, identifying a nearly linear progression from the early-century eugenics movement to family planning policy in the 1960s.[98] In *Woman's Body, Woman's Right: A Social History of Birth Control in America* (1976), Linda Gordon wrote, "Two major factors underlay the selling of population control in the [post–World War II] United States."[99] The first was the decision by John D. Rockefeller III and others to lobby for governmental family planning programs, thereby spreading the costs of population control across society. The second "was the desire to cut the birth rates of the poor, particularly nonwhites, in the United States. Stemming from the same hereditarian and blaming-the-victim assumptions as eugenic programs always had, population-control propaganda carried sometimes overt, sometimes covert, racist and elitist messages."[100] Gordon continued, "If the victims of our class society have seen in birth control a plot to exterminate them, there is a great deal of evidence, contemporary and historical, to support their analysis."[101] Concomitant to this racial analysis is a dismissal of the economic rationale of family planning advocates as little more than a watered-down desire to recreate nineteenth-century England's Malthusian-inspired poor laws and save on future welfare costs.[102]

Putting aside the unfortunate excess of Gordon's word "exterminate," much evidence supports this thesis. Throughout American history, many Malthusians and family planning advocates have been racists, and even nonracist arguments can have racist consequences. As Dorothy Roberts states in her history of African-American reproduction, "Reproductive politics in America inevitably involves racial politics."[103] Although the era of brutally racist forced sterilizations had largely passed, still more African Americans than whites were being sterilized in the 1960s.[104] The American demography profession and population interest groups were not entirely free from their eugenic roots as they sent experts to Capitol Hill to lobby for family planning, and other experts, such as FBI director J. Edgar Hoover, testified in unsavory terms about the dangers to society of differential fertility between whites and nonwhites.[105] At the least, advocates of federal family planning programs highlighted problems of the American city, including rising welfare rolls. Given the racist history of the birth control movement and the racialized nature of urban poverty by the 1960s, population policies were motivated in part by apprehension that nonwhite poor—and their offspring—were driving up taxes and crime.

Nonetheless, the ghost-of-eugenics argument has been pushed too far. The liberal campaign for better access to contraception in the 1960s cannot be equated with early twentieth-century population control efforts that targeted specific groups. (Similarly, assistance to population programs in developing nations should not be equated with imperialism.) A closer look at the triumvirate of family planning leaders in the Senate—Joseph Clark, Ernest Gruening, and Joseph Tydings—demonstrates that policy makers approached family planning from a broad array of economic, ecological, and quality-of-life concerns far removed from the crude assumption that a smaller birthrate among the (minority) poor would reduce poverty.[106] Each was a Malthusian who rejected eugenic ideas, and each believed that tackling population problems was integral to curing social and economic ills that extended far beyond the ghetto.

Sen. Gruening was a physician and muckraking journalist who had supported the birth control movement at its inception.[107] During the New Deal, he oversaw the development of maternal health and family planning clinics in Puerto Rico as head of the Puerto Rico Reconstruction Administration.[108] The knee-jerk reaction to such work developing family planning programs for people of color would be to label him a neo-eugenicist. But Gruening had long worked for racial justice as well as birth control, and had long opposed American imperialism.[109] During World War I, Gruening was offered the position of executive secretary of the New York City NAACP.[110] As managing editor of the *Nation* in the 1920s, he excoriated America's interventionist policies in Haiti and the Dominican Republic and supported the postrevolutionary Mexican state. In Puerto Rico, Gruening considered his charge "diminishing the territories' colonial status" and working with local reformers to rehabilitate the island's economy on a more egalitarian basis. "A democracy shouldn't have any colonies," he had told President Roosevelt upon first joining his administration.[111] After becoming governor of Alaska in 1939 and battling for statehood (obtained in 1958), Gruening was elected one of Alaska's first two senators, and he worked to bring the benefits of the civil rights movement to that state's indigenous people. During the Great Society, Gruening became a critic of President Johnson from the Left.[112]

Clark and Tydings were less activist crusaders for civil rights, but they supported the reforms of the day. Clark was an iconoclastic but dedicated liberal who as mayor of Philadelphia in the early 1950s had battled his party's political machine and observed a personal term limit of one. During the population hearings, Clark demonstrated his firm opposition to eugenic thought. When questioning the superintendent of Washington, D.C., schools, for example, he asked leading questions that clearly dismissed the notion of innate differences among racial groups.[113] Tydings, a young liberal often compared to John F. Kennedy, was elected to the Senate during the Democratic tidal wave of 1964. A loyal supporter of the Johnson administration, he had personal links to the Great Society: co-chair of "Citizens for Tydings" was Eunice Kennedy Shriver, sister of John and Robert Kennedy and the wife of Sargent Shriver, the head of Johnson's Office of Economic Opportunity.[114]

Clearly these lawmakers, as they linked the goals of reducing birthrates and poverty, had the inner city—and future social spending budgets—in mind, and they were not unaware that African Americans had more unwanted babies than European Americans.[115] As Tydings introduced several bills in the late 1960s that would have created a comprehensive, publicly funded family planning system, he said, "We'll never meet the problems of the slums, the ghettos, the poor in our great city until we face up to the tragic plight of the unwanted child. Every dollar that we spend for family planning instruction and assistance literally means a hundred dollars saved in welfare costs, institutional costs, support costs."[116]

Four aspects of the population–poverty connection, however, suggest that race was just one of many important factors. First, it would have been strange had policy makers not promoted better access to family planning as an antipoverty initiative. Simply put, poverty was the name of the game in the early 1960s. Moreover, population and poverty had been linked intellectually since Malthus—and procreation can indeed exacerbate poverty. Poverty investigators and social workers in this era were sympathetic to the traditional liberal argument that overpopulation is a symptom rather than a cause of poverty, but their research established that working-class families often suffered when they had more children than the norm.[117] Accordingly, reformers repeatedly emphasized that the economic beneficiaries of family planning programs would be not only taxpayers at large but the five million Americans without access to birth control.[118] The social science on these matters, some of it originating in the War on Poverty's bureaucracies, buttressed this position. "Poverty and Family Planning," a study by the research division of the Office of Economic Opportunity, maintained that children were both the cause and effect of poverty.[119] Another mid-1960s study reported that almost half the children in the United States in poverty belonged to families with five or more children.[120] From the vantage point of its supporters, promoting the right to plan one's family logically accompanied Great Society efforts to provide the poor with economic opportunities, not welfare.[121] Labor Secretary Willard Wirtz, for instance, argued that access to birth control should be part of the nation's manpower policy because the unemployed came disproportionately from large families.[122]

Second, although family planning advocates in Congress often alluded to the African-American ghetto, they did not equate "poor" and "black"; they frequently referenced high birthrates in poor and predominantly white areas as well.[123] Third, family planning policy was designed not only to help poor families but also to prevent middle-class families from descending into poverty. Tydings, for example, cited research showing that family planning would prevent downward mobility for adults as much as prevent those already in poverty from having children.[124] Responding on the radio to the criticism that family planning targeted the poor, Tydings observed that copious research money was already dedicated to developing new contraceptive technologies likely to be used by middle- and upper-income women who could afford birth control but could not safely use existing technologies.[125]

Fourth, family planning supporters highlighted the cultural aspects of contraception—for example, that it enhanced reproductive choice and control—and thus challenged prevailing gender norms. (A few went so far as to argue that contraception enhanced sexual freedom.) The family planning movement was predicated on the notion, supported by social science, that the high fertility among some segments of the population resulted from *unwanted* babies—hence, better access to and knowledge of contraception would lower the birthrate. Federal data in the early 1960s reported that 17 percent of all babies born to married couples in the United States were unplanned, and the percentage rose to well over 40 percent among the poor.[126] Hence Tydings always stressed that many poor women wanted fewer children; he rejected the argument that the poor had babies to secure additional welfare payments. At the same time, however, social scientists concluded that some poor women *wanted* large families for a host of psychological and societal reasons. A study funded by Planned Parenthood, *And the Poor Get Children* (1960), found that poor women had more children than their better-off counterparts because they were trapped in old-fashioned marriages and faced tremendous intraclass norms of reproduction; many were unable to stand up to their husbands and take control over their reproduction and sexual happiness.[127] Accordingly, family planning advocates tapped into the 1960s "rights revolution" to argue that the poor should have the same right of access to birth control as everyone else. Tydings, for example, told the press that "twenty percent of American families lack the effective freedom to make private decisions in the area of family planning.... I believe that a couple should not lose the right to plan the size of their family merely because they are poor."[128]

Central to this rights discourse was a reaffirmation of the voluntary nature of motherhood—of the freedom to have as many or as few children as one pleased. Tydings secured language in the 1967 Social Security Amendments that spelled out, as he put it, the "voluntary, non-coercive, non-punitive nature of the family planning services which are to be offered."[129] The ghost-of-eugenics camp suggests that a perfunctory insistence on the voluntary nature of family planning masked a racist project of population control—that beneath the rights talk lurked the belief minorities had a "duty" to have smaller families.[130] But the evidence does not support the claim. Gruening's advocacy of birth control stemmed from libertarian and feminist concerns.[131] The Tydings papers include more than two dozen references to the voluntary right to birth control, with no implication that the poor had an obligation to exercise it.

In addition, the economic rationale of family planning advocates extended well beyond the goal of individual-level poverty reduction. During the zenith of Keynesianism, the assertion that better access to contraception would diminish poverty was, in fact, also a *macroeconomic* argument. The new economics assumed not only that top-line economic growth trickles down to the poor but also that poverty reduction creates more consumers and provides a steady stimulus to the macroeconomy. In the context of his hearings on the "manpower crisis," Sen. Clark consistently claimed that population growth exacerbated automation-induced unemployment, and, in 1963, he and Sen. Gruening introduced a bill urging federal population research. After discussing what he optimistically described as waning Catholic resistance to birth control and reviewing the Coale-Hoover thesis that population growth in the Third World stunts economic development, Clark offered several reasons why the US had its own population problem. He contended that the "bumper baby crop" was exacerbating unemployment, noting President Kennedy's observation that twenty-five thousand new jobs had to be created every week to keep the employment rate steady.[132] Clark also predicted that the compounding effects of automation and "cybernation ... the union of the computer and the assembly line" would exacerbate unemployment.[133] Other lawmakers connected the developing "urban crisis" and automation. Sen. Henry "Scoop" Jackson (D-Wash.), for example, suggested that the "great issues" facing the nation in 1961 were the "population explosion in our metropolitan areas" and the related threat of automation leading to unemployed masses in depressed cities.[134]

Sen. Clark worried that population growth would increase public assistance expenditures, but he did so primarily in terms of unemployment relief, not welfare. His standpoint was essentially libertarian. "Can there be any doubt," he asked, "that the growth of population in this country will inevitably result in greater unemployment, higher taxes, and bigger government?"[135] Finally, Clark espoused the notion that the economy was running to stand still. "Our rate of economic growth in the last decade has been disappointingly low," he told the Senate. "Yet we persist in thinking in terms of spectacular increases in our gross national product, failing to convert these figures into a per capita rate of growth. If we get down to brass-tacks we will have to admit that, because of the constant increase in population, our annual rate of growth since the Korean War has been less than 2 percent per annum, probably the lowest of any of the major industrial countries."[136]

Sen. Tydings, too, thought about demographic change in wide-ranging economic, social, and geopolitical terms. He became interested in population matters during a trip to Latin America, which converted him to the Coale-Hoover thesis. As he introduced international and domestic family planning legislation in February 1966, Tydings gave a speech on the Senate floor, "Defusing the Population Explosion," often cited as a crucial turning point for family planning policy. "There is urgent need for the Congress to take decisive action to defuse the population explosion," he stated.[137] Demonstrating the lingering Cold War assumption that poverty begat left-wing political radicalization, he continued, "We cannot pretend that this problem has nothing to do with the goals which our nation is striving to foster both at home and abroad. We have made great sacrifices to help underdeveloped nations to improve their standards of life, yet hunger stalks the globe and the number of new mouths to feed outruns the ability of many nations, most notably India, to provide even a minimum diet."[138] Tydings did not identify a population bomb in the US, but he felt that the nation maintained a high standard of living despite steady population growth, not because of it. "Fortunately, it appears likely, at least for the immediate future," he said, "that the increases in our gross national product will continue to outrun our population increase.

Although the pressures upon our scarce land and water resources will become more intense, I do not doubt that we shall be able to feed, clothe, house, and educate our swelling citizenry at or above our present standards."[139] Tydings also held that the increasing ratio of dependent youth to taxpaying adults would drive up public expenditures well beyond the realm of welfare spending. Although the CEA largely ignored the dependency ratio, lawmakers did not, and concern with the "overburdening of our educational system," as Tydings frequently put it, was central.

Tydings also revealed the extent to which the quality-of-life critique of population growth extended beyond poverty and race. "But even if we can physically provide for a growing number of people," he said in the Senate, "there are disturbing social, psychological, and moral problems to consider."[140] In calling for a Joint Select Committee on Population and Family Planning, Tydings suggested that "the survival of millions in other nations and the quality of life in our own country" were at stake.[141] He frequently invoked the alleged loss of "joy" that would come with an ever more populated society.[142] While many quality-of-life laments centered on the countryside, they also focused on the problems of the city, which in the American context undeniably tapped into racial discourse. Yet antipathy to the unplanned city had been part of postwar liberalism long before most policy makers identified a racialized "urban crisis." Even as late as 1963, when John Kenneth Galbraith argued that "a growing population, and particularly a growing urban population, increases the friction of person upon person and the outlay that is necessary for social harmony," he wrote from the perspectives of postwar psychology and the critique of mass society rather than anxiety about racial tensions.[143]

In the end, the overall 1960s family planning debate mirrored the fate of one of the most famous studies of race and demography: the "Moynihan Report." In this 1965 report on the "breakdown" of the African-American family, formally titled *The Negro Family*, Assistant Secretary of Labor Daniel Patrick Moynihan suggested that the high rate of out-of-wedlock births among urban African Americans was a major cause of poverty.[144] The Moynihan Report gave the imprimatur of cutting-edge social science to the connection between urban population growth, concentrated among minorities, and poverty. It triggered immediate blowback from liberals and African Americans.[145] Moynihan was a racial liberal—but his liberalism was tainted with what historian Daryl Scott labels the "image of the damaged black psyche."[146] The Left quickly branded Moynihan a neoconservative at best and a racist at worst, and the original intent of his report was muddied by controversy.

Similarly, family planning programs emerged from a host of population-related concerns but were burdened with the racist legacy of population control. The racial politics sweeping the United States in the late 1960s clouded the complexity of these programs' origins. Lawmakers linked domestic population growth to macroeconomic and aesthetic concerns during the formative period of the Great Society, well before the crystallization of the "urban crisis." Advocates believed access to family planning programs was consistent with the Great Society's goal of providing economic opportunity to poor Americans. By the late 1960s, racial politics had not entirely superseded macroeconomic concerns surrounding population growth, but they had reduced their urgency. By focusing on poverty, the mid-1960s family planning debate was another vise pinching the political economy of population.

Population and cultural anxieties collided in another important area of Lyndon Johnson's Great Society: immigration reform. But here, too, race does not tell the whole story.

Opening the Immigration Gates to All—In Limited Numbers

The 1965 Immigration (Hart-Celler) Act was primarily designed to end the racist immigration system erected in the 1920s. A legacy of early-century eugenics and scientific racism, the 1921–65 immigration regime discriminated against prospective immigrants from Southern and Eastern Europe by assigning nations in those regions absurdly low quotas of immigrants (e.g., one hundred) while preserving huge quotas—often unfilled—for Western European nations and Great Britain.[147] But the Hart-Celler Act provoked significant unintended consequences. Its architects did not anticipate significantly altering either the total level of immigration or its ethnic distribution. Yet by establishing a system that favored "family reunification" as the grounds for immigration—the effects of which accounted for the vastly increased immigration to the United States in the last decades of the twentieth century, especially from Asia and Africa—the 1965 Immigration Act became the most significant piece of 1960s population policy from a demographic perspective.[148]

Apprehension over aggregate growth was vital in shaping immigration reform, but it was not the only factor. As historian Carl Bon Tempo has shown, ascendant cultural pluralism in the postwar United States, and especially a new, broader, and nonracial definition of "American," drove reform.[149] Cold War exigencies were also crucial; proponents of liberalization argued that a racist immigration system undermined efforts to sway nonaligned nations toward the American sphere. Because of the primacy of culture and the Cold War, and perhaps because many lawmakers presumed that the results of reform would be demographically neutral, some historians of immigration policy have ignored the backdrop of the population debate altogether.[150] Other scholars have considered at least some of the demographic variables that influenced the final makeup of the legislation. In particular, immigration restrictionists pointed to rising global population growth rates to buttress successful eleventh-hour demands for the imposition of a cap on annual immigration from the Western Hemisphere, whereas the pre-1965 system had no such cap.

According to conventional wisdom, fears of rising immigration were primarily culturally based—racist lawmakers feared a "horde" of dark-skinned newcomers—and talk of economic and quality-of-life impacts of increasing immigration was mere subterfuge. Most accounts suggest that it was principally conservatives who argued against immigration liberalization on the grounds it would overpopulate the United States. These opponents saw caps on total immigration, as well as stressing family reunification, as devices to largely preserve the status quo of immigration even as the national origins system was eliminated on paper.

As we have seen throughout this study, historians have focused so intensely on issues of population "quality" (that is, on the racist motivations of population movements) that they have neglected the very real anxiety about population quantity—even among racial liberals. Southern segregationists who opposed immigration reform may have deployed a disingenuous Malthusianism. But more importantly, many liberal advocates of reform, consistent with the unease with demographic change permeating the Great Society, not only argued that immigration reform would and should be demographically neutral but also expressed opposition to domestic population growth from any source. The prospect of population increase was the third rail of the 1960s immigration-reform debate: the range of options considered was limited by the prevailing sense that America already had too large a population. A truly radical policy shift toward nearly open immigration would have met opposition regardless of prevailing growth rates, but population anxiety narrowed the possibilities. Of the many proposals for reform batted about in the early 1960s, none envisioned more than a very modest increase in total immigration.[151]

The road to immigration liberalization began in the 1920s, when ethnic-based interest groups and some lawmakers rallied against the new restrictive regime. In the 1940s and 1950s, Congress "opened the door a little" in piecemeal fashion, eroding the quotas through special legislation and increasing the number of refugees from communist states allowed into the United States.[152] A coalition of immigration reform advocates coalesced among congressional liberals, religious leaders, and interest groups. Reformers were rejuvenated by the election of John F. Kennedy, a descendant of Irish immigrants and the author of the celebratory *Nation of Immigrants* (1959).[153] But Kennedy moved cautiously on the issue while his bureaucracy crafted a reform package, and immigration reform stalled in the 87th Congress (1961–63).

In early 1963, the president announced that immigration reform would be a priority,[154] and soon thereafter a major barrier to reform was cleared by the death of Francis Walter (D-Pa.), the virulently anti-reform chair of the House Subcommittee on Immigration and author of the restrictive 1952 McCarran-Walter Act, which became law over President Truman's veto. In the summer of 1963, Kennedy sent Congress a special message on immigration with a series of recommendations.[155] The Kennedy plan would have preserved nonquota status for the Western Hemisphere in keeping with America's "good neighbor" foreign policy. For immigration originating outside the Western Hemisphere, the administration proposed phasing out the national origins system over five years and replacing it with a new formula giving priority to potential immigrants with skill or talent, especially in areas of pressing manpower needs, to those with family in the United States, and to those who registered first (in other words, it partially adopted the first-come, first-served principle). The total number of immigrants that in theory would be permitted annually from the Eastern Hemisphere increased just a smidgen from the McCarran-Walter level to 165,000. This ceiling reflected the maintenance of a restrictive system, but the proposed quotas were to be allotted more equitably among nations, and the president could reallocate unused quotas (a usurpation of congressional power that did not survive into the final law, which eliminated the entire quota system).[156] Rep. Emanuel Celler (D-N.Y.), the dean of immigration reformers in Congress since the 1920s, and Sen. Philip A. Hart (D-Mich.) introduced legislation incorporating the administration's recommendations.

Lyndon Johnson called for immigration liberalization in his first State of the Union address.[157] During early 1964, reform was stifled by the uncertainty of the immigration views of Rep. Michael Feighan (D-Ohio), who replaced Francis Walter as chair of the Subcommittee on Immigration, as well as by a feud between Feighan and Celler, chair of the parent Judiciary Committee.[158] But Feighan's narrow reelection in 1964—in a Cleveland district with many voters descended from immigrants—put him solidly into the liberalization camp. Although Feighan was willing to agree to the elimination of national origins quotas, he opposed the Johnson administration in demanding a new cap on immigration from the Western Hemisphere. The suggested figure of 120,000, close to the number entering from the Western Hemisphere during the previous several years, allowed Feighan to sell immigration reform to conservative constituents as a restrictionist measure. Indeed, many social conservatives perceived caps as a way to have their cake and eat it, too—to oppose the end of the unpopular and blatantly racist national origins system yet still preserve the ethnic status quo of immigration, as well as limit total immigration. Feighan also had a logical point when he repeatedly asked, why, if the goal of the legislation was to end racial discrimination, would one half of the world remain subject to numerical quotas, however equitable, while the other half would not? Combining the elimination of racial discrimination with assurances of the numerical status quo appealed to the American people, who, according to polls, wanted to eliminate racial considerations from public policy but not increase net immigration.[159]

With cajoling from LBJ, including trips on Air Force One, the administration prevailed over Feighan on the most significant point of difference.[160] Feighan's bill, introduced in June 1965, continued the tradition of relatively unfettered immigration from the Western Hemisphere but placed greater emphasis on family reunification and less on recruiting skilled workers to the United States than did the administration's proposal (a reversal of priorities that survived into the final legislation). Liberal family reunification, like the overall proposal, was not expected to significantly increase immigration or alter immigration patterns. Feighan's bill reflected the stance of organized labor, which, although desiring the elimination of the racist system, sought neither a huge upturn in aggregate immigration nor an influx of skilled workers.[161]

When scholars discuss the role of population anxieties in shaping the 1965 Immigration Act, they generally do so in the context of the successful last-minute effort by restrictionists to insert into the Senate bill the numerical cap on the Western Hemisphere that Feighan had agreed to omit. This amendment was in fact crucial to the overall success of reform. LBJ's adviser Larry O'Brien told the president, "It is clear that some sort of compromise involving a worldwide quota may be necessary to spring a bill from the Senate Judiciary Committee."[162] Due to a real confluence of anti–civil rights, anti-immigration, and anti–population growth positions, many historians misconstrue the population argument as a tool exclusively used as cynical subterfuge by individuals more worried about an increasingly multicultural society than about resource scarcity, stagnant wages, or other alleged ills resulting from growth.[163] Many of the restrictionists were Southern Democrats and segregationists. For example, the South provided sixteen of the eighteen nay votes in the Senate on the final measure.[164] Clearly ethno-racial and cultural attitudes contributed for much of this Southern resistance. In addition, restrictionists claimed that liberalization would cause skyrocketing immigration to the US given the rapid growth of global population. Sen. Sam Ervin (D-N.C.), a segregationist who opposed the major civil rights legislation of 1964 and 1965, said, "This world is confronted at this moment by a population explosion, and soon millions of immigrants will be begging for, indeed demanding, admission to the United States."[165] Ervin concluded, "it is exceedingly unwise to relax our immigration laws and increase the immigrants coming the United States to any extent at a time when 7 million Americans are on public welfare, 3.8 million Americans are seeking in vain for jobs in which to earn daily bread for themselves and their families, the administration is asking the Congress to appropriate billions of dollars for the abolition of poverty in Appalachia and other areas of the Nation, and the Bureau of the Census is predicting that the population of the United States will increase to a total of approximately 280 million people within 20 years."[166] In the House, segregationist Ovie Fisher (D-Tex.) claimed that the nation already had "our hands full trying to handle our own problems with our 5 million unemployed."[167] He asked his colleagues, "Are we to become the dumping ground for the surplus population of other countries?"[168]

In this case, the economic case against immigration-based population growth was window dressing on a cultural agenda. Were economic concerns truly paramount when the Military Order of the World Wars, a patriotic veterans' organization, told Congress that population growth had exacerbated automation-induced unemployment and "inspired a so-called war on poverty"?[169] The Daughters of the American Revolution and the Savannah Citizens' Council, groups that wished to preserve an imagined "Anglo-Saxon" America, also professed fears of the economic effects of the population explosion.[170] Segregationists' use of the overpopulation argument reinforced the association, developed during the family planning debate, between racism and efforts to rein in population growth.

A slightly different scholarly approach takes the population concerns of the restrictionists at face value and accordingly criticizes reformers for not engaging the demographic social science available to them, much of which predicted that liberalization would spur large increases in immigration.[171] According to historian Betty Koed, the "key players in immigration policy were more interested in power than knowledge."[172] In this vein, reformers either ignored the issue of population growth altogether or brushed aside the overpopulation argument with the dubious claim that reform would not significantly increase net immigration levels. For example, the liberal and pro–immigration reform Rep. John Lindsay (R-N.Y.), who would soon become the embattled mayor of New York, not only dismissed the notion that reform would break open the floodgates but also concluded, "Mere numbers are not the problem. I am concerned, not with statistics, but with a philosophy."[173] Historian Steven Gillon agrees with Koed, pointing out that those who "expressed concern with population explosions and hordes of newcomers flooding across the border in search of work . . . had powerful evidence to support their fears."[174]

Yet Kennedy and Johnson administration officials, proponents of liberalization in Congress, and ethnic-based interest groups were all cognizant of worldwide population growth rates and the likelihood that future immigration to the United States would come primarily from areas of high growth. They claimed, however, that reform would neither dramatically increase total immigration nor alter the ethnic distribution of immigrants because the legislation was written with these goals in mind. To offer just one example among hundreds, Emanuel Celler said, "At this point I want to make it clear, since every discussion surrounding immigration changes is obscured by arguments about our unemployment, our lack of classrooms, our housing, and so forth, that these arguments are totally irrelevant since the bill before you in no way significantly increases the basic numbers of immigrants to be permitted entry. We are not talking about increased immigration; we are talking about equality of opportunity for all peoples to reach this promised land."[175]

Such comments reflected poor analysis of how the law's family-reunification stress would unintentionally expand immigration. But reformers had good reasons for pooh-poohing the notion of a looming surge. Although the potential pool of future immigrants was rising rapidly, the future *demand* for immigration was much less certain. Attorney General Nicholas Katzenbach assured Congress that in Western Hemisphere nations, "There is not much pressure to come to the United States."[176] In the optimistic early 1960s, many US policy makers assumed that the developing world would enjoy unbroken economic progress for decades to come. The future simply worked out differently than imagined. Many poor nations had higher economic growth rates then than they have today, and reformers failed to anticipate how revolutions in consumer culture and technology would cause many in the developing world to crave the American lifestyle.

The support of reform by lawmakers with a demonstrated aversion to domestic population growth reveals the extent to which reformers believed in the numeric insignificance of immigration. Sen. Tydings was so confident of the demographic unimportance of immigration reform, which he deemed a civil rights measure, that he actually co-sponsored some of the legislation. Tydings argued, "The immigration reform bill will not increase the number of migrants to this country. It will not open the flood-gates or swamp our labor market."[177] Beyond the small group of leaders on population issues, many liberal reformers not only sought reassurances that immigration reform would be net population neutral but also believed the domestic population growth rate was already too high. This stance centered on the traditional argument—magnified by the unemployment concerns of the early 1960s—that immigrants would take jobs away from Americans. In addition, proponents of immigration reform echoed the running-to-stand-still thesis that population growth was a drag on the economy. Liberals made these points copiously during the 1964–65 debate. Rep. Lindsay may have said the immigration issue was one of "philosophy" not "numbers," but he nonetheless feared the economic consequences of domestic population growth. He testified in running-to-stand-still terms:

> In devising reforms in our quota system, it should be recognized that a return to the wide open, unrestricted policy of pre–World War I is out of the question. American immigration policy cannot solve the problem of world overpopulation. When our nation was young and underpopulated we could absorb an unlimited number of immigrants. This is not the case today. Our rate of economic growth lags behind the rate of growth of our population. Chronic unemployment would be aggravated by a return to the immigration policies of a less complicated age.[178]

Rep. Peter Rodino Jr. (D-N.J.), who represented an Italian-American district in Newark, had introduced bills to repeal the national origins system since 1949 and almost got his name on the 1965 act. He also positioned population growth as a zero-sum game for the nation. "We will not be admitting substantially more immigrants," he stated. "Times and possibilities have changed. We can no longer admit everyone who wishes to come here and it is with sadness that we modify Miss Liberty's invitation. We must be able to provide for those who come here—with jobs, with homes, with futures—a modern society is limited as to the rate at which it can expand and accommodate new settlers."[179]

Many individual restrictionists who testified before Congress also accentuated economic arguments against population growth rather than cultural ones. A Franciscan monk, for example, professed his desire to help the peoples of the developing world but noted, "America was a vast empty undeveloped land when Christopher Columbus discovered it in 1492. Since then more than 43 million have come from abroad to the United States of America. They with their offsprings have filled the land with more than 196 million people causing thoughtful patriots to question how many more this land can now absorb and support with its diminishing natural resources. We have more workers than we have jobs."[180] The president of the conservative National Economic Council said, "If overpopulation within the United States is becoming an underlying factor in more and more of the problems of our society, why continue immigration blindly and in disregard of trends?"[181]

In the end, population concerns did not block immigration reform. The desire to dismantle a racist regime was paramount, and reformers believed that the new system would not significantly increase immigration. However, the immigration debate further reveals the central role that demographic unease played in shaping of major New Frontier and Great Society reforms. Fears of overpopulation, shared by liberals as well as conservatives, did more than lead to the imposition of the eleventh-hour cap on immigration from the Western Hemisphere; they set the parameters for the overall discussion by insisting that reform should not produce aggregate population growth.

Although the idea was not central to their case, opponents of immigration reform also argued that population growth would outstrip the supply of natural resources and harm ecosystems. The early 1960s was a crucial period for the evolution of the population–resources debate in the United States, and the next chapter shows how moderate concerns about population and resources, emerging under the rubric of postwar abundance and centered on amenities, influenced the environmental policy making of the 1960s—and how what began as a sanguine discussion transformed into a doomsday doctrine of population-induced ecological collapse.

CHAPTER SIX

The New Environmental State and the Zero Population Growth Movement

As we have seen, Malthus was never a prophet without honor in the United States. But in the 1960s, the eruption of dire Malthusianism was unprecedented. Between 1900 and 1960, the world's population had doubled, and a growing cadre of social scientists expressed grave concern that the global supply of resources might not withstand the next expected doubling, projected to occur in a mere thirty years. In the late 1960s, mass environmentalism emerged, the US population crossed the 200 million mark, global population growth rates peaked, and northern India endured drought and famine, and, in response, Malthusianism rose to the surface once again.[1] Now infused with an ecological sensibility, this doomsday population discourse emphasized pollution and the prospect of environmental collapse more than simply the depletion of natural resources and food. The natural scientists, birth control advocates, foundation officials, and radical economists who nurtured postwar Malthusianism generally assumed that the developing world faced a more urgent population problem than the United States and the rest of the developed world. However, most of these population experts also insisted that every corner of the globe faced population-induced ecological and human crises in the long run.[2] Paul Ehrlich, a Stanford biologist, expressed this viewpoint in *The Population Bomb* (1968), the most famous population treatise since Malthus, and helped spark the creation of an organized "zero population growth" movement in the United States.[3]

Before this radical Malthusianism peaked, however, trepidation over overpopulation significantly influenced federal environmental policy making, showcased in the 1964 Wilderness Act, which set aside nine million acres of public land to remain wild in perpetuity. The Wilderness Act was the policy capstone of the 1950s aesthetic critique of population growth, but it also foreshadowed the ascendance of late-1960s Malthusianism. By mid decade, many demographers, economists, and natural scientists no longer saw population growth simply as an aesthetic or abstract hazard but as a concrete danger to a fragile ecosystem. These concerns spawned a powerful grassroots zero population growth movement and a new "ecological economics," which articulated a formal theory of limits to growth. During the late 1960s, mainstream economists and policy makers forged an ephemeral alliance with Malthusians, and Malthusianism became part and parcel of public policy.

Yet the zero population growth movement began to fracture just as its influence spiked. Moderates and radicals within the movement differed on the appropriate policy disincentives to childbirth, with a miniscule minority (but one well covered in the press) going so far as to seek compulsory fertility reduction measures that would eliminate the right to voluntarily control family size. And the movement could not overcome significant contradictions in its economic thinking. Meanwhile, it came under blistering attack from ethnic-minority leaders who believed that population policies targeted nonwhites and from environmentalists who argued that the emphasis on population growth was distracting attention from the polluting nature of modern capitalism and technology.

Population and Resources in the Kennedy Years: Toward the Wilderness Act

Before Malthusianism crested in the late 1960s, the specter of overpopulation caused many conservationists and policy makers to fear that little time remained to save America's most spectacular undeveloped lands. Apprehension of demographic trends served as an important bridge between the optimistic environmentalism of the postwar years and the radical, limits-to-growth environmentalism of the late 1960s.

Though personally uninterested in conservation, presidential candidate John F. Kennedy sensed that the political key to natural resource matters was to recommend resource development to some audiences and preservation to others.[4] "I get it," he joked to his advisers regarding resources policy, "we're for everything."[5] During his presidency, conservationists could take heart at the strengthening of the Water Pollution Control Act and other minor measures, but like much of Kennedy's domestic agenda, the bulk of his environmental proposals became law only after Lyndon Baines Johnson became president.[6]

In addition to laying the policy groundwork for the expanded environmental regulation of the late 1960s, the Kennedy administration nurtured the intellectual transformation underlying this expansion.[7] During the early 1960s, three broad attitudes toward natural resources and population coexisted in the US. The first was developmental. For most of the nation's history, the minority who questioned using resources in a scorched-earth manner argued that the efficient management and development of them was necessary to serve economic progress. These advocates of conservation cum development did not consider population growth a problem, provided resources were used wisely. Second, romantic preservationists had long celebrated natural areas simply on the merits of their beauty (which is not to say that many, such as John Muir, did not also offer a serious critique of human despoiling of the planet). This romantic perspective took off after World War II and helped launch modern environmentalism.[8] In a society that had supposedly moved beyond the quest for economic security and entered an era of permanent abundance, many Americans came to view natural resources primarily as amenities. As we have seen, aesthetic environmentalists were also critical of population growth and a crowded society.

The era's third population–resources perspective involved an ecological framework, which at its extreme morphed into limits-to-growth thought. During the early 1960s, experts continued to proffer anti–population growth arguments regarding both the developing and developed worlds, though they generally adopted a more sober tone than the Malthusian treatises of the late 1940s and stopped short of predicting starvation and other doomsday scenarios. At a 1963 forum on population at Columbia University, Donald Bogue, president of the Population Association of America, argued that the Baby Boom had already caused short-term economic and social problems and, due to demographic momentum, augured more serious problems despite declines in the birthrate since the peak of 1957. "When the demographic facts for the United States are assembled," Bogue wrote, "they suggest that instead of smugly patting ourselves on the back for escaping the impact of the population explosion, we must realize that we are participants. At present we are on a collision course that could lead us to catastrophe, timed to arrive only a very few decades after our sister nations (if they too do not alter their growth rates) have crashed on the Malthusian reefs."[9] Although Bogue stayed within the traditional paradigm of diminishing returns from finite resources, especially food, many other supporters of population limitation were embracing newer ecological themes such as the interconnectedness of natural systems. It was a fusion of older concepts of resource exhaustion and newer ones of ecological collapse that drove the Malthusianism resurgence.

The Kennedy administration schizophrenically reflected all three perspectives. The president and his economic advisers often spoke the old progressive-era language of managing resources wisely for economic development. The slogan "New Frontier" suggested something of the old sense of conquering the land. At the May 1962 White House Conference on Conservation, Kennedy said that "natural resource development is a key to long-run economic growth and national strength."[10] He echoed 1950s optimism about the long-term supply of natural resources, predicting that scientific advances could dramatically improve the food yield from the ocean. Kennedy's Council of Economic Advisers (CEA), meanwhile, deemed the wise management of natural resources essential to economic growth.[11] As historian Paul Milazzo has shown, the pursuit of economic growth played an influential role in the environmental policy making of the 1950s–70s, especially in the promotion of clean water.[12]

At the same time, the Kennedy and Johnson administrations embraced the new postmaterialist, quality-of-life sensibility, becoming the only administrations in US history to make the quest for beauty a priority.[13] From this point of view, the population surge was primarily a problem of abundance. It might cramp Americans' wide-open lifestyle, especially as higher incomes spurred more people to seek outdoor recreation, but it did not threaten the economy or the supply of raw materials. Kennedy himself often wed developmental and quality-of-life themes. "Because we have so much in surplus in the United States, there is some feeling . . . we can afford to waste what we have," he said in 1963. "I don't believe it at all. I think what we have to decide is how we can put it to best use, how we can provide . . . a use of our natural resources and scientific and technological advances so that . . . the 350 million who will live in the United States in the year 2000 can enjoy a much richer and happier life than we do now."[14]

Ecological concerns received less attention in the White House than the developmental and aesthetic ones. Nevertheless, *Silent Spring* (1962), marine biologist Rachel Carson's best-selling and profound warning against pesticides, "caused a furor in scientific and business circles that spilled over into the highest levels of government" and "catapulted the concept of ecology into millions of minds—and into the global dialogue," according to Stuart Udall, Kennedy's and Johnson's secretary of the interior.[15] Policy makers began to feel that the nation needed more conservation and stronger environmental regulation not only for economic and aesthetic reasons but also to preserve ecosystems.[16] In 1965, Supreme Court Justice Abe Fortas publicly stated, "Life is a seamless web."[17]

On the specific matter of population, the developmental and quality-of-life perspectives countered a sense of ecological crisis, but the Kennedy administration nonetheless expressed an ascendant limits-to-growth perspective well before the zero population growth movement appeared. Stuart Udall managed to mingle all of the various perspectives. A former US representative from Arizona, Udall eloquently articulated the aesthetic viewpoint, even as he remained committed to dam building and other traditional forms of resource development.[18] In *The Quiet Crisis* (1963), which included an introduction by President Kennedy, Udall discussed population expansion primarily in quality-of-life terms. He questioned the assumption that with the expected doubling of the American population by the year 2000, "life in general—and the good, the true, and the beautiful in particular—will somehow be enhanced at the same time. We have growth room in this country, but the time has come for thoughtful men and women to ask some basic questions about our land-people equation. . . . It is obvious that the best qualities in man must atrophy in a standing-room-only environment."[19] Udall remained optimistic, writing, "The creation of a life-giving environment can go hand-in-hand with material progress and higher standards of husbandry, if, in President Kennedy's words, we make time 'our friend and not our adversary.'"[20] But this rosy conclusion came with a warning: "In the years ahead, nations can either compete ruthlessly for resources, in a context of scarcity, or co-operate, respect the laws of nature, and share its abundance."[21] Separately, Udall rejected the notion that "science and technology hold the keys to the kingdom of abundance" and maintained that "population pressures compound all of our [environmental] problems."[22]

The dance between the aesthetic and the limits-to-growth perspectives was on full display preceding passage of the 1964 Wilderness Act. Measuring the precise role played by population anxiety compared to other resource concerns is a bit like trying to divide ice from snow, but clearly the population question permeated environmental policy making. Similar to employment policies designed to smooth the transition of the Baby Boomers into the labor force, the Wilderness Act was designed in part to manage—not reverse or fundamentally question—the postwar population surge. Yet it simultaneously showed the blossoming of ecological Malthusianism.[23]

Adoration of wilderness has a long history in quality-of-life policy making. In the 1930s, a wilderness lobby began pressing for a federal response to the threat the automobile posed to natural lands.[24] In the 1950s, rising prosperity increased demand for outdoor amenities such as suburban open space and vast parcels of protected lands.[25] Thereafter, the population question was at the heart of the debate leading up to the 1964 Wilderness Act. The American Planning Association said simply in 1953, "As our population grows, our needs for rest, recreation, and spiritual refreshment become greater."[26] President Eisenhower, too, saw the population–resources issue through the lens of recreation. "With the steady growth of our population, there is an increasing need for recreation under natural conditions," he wrote to a wilderness advocate. "This is of major significance to the physical and mental health of the nation."[27] Lawmakers promoted wilderness preservation as a way to manage population growth by relieving the environmental and recreational strains that resulted from it. Introducing the first wilderness bill in 1955, Sen. Hubert Humphrey (D-Minn.) said that he was motivated by "the rapid growth of our population, and the resulting tremendous pressures for opening up these wilderness areas for commercial and economic purposes."[28] References to demographic pressures steadily increased in the following years as the overpopulation issue picked up steam.[29]

The environmental community emphasized population as it pushed for wilderness protection.[30] The bulletin of the Wilderness Society, the leading pressure group, noted in 1958, "The wilderness is limited. The population is not."[31] Several environmental conferences in the late 1950s addressed the "wilderness-to-person" ratio. For example, the theme of the 1959 annual North American Wildlife Conference was "Resources, People, and Space." David Brower, who headed the Sierra Club from 1952 to 1969, articulated Malthusian themes at this conference.[32] Ecologists increasingly forecast a collision between population growth and environmental health. Some even suggested that the wilderness campaign was an unwise diversion from the central goal of reining in population growth.[33]

The media also connected wilderness and demography. The *San Fran-*

cisco Chronicle observed in 1957, "Recognizing that population pressures and economic growth are swiftly crowding the American land, a bipartisan group in Congress is now sponsoring legislation to create a National Wilderness Preservation System."[34] The next year the *Chronicle* titled an editorial in favor of wilderness protection "One Hundred Million Arguments," referring to the expected increase in population by century's end.[35] The *Washington Post* argued that wilderness would "guarantee a refuge from man's dominion, a haven of escape which will be all the more desired as the growth in population increases the hunger for the forest's peace."[36] And the *Boston Globe* warned, "The wilderness of the United States is threatened with erasure before population and industrial growth unless the government intervenes with a positive program to keep it in its primitive state."[37]

During the congressional hearings, pro-wilderness citizens and interest groups used an array of important arguments, for example that the land should remain as God made it and that wilderness areas are boons to nearby communities.[38] Yet most tapped into the quality-of-life critique of population growth—and many emphasized it. Echoing a prevalent lament by the youthful "New Left" that American capitalism had become an industrialized, bureaucratized "machine," conservationists argued that setting aside wilderness areas would stave off the harmful effects of population growth and urbanization. They frequently described wilderness as "something quite rare and extremely valuable in this day of smog and crowds"[39] and asserted that "something must be done to preserve a small portion of our great outdoors for the health and sanity of our mushrooming population."[40]

Some scientists and environmentalists viewed the problem more starkly, seeing wilderness as the preventer of population-induced scarcity. A professor of zoology, for example, told Congress, "The most serious problem facing the world today is the human population explosion. . . . In the race to provide more things for more people we may finally lose by overshooting the capacity of our natural resources to support humans and their industries."[41] Experts frequently cited Fairfield Osborn's 1948 Malthusian book, *Our Plundered Planet*. Many experts claimed that because the American population would not stabilize for a century, wilderness areas would ensure a supply of raw materials in the interim.[42] Environmentalists averred that wilderness was not merely aesthetically pleasing but performed ecologically necessary tasks such as protecting watersheds and providing natural bridges for migrating wildlife.

Ecological and Malthusian arguments were moderated by their assumed time scale. Since development on wild land is virtually irreversible, apprehension of long-term demographic trends fostered an intergenerational environmental social contract: the current generation has an obligation to preserve as much land as possible for future, larger generations. This compact reflected the moderation of the wilderness debate. Most advocates of wilderness preservation did not assume that population-induced resource scarcity lurked just around the corner. After all, the Wilderness Act essentially decommissioned millions of acres of potentially economically productive land. Although the specter of scarcity loomed in the distance, and some wildness activists were Malthusians immersed in the population debate, most lawmakers and citizens viewed wilderness simply as a way to guard against the quality-of-life threat posed by unchecked population growth, as a way to hold onto a disappearing, less crowded America even as the number of inhabitants kept expanding.

Opponents of federally designated wilderness, led by Western chambers of commerce and the mining and forestry industries, argued that "locking up" large areas of land amounted to an unfair—and, to some, unconstitutional—check on economic growth. They claimed that a formal wilderness system would serve the narrow special interests of wealthy, outdoor-enthusiast urbanites while harming millions of Americans, especially in the Western states, who depended upon the land for their livelihood. (This logic ignored the economic benefits enjoyed by towns located near wilderness areas.) The anti-wilderness camp noted that a "multiple-use" concept had dominated management of public lands since the turn of the twentieth century and thus suggested that a reasonable amount of wilderness could be protected though present law. A small-town councilman testifying before the House summed up the matter this way: "I feel strongly that the economy of the State of Idaho cannot survive on sentiment alone."[43]

The anti-wilderness camp also tapped into—but tried to reorient—growing unease about population growth. Conservative, pro-industry voices deployed arguments of impending demographic pressure and resource scarcity to argue that, as the nation's number of residents continued to climb, it could not afford to frivolously decommission natural resources in the interest of recreation and natural beauty. Noting Census Bureau projections, one rancher told Congress, "The battle for biscuits to feed 400 million empty bellies will leave little time for the vast majority to use the solitude of the forests to refresh their esthetic souls."[44]

Other opponents of wilderness believed that a rapidly rising population (and one moving westward) would demand the creation of new industries supported by raw materials from the public lands. Resource officials within the federal government concurred. The Forest Service promoted the "multiple use" of public lands; indeed, a 1960 law had codified this approach by permitting the creation of wild areas within national forests but emphasizing timber production.[45] The Forest Service also opposed the proposed new wilderness system because it yielded authority to Congress and because, in its view, new formal wilderness areas would serve too narrow a constituency of outdoor enthusiasts.

The preamble to the Wilderness Act, written by Wilderness Society president Howard Zahniser, captures the era's confidence that population growth could be managed for future generations: "In order to assure that an increasing population, accompanied by expanding settlement and growing mechanization, does not occupy and modify all areas within the United States and its possessions, leaving no lands designated for preservation and protection in their natural condition, it is hereby declared to be the policy of the Congress to secure for the American people of present and future generations the benefits of an enduring resource of wilderness."[46] Today this preamble remains on the books as testament to the postwar aesthetic critique of population growth. The Wilderness Act reflected the goals of a century-old American conservation movement yet also a more recent phenomenon: the liberal postwar critique of "mass society" and materialism that incorporated anxiety about continued population expansion. The wilderness debate also offers lessons for today's advocates of a smaller population since it shows that disparate Americans can agree on anti–population growth ideas when they are couched in non-radical, quality-of-life terms.

Building a Zero Population Growth Movement

In February 1965, President Johnson sent Congress a special message on natural beauty. "A growing population is swallowing up areas of natural beauty with its demands for living space, and is placing increased demand on our overburdened areas of recreation and pleasure," the message stated.[47] Johnson then convened a White House conference on beauty. Further, in an important decision for the course of environmental law, a federal court ruled in 1965 that an environmental organization had the right to bring suit against a power company seeking to build a pumping station on "aesthetic, conservational, and recreational" grounds.[48] However, the quality-of-life perspective waned after the mid 1960s. This is not to say that environmentalists, policy makers, or even avowed Malthusians stopped linking population growth to a range of quality-of-life concerns, from traffic congestion to noise pollution to crowded schools and hospitals.[49] The subsequent major environmental laws of the late 1960s and early 1970s primarily combated air and water pollution but also incorporated such quality-of-life goals as noise control and the creation of urban parks. Nonetheless, limits-to-growth concerns dominated both the overseas and domestic population growth debates by the late 1960s.

The population movement's goal became "zero population growth," a somewhat fuzzy term. It could imply the immediate cessation of population growth, which, in the American case, would have required a drastic 50 percent reduction of the fertility rate. Alternatively, the term could simply refer to the onset of a replacement fertility rate (about 2.11 births per woman), which, if it held steady, would have stabilized the American population in seventy years after a further gain of about 30 to 40 percent.[50] Either way, the goal of lowering the population growth rate was unambiguous. Some Malthusians remained moored to the food-to-people paradigm,[51] but this traditional perspective fused with ecological science to form a potent new ideology of pending overpopulation-induced collapse. A rejuvenated Malthusianism came before—and spurred—the new mass environmental movement of the late 1960s.

The fusion between older concerns about limited resources and newer themes of ecological fragility and finiteness reflected a consensus among natural scientists that population growth was harmful.[52] It was the economists, however, who first constructed a more formal new theory of the "limits to growth," launching a heretical "environmental economics," followed by its offshoot, "ecological economics," which rejected the cult of "growthism" and identified limits to the economy and number of inhabitants in a finite and fragile world.[53] In its moderate guise, environmental economics implied efforts to integrate environmental concerns into orthodox economic thought and public policy, for example by taxing negative externalities (spillover effects) like pollution so that consumer prices reflect true environmental costs. It also reserved room for beauty and other intangibles. In the memorable phrase of Herman Daly, a leading environmental economist, the trampling "invisible foot" of market activity was as important as the more famous and benign "invisible hand."[54] Environmental economics quickly gained acceptance in mainstream circles. In a 1967 essay that critiqued but ultimately defended the "aesthetically concerned minority," political scientist Aaron Wildavsky suggested that the takeoff of the environmental movement was closely associated with a "new economics" of the natural environment in which intangibles were assigned large if imprecise values.[55]

Environmental economics offered not merely an insistence on market failure but also a powerful attack on core assumptions of neoclassical economics, including the rationality of the consumer and the desirability of letting the market reduce all goods and human activity to commodities.[56] The more radical ecological economics offered a fundamental rejection of the compatibility of economic progress—as traditionally defined—and ecological sustainability. And it demanded immediate population stabilization. Ecological economics drew on John Stuart Mill's sympathetic discussion of the "stationary state," the supposed end point of economic and population growth. It was also inspired by the first law of thermodynamics: energy can be transferred from one system to another in many forms but can be neither created nor destroyed. Accordingly, ecological economics emphasized the finite "stock" of natural wealth and the "scale" of economies as opposed to the "flow" of income and consumption put forth by orthodox economics. Scale referred to not only the physical scale of the planet but also the time scale of economic growth; ecological economists were adamant that perpetual growth was a seductive illusion over the long run because natural systems are "closed loops" and all human activity increases entropy, the energy unavailable for productive use.

A small coterie launched ecological economics. Romanian-born Nicholas Georgescu-Roegen, who studied under Joseph Schumpeter at Harvard, deserves credit for giving birth to the field—which he called bioeconomics—in the mid 1960s. Georgescu-Roegen argued, in simplest terms, "Matter matters, too." Seeing the earth as a closed system—he used the analogy of an hourglass—Georgescu-Roegen urged the reorientation of economic activity toward sustainability.[57] Better known today is Kenneth Boulding, president of the American Economic Association in 1968, who began the 1960s as an orthodox economist at the University of Michigan, though one who had identified planetary limits in an introduction to Malthus's *Essay on Population*.[58] Boulding's classic 1966 essay, "The Economics of the Coming Spaceship Earth," pleaded for a transition from a reckless "cowboy economy" to a "spaceman economy."[59] This new economy would recognize that "the earth has become a single spaceship, without unlimited reservoirs of anything, either for extraction or pollution, and in which, therefore, man must find his place in a cyclical ecological system which is capable of continuous reproduction of material form even though it cannot escape having inputs of energy."[60] A spaceman economy would emphasize the total stock of resources, not current consumption (called "throughput" by environmental economists). Notwithstanding his radical stress on the biosphere, Boulding's work stayed within a market-oriented paradigm. (In 1964, Boulding even argued that in order to bring about population stabilization, procreation licenses should be issued by the state and bought and sold on the open market.)[61] Finally, Herman Daly, who studied under Georgescu-Roegen, emerged as a leading ecological economist as the population movement peaked in the late 1960s and founded the *Journal of Environmental Economics*.

As these economists engineered a fundamental paradigm shift beneath the radar, Malthusian activists—social scientists, conservationists, and natural scientists—catapulted doomsday rhetoric into the headlines. Building on classic Malthusianism but also on ecological science and the emerging environmental economics, these activists predicted that overpopulation overseas and in the US would cause catastrophic environmental deterioration and possibly even societal collapse. Some, such as the Swedish food scientist Georg Borgström, author of *The Hungry Planet* (1965), updated older models of resources scarcity with ecological variables. Although their estimates erred badly (Borgström, for example, labeled Japan—which today faces the prospect of population decline—a ticking demographic "time bomb"), ecological economists launched a powerful critique of mainstream economics. Opponents of ecological economics have successfully challenged its skepticism of human ingenuity but have not overturned its central insistence that humans operate within a closed system.[62]

The term "zero population growth" entered the mainstream after sociologist and demographer Kingsley Davis used it in a 1967 *Science* magazine article.[63] Attacking the population establishment represented by the Population Council and the Ford Foundation, Davis argued that current family planning programs in the developing world would be ineffective at reducing fertility unless they confronted the motivations behind high fertility (in other words, offered more than the technical fix of contraception). Davis did not support compulsory measures to regulate fertility, regardless of their political impracticability, and instead advocated child taxes, subsidized abortions and sterilizations, and later marriages.[64] He also urged family planning program officials to explicitly state a goal of zero population growth, not merely of lower birthrates.[65]

Although members of the established population network generally ascribed to the new Malthusianism, a new generation of scholars and activists popularized it. Among dozens of such examples, conservationists Robert and Leona Rienow wrote in *Moment in the Sun* (1967), "For it is painfully, even disastrously, evident that as this nation streaks ahead at its breakneck pace, it cannot much longer cling to the same rough pioneer doctrines that carried it to its present material heights. The old frontier idea of producing armies of offspring to overcome infant mortality and push forward to conquer the continent is as discredited as bundling, witch-burning, and pond-dunking for shrews. Let all lovers of life plead for a new philosophy, a transformed social code, so that this nation and the world may survive."[66] A famous proponent of draconian population control was biologist Garrett Hardin, an enormously polarizing figure whose radicalism encouraged many to view the population movement as nothing more than the old wine of eugenics in new bottles. In "The Tragedy of the Commons," which appeared in *Science* in 1968, Hardin called for a "new morality" to solve the population problem.[67] He invoked a classic market failure: when land (in his example, a pasture) is owned in common, any one individual has every incentive to work this land as hard as possible because the grass is free. He or she has little incentive to conserve the land because if everyone else maximized his or her profit, such conservation merely bankrupts the individual while having little impact on the total supply of grass. Extending his model to the population question, Hardin insisted that babies are negative externalities: they incur modest cost for their particular parents but great cost for society as a whole. As a result, he resolved that the time for voluntary population control had passed, opining, "Freedom to breed is intolerable."[68] Hardin famously called for "mutual coercion, mutually agreed upon," to remove family size decisions from the individual.[69] Elsewhere, Hardin rejected the "sharing ethic" and promoted a new "lifeboat ethic," arguing that each nation is its own lifeboat with limited carrying capacity. Wealthy nations should not aid poor ones (or absorb their populations through immigration), unless the recipients agreed to limit their procreation.[70] As he saw it, some people need to be thrown off the lifeboat for the majority to survive. Hardin's critics branded these arguments authoritarian, but he claimed they were rooted in social contract theory—individuals in a society agree to give up some of their rights to advance the greater good. Hardin indeed flirted with eugenic thought, which explains why critics pointed to him as they invented racist motivations behind the zero population growth movement.[71]

The most famous alarmist treatise was Paul Ehrlich's *The Population Bomb* (1968), the best-selling environmental book of the 1960s. Converted to Malthusianism after a 1966 trip to India, Ehrlich argued that an overpopulation crisis was not around the corner but had in fact arrived.[72] "The battle to feed all of humanity is over," the book famously begins.[73] "I'm scared," Ehrlich told *Look* magazine. "My world is being destroyed. I'm 37, and I'd kind of like to live to be 67 in a reasonably pleasant world, not to die in some kind of holocaust in the next decade."[74] Notwithstanding his cataclysmic tone, Ehrlich followed the prevailing social science, claiming that rapid population growth in the developing world impeded economic development. He also predicted another surge of population when the current young cohorts came of age.[75] Ehrlich further alleged that the US was in the midst of its own population explosion.[76] In copious publications, he and his wife Anne asserted that the planet could not sustain the rest of the world catching up to American levels of consumption.[77] Ehrlich hoped a combination of policy carrots and sticks would reduce fertility sufficiently and preserve voluntary family planning, but he held out the possibility that compulsory measures, including compulsory sterilizations, might be necessary down the road.[78]

Although *Population Bomb* became the iconic statement of the zero population growth movement, the Sierra Club and other mainstream American environmental organizations had been engaging the population question more vigorously since the late 1950s, as we saw in the context of wilderness policy. The Sierra Club's David Brower announced in 1966, "We feel that you don't have a conservation policy unless you have a population policy."[79] It was actually Brower who urged Ehrlich to write a book on the population explosion.[80]

Even prior to *Population Bomb*, opinion polls revealed a steady upswing in the percentage of Americans who considered the population explosion to be a major problem.[81] But *Population Bomb* was clearly the tipping point. It spread the overpopulation message to a mass audience, just as American youth were rebelling against their parents and the "Establishment."[82] Ehrlich became the public voice of the zero population growth movement, even making more than twenty appearances on NBC's *Tonight Show*![83] Ehrlich and the population movement would soon face an effective backlash from the political Right, but his powerful if overstated message cut through the media clutter and catapulted the overpopulation critique to center stage in American public discourse. By 1971, after over twenty printings of *Population Bomb*, 46 percent of Americans believed that by the year 2000 the nation would have to limit its population to maintain its current standard of living.[84]

The new ecological perspective transformed the population-policy community, with older organizations such as the Population Council now emphasizing environmental arguments in support of family planning programs. More importantly, *Population Bomb* helped launch the organization Zero Population Growth (ZPG) in December 1968.[85] ZPG was not the first organization of its kind formed in the 1960s. Hugh Moore, the ultra-Malthusian founder of the Dixie Cup Corporation, had launched the Population Crisis Committee in 1965, but his strident scare tactics alienated the mainstream family planning movement (to say nothing of mainstream policy makers). ZPG, in contrast, rode the wave of the expanding environmental movement and the youth rebellion against the "consumer society," emerging during a brief moment when it could influence the population and policy-making establishments.

Charles Remington, a Yale entomologist, and Richard Bowers, a New Haven attorney, founded ZPG in Old Mystic, Connecticut.[86] Bowers had become convinced of the need for a new interest group after unsuccessfully lobbying the Nature Conservancy to take up the population issue, and he contacted Ehrlich. The organization's headquarters were in Palo Alto, California, because Ehrlich taught at Stanford, but its local branches enjoyed considerable autonomy.[87] With slogans such as "Stop at Two," "Stop Heir Pollution," and "Make Love, Not Babies," ZPG quickly became a significant political force lobbying to halt what it saw as the federal government's subsidization of population growth.[88] ZPG grew with remarkable alacrity, from just over 100 members in 1969 to 20,000 in 1970. Membership likely peaked at 35,000 in the summer of 1971, with more than 400 local and state chapters.[89]

ZPG was the culmination of the post–World War II Malthusian revival, but it was also an extension of 1960s environmentalism.[90] ZPG and leading radicals acknowledged traditional concerns about dwindling raw materials. And they proposed that a smaller population would have quality-of-life and psychological benefits. Carl Pope, an early leader in the group (and later executive director of the Sierra Club) warned of the unpleasant side effects of growth by pointing out that laboratory rats subjected to overcrowding developed social pathologies.[91] ZPG's primary message, though, was that population growth and environmental deterioration were inseparable.

An offshoot of 1960s radicalism, ZPG also promoted racial and gender liberalism. In particular, it worked assiduously to keep the ghost of eugenics locked in the attic. Echoing leading demographers, the group pointed out that population growth in the United States resulted primarily from the voluntary fertility decisions of the white middle class,[92] and it stressed that this class was principally responsible for pollution in the United States because it constituted the largest bloc of consumers.[93] ZPG barely mentioned immigration.[94] When the organization formed, the surge in immigration that resulted from the 1965 Immigration Act had not yet begun. According to the later recollection of one official, "We regarded ourselves, or at least many of us did, as liberals, and immigration was not an issue that liberals looked at."[95] In the mid 1970s, ZPG would splinter over the immigration issue. But during the peak of its popularity, the organization accurately emphasized that the Baby Boom, not immigration, was the chief cause of domestic population growth.[96]

ZPG desired a significant state role in reducing fertility. It supported all of the environmental and family planning legislation of the day and lobbied for additional measures designed to roll back demographic trends. With Carl Pope serving as lobbyist when its Washington office opened in February 1970, ZPG sought to neutralize the pronatalism built into American family policy. Hence it supported eliminating the income tax savings enjoyed by married couples, ending deductions for dependents after two children, and making the costs of adoption deductible. More drastic ideas floated included imposing a tax surcharge on parents and charging tuition in the public schools. Further, ZPG conducted letter-writing campaigns against companies that depicted large families in their advertisements and called for additional federal population research. Given the prevailing view that fertility decisions should be left to the individual, ZPG struggled with how to *directly* confront population growth. The head of a short-lived organization in the 1970s called the Coalition for a National Population Policy observed, "If Congress came to ZPG advocates today and announced its readiness to use any means to stabilize population size short of making the conception of a third child a felony, we would be hard put to tell them precisely what to do."[97]

Ultimately, ZPG's social theories were more radical than its proposed policies. For example, it opposed compulsory birth control and other proposed draconian measures, but its Board of Directors resolved that "parenthood is not an inherent right of individuals but a privilege extended by the society in which they live."[98] Under the umbrella of its stress on population and ecology, ZPG made a significant but often overlooked contribution to one of the most important policy shifts of the era: the liberalization of abortion law. From its inception, ZPG firmly supported the burgeoning women's movement. Following the lead of Berkeley's Judith Blake and other feminist demographers who advocated a smaller population, the organization argued that modern society denigrated women by making childbearing their primary role. It deployed a radical feminist critique of prohibitions against abortion and contraception and other reproductive laws, such as those denying voluntary sterilization to a woman until after she bore a certain number of children. ZPG's primary goal was to reduce the American birthrate to save the environment, not to transform the American family, but its feminist arguments were vital.[99] Indeed, sympathetic critics sometimes complained that ZPG overemphasized questions of gender at the cost of the core population–resources discussion.

The links between the population and abortion issues have become shrouded over time. To be sure, historians of the feminist movement and of abortion politics have noted the general confluence between the family planning movement and the promotion of abortion liberalization.[100] It is well known that in 1959, Planned Parenthood helped the American Law Institute draft a model law subsequently used by the few states that liberalized their abortion laws in the 1960s.[101] In addition, scholars have recognized that Garrett Hardin and other population activists worked with leaders of the women's movement to spur the creation of the National Association for the Repeal of Abortion Laws (NARAL), founded in 1969.[102] Historian Suzanne Staggenborg notes in her study *Pro-Choice Movement* that the national ZPG organization—initially leery of engaging the abortion issue due to the group's ecological emphasis and the recognition that the full legalization of abortion, though obviously consistent with the group's mission, would only marginally affect aggregate population—officially endorsed the repeal of abortion restrictions in 1969. Staggenborg also mentions that local ZPG chapters lobbied to liberalize abortion laws.[103] But scholars and journalists are as often wrong as right on these topics.[104] Many studies on modern abortion politics simply elide the role played by the overpopulation issue.[105] Moreover, both opponents of abortion rights and some pro-abortion historians have described the union of population concerns and support for abortion rights primarily to tag population activists with the neo-eugenicist label.[106] The full history of how population concerns contributed to the legalization of abortion in the United States remains unwritten. At the least, ZPG took the lead in several lawsuits that helped liberalize abortion at the state level, bussed advocates to pack state legislative hearings on abortion, and secured a number of state resolutions in favor of population stabilization.[107] In Colorado, for example, zero population growth advocate and state representative Richard Lamm—later governor of Colorado—was instrumental in securing passage of that state's liberalized abortion law in 1967, the first of its kind in the nation.[108] The *ZPG Reporter* called abortion "the weathervane of the population issue."[109]

Writing for the majority in the US Supreme Court's *Roe v. Wade* decision (1973), Justice Harry Blackmun left a tantalizingly vague line of inquiry. Reflecting on the contentious nature of the abortion issue, Blackmun wrote:

> One's philosophy, one's experiences, one's exposure to the raw edges of human existence, one's religious training, one's attitudes toward life and family and their values, and the moral standards one establishes and seeks to observe, are all likely to influence and to color one's thinking and conclusions about abortion. In addition, population growth, pollution, poverty, and racial overtones tend to complicate and not to simplify the problem.[110]

Mainstreaming Malthus

During a brief window from 1968 to 1972, the overpopulation critique resonated in America's public imagination on a level never seen before or since. A stream of Malthusian books flowed from popular and scholarly presses alike,[111] the popular culture echoed the Malthusian craze, and several novels incorporated themes of population-induced resource exhaustion.[112] Marvin Gaye sang in his 1970 hit "Mercy Mercy Me (The Ecology)," "Oh mercy, mercy me / Ah things ain't what they used to be / What about this overcrowded land? / How much more abuse from man can she stand?" And in "Five Years," the opening track on his *Ziggy Stardust* album (1972), David Bowie sang "So many mothers sighing / News had just come over / We had five years left to cry in / News guy wept and told us / Earth was really dying."[113] Meanwhile, several commentators used the occasion of the lunar landing in 1969 to comment on the fragility of a finite, ever-more populated and interconnected world.[114] R. T. Ravenholt, head of the Office of Population at the Agency for International Development, noted, "The cameras of the Apollo expeditions focused not only on the Moon but were turned back to give us the beautiful views of the planet Earth, the most wonderful space ship of all. These views dramatized more powerfully than previous earthbound views the visible fact that our planet is a finite body, that our air, water, soil, and mineral resources are limited, and that the Earth—large and generous though she is—can be mother to only a limited number of inhabitants."[115]

That novelists, popular musicians, and family planning bureaucrats adopted the Cassandras' message is not especially remarkable. More striking and less well known is the extent to which mainstream policy makers, economists, and journalists bought into population fears, even if they tended to talk about environmental quality rather than impending doom.[116] Reviewing the environmental arguments in favor of a smaller population, *Business Week* wrote, "As compelling as these arguments may be, the very prospect that population growth might halt is to some people a chilling idea for an economy conditioned to expect an annual 1% population increase. . . . Yet the idea does not chill most economists." *Business Week* pointed to Lester Thurow, a well-known economist who concluded in Stable Population Keynesian terms, "Our economic growth is definitely not dependent on population growth."[117] Other economists tried to incorporate population size into definitions of social welfare.[118] The small coterie of congressional leaders on the environment absorbed the new Malthusianism that had previously been the domain of family planning leaders, though they generally stopped short of calling for zero population growth. Edmund Muskie (D-Maine), the dean of congressional environmentalists known as "Mr. Clean," frequently warned of the dangers accompanying population growth.[119] Sen. Gaylord Nelson (D-Wis.) was friends with Paul Ehrlich and frequently claimed that overpopulation was the greatest environmental threat.[120] Nelson wrote in *America's Last Chance* (1970), "Measured in terms of our past performance in protecting our environment the United States is already overpopulated. If we cannot manage the wastes produced by 200 million people, it will be a catastrophe when we reach 300 million as predicted within the next thirty years."[121]

Major blocs of American society came on board as well. The American business community was not the unified and enthusiastic supporter of population growth that scholars often assume it was.[122] Some business leaders continued to espouse the traditional "chamber of commerce" view in favor of population growth (and implicitly the cheap labor they imagined it engendered). But in 1970, a *Fortune* magazine poll revealed that 80 percent of Fortune 500 CEOs supported some effort to reduce population growth.[123] The retired CEOs serving on Planned Parenthood's Commerce and Industry Committee asserted that rapidly rising numbers of people lead to diminishing returns in the economy.[124] Even Dan Gerber, CEO of the baby food company bearing his name, favored zero population growth, stating, "We are not in the least alarmed at the possibilities of population limitation."[125] Carl Madden, the chief economist of the US Chamber of Commerce, told Congress that the US should work toward an optimal population. He said, "The realization is growing that economic activity has to respect the laws of thermodynamics."[126] Moreover, the mainstream business press offered ample support for the idea of zero population growth. In June 1970, the editors of *Fortune* concluded that "experts tend to agree that the birth rate must drop if we are to avoid a 'popullution' problem."[127]

Religious voices, especially the old mainline Protestant churches, called for voluntary population control. In 1965, the General Assembly of the Presbyterian Church (U.S.A.) urged support for overseas population programs, and in 1971, the Assembly stated that fertility voluntarism could not be preserved without a major change of attitude. "The assumption that couples have the freedom to have as many children as they can support should be challenged," it concluded. "We can no longer justify bringing into existence as many children as we desire."[128] The Presbyterian Church called on the government to work toward population stabilization. Some liberal Catholics also continued to press the church on population matters, despite the Pope's reaffirmation of the Church's traditional views on reproduction in the 1968 encyclical *Humanae Vitae*.

Labor was the most tepid participant in the new consensus. (Recall that in the late nineteenth and early twentieth century, the American labor movement had espoused a working-class Malthusianism.) In 1971, Howard Samuel, a labor leader who served on the national population commission detailed in the next chapter, suggested in the AFL-CIO's *American Federationist* that neither rapid growth nor stabilization had ever eliminated unemployment and poverty. Nonetheless, he concluded, "We used to think that [population] growth went along with progress. That philosophy belongs to the past. But neither is the opposite extreme justified—the extreme of crying for population to come to a screeching halt, which is impossible anyway. The answer is to aim for a stabilized population through voluntary means."[129]

The broad consensus regarding the dangers of population growth not only helped spur but also was an explicit part of the expanded federal environmental policy making of the late 1960s. Congress extensively investigated the assumed population–resources problem. The House subcommittee on Conservation and Natural Resources, for example, held hearings in 1969 on the "Effects of Population Growth on Natural Resources and Environment."[130] Rep. George Bush (R-Tex.) convened hearings with his Republican Task Force on Earth Resources and Population, and he suggested renaming the Department of the Interior the Department of Resources, Environment, and Population.[131] Bush's rhetoric matched that of radical population activists. He said on the House floor in 1969:

> We now know that the fantastic rate of population growth we have witnessed these past 20 years continues with no letup in sight. If this growth rate is not checked now—in this decade—we face a danger that is as defenseless as nuclear war.... Unless this problem is recognized and made manageable, starvation, pestilence, and war will solve it for us. As our task force seeks solutions to the problems of resources, environment, and population, it becomes apparent to us that the present rate of population growth is related to many of our economic and social ills.[132]

In terms of specific policy, the new Malthusianism helped spur passage of and was written into the 1969 National Environmental Policy Act (NEPA), which created the Council of Environmental Advisers in the executive branch, instructed federal agencies to incorporate environmental concerns into their decision making, and required agencies to conduct environmental impact studies of potential major actions. Sen. Henry Jackson (D-Wash.), its primary author, called NEPA "the most important and far-reaching conservation-environmental measure ever enacted upon by the Congress."[133] In the summer of 1968, Congress held a joint colloquium on the possibility of a comprehensive national environmental policy that would unify the disparate efforts of various agencies.[134] In the words of Sen. Clifford Hansen (R-Wyo.), they were "trying to react to some circumstances that have sort of come upon us, and, so far, to which we have given all too little concern. I refer to the fact that we have had a very sharp expansion in our population."[135] Secretary of the Interior Udall said that Congress "must establish as a principle of national policy that the relationship between our population and finite resources is a major concern of the Federal Government. No comprehensive policy for our environment can fail to include recognition of the hazards of irresponsible population growth. The Federal Government has for too long resisted involvement in this central issue."[136] In a report leading up to the joint colloquium, Sen. Jackson's Committee on Interior and Insular Affairs declared, "The threat of environmental deterioration, which the President of the United States has described as 'a crisis of choice,' is largely the result of the unprecedented impact of a dual explosion of population and technology upon limited resources of air, water, land, and living space."[137]

Title 1 of NEPA begins by declaring that Congress "recognizes the profound impact of man's activity on the interrelations of all components of the natural environment, particularly the profound influence of population growth."[138] In its declaration of policy, NEPA states that one of the law's six objectives is to "achieve a balance between population and resource use which will permit high standards of living and a wide sharing of life's amenities."[139]

Congress had written the goal of balancing population and resources into law. Yet this directive quickly became a dead letter. Under any circumstances, putting teeth into the population provision would have been difficult, as the drafters did not make it clear how agencies were supposed to incorporate demographic variables into their decision-making process. Moreover, the courts and the executive branch have generally ignored the statement of principles.[140] Not surprisingly, ZPG soon complained that environmental impact statements "continue to ignore population."[141]

Other legislation incorporated population concerns more concretely. The Environmental Education Act (1970), spearheaded by Sen. Nelson, authorized the Department of Health, Education, and Welfare to establish and promote environmental curricula and training programs.[142] Nelson said that the measure "would be a first step toward making every day a national environmental teach-in day."[143] Alan Cranston (D-Calif.), another senator immersed in the population issue, introduced a successful amendment that instructed the commissioner of education to "ensure that full consideration is afforded to the relationship of population to environmental deterioration and ecological imbalance."[144] ZPG also secured language allowing small grants to citizen environmental groups.[145] The Environmental Education Act enjoyed a decade of full funding before President Reagan effectively repealed it.[146]

Malthusianism had entered the policy mainstream. Nevertheless, the anti–population growth consensus began to erode just as it peaked in the popular imagination.

The Population Movement Buckles

The population movement suffered from internal divisions and from the external criticisms of dissident environmentalists, minority voices, and feminists, all of which took some of the wind out of the sails of the overpopulation critique. The population movement also articulated a muddled political economy. The failure to maintain a consistent mainstream economic critique of population growth further set the stage for quick demise of the zero population growth movement in the early 1970s.

Population activists divided into two primary groups: radicals (e.g., Hugh Moore and Paul Ehrlich) and moderates aligned with the Population Council and the large foundations.[147] The radicals doubted the sagacity of the voluntary approach to fertility reduction and the effectiveness of improving access to contraception. Building on Garrett Hardin's belief that overpopulation warranted curtailing the right to procreate freely, some radicals sought compulsory measures to arrest population growth, such as capping by law the number of children a person could have. (The most extreme voices—never more than a minute band of population activists—even called for measures such the use of anti-fertility agents in the water supply.)[148] Hardin and other "coercionists" orbited ZPG, and ZPG founder Richard Bowers declared, "Voluntarism is a farce. The private sector effort has failed."[149] ZPG "carried a chip on its shoulder" against the population establishment, according to historian Donald Critchlow.[150] In return, John D. Rockefeller III refused to meet with or join ZPG.[151]

Nonetheless, it is easy to overstate the strength of the radicals and the intensity of their battles with the moderates. As an organization, ZPG never officially condoned or promoted compulsory let alone coercive measures. Even Hardin fought to prevent the ZPG board from taking a stand in favor of compulsory measures, despite his personal support for them, and ZPG stayed silent on the issue.[152] Even as the group targeted "wanted" (that is, intended) births, it always stated that reducing unwanted births—which contraception prevented—would go far toward the goal of population stabilization. The moderates' accusations that radicals sought immediate zero population growth were unfair because ZPG simply urged families to "stop at two," and a birthrate of two would have brought about population stabilization only after several decades. Meanwhile, the population establishment moved closer to the radicals in embracing the goal of eventual population stabilization. By 1970, both moderates and radicals were pushing for a series of public policies, especially the creation of an antinatalist tax system, to put the nation on a path toward zero population growth without compulsory measures. Although John D. Rockefeller III never joined ZPG, he did maintain a friendly posture toward the group, writing a board member that he was "appreciative of the important contribution that ZPG has made towards alerting the American public to the fact that we too have a population problem. It really has been amazing to me how rapidly the idea had caught hold. And your group deserves much of the credit."[153]

Notwithstanding the very real crossover between the radical and mainstream camps, racial politics revealed harmful divisions in the population movement. As already noted, some ethnic-minority activists, mainly male, detected racist motivations in family planning policies, or, at the least, felt that these policies limited minorities' political empowerment. Minority leaders ratcheted up their critique when confronted with the prospect of coercion. Some claimed that the newly liberalized abortion laws at the state level were designed to regulate minority reproduction.[154] Meanwhile, the establishment also accused radicals of fueling the racial fire. Hugh Moore's Population Crisis Committee, for example, ran an ad, "Have You Been Mugged Today?" which, to quote Critchlow, featured "what many perceived as a young black man mugging a victim."[155]

But advocates of population limitation were not, in the main, the racists depicted by their critics and by scholars ever since. Planned Parenthood called the mugging ad "racist."[156] ZPG largely steered clear of the incendiary and erroneous assumption that population density correlates with crime. Although many population social scientists assumed that population growth exerted an aggravating effect on America's social problems, including crime and juvenile delinquency,[157] this was usually a secondary argument to the ecological one for zero population growth. Studies reported that, despite suspicion of family planning programs, African Americans were only a bit less likely than white Americans to perceive population growth as a problem.[158] The relatively modest difference of opinion was all the more surprising considering many African Americans were dubious of the environmental movement. Research also undercut the claim of racist motivations by revealing that among whites, a "favorable attitude toward Blacks was associated with favorable attitudes toward population control."[159]

Finally, a feminist critique within the camp sympathetic to population reduction prevented a united front from pushing for zero population growth. The most prominent figure here was demographer Judith Blake, who bemoaned "coercive pronatalism" and charged the mainstream movement with exaggerating the extent of unwanted fertility. Blake believed that many poor women simply desired larger families, and hence that family planning programs targeting them were inevitably tinged with classism and racism. She claimed that the solution to overpopulation was not more birth control but a change in gender norms so women would no longer identify themselves primarily as mothers.[160] Though the population establishment criticized Blake, it soon incorporated her premise that enhancing women's rights was essential to combating overpopulation.[161] As discussed, ZPG espoused a radical critique of women's place in American society, over and above its use of feminist themes to argue for abortion rights.

The external criticisms of the population movement received more attention in the media and were probably more damaging than these internal fissures. Most importantly, population activists clashed with a minority of environmentalists on the question of whether population growth or technology was more responsible for environmental destruction. Environmental economists and ZPG agreed, as Garrett Hardin said, "The pollution problem is a consequence of population."[162] Some environmentalists, however, argued that stabilizing population growth—which could take half a century—would be either irrelevant to a sick environment or, at the most, meager medicine. They claimed that technology, consumption, and capitalism run amok, rather than population growth, were the primary causes of environmental ills.[163] In oversimplified terms, this chasm pitted the older American conservation movement against the New Left. Whereas the old guard stressed the harms of population growth, younger environmentalists offered a more holistic critique of capitalism that downplayed the population issue.[164] As one journalist observed in 1972, some on the radical Left saw the zero population growth movement as a "copout, and a misanthropic one at that, a middle class diversion from the need to redistribute wealth as the real answer to America's problems."[165] This viewpoint gelled with increasing efforts, loosely organized as the Alternative Technology Movement, to impose better social controls over technology.[166] A few demographers, including Ansley Coale, also argued that American economic organization itself was the primary cause of environmental degradation.[167] Some individuals came to this position from a longstanding rejection of unplanned technology. For example, the great critic of the city Jane Jacobs wrote that American environmentalists were "laboring under the delusion that population and affluence are causing environmental deterioration."[168]

The dominant figure arguing that technology harms the environment more than rising numbers of people was biologist Barry Commoner. By the late 1960s, Commoner had already established himself as a leading ecologist and critic of capitalism's myopia. Paul Ehrlich, Garrett Hardin, and Commoner participated on a panel together at the 1970 meeting of the American Association for the Advancement of Science. In response to Ehrlich's and Hardin's population-centric talks, Commoner declared, "Saying that none of our pollution problems can be solved without getting at population first is a copout of the worst kind."[169] Commoner never denied that population growth was a serious problem in the developing world, but in *The Closing Circle* (1971), he assumed that material prosperity would induce the demographic transition toward lower birthrates.[170] Instead of a mere emphasis on fertility reduction, Commoner sought a more ecologically sensitive capitalism and a new ethos of how humans should use technology. He vehemently rejected the idea that the US was overpopulated, and he pointed out that since World War II, the rate of pollution increase far outpaced the rate of population increase.[171] Elsewhere, Commoner called the talk of compulsory birth control "faintly masked barbarism."[172] In response, Paul Ehrlich and the rest of the zero population growth camp countered with new multivariable models that reaffirmed a "disproportionate" role for population growth in environmental degradation.[173] These models concluded that it was useless to attribute predominate blame for environmental woes to either population growth or consumption because the two variables acted in tandem.

Despite the Commoner/Ehrlich divide, many in the zero population growth movement were sympathetic to a deep critique of capitalism, even though the pioneers of environmental economics had only begun to integrate concerns about economic inequality into population theory.[174] Zero growth advocates did not believe that population control would quickly solve the nation's ecological and social problems; they simply deemed it the paramount first step. Many supporters of population reduction also worried that new technologies were unplanned and excessively polluting. Moreover, few observers approached the causal impact of technology and population along purely dichotomous lines. One prevalent argument, for example, was that the pressure of population growth in fact drove the development of harmful and polluting technologies.[175] A few years later, British economist E. F. Schumacher, another pioneer of environmental economics, argued in the best-selling *Small Is Beautiful* (1973) for "technology with a human face" while taking the "population explosion" for granted.[176] Theodore Roszak, one of the leading anti-technology theorists of the counterculture, wrote the introduction to the American edition. Policy makers also expressed technological concerns. Sen. Muskie, for example, introduced a resolution to establish a Select Senate Committee on Technology and the Human Environment.[177]

From today's perspective, the Commoner/Ehrlich divide appears to be hairsplitting. Clearly, a global population of five hundred million, assuming current technologies, would leave a significantly reduced ecological footprint than today. Conversely, the planet might happily sustain many more billions if everyone lived as do the Amish. Assessing the ecological effects of population growth and harmful technology are both important to creating environmental policy.[178]

The Zero Population Growth Movement and the Economy

The Commoner/Ehrlich debate revealed additional contradictions in the economic thought of the population movement. Commoner's camp charged the population movement with using the fix of a lower birthrate to paper over the inequalities and polluting nature of American capitalism. This argument resonated because, by this time, the majority of population activists had abandoned the traditional links between population growth and economic welfare, which had animated the movement for over a century, and refocused on pending environmental collapse. In doing so, zero population growth advocates turned away from older arguments in favor of population reduction that located virtue in both economic growth and more equitable distribution of wealth.

At bottom, the 1960s population movement faced a central conundrum regarding economic growth. Since Malthus, population theorists had believed that a smaller population aids economic growth and per capita welfare, and creates a more equitable society. The emergence of Stable Population Keynesianism (SPK) in the 1930s reconfigured this basic idea, treating population growth as largely irrelevant to full employment, given vigorous state economic policies. In the 1950s and 1960s, SPK weakened due to several factors: the new aesthetic critique of population growth; a focus on the age distribution left by the Baby Boom; and social scientists' emphasis on the connection between population growth and household-level poverty. Nevertheless, the general idea that population dynamics are tangential to macroeconomic progress remained. With the rise of limits-to-growth thought, however, population activists faced the following problem: should they promote the cessation of population growth on the grounds that such cessation would aid economic growth as traditionally defined, or on the grounds that population growth was a concomitant to ecologically damaging economic growth?

During its late-1960s heyday, the population movement evaded this central dilemma. The relationship between zero population growth and zero economic growth remained largely unexplored. On the surface, population activists generally followed environmental economists in asserting that unrestrained population growth, economic growth, and consumption were all unsustainable. Most ZPG materials concluded that policy makers needed to anchor the economic growth ship, not merely change its course, in order to save the air and water and prevent the collapse of America's housing, education, and transportation systems. In particular, ZPG claimed that the combination of a growing population and a rising standard of living (that is, higher consumption) was a dangerous amalgam. The group also railed against what it saw as America's unethical and disproportionate consumption of world resources (it estimated that the nation had 6 percent of the world's population and consumed 40 percent of its natural resources). The *ZPG Reporter* summed up the organization's prevailing adherence to a limits-to-growth philosophy when it called for the end "of an economic system based on material growth" and invited economists "to join us and see whether they can develop a system based on materials equilibrium to replace the present one."[179]

At the same time, the radical zero population growth tide had not entirely swept away SPK. On some occasions, ZPG continued to claim that the cessation of population growth would in fact enhance economic growth, worker productivity, and the individual standard of living.[180] Indeed, the organization sometimes maintained that an expansionary economic policy was needed to smooth the transition to a stable population.[181] Some outside observers took it for granted ZPG adhered to the argument that a smaller population would drive economic growth. One journalist concluded: "The ZPGers are at least generally spared the need to dispute the proposition that a larger population is economically desirable. This traditional wisdom has largely evaporated in the face of the Keynesian theory and practice by which governments can provide direct stimulation to the economy."[182] More often, the moderate voices in the population establishment, such as the Population Council, promoted the idea that a smaller population would aid individual economic welfare.[183] Whereas the radical ecologists rejected America's mass consumption–based economy, moderates argued that a reduction in population levels would increase personal consumption.

These tensions might have been resolved had population activists called for the cessation of population growth without the cessation of economic progress. But to do so would have entailed more than arguing that the correlation between population growth and economic growth is theoretically tenuous; within the prevailing ecological paradigm, it would have meant embracing the highly controversial supposition that economic growth need not be ecologically destructive. Reconciling a steady population, economic growth, and environmental sustainability would have updated SPK for the ecological era. But for radical population experts, this would have brought their position uncomfortably close to that of Barry Commoner, who believed that it was not economic growth per se that was destructive but the form that growth took.[184] Such a position would have anticipated today's environmental optimists, who conclude that technology can solve our problems and that economic growth is good for the environment because it turns poor polluters into middle-class environmentalists. Given Americans' overwhelming support for economic growth, retooling the definition of growth would have provided a more viable approach than rejecting it outright.[185] Only later, in the 1980s and 1990s, did several theorists more attuned to the good that economic growth has done in the last few hundred years try to reconcile environmental health and economic expansion.[186]

Finally, the zero population growth movement's economic case lost steam by injecting a heavy dose of localism into the American population debate. Due to the local-branch nature of the organization, ZPG members spent much of their time trying to combat local sprawl rather than educating Americans about aggregate growth. Judith Morgan, a ZPG vice-president, said that the organization's chapters were "local salespersons for land use planning, discussions of growth control mechanisms" and the "advocacy of [local] population 'caps.'"[187] Given the dramatic increase in the suburban population in midcentury America, ZPG hardly could have avoided the issue of urban sprawl. Yet the emphasis on local growth fostered a certain amount of middle-class, "not in my backyard" (NIMBY) sentiment, which diluted the critique of aggregate population and consumption increases.

Reservations about population growth helped shape American environmental policies well before the takeoff of the zero population growth movement of the late 1960s. Yet the center of anti–population growth thought—the simple notion that fewer people promote the Good Life and a better standard of living—practically disappeared during the decade. Radicals launched an ecologically based movement that briefly entered the mainstream but engendered fissures that contributed to its ultimate demise. American Malthusianism was wobbly even before conservatives kicked the chair out from under it.

CHAPTER SEVEN

Defusing the Population Bomb

Ever since the Truman administration's "Point Four" foreign aid program, which assumed that population growth–induced resource scarcity bred communism, the US government had incorporated Malthusian concerns to some degree. But state action came haltingly. Neither President Eisenhower nor Kennedy believed direct action to combat population growth, whether domestic or international, fell within the proper purview of government policy. As we have seen, President Johnson spoke forcefully about what he saw as the global population crisis and promoted the inclusion of family planning training and education in overseas USAID programs. His administration also launched federally sponsored family planning programs as part of its War on Poverty. Despite this dramatic policy evolution, Johnson did not seriously consider assertive policies to decelerate domestic population growth, and his administration held up even the modest proposal of creating a national commission to study population issues.[1]

From 1969 to 1972, however, disparate actors in the federal government embraced the new Malthusianism and elevated the population-policy debate far beyond the birth control programs that had emerged in the mid 1960s. Cresting concerns about overpopulation among the general public and experts' frustration that global population growth rates were unaffected by two decades of accelerated family planning aid combined to create a sense that the moment had arrived to move "beyond family planning."[2] Lawmakers sympathetic to the zero population growth movement now considered not merely managing domestic population growth and its supposed social, economic, and environmental consequences but intervening comprehensively to "control" this growth. Americans' faith in liberal individualism and puritanical resistance to public debate about sex and reproduction prevented draconian measures, such as capping the allowable number of children per family. Nonetheless, the state had several tools at its disposal, including creating tax disincentives for large families and early marriage, legalizing abortion, dramatically increasing access to family planning, and reducing immigration.

The Nixon administration initially jumped on the zero population growth bandwagon. In a special 1969 message on population drafted by his urban affairs adviser Daniel Patrick Moynihan, the president framed the issue in both foreign and domestic terms, calling the planet's rising numbers "one of the most serious challenges to human destiny in the last third of this century."[3] At Nixon's urging, Congress created the Commission on Population Growth and the American Future, chaired by philanthropist and Malthusian John D. Rockefeller III, to investigate all facets of the population problem. The commission's final report, issued in 1972, called for a series of policies designed to encourage population stabilization.[4]

Yet even before the commission's report, the administration was rapidly phasing out the "overpopulation" critique, and Nixon all but ended the possibility of state intervention to slow population growth when he perfunctorily thanked the commission for its labors but rejected its final report. Behind the scenes, his administration ensured that the commission's recommendations never saw the legislative light of day.

The events surrounding the ineffectual population commission provide a wonderful window into policy making in the Nixon White House. More germane to the present study, this policy turnaround was a crucial moment in the centuries-old debate about population, natural resources, and the economy. What emerged during Nixon's tenure was a new political economy of population in the United States: a widespread embrace of population growth that survives to this day. Granted, some population concerns remained in the 1970s, as talk of a "zero-sum society" thrived and some liberals questioned the virtue of all kinds of "growth." By any measure, however, unease with "overpopulation"—especially domestic US overpopulation—dwindled dramatically.[5] Indeed, by the late 1970s, most policy makers had traded in overpopulation fears for an unabashed embrace of steady population growth, at least in regard to America's demographic trends.

The reversal from prevailing skepticism to prevailing optimism about population growth was closely connected to a broader revival of laissez-faire economic ideas that dominated the American political economy in the final third of the twentieth century. New optimism about the benefits of population growth not only responded to but also contributed to the resurgence of a conservative political economy. Examining the course of the population issue in the Nixon White House within the context of shifting social science expertise, two developments emerge that drove the turnaround in demographic discourse. First, the Nixon administration helped defuse the "population bomb"; it narrowed the scope of the overpopulation critique by concentrating on the shibboleth of altering the geographic distribution of Americans rather than on the possibility of addressing aggregate growth. In doing so, President Nixon came to reject the goal of zero population growth. In part, this refutation simply revealed an instinctual defense of economic growth, given that some in the population-control movement called for a radical brake on economic activity. The administration's dismissal of an overpopulation problem, however, also reflected the second development spurring an about-face in population thought: the ascendancy of a new pro–population growth economics, which had been building momentum among social scientists since the early 1960s.

This account challenges the conventional wisdom on the waning of the domestic overpopulation critique. Most historians emphasize two main factors. The first is shifting demographic fundamentals: the clamor for population control took place during a unique interregnum when a significant slowdown in US aggregate population growth seemed possible. The birthrate of American women declined from 1960 to 1967, briefly increased in 1968 and 1969, and then dropped again from 1970 to 1972, slipping below the replacement level of 2.1 births per woman. Moreover, the dramatic and surprising rise in immigration stemming from the 1965 Immigration Act had not yet gathered steam. Scholars have emphasized that these trends undercut calls for population control.[6] Second, historians have stressed that America's "culture wars" sucked the population issue into its vortex.[7] In this interpretation, the new battle over abortion rights was paramount, both for politicizing the population issue and for creating an organized constituency—the "pro-life" movement—that considered population control an anathema.[8]

In accounting for the trajectory of the population issue in recent decades, these demographic and cultural analyses illuminate much of the story but are insufficient. To begin with, historians have exaggerated the role of the declining birthrate in weakening the overpopulation critique. Many demographers, lawmakers, and the Nixon administration predicted that birthrate declines would be short-lived and that a new Baby Boom was just around the corner.[9] Also, most participants in the debate were not surprised that the birthrate was decreasing; they understood that populations cannot grow indefinitely. Even population alarmists conceded that American fertility, the Baby Boom aside, was likely to resume its historic pattern of decline.[10] The question was never whether the US (or world) population would stabilize but rather at what level, when, and at what cost along the way.

The culture wars argument is also important. As we will see, Nixon distanced himself from the report of his population commission in part because he opposed its advocacy of legalized abortion and was mindful of criticism from the Catholic Church. Moreover, a stepped-up battle over immigration during the 1970s reinforced the politicization of population issues and drove many environmentalists away from them out of fear of being branded anti-immigrant and racist. The scholarly stress on cultural fissures, however, slights the vital role that broader shifts in economic ideas played in remaking the American population debate—before the culture wars engulfed it. Accounts of the eclipse of the overpopulation issue that do mention the confluence between conservative economic theory and anti-Malthusianism focus on the 1970s but miss the critical developments of the 1960s, when a conservative veneration of population expansion took shape.[11] As with so much of what took place in 1960s America, a veneer of liberal success on the population issue temporarily masked a budding and ultimately more successful conservative response.

Nixon's Brief Bout of Malthusianism

The election of Richard Nixon was initially unsettling to advocates of population control. Although the GOP's 1968 platform mentioned the "menace" of the "world-wide population explosion," his views on these matters were inchoate.[12] Nixon, however, assumed the presidency as popular and media concern about overpopulation crested, and his initial response was in step with the public's mood. In his special message calling for a population commission, Nixon stated, "I believe that many of our present social problems may be related to the fact that we have had only fifty years in which to accommodate the second hundred million Americans."[13] The president predicted that the additional 100 million people expected by the end of the twentieth century would cause further economic and social strains. Nixon indicated elsewhere that he was serious about combating international population growth,[14] and neither government officials nor the press doubted his commitment.[15]

At this juncture, four factors moved the administration to favor population alarmism. Most obviously, popular apprehension was peaking. Second, the congressional movement for population control remained bipartisan and vibrant. The late 1960s saw the introduction of dozens of pieces of family planning legislation, and although several congressional Malthusians were Republican (e.g., Rep. George H. W. Bush),[16] the White House wanted to "seize the initiative" from Democratic leaders.[17] Third, the population establishment, and especially the John D. Rockefeller III–led Population Council, continued to highlight what it saw as the overpopulation problem and to lobby aggressively for federal spending on family planning programs and population education. The Republican Rockefeller enjoyed positive relationships with several administration members friendly to family planning.[18] Fourth, the Cold War sustained the notion that the US had to put its own population house in order as an example to Third World nations. For instance, Donald Rumsfeld, who headed Nixon's Office of Economic Opportunity before becoming his counselor, noted that Nixon and his three predecessors had all supported efforts at easing overseas population growth for national security reasons. Rumsfeld eventually testified to the population commission that "the credibility of this [presidential] support hinges in part upon the degree of responsibility we in the United States display in population affairs here at home."[19] Commenting on the landmark population legislation of the Nixon era—the 1970 Family Planning Services and Population Research Act, which greatly extended federal support for birth control programs—the *New York Times* concluded: "Perhaps most important of all, the family planning bill demonstrates to a sometimes skeptical international public that the United States intends to practice at home what it has been preaching to the world with increasing urgency in recent years."[20]

A vocal minority in Congress promoted even more aggressive population policies. In 1970, for example, Sen. Joseph Tydings (D-Md.), one of the issue leaders since the mid 1960s and a sponsor of the Family Planning Services and Population Research Act, introduced a joint resolution declaring it official policy for the federal government to "develop, encourage, and implement, at the earliest possible time, the necessary policies, attitudes, social standards and actions which will, by voluntary means consistent with human rights and individual conscience, stabilize the population of the US and thereby promote the future well-being of this nation and the entire world."[21] That same year, Sen. Bob Packwood (D-Ore.) and Rep. Pete McCloskey Jr. (R-Calif.) introduced bills to eliminate tax deductions for all but the first two children.[22]

But the policy window was not wide. Most lawmakers were content to merely study the population issue, and, in 1970, they turned their attention to perhaps the most famous—or infamous—legacy of the population issue during the Nixon years: the Commission on Population Growth and the American Future.[23] Nixon's point person on population was his domestic policy adviser Daniel Patrick Moynihan, the maverick Democrat and future senator who had written the "Moynihan Report" on the African-American family in Kennedy's Department of Labor. Moynihan was the main author of Nixon's population message,[24] and in 1969 he steered the commission's enabling legislation through Congress.[25]

The legislation did not specify whether the commission was charged with recommending policies simply to adjust American society to population increase or to slow down this increase. House amendments pointed the commission in a more radical direction, but Nixon's population message—and his advisers—emphasized planning for population increase rather than arresting it.[26] Moynihan, for example, told the president that "the first function of the Commission is to chart the expected growth of the population between now and the year 2000 in terms of numbers and location, and the resources of the public sector that will be required to deal with this anticipated growth."[27] Moynihan revealed his technocratic approach to the issue at a June 1970 press conference, when he told reporters, "By and large, the average cat food company knows more about the demographic structure of the American public and what it is likely to be than does the city of Chicago. We don't have any forward thinking this way and we are trying to build it into our concerns, medicine and aging and things like that."[28] At the other end of the spectrum, advocates of population reduction bemoaned what they saw as the commission's narrow mission.[29] Rep. Morris Udall (D-Ariz.) complained about the "implied assumption that these other 100 million Americans, this additional population, is inevitable, that we simply accept it and begin to plan for how we are going to take care of it. I don't think we ask the ultimate question if we make that assumption."[30] "Let's see if we can't slow down the assembly line," he wrote elsewhere.[31] Udall introduced more forceful legislation that would have made population stabilization the official policy of the United States, but it received only perfunctory debate.[32]

During the first half of 1970, a small group within the administration led by Moynihan selected the commission's members.[33] The process quickly became politicized, and in June an exasperated Moynihan complained to John Ehrlichman, the Assistant to the President for Domestic Affairs, "With any luck we may yet appoint a Population Commission. That is, after the FBI has gone through its pathetic inquiries into the prospect that a Negro doctor had an Aunt whose girlfriend slept with a Communist."[34] In addition to Sen. Tydings and three other members of Congress, all of whom were deeply concerned with population growth,[35] the commission included what we might now call a "politically correct" mix of representatives from various interest groups.[36] "Politically," its research director concluded, "the group was conservative by college student standards, liberal by national and White House standards. By no stretch of the imagination could the group be characterized as radical."[37] Moynihan's first choice for chair was William Scranton, the former governor of Pennsylvania whom liberal Republicans had drafted in 1964 to unsuccessfully challenge Barry Goldwater (at the time he was a vice chairman of the Urban Institute), but Moynihan also approved of the final selection of John D. Rockefeller III.[38]

In March 1971, the commission's interim report used safe language—and the moderate critique of population growth rooted in aesthetic rather than scarcity concerns—to warn against the dangers of continual population increase. Rather than sounding the resource-exhaustion alarm, the commission maintained that population growth acted "as an intensifier or multiplier of many problems impairing the quality of life in the United States."[39] Yet as the Commission on Population Growth and the American Future gathered steam, the Nixon administration began to pull back from even this moderate, quality-of-life-centered response to the population question, setting the stage for a collision.

The Urban Crisis and "Balanced Growth"

The development of a contentious abortion politics in the United States helps explain the eventual dénouement of the Malthusian revival.[40] Individuals who today would be called "cultural conservatives" increasingly rejected the zero population growth movement, emphasizing its ties to the abortion legalization movement.[41] This abortion-related backlash against population policy filtered into the White House. In April 1971, Nixon issued an order insisting military bases follow state abortion laws, declaring abortion an "unacceptable form of population control."[42] Yet abortion was just one of several issues that reshaped population politics. Before a showdown over abortion at the end of the population commission's life, the White House undercut the urgency of the zero population growth critique by instead thinking about population problems primarily in terms of controversial social-demographic issues surrounding the American city (and not, therefore, in terms of aggregate population growth).

On one level, poverty and social decay provide conceptual links between the population and urban debates. During the mid 1960s, and especially after the Watts uprising in Los Angeles, a so-called "urban-crisis" captured policy makers' imaginations. The population debate overlapped with this racialized urban crisis because several hot-button social issues with demographic overtones—for example, rising teenage pregnancy—were seen primarily as urban problems. The purported connection between population growth and the urban crisis, therefore, injected a fresh dose of racial politics into a population discussion already tainted by the legacy of eugenics.[43]

On another level, the paradigm of controlling "growth" linked the population and urban debates. Because urban and suburban growth accounted for most of the overall population growth in 1960s America—as they did throughout the twentieth century—population controllers and urban planners shared overlapping goals. The former wanted to reduce aggregate population growth, and the latter sought a national growth policy that would reduce urban densities or at least induce "balanced growth" between the city, suburb, and countryside.

Within a Nixon White House engaged in the quest for a national urban policy, the question "Where shall they live?" subsumed the question "How many of them shall there be?" In other words, the administration stressed the geographic distribution of the population—in particular, the increasing concentration of Americans in and around major cities—rather than aggregate growth. A June 1971 meeting of Nixon's Domestic Council showed that the administration thought about population primarily in terms of distribution when John Ehrlichman, Nixon's domestic policy chief, scribbled two notes under the agenda heading of "population" for this meeting: "what growth among poor" and "<u>where</u> will growth be in U.S."[44]

Because of the historical racialization of poverty discourse in the United States, critics of the administration and of the population movement dismissed the population–urban crisis link as race-baiting (even though the anxiety about "growth among the poor" was always expressed in race-neutral terms). Given that one interpretation of Nixon labels him "Tricky Dick"—a schemer who undermined policy goals by publicly endorsing them while simultaneously letting his henchmen destroy them—it is tempting to surmise that the administration's emphasis on population location was a clever way of dooming the population issue through controversy even as it scored short-term political gains.[45] However, the emphasis on the question "Where will they live?" should be seen against the backdrop of not only the urban crisis but also of a broad bipartisan movement to develop a comprehensive "growth policy" for the United States.

The quest for a national growth policy fused demographic and environmental planning; proposals for government-induced population redistribution reflected a longstanding belief that more efficient distribution of the US population would protect the land.[46] More specifically, "growth policy" in the 1960s implied measures to minimize the damage to landscapes that resulted from the nation's explosive postwar economic growth (and from the localized nature of land-use planning). Advocates of a national growth policy acknowledged the increase of the aggregate population, but their primary concern was the deleterious effects of distribution, for example, the "sprawl" created by the expanding megalopolises concentrated along the Atlantic and Pacific coasts.[47] Hence, many proposals for a national growth strategy included efforts to subsidize population relocation.[48] The campaign for growth policy united liberals, who opposed the ecological effects of urban sprawl, and conservatives, who focused on the social ills of the city.

Within Nixon's inner circle, Moynihan personified the connections between growing fears of an urban crisis, the drive for growth policy, and the broader population debate. He chaired the White House's informal Urban Affairs Council, and it was no coincidence that he subsequently spearheaded the population issue. After Nixon's special message on population, Moynihan noted that "many of the points the President makes are closely linked to concerns of the Urban Affairs Council."[49] In a 1969 *Public Interest* article, "Toward a National Urban Policy," Moynihan wrote: "The federal government must assert a specific interest in the movement of people, displaced by technology or driven by poverty, from rural to urban areas, and also in the movement from densely populated central cities to suburban areas."[50]

In his 1970 State of the Union address, Nixon called for a federal "growth policy" to "create a new rural environment which will not only stem the migration to urban centers, but reverse it."[51] The congressional drive for such a policy began with promise but ultimately failed, primarily because of the overwhelming antipathy to government planning in the United States.[52] Although the question "Where will they live?" was embedded in an ultimately futile policy campaign, it still exerted significant influence over the course of the population debate, deflecting attention away from the traditional discourse centered on aggregate population growth, the economy, and the environment. Nixon explicitly moved toward the position that the "population problem" was primarily one of location. Historian J. Brooks Flippen writes that Nixon signed the 1970 Family Planning Act reluctantly: "Concerned with conservative objections and now questioning whether the problem was distribution and not growth, Nixon initially resisted the new proposal."[53]

Although concerns about the geographic location of the population are compatible with a preference for a smaller aggregate population, within the Nixon White House, the demographic aspects of the "urban crisis" and the interest in population location crowded out the overpopulation critique. Moynihan, for instance, vaguely approved of a slower aggregate rate of domestic population growth but advised Nixon to emphasize population redistribution away from the cities as the solution to the "population problem."[54] In a tense early 1970 meeting, the president of the Sierra Club, Phillip Berry, urged Nixon to pursue aggressive policies to promote national population stabilization.[55] Moynihan followed up with a letter to Berry that conceded global population growth was an urgent problem but defined the domestic issue primarily in geographic terms. "We are highly concentrated, with a large majority of our people living on a small fraction of our land," Moynihan wrote. "In the past eight years one out of every three counties lost population. If this trend continues unattended we shall become increasingly concentrated in the coming decades—our large metropolitan regions will become more congested while valuable rural areas continue to decline."[56]

Nixon himself increasingly thought about the population issue in terms of the city, though his analysis of urban population growth contained more racial rhetoric than concerns about urban planning. In a taped discussion with Ehrlichman about the population commission, Nixon bluntly stated that many people thought about population control in terms of controlling the "Negro masses." After Nixon then suggested individuals not using birth control "are the people who shouldn't have kids,"[57] the conversation turned immediately to Black migration patterns. Nixon expressed wonderment that the African-American population of San Francisco had reached 30 percent due to black in-migration and white flight.[58] Nixon's casual racism is not noteworthy; the point is that he thought about population in terms of the increasing concentration of Americans, especially African Americans, in cities. There is no evidence that Nixon saw the issue of population location as a way to divert attention from the question of aggregate growth (or as a way to create more conservative suburban voters). Yet Nixon must have known that throughout the twentieth century, calls for government-sponsored population redistribution usually went nowhere, especially after the waning of the New Deal's relocation programs. And he likely knew that Malthusians deemed geographic redistribution a "dangerous pseudosolution to the population problem," as Paul Ehrlich put it.[59]

Not only the racial and geographic-distribution aspects of growth policy but also the evolving macroeconomic discourse surrounding it deflated the overpopulation issue. Early in his tenure, President Nixon had flirted, if not with anti–economic growth thought, then at least with themes of balance and scarcity. "The time has come for a new quest," Nixon stated in his 1970 State of the Union address, "a quest not for a greater quantity of what we have, but for a new quality of life in America."[60] By late 1970, however, in response to recession and the Left's assault on the growth ideal, Nixon returned to the robust celebration of economic growth that had dominated the postwar political economy. Nixon's retreat to growthism reinforced a developing disdain for the zero population growth movement. Already in his meeting with the Sierra Club's Berry, he had announced that the population issue was exaggerated.[61] In part, this stance simply reflected Nixon's growing antipathy to environmentalism, which he had dismissed by telling Berry, "All politics is a fad."[62] Nixon and his staff also assumed that population growth and economic growth were concomitants, and, thus, that zero population growth would lead to unemployment. He also assumed erroneously that the population movement called uniformly for the cessation of economic growth. Because of the perceived link between population and economic growth, Nixon's renewed emphasis on economic growth vitiated support for population control.

Nixon's call for "balanced growth" continued to incorporate population concerns, but it stressed only the locational concerns, not a slower rate of population growth or an improvement in the quality of life.[63] Accordingly, Nixon's bureaucracy combined the pursuit of balanced growth, couched in geographic terms, with a minimization of the alleged overpopulation problem. In March 1970, Nixon's National Goals Research Staff (NGRS) reported internally that the US could handle the population growth expected by the end of the century, even if the potential environmental effects were indeed worrisome. "There is no present need for incentives to reduce population growth in the US," the group concluded.[64] In its main report, *Toward Balanced Growth: Quantity with Quality*, the NGRS claimed that the "question of population size in the United States is not Malthusian" but rather one of paying the price for the problems created by affluence ("congestion and contamination").[65] The report also suggested that zero population growth would be achieved without any government action. It concluded that among the various decisions facing the nation on population, "One which appears not to be urgent is that of overall size of the population—even after the effects of a considerable amount of immigration are taken into account."[66] The NGRS, however, reported that the question of population redistribution was "a different matter, and one to be taken seriously regardless of what may be the upper limit of the population size."[67] Accordingly, the only population policies called for in *Toward Balanced Growth* concerned geographic redistribution. The report advocated subsidizing population relocation to "alternate growth centers" and "new towns."[68]

Well before the Commission on Population Growth and the American Future issued its 1972 final report, then, the Nixon White House had changed the tenor of the population issue. But it was not simply recoiling against radicalism. It was also increasingly imbibing a new celebration of population growth percolating among conservative economists.

Toward a "Market-Knows-Best Demography"

In the 1930s, when the birthrate slumped in the industrialized nations and threatened to eventually snuff out population growth, John Maynard Keynes argued that higher birthrates would spur economic recovery. During the 1930s, American economists sympathetic to Keynes's broader anti–laissez-faire project developed a new demographic-economic doctrine that broke from Keynes on the specific question of population growth but still used Keynes's new economics of consumption. Stable Population Keynesianism (SPK) maintained that Keynesian policies, especially the promotion of mass consumption, would render population growth economically irrelevant. The state, not the stork, would sustain economic growth, leaving society to enjoy the environmental and aesthetic benefits of a smaller population.

In the 1960s and 1970s, SPK was eviscerated by the development of a basket of populationist and pro-market ideas that may be termed "market-knows-best demography" (MKBD).[69] MKBD boils down to five propositions. First, population growth unleashes economies of scale and hence economic growth. Second, demographic density propels innovation and scientific progress, which are essentially unlimited. Short-term population pressure induces creative responses to maintain living standards, and higher population densities encourage the diffusion of information, technology, and skills; lower per capita infrastructure costs (for example, in transportation); and allow industries to reap the benefits of clustering. Moreover, more people equal more geniuses. Third, individual fertility decisions serve the common good. Fourth, even if a healthy economy amid a stable population is theoretically possible (as SPK insists), the state cannot be relied upon to make the necessary adjustments. Fifth, population growth advances human liberty.

The ascendancy of MKBD was in step with the overall withering of Keynesianism during the 1960s and 1970s, but, at the time, it was not the exclusive domain of conservatives. Guided by the central laissez-faire premise that the invisible hand produces socially optimal results, however, the doctrine was constitutive of the political "New Right" and the new classical economics that swept American politics in the 1970s. MKBD articulated many themes amenable to the New Right's worldview: faith in the market, the importance of innovation, entrepreneurship, and liberty, and unabashed celebration of economic growth. Many leaders of the late twentieth-century conservative intellectual movement would subsequently draw from MKBD.

MKBD sprang in part from the very old idea (ironically attributable to late-career Malthus as well as Adam Smith) that wealth and freedom lower fertility. This idea was already central to midcentury demographic transition theory, and Ludwig von Mises, one of the early giants of modern conservatism, offered an important statement of it in 1949.[70] Yet MKBD matured within four specialized debates of more recent lineage. The first, overlapping with the broader postwar evolution of economic growth theory, entailed a rejection of the prevailing idea that rapid population growth in the developing world stunted incomes due to an excess of dependent children who drained savings into unproductive investment. During the 1960s, doubts emerged about whether high fertility produced shortages of savings and capital, and optimists concluded that increased family size motivates families to positively change economic behavior.[71]

The second specialized debate concerned natural resources. By the 1960s, many economists downgraded the importance of natural resources to modern skills-based economies and, separately, suggested that market forces obviate resource scarcity. This debate revealed the developing links between modern conservative ideas and population optimism. For example, seminal anti-statist economist Friedrich Hayek argued in *The Constitution of Liberty* (1960) that natural resources could in fact become more plentiful.[72] In a classic cornucopian statement from 1963, two leading resource economists concluded, "Nature imposes particular scarcities, not an inescapable general scarcity."[73]

Also fostering a more optimistic posture toward population growth was the maturation of human capital theory, which holds that investment in people, via education, training, etc., unleashes economic growth.[74] Led by the University of Chicago's Theodore Schultz (also an official at the Population Council),[75] human capital theorists proposed that population growth promotes the expansion of intermediary institutions (e.g., schools) that enhance human capital.[76] Moreover, they argued that the public investment necessitated by rapid population growth is not economic deadwood but contributive to economic growth. Schultz was not a conservative activist, but he espoused the basic tenets of the conservative "Chicago School" of economics. Schultz's work on human capital theory reveals not only an unexplored connection between the population debate and a major component of economic thought since the 1960s but also the affinities between population optimism and an unbridled faith in markets.[77]

The fourth and final debate concerned the microeconomics of fertility—that is, not the *consequence*s of population growth but its *causes*. Market-oriented economist-demographers theorized that fertility decisions at the micro, family level result in macro efficiencies for society. In short, they located an "invisible hand of fertility."[78] Human capital theorists, especially Chicago's Gary Becker, Jacob Mincer, and Theodore Schultz, were innovators of what economists often refer to as "new household economics."[79] This school of thought did not have an immediate influence on the mainstream population debate, but it would eventually provide an essential plank in pro–population growth thought.[80] The central idea of the new household economics was that parents, managers of what Becker called the "small factory" of the household, are rational actors who weigh the costs and benefits of having children, at least subconsciously. (The theory downplays the reality that the act of producing babies is usually pleasure, not work, and sometimes immune to rational calculation.) In particular, well-off parents treat children as "consumer durable goods" that provide them with "psychic income." Families thus increasingly prefer to have a few "high quality" children—those on whom they can lavish human capital, whether in the form of better education or piano lessons—rather than many "low quality" children. Higher incomes, in other words, translate into spoiled children, not additional siblings. Individual households rationally maximize their numbers of children, and the end result is a socially optimal population.

Since the 1960s, perhaps the single leading figure in the economics of American fertility has been economist Richard Easterlin. Building on the consumption theories of Milton Friedman, the dean of the "Chicago School"—and, in particular, the argument that expected lifetime earnings, not immediate income, guide an individual's consumption habits—Easterlin posited a cyclical theory of American fertility based upon "relative expectations" or "potential income." Members of a large cohort face stiffened labor market competition, and as a result they have fewer babies than their parents did.[81] Easterlin's emphasis on "intergenerational relative income" differed from Becker's emphasis on household consumption, but the thrust of both was that population growth rates naturally adjust to the economic and social environment, a conclusion that cuts against overpopulation concerns.[82] True to the broader philosophy of the "Chicago School," any externalities associated with children (e.g., pollution effects) were deemed marginal.

Apart from their work on fertility, the new household economists also praised the broader economic virtues of population growth.[83] Whether they focused on population growth's inducement of harder work, technological innovation, or reduced fertility, all of these economists stressed the motivations and initiative of the individual, a stress that dovetailed with the ascendant New Right's stress on the entrepreneur.[84] This is not to say that MKBD became dominant in the late 1960s. A majority of American economists remained convinced of population growth's adverse capital-absorbing tendencies, and some even incorporated the metaphors from the new radical ecological economics.[85] Others rejected the assumptions of the new household economics.[86] Nonetheless, skepticism of MKBD was increasingly becoming the domain of an old guard of economist-demographers with links to the population movement. Just when population doomsdayism was enjoying its day in the sun, pro–population growth views were bubbling to the surface.

The Conservative Press and the Population Issue

We have seen that American business leaders and the business media did not oppose the zero population growth movement during its heyday, and to a modest degree even supported it. Such support continued during the height of the population commission's work. In 1971, the *Wall Street Journal* did express libertarian concerns about population policy, suggesting that Americans "ought also to talk about how the quality of life might be affected by, to take the extreme example, having a computer or a bureaucrat decide who is and who is not allowed to have a child." And yet the *Journal* concluded, "It seems clear to us that some measures to limit population will be needed."[87] Members of the embryonic conservative movement, however, were quicker to embrace the new pro–population growth ideas. In the 1960s, conservative intellectuals had begun supporting the general consensus that domestic population growth represented a challenge. Even before the formation of the population commission in 1970, though, they had largely reversed course and adopted populationist themes.

The *National Review* demonstrates this shift. In 1965, editor and founder William F. Buckley Jr. argued that population growth was poised to outstrip human ingenuity: "Solutions for today and tomorrow are perhaps not so difficult to contrive—send tractors to India, and hybrid corn to Egypt. But the day after tomorrow?" And Buckley warned his readers that the US was not immune from the population dilemma. "The fact of the matter is that a solution must be found," he wrote. "That old dog Malthus turned out to be very substantially correct in his dire predictions, and there seems to be no point in waiting until the United States is like India before moving in on the problem."[88] Buckley was thus hopeful that the Catholic Church would reverse its position on birth control. Also in 1965, the *National Review* printed a supplement called "The Population Explosion," which yielded nothing in apocalyptic rhetoric to the liberal doomsday literature of the era. In the lead article, "The Avalanche," as the editors summarized it, "A science fiction novelist takes a hard look at the earth's skyrocketing birthrate and admits it portends horrors even he finds hard to imagine."[89] The author identified as the true science fiction of the era the food optimism promulgated by the "nutritional technological cohorts—the algae-and-yeast boys, the ranch-the-oceans fellows, and the transmutation-of-petrochemicals-into-proteins enthusiasts."[90] "The Avalanche" also proffered the typical Cold War–inspired, libertarian argument against population growth: that it would engender big government and Sovietize the US. "The very presence of these new masses of humanity [in the United States], the weight of their parents' votes and, so soon, their own, makes bigger bureaucracy—bigger Big Brother bureaucracy—so probable that without a miracle it is a certainty."[91] Another article in the supplement, meanwhile, affirmed the traditional view that population growth stunted capital formation and economic growth.[92]

Yet just a few years later, even as the population scare achieved critical mass, the *National Review* rejected the overpopulation critique and printed the conservative economists who believed that population growth expands the market—and that the market can solve ecological dilemmas. These included the Australian economist Colin Clark, an early critic of the prevailing wisdom regarding economic development who claimed that the world could feed at least forty billion people. Clark maintained that technological innovation was a function of population.[93] And he reached deep into the intellectual toolkit of populationists, articulating the militaristic and mercantilist view that the US needed continual population growth to remain a world power.[94] Further, Clark believed that population expansion enhances liberty. In contrast, nations with stable populations have less social mobility and freedom and more expensive government.[95]

Milton Friedman, one of the leading economists of the American neoliberal revival, echoed the notion that population growth not only grows the economy but also reduces the size of government. In a 1970 *National Review* piece on the new environmentalism, Friedman wrote, "[The] growth of population and improvements in transportation and communication have greatly widened the scope for effective competition and so have reduced the need for governmental concern with monopolist behavior."[96] A final example of the new libertarian embrace of population growth came from Robert Moses, the famous urban planner who did more than any other to build (and some say ruin) modern New York City. By the 1960s, Moses was out of favor with the establishment, and he turned against the New Left and its social planners with vigor. Failing to recognize that the vast majority in the population movement embraced a laissez-faire approach to population, in the sense that they had no more ambitious goal than eliminating unwanted fertility, Moses wrote in the *National Review*: "The planners already predict drastic regulation of the population by law to insure a future stable, comfortable, balanced society and economy. This consummation will be arrived at on the basis of scientific, impartial, unbiased study of long-haired, bewhiskered, sideburned experts who will of course be completely divorced from politics."[97]

Proponents of population control continued to argue that rising numbers of inhabitants erode freedom.[98] Nevertheless, conservatives, who increasingly captured the discussion of "liberty" in the United States, effectively built a libertarian case in favor of population growth. Their views represented a shift from the 1950s and 1960s, when many conservatives had insisted that population growth produced Big Government. This shift also filtered into the mass media.[99] Also, if Moynihan's case is indicative, many liberals drifting rightward toward neoconservatism were similarly unimpressed by the possibility of state-directed demographic management. Appearing on *Face the Nation* in early 1970, Moynihan said, "There is no government in history that has ever had any effect whatever on population." He continued, "One of the nice things about people is they don't pay too much attention to Government . . . particularly with respect to the number of children they have."[100]

Nixon Spurns the Population Commission

Against the backdrop of this rising conservative critique of the (over) population issue, the Commission on Population Growth and the American Future released its interim report in March 1971, which was well received in the press and stirred few feathers in the administration. That summer, Milton Eisenhower and Sen. Tydings, who had just lost his seat, launched a group called the Coalition for a National Population Policy. Membership in ZPG peaked, the popular press still rode the population bandwagon, and lawmakers reintroduced joint Senate and House resolutions calling for population stabilization.[101] The administration, however, increasingly thought about the population issue in terms of geographic redistribution and the urban crisis—indeed, ZPG proposed that the interim report dealt a blow to "the Nixon Administration's contention that the US population problem is one of distribution, not growth"[102]—and the president specifically rejected the goal of zero population growth. Abortion politics were becoming more salient, and, according to the *National Journal*, doomed the population stabilization resolutions.[103]

The contours of the commission's final report, *Population and the American Future*, were well known before its official release in the spring of 1972. Arguing that population stabilization would yield significant environmental and modest economic benefits,[104] the report called for a series of antinatalist policies,[105] including population and sex education in schools, the liberalization of abortion laws, passage of the Equal Rights Amendment, more access to contraception, and stepped-up enforcement of existing immigration restrictions.[106] In addition, the commission proposed a series of measures to promote the geographic redistribution of the American population.[107] In sum, the commission did not identify a population "crisis," but it suggested that slowing growth would make various economic and social problems easier to solve.

Initially, the White House and the commission each sought to control the diffusion of the commission's findings.[108] During March and April, however, the Nixon administration moved toward outright rejection of the body, stonewalling Rockefeller's designs for a successful launch of *Population and the American Future*.[109] Abortion politics were central to the White House's posture and the ultimate "fiasco" surrounding the final report,[110] but several other factors fueled the White House's treatment of the commission, including the new conservative economic ideas about population growth and intra–Republican Party politics.

In March, the White House debated a full range of options for responding to the commission's final report, ranging from issuing no response at all to praising but dissenting on the abortion issue to attacking on all fronts.[111] At least two teams drafted the president's potential statement upon receiving *Population and the American Future*. One was written by Ray Waldmann, a White House staffer, and David Gergen, the longtime editor of *US News & World Report*, who served as an adviser to presidents Nixon, Ford, Reagan, and Clinton. The Waldmann-Gergen draft praised the commission for its work and had Nixon saying noncommittally, "questions related to population and economic growth are among my concerns." Although it encouraged further dialogue on population matters and reaffirmed support for the Equal Rights Amendment, this draft firmly opposed "unrestricted abortion rights."[112] Patrick Buchanan, the conservative television commentator and sometime candidate for president, who was then a young Nixon speechwriter, wrote the other draft.[113]

More than anyone in the Nixon White House, Buchanan seems to have engaged the new populationist economics and the libertarian critique of population control. Buchanan still assumed rapid population growth would place a "drain upon limited economic and material resources,"[114] so he pointed to the moderating birthrate, not pro–population growth theorists, when identifying as "a chimera" the idea that "the American people are in danger of procreating themselves into poverty."[115] Using the new conservative population ideas, however, Buchanan also cast doubt on the entire range of economic assumptions guiding the population commission, writing, "The central conclusion of the commission—that there is nothing substantive for America to gain from an expanding population—is clearly open to challenge. Just as the commission has enumerated arguments for this novel view—so powerful arguments can be marshaled on behalf of its antithesis."[116] Elsewhere Buchanan wrote, "Malthusian spectres, like the old soldier of the barracks ballad, as often as not just fade away."[117]

The Buchanan draft directly challenged several other recommendations of the population commission. It had Nixon stating that the federal government should assume no role in sex education and that he was "utterly opposed to abortion."[118] Buchanan also cleverly tried to steal the quality-of-life argument back from opponents of population growth. The draft suggested that although one child might promote happiness for some people, "To other middle or lower-income couples from religious or ethnic or racial minorities, the good life may reside in many children and few material possessions."[119] Finally, the Buchanan draft tried to marginalize the Rockefeller commission more directly. It thanked the group for beginning a national conversation about population but cautioned that it had offered "deeply controversial recommendations."[120] It also remarked that in a sprawling democracy, population issues were too important to be decided by a commission or even by the president.

Nixon's growing disdain for the commission and the population issue—and support for the Buchanan position—was evident in the days leading up to the publication of the final report.[121] In a conversation with Ehrlichman on March 30, 1972, Nixon said that Buchanan was the only one capable of writing a speech "to kick that population commission in the ass."[122] The new political calculus surrounding abortion was crucial, and Nixon summed up the issue this way: "Those that vote for abortion, except for a few fanatical libs [liberals?], are not going to vote for Nixon because he comes out for abortion. Those who are against abortion, however, feel so strongly about it from a moral standpoint that they sure as hell will vote against Nixon because of that issue."[123] Ehrlichman echoed the president's reasoning: "The people that are pushing for zero population growth, like the Sierra Club and others, are never going to be pro-Nixon. . . . The people who are offended by abortion can be won over."[124]

Nixon's observations came amid a public relations battle between anti-abortion Catholic leaders and the pro-abortion forces marshaled by Rockefeller and the population lobby. On March 15, the National Catholic Welfare Conference excoriated the commission for walking into an "Ideological Valley of Death."[125] Rockefeller, for his part, met with Catholic leaders, secured the support of the Protestant National Council of Churches, and had his allies at major newspapers write favorable editorials about the commission. Nixon's accurate assessment of abortion politics circa 1972 and his trepidation about supporting the commission were both part of his developing "Catholic Strategy" to win reelection in 1972.[126]

Apart from the abortion issue, Nixon also voiced his disdain for the general anti-growth thrust of the population movement. In a conversation with Henry Kissinger on March 31, Nixon brought up a recently published Malthusian bestseller, *The Limits to Growth*, which he referred to as the "MIT computer study."[127] (The study predicted the collapse of world systems within a century.) "What is the reason, Henry," Nixon asked, "for the total negativism of people in the intellectual community? What in the heck is the reason for it? May I ask why? You know these people."[128] At the same time, Nixon's economic advisers were embracing pro–population growth positions. For example, Hendrick Houthakker, one of the economists on Nixon's Council of Economic Advisers, downplayed overpopulation in a speech at American University and called population control a "simple-minded idea" and a "panacea."[129] "As far as I am aware," Houthakker said, "it has not been demonstrated that there exists any close causal relation between the growth of per capita gross national product and the growth of population, and there is no obvious reason why there should be. The use of facile biological analogies obscures the fact that man is a producer as well as a consumer."[130] There is no smoking gun in the record that Nixon had an epiphany after reading conservative economists on population, but certainly conservative advisers such as Milton Friedman, who met with Nixon four times in 1970 and 1971, would have explained the Right's growing rejection of Malthusian economics.[131]

Nixon chose the milder response to the commission, but the tapes reveal that he would have preferred the much stronger Buchanan draft that forcefully refuted the economic logic of population pessimists. The decision to soft-pedal the rejection of the commission resulted in part from a desire to appease Nelson Rockefeller, the powerful Republican governor of New York and brother of John D. Rockefeller III, or, more precisely, to appease the liberal, eastern, Rockefeller wing of the Republican Party.

On April 3, 1972, Nixon and Ehrlichman discussed the potential results of issuing Buchanan's strong statement. Ehrlichman informed the president that in his many conversations with Nelson Rockefeller, the latter had frequently expressed his appreciation of the White House for appointing his brother chair of the commission. Ehrlichman told Nixon it was "as if Nelson were trying to find some healthy activity for his brother."[132] Ehrlichman said that "the proposal that's coming to you is that you blast them out of the water."[133] He confided, however, "I'm awfully afraid of the effect on our relationship with Nelson if we tee off on this commission."[134] The president agreed, proposing that they "treat with kid gloves" all issues other than abortion.[135]

After the Commission on Population Growth and the American Future issued its majority report on March 27, 1972, the White House delayed comment, prompting several pleading letters from John D. Rockefeller III, who suspected Catholic leaders were pressuring the White House to denounce the report.[136] On May 5, Nixon released his official statement, which after bland words of praise and calls for further research included the now-familiar statement against unrestricted abortion rights (as well as against contraception for adolescents).[137] That same day, Nixon greeted Rockefeller and several members of the commission at the White House, but he failed to invite them to sit on the Oval Office sofa, as was customary on such occasions.[138] During this polite but perfunctory meeting, Nixon asked questions only about overseas population growth.[139]

Nixon's response to the commission's report effectively tabled the issue of domestic population growth. The White House did form an interagency task force to study the commission's finding,[140] but it blocked the distribution of a film that the Department of Health and Human Services had made on population issues and refused to participate in an *ABC News* special on the commission called "Doom or Boom," which aired in January 1973.[141] It was thus anticlimactic when the task force's chair wrote the White House that the "Commission's primary recommendation, namely 'that the nation welcome and plan for a stable population' seems premature and is not adequately supported by the arguments set forth in the report."[142]

Ironically, even as the White House rejected the Commission on Population Growth and the American Future, this body was turning away from the prevailing overpopulation critique. The commission was historically significant not only as an initial skirmish in the culture wars but also because it provided evidence for—and in part faltered because of—the progress of populationist thought. In particular, many of the studies initiated and subsequently published by the commission challenged population alarmism. The research volume on environmental topics, undertaken by Resources for the Future, did suggest that slower population growth would give the nation more time to address its environmental problems but concluded that population growth would play only a minor role in determining pollution levels over the next thirty to fifty years compared to technological development and government resource policy.[143] In the economic volume, Richard Easterlin wrote, "In the case of pollution, the causal role of population seems vastly exaggerated."[144] A majority of papers published by the commission that served as the basis for a conference at the National Bureau of Economic Research undercut the overpopulation paradigm that had launched the commission.[145] These papers claimed that continued population growth would: spur entrepreneurship, new knowledge, and technological innovation; increase savings (and hence investment) while increasing consumption; augment economies of scale; create a more productive labor force; and foster optimism in the future.

Allen Kelley, who would emerge in the 1970s as a leading "revisionist" economic demographer, actually switched from an anti– to a pro–population growth position in the course of his commission-sponsored research. In other words, he came to reject the basic intellectual premise of the commission's work. As Kelley saw it, "the 'population problem' as commonly conceived—too many people—may be a non-problem."[146] He also stressed that the commission erroneously treated population growth rates as a given, when in fact they would decline further in response to continued economic growth.[147] Commenting on Kelley's about-face, Richard Easterlin wrote, "Kelley's experience is representative, I think, of that of many of us who have tried to look into the arguments and evidence about the 'population problem.'"[148]

Population and the American Future did claim that "from an economic point of view, a reduction in the rate of population growth would bring important benefits," including lower poverty rates.[149] It challenged the "growth mystique" at the center of the American political economy.[150] Yet it also noted, "Population Policy is no substitute for social, economic, and environmental policy."[151] Moreover, growing uncertainty regarding the deleterious effects of population growth produced an important shift in perspective; instead of highlighting the costs of continued demographic expansion, commission members were more comfortable challenging critics to explain why more people would be beneficial. Research director Charles Westoff asserted, "The 'costs' of the most likely magnitudes of population growth for the US to the year 2000 will probably not add up to an overwhelming case for a national population policy aimed at achieving ZPG as soon as possible. . . . One change in the frame of reference that might finesse these difficulties is to try to shift the burden of proof to question the argument that increasing the rate of growth or continuing current rates of growth are desirable."[152] In its letter transmitting its final report to Congress, the commission adopted this strange posture of pointing out the lack of future benefits rather than tallying present or future costs. It wrote, "After two years of concentrated effort, we have concluded that, in the long run, no substantial benefits will result from further growth of the Nation's population, rather that the gradual stabilization of our population through voluntary means would contribute significantly to the Nation's ability to solve its problems. We have looked for, and have not found, any convincing economic argument for continued population growth."[153] Privately, Rockefeller seemed perplexed that this was the strongest language a commission created to study the population crisis could muster. "Sort of back door approach," he scribbled across a draft.[154]

Regardless of these subtle distinctions, the commission's moderate (and increasingly challenged) arguments in favor of slowing population growth, as well as its stress on population redistribution, were caught between a new classical economics on the Right and population doomsdayism on the Left. The Commission on Population Growth and the American Future—and the "center" of the population debate that it embodied—was stillborn even before Nixon dismissed its final report.

One additional idea served to dampen zero population growth sentiment within the commission.[155] Increasingly, experts predicted that the increase in the average age of the population resulting from zero population growth would stress America's economy and society. Even Ansley Coale, who in 1958 had authored the leading book arguing that rapid population growth stunted per capita income, now mused that proponents of zero population growth might regret seeing their wishes fulfilled.[156] A focus on aging is not necessarily part of any political or economic program, and indeed, demographers quite reasonably turned their attention to aging when fertility declines followed the Baby Boom. Nevertheless, the emergence of an "aging crisis" in the 1970s reflected the vagaries of the long population debate at a particular moment in time, as well as the triumph of New Right economics.

CHAPTER EIGHT

Population Aged

During the 1970s, fears of a "population explosion" gave way to fears of an "aging crisis," an increase in the average age of the populace that augured dire fiscal consequences. Although it was rooted in very real and apolitical demographic trends—the lower birthrates of the 1970s that followed the huge Baby Boom generation—the preoccupation with the "graying of America" was also a product of, and helped to cement, the pro–population growth perspective. More than three decades later, especially after the Great Recession has wreaked havoc on the nation's balance sheet, and the first Baby Boomers have turned 65, this fiscal apprehension about the graying of America remains the dominant paradigm through which policy makers and the media think about domestic population.[1] The point of this chapter is not to deny that the United States currently faces significant problems associated with funding its entitlement obligations. The Boomers' retirement, which will begin in earnest in 2015, will throw gasoline on the fiscal fire if real reform does not take place. But it is to suggest that our current preoccupation has surprising roots in both the much longer population debate chronicled in this book and the peculiar political economy of the 1970s.

Due to steady gains in life expectancy, the average age of the population had been increasing throughout the twentieth century.[2] The percentage of Americans over age 65 increased from 5.4 percent in 1930 to 10.7 percent in 1976.[3] (The 2009 figure was 12.9 percent.)[4] The Baby Boomers initially slowed the trend but simultaneously put the nation on a path toward an accelerated increase when they had far fewer children than their parents. More than 3.7 million babies were born in the US in 1970, but only about 3 million each year from 1973 to 1977.[5] Beginning in 1972 and for the remainder of the decade, the American fertility rate sat below the "replacement" level of 2.1 births per woman. (The American rate remained higher than in most Western European nations and would move back above the replacement level in the 1980s).[6] During the 1970s, Baby Boomers were still young, but they promised to dramatically increase the average age of the American population as they passed through life. The most dramatic burst of population aging in the US is expected to occur from the present through 2050, when those over 65 will represent 20 percent of the population.[7]

Demographers logically turned their attention to population aging in the 1970s. However, political ideology and the twists and turns of the broader American population debate also drove the new concern. Indeed, the idea of an "aging crisis" continues to be intertwined with politics. During the 2000s, for example, President George W. Bush stressed the fiscal predicament created by an aging populace to drum up support for his plan—rooted in a much broader conservative critique of the state—to privatize Social Security. Yet because the idea of an aging crisis enjoys such expansive and bipartisan acceptance, journalists and policy makers focus on the disagreements about how to combat the perceived problem rather than questioning its existence. Only a distinct minority, for instance liberal *New York Times* columnist Paul Krugman, has challenged the concept that an aging populace is a significant fiscal and macroeconomic problem.[8] Fewer still have paused to consider the concept's origins. The results have been an ahistorical policy debate about aging and an underestimation of the role that the broader population debate played in shaping the contemporary American political economy.

Raw demographics plus political economy propelled the sense of pending calamity. More specifically, the emergence of the aging crisis cannot be understood unless it is placed in the context of two related 1970s shifts that we have already encountered. The first was the erosion of limits-to-growth thought and the concomitant broadening embrace of pro–population growth ideas, which reversed the pessimism that had prevailed throughout the twentieth century. In calling for more babies to support the growing elderly population, the perception of an aging-policy problem gelled smoothly with the rejection of Malthusianism.[9] The rising population optimism of the 1970s reflected the maturation of market-knows-best demography. Moreover, many economists, echoing the 1930s discussion about the role that demographic trends played in a poor economy, claimed that the "stagnation" of the American economy resulted from the declining birthrate, and thus that a higher birthrate was necessary for recovery. The new stagnationists assumed that an aging economy was an unproductive one and that the Baby Boomers' future retirement would require a bumper crop of babies to support it.

The second development propelling the heightened disquiet with the aging population—which was also paramount to the development of pro–population growth economics—was the erosion of the Keynesian consensus among American economists and subsequent revival of conservative "new classical" or "neoliberal" economics. The demise of Keynesianism provided three important theoretical underpinnings for the transformation from a focus on overpopulation to a focus on population aging. First, it robbed opponents of population growth of the Stable Population Keynesian argument that the state could manage economic growth without the stork. Second, although one hardly needed to be anti–welfare state to see that the Social Security system could not pay what was owed, eroding support for Keynesian progressive social and fiscal policy bolstered the idea that public spending on the elderly was poised to spiral out of control. It was primarily members of the political "New Right," motivated by the goal of shrinking the welfare state, who propelled acceptance of the crisis paradigm. Third, the New Right's "supply-side" economics, which replaced the prior Keynesian stress on consumption with a stress on the supply of business investment, fostered specific concerns about the macroeconomics of an aging society. The aging, limits-to-growth, and stagnation debates of the 1970s were interconnected, culminated in the triumph of population optimism, and contributed to the broader laissez-faire revival in the United States.

The Last Gasp of the Zero Population Growth Movement

During the 1970s, the demographic-economic debate in the United States arrived at a place familiar to us today. The theoretical embrace of population growth became the default position in most economic and policy-making circles, with population aging the primary demographic fixation. Although a few environmentalists and ecological economists tilted against the pronatalist windmills, the media and policy makers mostly ignored these Don Quixotes. Even the debate about overseas population growth, long dominated by the Malthusian perspective, evolved into a stalemate between pessimists and optimists, with the latter encompassing those who insisted that population growth is a neutral or even positive phenomenon and those who simply predicted that population growth would level off sooner than expected.[10] Finally, although the field of ecological economics continued to mature and to offer a powerful critique of population growth, it moved to the margins of the American political economy, where it has resided ever since.

Even after the zero population growth movement declined from its late 1960s peak, the Nixon White House helped to defuse the population bomb, and the Commission on Population Growth and the American Future disbanded with little trace in 1972, Malthusian ideas were not entirely expunged. As the rate of population growth in the developing world began outpacing gains in food production,[11] interest groups such as Zero Population Growth and the Population Crisis Committee continued to insist that global population growth acted as a multiplier of environmental damage and was unsustainable on a finite planet, and that America's inordinately large share of global resource consumption carried with it ominous geopolitical ramifications.[12] Although many economists moved toward a pro–population growth posture regarding the United States, most American policy makers continued to believe that rapid population growth in poorer nations impeded their economic development.[13]

Ironically, limits-to-growth ideas received a very temporary shot in the arm just as the population commission fizzled. Recall that President Nixon told Henry Kissinger in 1972 of his distaste for a pessimistic "MIT computer study," which harnessed an algorithm based on crude projections of resources, pollution, and population to predict the collapse of the world system in one hundred years. This study, conducted by a team of MIT researchers and funded by a small multinational organization of business leaders, academics, technocrats, and philanthropists called the Club of Rome, was published as *The Limits to Growth* (1972).[14] Its authors were protégés of Jay Forrester, a computer scientist at MIT's Sloan School of Management who had applied the military's computer-based "systems analysis" approach to a variety of civilian problems. *The Limits to Growth*'s model ("World 3," an update of earlier models by Forrester) contained five variables: "world population, industrialization, pollution, food production, and resource depletion."[15] Assuming unchanging trends in these variables, the authors concluded that "the limits to growth on this planet will be reached sometime in the next hundred years. The most probable result will be a rather sudden and uncontrollable decline in both population and industrial capacity."[16] Although it was "possible to alter these growth trends and to establish a condition of ecological and economic stability that is sustainable far into the future," doing so would require a radical retreat from the pursuit of economic growth and an embrace of the stationary state.[17]

The Limits to Growth has since sold over thirty million copies in dozens of languages, but it failed to move the needle toward Malthusianism. Indeed, the firestorm of controversy it set off within both scientific and lay circles, detailed in a moment, helped erode support for zero population growth sentiment even as it temporarily directed attention toward it.[18] Nonetheless, in the mid 1970s, the ecologically based critique of population growth morphed into a deepening attack not so much on population trends but on the desirability of "growth" of all kinds. After the campaign for far-reaching national population policy failed during the Nixon years, this broader debate about growth became the primary lens through which Americans engaged population–resource issues. The conversation moved from the potential costs and benefits of "zero population growth" to those of "zero economic growth."

Now, aesthetic, moral, and psychological critiques of growth, which had been popular at midcentury but recently were subsumed under the population movement's ecological critique, briefly returned to the fore. A leading figure espousing these new critiques was Ezra Mishan of the London School of Economics. In the tradition of John Kenneth Galbraith's *The Affluent Society*, Mishan bemoaned the never-ending quest for higher production—"growthmania"—and the assumption that technology is a panacea. He yearned for a more humane, less polluting, and decentralized capitalism that does not equate consumption with happiness.[19] Mishan argued that societies should prioritize social welfare and happiness, not GNP, claiming he was "not a zero economic-growth man because, in fact, if we could measure some standard of human contentment, we'd find out that we've been on the negative growth path a lot already."[20] Mishan believed that, due to the "Jones effect" (i.e., the felt need to maintain one's relative wealth regardless of absolute improvement), "The goodies proliferate but society feels no better off."[21] Perhaps the most widely read antigrowth treatise of the 1970s was E. F. Schumacher's *Small Is Beautiful*, which we have already encountered.[22] Schumacher's larger project was to build a new "Buddhist economics" that would value the worker above the product and achieve harmony with natural resources. Other writers anticipated myriad salutary outcomes from a zero-economic-growth society, including an economy geared less toward producing new needs than toward enhancing services and the quality of life, a less frenzied work life and ethic, and a heightened sense of community.[23]

During the 1970s, the challenge to the sacred cow of economic growth resonated with a contingent of liberals who advocated a postmaterialist society, reflecting what scholars have labeled a "therapeutic" cultural turn.[24] Also some policy makers, primarily but not exclusively liberals, sought a balance between higher production and quality-of-life and environmental goals. Congress convened a series of hearings in 1973 and 1974—framed primarily by the OPEC oil embargo–induced energy crisis—on *Growth and Its Implications for the Future.*[25] The Carter administration initially embraced the critique of growth, convening a 1978 White House Conference on Balanced National Growth and Economic Development and inviting E. F. Schumacher to the White House.[26]

By 1980, however, the limits-to-economic-growth critique (along with its zero-population-growth predecessor) was a mere shadow of its former self.[27] The concept of "balanced growth" was so vague and embodied so many contradictions that its definition depended on whom one asked. Environmentalists, for instance, imagined a fundamental recalibration of the American growth machine, whereas business interests imagined a slightly less polluting form of the status quo. For policy makers, the concept of "balanced growth" could not deal with variations below the highest level of generality. For example, it could not ameliorate the tensions between lawmakers in the booming "Sunbelt" region of the South and West and those in the stagnating northeastern "Rustbelt." Not could it address the intransigent racial and social inequalities of the city. Even if policy makers could have agreed on a definition of balanced growth, the waning of the Keynesian consensus cast doubt on the premise that they could ever engineer this growth.

In addition, mainstream environmental groups, as well as reproductive rights groups traditionally interested in demographic matters (e.g., Planned Parenthood), abandoned the population issue during the 1970s. And the mainstream press dramatically reduced its coverage of population matters.[28] Three factors go far in explaining this retreat. The first is increasing immigration to the US, which remade American politics and caused many elite Americans, regardless of political persuasion, to shy away from the topic of population growth because they associated it with anti-immigrationism and hence bigotry.[29] (And as a result, anti–population growth positions became disproportionally expressed by anti-immigration organizations.) Second, the maturation of abortion politics and the culture wars made all reproductive issues fraught with peril. Finally, lower fertility in the 1970s (which demonstrated the partial demographic if not institutional success of the zero population growth movement) reduced the urgency of the population debate. This was true even though, given the momentum of population growth and the vagaries of fertility—and the widespread acceptance of the cyclical fertility theories of Richard Easterlin and others—the birthrates of the 1970s hardly signaled zero population growth ahead for the United States.[30] The Census Bureau estimated that zero immigration and an immediate movement to the replacement fertility rate would lead to population stabilization in 2039, whereas a gradual movement to replacement fertility (a much more realistic scenario, but of course an incorrect one as the US has become the fast-growing outlier in the industrialized world) would lead to stabilization by 2062.[31]

Although the culture wars and the declining birthrate were important to the disavowal of Malthusianism, the shifting political economy in the United States—specifically, the laissez-faire, neoliberal revival—was as important if not paramount. During the 1970s and 1980s, the political Right stepped in to fill the vacuum left by the fractured population debate; market-knows-best demography expanded as it fused with supply-side economics.

At first, the revolt against Malthusianism, taking the form of a backlash against *The Limits to Growth,* was broader than any particular political-economic agenda. All sides of the political spectrum castigated the book. The *New York Times* declared it to be an "empty, misleading work."[32] Other critics suggested that *Limits to Growth* was a crude rehashing of the principle of diminishing returns based on poor data (excepting its valid population projections). They also emphasized that the study was oblivious to the ability of the market to adjust to scarcities and to humanity's capacity to regulate its environment and technologies and improve its productivity. William Nordhaus, a Yale economist on President Jimmy Carter's Council of Economic Advisers, wrote in the *American Economic Review*, "Economists have for the most part ridiculed the new [Malthusian] view of growth, arguing that it is merely Chicken Little Run Wild."[33]

Still, Nordhaus believed that the limits-to-growth paradigm warranted serious consideration, and other mainstream economists praised the book for opening eyes to the ultimate finiteness of the earth's resources. Paul Samuelson, an MIT Nobel laureate and leader of his generation of American Keynesians, noted, "It may be that in order to convince public opinion on the need to do something about ecology and not just talk about it, the overselling of . . . the Club of Rome, of biological scientists like the distinguished Paul Ehrlich . . . may still be found to earn a gold star for good performance in that court of final judgment."[34] Nobel laureate and theorist of economic growth Robert Solow roundly dismissed the MIT study and yet wrote, "I hope nobody will conclude that I believe the problems of population control, environmental degradation, and resource exhaustion to be unimportant, or that I am one of those people who believe that an adequate response to such problems is a vague confidence that some technological solution will turn up. On the contrary, it is precisely because these are important problems that public policy had better be based on sound and careful analysis."[35] Other economists who aligned themselves with neither the Malthusians nor the cornucopianists advocated new controls over technology and public policies (e.g., pollution taxes) to correct for the negative externalities of market activity.[36] Those who favored reform rather than cessation of economic growth also sought to redefine economic growth to account for goods not traded on the open market and, most important, to account for human welfare.[37] Richard Easterlin, whose work supported the optimists, reminded his readers that economic growth for its own sake is little more than a treadmill.[38]

A coterie of conservative and market-oriented economists sought to bury the limits-to-growth idea. These conservative leaders of a new classical economics reinvigorated a defense of economic growth, which, combined with the market-knows-best demography gaining strength since the 1960s, ironically challenged the population skepticism of the original classical economists of the eighteenth and nineteenth centuries.[39] Pro-growth economists stressed that economic and population growth had revolutionized standards of living since the Industrial Revolution and claimed that further growth would enhance human happiness. As resource optimists had done since the 1930s, defenders of growth maintained that the market would produce and allocate goods efficiently so as to prevent scarcities. In addition, they claimed that economic growth need not increase pollution and might, in fact, create the demand for a clean environment and provide societies with the wealth to combat pollution.[40]

In the late 1970s, pro-growth advocates also used arguments rooted in the goal of equity. "A no-growth society would work most severely against the interests of the poorer members of society," wrote economist Richard Zeckhauser, who also claimed that the anti-growth campaign was a misguided project of the contented affluent.[41] Wilfred Beckerman, a British economist who titled one of his books *Small Is Stupid* in a rebuke to Schumacher, argued, "A failure to maintain economic growth means continued poverty, disease, squalor, degradation and slavery to soul-destroying toil for countless millions of the world's population."[42] Finally, futurists dismissed limits-to-growth thought on less traditional grounds, for example, by promoting space colonization as one way to create a safety valve for human activities and engineer a "limitless future."[43]

Even if scholars have exaggerated the novelty of his ideas, Julian Simon was a pivotal figure in the modern US population debate, an extender of market-knows-best demography and a key link between population optimism and the broader neoliberal revival. An economist at the University of Illinois for most of his career, Simon had begun his population studies in the late 1960s as a conventional Malthusian. He recalled in his memoirs, "I believed that rapid population growth was the main obstacle to the world's economic development and one of the two main threats to humankind (nuclear war being the other)."[44] Simon's first article on population, drawing on an earlier focus on the economics of advertising, recommended methods for marketing family planning programs in the developing world.[45] Almost immediately after joining the population movement, however, Simon's views shifted 180 degrees to a full rejection of Malthusianism. Simon's about-face came partly from studying the historical analyses of Simon Kuznets, Richard Easterlin, and others who noted the absence of a strict relationship between population and economic growth, as well as the work of the agricultural and resource economists Ester Boserup, Theodore Schultz, Harold Barnett, and Chandler Morse. Simon's main epiphany, however, came during a 1969 trip to Washington, D.C., ironically to visit USAID to discuss family planning programs. Seeing a road sign for the Iwo Jima Memorial, Simon remembered a eulogy by a chaplain who had wondered how many geniuses had unnecessarily perished at that battle. Simon recalled: "Then I thought, have I gone crazy? What business do I have trying to help arrange it that fewer human beings will be born, each of whom might be a Mozart or a Michelangelo or an Einstein—or simply a joy to his or her family or community, and a person who will enjoy life?"[46]

Simon accelerated trends among professional demographers. Although still concerned about rapid population growth, especially in the developing world, "demographic revisionism" adopted a more optimistic view regarding the economic and social consequences of such growth than had been the norm throughout the twentieth century. By the 1970s, a majority of demographers, though not celebrating population growth to Simon's unbridled extent, did point to several factors that mitigated overpopulation concerns, especially the ongoing Green Revolution in agriculture and the continued diffusion of family planning in the developed world.[47] Simon, however, went well beyond most demographers not simply by making peace with population growth but by enthusiastically embracing its unlimited continuance.[48]

Much of Simon's effort to dismantle Malthusianism involved demonstrating that the costs of many commodities were declining and bore little relationship to demographic trends. Simon wagered Paul Ehrlich in 1980 that the cost of five metals would be lower in ten years. Simon famously won, although metal prices hardly indicate environmental quality, and Simon later refused a bet that would have incorporated diverse measures of environmental decline.[49] Simon highlighted the long-term consequences of population change as opposed to what he saw as the population movement's short time horizon (a generation or sometimes "a single hot summer").[50] Simon emphasized that population density drives economic growth by producing economies of scale, not only in transportation, markets, job creation, etc., but also in expenditures on human capital. (One of population pessimists' main arguments is that societies cannot keep pace with the human capital needs of rapidly increasing populations.) Above all, in keeping with his original inspiration from Iwo Jima, Simon argued that human beings, not only geniuses, are the *Ultimate Resource*, and that their steady increase in numbers is all the better for driving scientific innovation and human happiness.[51] Consistent with his libertarianism, Simon believed that people have the right to a wide range of options for controlling fertility, including abortion. Ironically, today's pro-life movement has adopted many of his economic arguments.

Simon was an important conduit between market-knows-best demographers and the economists and conservative intellectuals who propounded the American revival of classical economics. Friedrich Hayek sent Simon his only "fan letter to a professional colleague."[52] Simon became a senior fellow at the Heritage Foundation, where he helped shape the Reagan administration's "neutral" position on population growth in the developing world and participated in the conservative critique of the environmental movement. (Reagan spoke the language of overpopulation in the 1960s, but, like so many conservatives, subsequently switched to the anti-Malthusian camp.)[53] Simon also had links to such futurists as Herman Kahn, with whom he edited a book espousing the resource-optimism position.[54] By the 1980s, Simon's ideas had become ingrained in the philosophy of leading conservative intellectuals. For instance, activist George Gilder summed up the new conservative mantra regarding population and the limits to growth in his well-known *Wealth and Poverty* (1981). After criticizing the population scare and what he saw as the fantasy that resources can run out, Gilder proffered, "Our greatest and only resource is the miracle of human creativity in a relation of openness to the divine."[55]

Simon and other market-knows-best demographers provided a necessary corrective to the excessive rhetoric of the zero population growth movement (which takes nothing away from the thinking of serious ecological economists such as Herman Daly). Paul Ehrlich and those sympathetic to his perspective complained justifiably that the optimists' environmental thought was myopic; it emphasized improvements in pollution control, for example, but ignored issues related to the total ecosystem, such as declining biodiversity. In addition, conservatives largely ignored the alleged aesthetic benefits of a smaller population identified by theorists ever since John Stuart Mill. Simon, for example, suggested that one of the primary benefits of population growth is increased road development, which spurs economic development, but he did not pause to consider the aesthetics of roads. The fact of human-induced climate change did not trouble population optimists in the 1970s. During that period, a few scientists did propose that human activity was warming the planet, but others predicted a new ice age,[56] and, overall, climate change was a fringe topic. Conservative participants in the population–resources debate focused on their opponents' exaggerated claims of resource exhaustion and on the ability of markets to solve pollution problems.[57]

Some economists adopted more nuanced positions than either the blanket rejection or boisterous celebration of population and economic growth. One inspiration was that economic growth could be retooled and reformed to make it less polluting and ultimately compatible with population growth. Whereas Stable Population Keynesians tended to define economic growth in standard terms, a new generation of resource theorists held that zero population growth and positive economic growth could coexist harmoniously if the latter were reformed so that it produced "zero net environmental destruction."[58]

But in the end, market-knows-best demography made significant inroads by the late 1970s.[59] Demographers and a wider swath of social scientists and political writers adopted an upbeat view of the economic consequences of population growth. In addition to affirming the pro–population growth precepts previously laid out (e.g., population growth drives innovation and creates economies of scale), new lines of argument treated population growth as endogenous—that is, responsive to economic change. These models viewed population growth as more cyclical and less threatening than did earlier theories, which treated it as exogenous.[60]

Populationist ideas strengthened in the context of a traditional debate that assumed ongoing population and economic growth. Yet as the lower birthrates of the early 1970s persisted and the economy weakened after 1973, ensuring future economic growth became a more pressing problem than identifying the ecological limits to it. The triumph of pro–population growth ideas resulted as much from a debate about the potential *decline* or stagnation of the US population as it did from the rise of conservative optimism regarding population *growth*. The pronatalist position is strengthened when a sluggish birthrate occurs amidst an equally sluggish economy.

The New Stagnation Debate

The 1970s dialogue about the prospect of future population decline harked back the 1930s one about economic-demographic "stagnation," but at the same time it was wrapped up with and contributed to the more recent ascendancy of conservative economic ideas. Writing in the 1970s, demographer Norman Ryder observed, "Little is heard currently of the stagnation thesis, probably because we have had a moderately high [economic] growth rate for a long time, and we have acquired some confidence in the efficacy of contracyclical fiscal and monetary mechanisms to check persistent large-scale unemployment."[61] A serious economic downturn and shifting political winds, however, shattered the Keynesian consensus shared by American policy makers and economists since the late 1930s.[62] As a result, economists flailed in all directions to explain the weak economy. Some economists drew inspiration from preeminent midcentury conservative Joseph Schumpeter and averred that the Western economies were in the trough of a long-term cycle determined by the waxing and waning of technological innovation. Even Jay Forrester, the MIT business professor whose work inspired *Limits to Growth,* pointed to long waves in the economy, rather than the normal fluctuations of the business cycle or demography, to explain macroeconomic lethargy.[63]

By the end of the decade, the economists who held sway were adherents of laissez-faire, and many were aligned with the "monetarist" school of Milton Friedman, which rejected the Keynesian stress on personal consumption and asked little of government in economic policy making except sound monetary policy. The conservative body of ideas that came to be known colloquially as "supply-side" economics countered the Keynesian stress on consumption and emphasized the supply of investment. And as Americans debated 1970s economic "malaise," demographic variables, especially the lower birthrates, loomed large.

Historian Robert Collins writes that by the end of the 1970s, a "political economy of stagflation" had emerged in the US.[64] ("Stagflation" connoted the combination of high unemployment and high inflation.) More specifically, worries that the supposedly mutually reinforcing factors of reduced population growth and listless economic performance would engender secular (long-term) economic stagnation united many liberals and conservatives in a revitalized celebration of population growth. (The revival of Keynes-Hansen stagnation theory, which theorized that lethargic population growth had exacerbated the Great Depression, was a decidedly ironic development given the overall evisceration of Keynesianism!) By the end of the decade, the debate was increasingly framed not as "Should we move toward zero growth and how?" but as "What are the consequences of the coming zero-growth society?" New stagnationists, like their predecessors in the 1930s, worried that a zero population growth society would: (1) sap productivity; (2) stunt labor mobility; (3) produce a less creative workforce; and (4) ultimately prevent full employment.[65] They also suggested that a no-growth society would suffer from an excess of expensive, elderly dependents. For example economist Clarence Barber, who had been an important population optimist during the 1950s debate, asserted that the return on capital decreased in tandem with the population. He reaffirmed the stagnationists' demographic interpretation of the Great Depression and thought that the sluggish birthrate of the modern era augured future economic malaise.[66] Even some scholars who considered the 1970s economic downturn to be temporary, such as Larry Neal, today a well-known economic historian at the University of Illinois, contended that the "birth dearth" was "primarily responsible for the current [economic] slowdown."[67] Although he conceded that a demographically stagnant America would not be "the Greek tragedy outlined by [Alvin] Hansen," neither would it be a "lighthearted romance."[68]

Most economists who wrote about these matters did not have a political agenda. And avowed conservatives and liberals alike warned that the sluggish birthrate contributed to economic malaise. But importantly, conservatives linked stagnationist ideas to their new stress on the supply of investment (even if they tended to be uncomfortable with the word "stagnation," which evoked memories of Keynes and also implied that capitalism had run its course). Whereas Keynes's analysis of the weak economy in the 1930s had linked insufficient consumption to the declining birthrate, economists at the vanguard of the neoliberal revival argued that the lower birthrate caused *overconsumption* and thus a poor supply of investment. Even if they doubted the arrival of a new stagnation, many conservative economists who had rejected the Malthusianism of the late 1960s and early 1970s readily connected the fertility decline of the 1970s to that decade's "stagflation" and flat productivity.[69] Simply put, supply-side economics prominently integrated demographic variables. In the bluntly titled *Grow or Die!,* libertarian James Weber argued, "In today's Welfare State, inflation is not a solution to the problems caused by a declining rate of population growth but a major problem resulting from the population decline."[70] (Weber also showed the affinities between the pro-life and pro–population growth positions.)[71] Although conservatives did not necessarily list the sluggish birthrate as the leading factor in America's economic decline compared to burdensome regulations and other policies, which, in their view, stunted investment and productivity, they took for granted that a listless birthrate harmed the economy.[72]

Not everyone abided stagnation theory and its implied call for a new Baby Boom. An old guard of population pessimists approved of the zero-population-growth and zero-economic-growth society that seemed to be approaching. Joseph Spengler, for instance, continued to argue that population limitation would enhance aggregate economic welfare and income per worker, especially by boosting savings.[73] "It should prove easy for societies to adjust to slow, zero, or slightly negative rates of population growth," Spengler wrote in 1975.[74] Further along Stable Population Keynesian lines, others stressed a potential boost to personal consumption,[75] and Norman Ryder argued that "purely demographic characteristics are probably of relatively small importance as determinants of the development of capital equipment, employment levels, and the pace of social change, and therefore of the economic efficiency of a society."[76] Cal Tech's Alan Sweezy claimed that appropriate fiscal and monetary policies could smooth out any economic difficulties resulting from zero population growth, which ultimately might enhance macroeconomic performance.[77] Even Richard Easterlin, in general a friend to the populationists, wrote a few years after this debate, "If population growth were a major stimulus to economic growth, as the stagnation arguments imply, then one might expect to find that higher population growth and higher economic growth go together. . . . The answer is yes for the period through 1870–1913 . . . and no for the period since then."[78] A few scholars tried to resuscitate the traditional argument that population growth exacerbates inequality; they believed, among other points, that such growth limits the economic mobility of poor families (who have more children than the rich) and concentrates wealth among real estate holders.[79]

However, the prevailing sense of population growth's distributional effects had reversed since the 1930s—and indeed represented an about-face from two hundred years of economic-demographic theory. Especially within the liberal camp, several economists who just a few years prior had supported the economic logic of the zero population growth movement now bemoaned the prospect of zero growth when it became a distinct possibility, as if they had finally reached the river crossing to a beautiful meadow but then decided it was too dangerous to cross. In addition to the prevailing worry that slower population growth was exacerbating the economic downturn, liberals now proposed, as did market-knows-best demographers, that slower growth would produce a less equitable society.[80] For example, MIT economist Lester Thurow, who had been sympathetic to the zero population growth movement during its heyday, now wrote that in a zero-growth economy, "the distribution of family income would gradually grow more unequal, blacks would fall farther behind whites, and the share going to female earnings would fall below what it would otherwise be."[81] Thurow suggested that in the absence of growth, markets become "zero-sum."[82] Well-known political scientist Mancur Olson believed that it was "entirely possible that a no-growth society would be torn by conflict over distribution."[83] And Willard Johnson, an MIT economist who specialized in the developing world, urged that society not make the poor "buy" a zero-growth society; he asserted that no-growth advocates such as Ezra Mishan ignored the values of the poor and their reasonable desire for a higher material standard of living.[84] Although this was an exaggerated charge, it was not unwarranted. When pressed on the question of what advice to give the developing world, Mishan had said: "Don't take the Western path. If you want to take any path, take the path that Gandhi outlined: intermediate technology. Learn to be satisfied with little. It can be done. It has been done for centuries."[85] Even Kenneth Boulding, who had called for a "spaceman economy" cognizant of ecological limits, now voiced concerns that the stationary state would be dull, tend toward a net investment of zero, and be fraught with distributional difficulties. "In the stationary state, there is no escape from the rigors of scarcity," he argued, predicting increased conflict between the generations and the development of "mafia-type societies in which government is primarily an institution for redistributing income toward the powerful and away from the weak."[86] Boulding hoped that political innovation would ameliorate these problems, but his views still represented a stunning retreat from his earlier position.

Due to the weak economy, the 1970s debate about growth focused on the alleged effects of a zero-*economic*-growth society, which can exist with any number of demographic scenarios. But importantly, the zero-population-growth critique also shrank because now, more than ever, economists and demographers treated zero population growth and zero economic growth as synonymous. Although 1970s theorists sometimes allowed that a smaller population would increase ecologically sustainable consumption per capita, they generally claimed that population growth fueled the economy, environmental considerations aside. Stable Population Keynesians, in contrast, had put forward that zero population growth need not cause zero economic growth.

Interestingly, a theoretical separation between zero population growth and zero economic growth remained in the context of the developing world, since demographic transition theory assumed that economic growth there was an essential precursor to lowering birthrates. And occasionally, population economists imported this premise to the domestic debate. Following the new household economics outlined in the previous chapter, some theorists supposed that a higher standard of living would induce Americans to have fewer babies but lavish upon them more human capital. Harvard economist Marc Roberts summed up his opposition to zero economic growth and support for zero population growth this way: "I can hope to improve the lot of all living individuals but still wish to limit the number I need to worry about."[87] Yet in the main, individuals who rallied passionately to the defense of growth in the industrialized world—and also those who attacked it—drew few distinctions between population and economic growth. They assumed that the two necessarily operated in tandem. Thus even demographers who worried about environmental degradation and advocated further reductions in global fertility increasingly tended to reject the goal of zero population growth. For instance, leading French demographer Alfred Sauvy had long been skeptical of what he saw as the "mysticism" and sloppy empiricism of the zero population growth movement. He was concerned about the social and economic disruptions resulting from a sudden shift to zero economic and population growth. In the context of France's declining fertility during the 1970s, he espoused an explicitly pronatalist position and argued that higher fertility would ameliorate inflation and poor economic performance.[88]

The marriage of antinatalism and support for economic growth has always offered the best chance for anti–population growth ideas to resonate in mainstream American discourse. Due to the perceived conflation of zero population growth and zero economic growth, however, few observers urged a population reduction in tandem with robust economic progress. And increasingly few economists wanted the state to actively pursue any economic or demographic outcomes. Liberals' dwindling support for zero population growth and anxiety about demographically induced stagnation reflected not only a continued withering of Stable Population Keynesianism, with its principle that a smaller population would create a more equitable society, but also a broader decline of the overall Keynesian paradigm among American economists as an explanatory and policy-making tool. Almost by definition, the decline of Keynesianism carried with it waning confidence in macroeconomic policies and policy makers, and doubt that state policy could alleviate any short-term economic difficulties resulting from the transition to zero population growth.

It is telling that Alfred Sauvy also fretted about the economic and social consequences of the increase in average age that initially comes with zero population growth. The new population optimism and the new stagnation debate were both intimately related to the emergence of aging as a social-policy problem, and all three developments combined to create today's pro–population growth political economy.

Rethinking the "Aging Crisis"

The aging crisis paradigm resulted not only from shifting demographic fundamentals but also from the significant economic downturn of the 1970s, the rise of the New Right and anti-tax sentiment, and the Republicans' victory in the 1980 elections. But its origins stretch far back to 1935 with the beginning of Social Security and into the postwar years, when projections of the program's finances (and later of the new Medicaid and Medicare programs) assumed a buoyant birthrate. In 1958, Paul

Samuelson claimed that the Social Security system's pay-as-you-go nature increased aggregate economic welfare and that the elderly fared better amid a growing rather than a stable population.[89] In 1966, the Brookings Institution's Henry Aaron confirmed Samuelson's findings by locating a "social insurance paradox": given steady population growth, the reserve fund for a public pension program grows at the same rate as population because current contributions happily exceed future benefits.[90] The logical extension of Samuelson's and Aaron's work was that a slowing population undermines the rationale behind a pay-as-you-go pension system. Under such conditions, younger workers are required to accept a lower future rate of return, steadily increasing the redistribution from the young to the old and creating the prospect of intergenerational conflict. Furthermore, the idea that a "generation gap" based on social attitudes had formed in the 1960s reinforced pessimistic predictions of fiscal intergenerational battles.[91] Samuelson and Aaron were supporters of increased social spending and worried about the ability of the Social Security system to absorb an aging population. More conservative economists directly attacked the macroeconomic consequences of Social Security. Milton Friedman argued as early as 1957 that the program depressed savings (because citizens assumed that the state would provide for them in old age), though Aaron and others vigorously contested this hypothesis in the 1960s.[92]

Three main economic reservations surrounding a graying population picked up steam in the 1970s. The first two derive from the fact that a population growing older increases the ratio between "dependent" retirees and workers who pay employment taxes. (The ratio of workers per Social Security beneficiary was 16:1 in 1950, and 5:1 in 1960, and is currently about 3:1. By 2025 it may decrease to 2.3:1.)[93] This increase in the dependency ratio could, pessimists feared, lead to one of two undesirable outcomes. First, if benefit levels were maintained, the result would be fiscal havoc—either massive tax increases or an ultimate bankrupting of America's pension and healthcare systems.[94] But second, if benefit levels were cut, population aging would reverse the significant reduction in poverty among the elderly that followed the creation of Social Security; being able to draw on fewer working-age taxpayers to fund the system would undoubtedly put a squeeze on entitlements.[95] To these two outcomes some economists added a third: they linked the slowly aging workforce to the negligible productivity gains, slow growth, and myriad other macroeconomic problems of the 1970s—and predicted that the aging of the Baby Boomers would exacerbate them.[96] In this vein, economies with a large share of young people are more dynamic and productive than older ones.[97]

In contrast, those who were (and are) sanguine about an aging population held that economic growth can pay for an older society. These 1970s optimists asserted that the elderly should be seen not as a burden but as productive members of society. The rising share of older workers could, in fact, increase living standards and productivity because the elderly tend to work harder and offer more human capital and experience than the young, and because the elderly of the future should be healthier and able to work longer than their predecessors.[98] Most healthcare costs occur in the last few months of life—regardless of when they come. In theory, gains derived from these trends could offset higher benefit costs. The optimist camp also noted that modern societies have long coped with population aging and that the social and legal definitions of "old" are constantly evolving. Some economists argued for abandoning mandatory retirement ages, not on fiscal grounds but because, in their view, they discriminate against the elderly. The camp sanguine about population aging further argued that the "total dependency ratio"—which takes into account children as well as the elderly—would be lower in 2040 than it was in 1970 because of a smaller number of children. And the elderly would gradually become less dependent.[99] (The pessimists vehemently countered the "total dependency ratio" argument by noting that the elderly are more expensive to care for than the young, particularly in terms of federal expenditures.)[100] If they did identify a problem for policy makers at all, optimists maintained that policies such as modestly increasing immigration, taxes, and/or the retirement age would be sufficient.[101]

Policy makers moved toward a "crisis" outlook gradually. After he departed as Social Security's chief actuary in 1970, Robert Myers fired one of the first warning shots in the future pension-policy war, suggesting that lower birthrates threatened the program.[102] Early in the 1970s, Social Security's advisory council was still optimistic about the program's long-term fiscal future, and benefits expanded significantly in 1972.[103] Beginning in 1975, however, as Social Security ran a deficit and the overall economy remained weak, the advisory council adopted a pessimistic posture based on lower fertility, slowing wage growth, and higher inflation, which ratcheted up benefits and unemployment and sucked away revenue.[104] The deteriorating macroeconomic climate spurred private and public research on aging and the welfare state as well as the creation of a Special Senate Committee on Aging.[105]

By the second half of the 1970s, many social scientists regardless of political persuasion were worried about the economic effects of an increasing average age of the population (and the decreasing birthrate), but the tone remained moderate, and few predicted calamity. After all, the pace of population aging had remained fairly consistent throughout the twentieth century, and Social Security had recently returned to a surplus footing.[106] Economist Robert Clark, for example, put the problem this way: "All of our projections indicate that the movement toward zero population growth will require even greater transfers of income to support the elderly, with the Social Security system being forced to bear much of the burden."[107] Leading demographer Nathan Keyfitz worried that older, less free-spending consumers might act as a drag on economic growth, but he observed that the empirical links between aging and economic performance were tenuous.[108] Keyfitz was also concerned that a stagnant population would stunt individuals' labor mobility as older workers clung to their jobs, but he concluded that the system could adjust, with workers becoming "more concerned with pay and the goods they can buy than with rank and title."[109] Several economists emphasized that the fiscal consequences of an increasing old-age dependency ratio would be offset by a reduction in social spending on the young.[110] Brian Reddaway, the British Stable Population Keynesian who gained prominence in the 1930s, declared that "one should dismiss the increased pensions bogey as quantitatively negligible, so far as it rests on demographic factors."[111] A notable exception to the prevailing view was conservative Harvard economist Martin Feldstein, who later chaired President Reagan's Council of Economic Advisers; in the mid 1970s, he unambiguously identified a "social security crisis."[112] Feldstein also claimed that Social Security reduced savings and stunted capital accumulation.[113]

In the short term, the new anxiety only modestly affected policy.[114] The 1977 Social Security amendments addressed the deficit by raising taxes slightly and lowering benefits but kept intact the expansionary trajectory of the program.[115] At the end of the 1970s, the Carter administration incorporated a warning about population aging into its budget projections, estimating that current demographic trends augured an increase in the total tax burden from 33 percent of GDP in 1980 to 50 percent in 2030.[116] Moreover, the 1970s had exposed a fundamental weakness of Social Security: its tax structure left it vulnerable to economic downturns. And after skyrocketing interest rates and inflation, and two recessions, in the early 1980s, demographers adopted a more urgent tone. In 1980, for example,

Keyfitz compared Social Security to a chain letter that would inevitably fail.[117]

The Republican victory in the 1980 election helped turned a simmer into a boil, as the accompanying attacks on the social contract and Keynesian progressive fiscal policy reinforced the preoccupation with the budget-busting threat of an aging population. In 1981, President Reagan declared a Social Security crisis.[118] That year also saw the creation of the bipartisan National Commission on Social Security Reform, often referred to as the Greenspan Commission after its chair, future Federal Reserve head Alan Greenspan. The commission's recommendations, issued in early 1983 and brokered by Senators Robert Dole (R-Kan.) and Daniel Patrick Moynihan (D-N.Y.), were the basis for that year's Social Security amendments,[119] which increased coverage (a clever way to augment revenue in the short term), delayed cost-of-living increases, imposed taxes on the Social Security benefits of better-off recipients, raised the Social Security payroll tax rate, created what we know as the Social Security Trust Fund, and instituted a gradual increase in the age for full benefits from 65 to 67.[120] The committee was optimistic that it had solved the problem for at least seventy-five years, with Greenspan reporting that it would take "a very adverse economic scenario" to jeopardize retirement benefits.[121]

Yet Reagan's (and Feldstein's) crisis tag stuck. The early-1980s recession, which occurred when the American birthrate was only beginning its recovery, shored up the notion that an aging workforce would exacerbate macroeconomic malaise. In other words, the graying of the American population was seen as not only worrisome for the future of Social Security but also contributive to the current economic doldrums. Less tied to the immediate business cycle, however, belief that there was an aging crisis also reflected growing antipathy to the state among policy makers and the general public; it was inextricably linked to and helped consolidate the anti–welfare state agenda of a conservative movement rejuvenated by Reagan's election. Put another way, the current fiscal crisis in America, and the fact that balancing the budget without deep cuts in Medicare, Medicaid, and Social Security now seems next to impossible, has masked the contingency and ideological origins of the aging issue. Three decades ago, the potentially significant problems associated with the Baby Boomers still resided in the distant future, but the immediate politics of a splintering Democratic coalition and a rising conservative critique of the New Deal loomed large. Yes, liberals and conservatives alike expressed concerns about aging, but it was primarily conservatives who deployed demographic trends as a powerful tool in their larger project of welfare state retrenchment. An emphasis on demography allowed opponents of the welfare state to point to fiscal forces seemingly out of their control as they called for retrenchment rather than stating their ideological preferences unambiguously. Engaged in a larger critique of escalating social welfare spending, many conservatives prematurely claimed that Social Security was a fiscal house of cards and proposed that the system become entirely voluntary. In the words of economist Phil Mullan, "Ageing is used as a neutral, non-ideological, apolitical pretext for legitimising reductions in public and especially, welfare spending. The assumption of 'too many old people' impresses the need and urgency for welfare reform."[122]

Put in the simplest terms possible, the aging of America moved from policy challenge to crisis because taxing the wealthy to fund the welfare state, or sustaining large deficits (at least politically popular ones) were both taken off the table in the United States in the 1970s and 1980s. Moreover, the waning of Keynesianism and the concomitant embrace of the new classical economics buttressed the theoretical conception of an aging crisis. First, the erosion of the Keynesian consensus weakened a basic counterpoint to the fiscal anxieties surrounding the graying of America, namely that the US could simply borrow the money to finance the Baby Boomers' retirement and then pay off the debt when the Boomers had died and been replaced by the smaller cohorts born after them. A society can choose to redistribute resources from one group to any other in any way it sees fit. (Some experts in these years indeed worried that public spending was skewing too heavily toward the elderly at the cost of children.)[123] But in an era of declining top tax rates and anti-tax sentiment, the idea of increasing taxes on the rich to cushion the pension system became a non-starter. Second, the supply-siders' emphasis on investment, as opposed to the Keynesian emphasis on consumption and aggregate demand, further promoted the aging preoccupation. During the middle of the twentieth century, proponents of population growth, following Keynes, opined that an aging population was problematic because the elderly consumed less than the young. In the 1970s, however, experts who promoted population growth to help counteract population aging flipped assumptions about savings and consumption around. Following the lead of supply-side economists who downplayed the importance of consumption in determining future investment, these pro–population growth individuals now lamented that the elderly over-consumed (and dis-saved), and thus that an increasing elderly dependency ratio stifled investment.[124]

Belief in the onset of an aging crisis also meshed with broader pro–population growth economic doctrine.[125] British sociologist Frank Furedi notes, "Concern with the greying of society is often linked to a preoccupation with apprehensions about declining fertility rates."[126] Indeed, most aging doomsayers wished for a new Baby Boom to counteract the fiscal dilemmas of population aging and found much common ground with market-knows-best demographers such as Julian Simon, who proposed that the nation double immigration levels and return to its 1957 fertility in order to support the elderly.[127] Even moderate participants in the aging discussion discredited Malthusian ideas and sardonically dismissed the zero population growth movement for peaking just before birthrates reached their nadir.[128] Today, even some theorists who *dismiss* the notion of an aging crisis are populationists, noting that fertility rates have fluctuated wildly and suggesting hopefully that the US may return to high fertility of the 1950s and early 1960s.[129] Above and beyond questions related to the age pyramid and social spending, the larger community of intellectuals who drove the new classical economics in the 1970s was prone to identifying the economic benefits of population growth.

The fear of aging fit well with conservative cultural views, as well. Since the decline of the eugenics movement in the middle of the twentieth century, Malthusians had often come under fire for allegedly keeping eugenic discrimination alive by focusing on the fertility patterns of the poor and minorities. Recently, however, it has been anti-Malthusians who link demographic change to supposed ethnic and cultural decline. Pat Buchanan and other conservative commentators claim that Western culture will diminish as industrialized countries age and developing nations continue to enjoy rapid population growth. These accounts generally lump the United States with Italy and Japan and downplay the fact that the US has the highest rate of population growth in the industrialized world.[130]

Despite diametrically opposed conclusions, the aging panic echoes Malthusianism in one other significant way. Richard Easterlin, whose fertility theories helped defuse the population bomb during its heyday, wrote in his wonderful summary of growth in the twentieth century that those focused on aging are guilty of using rhetoric as exaggerated as that of late 1960s Malthusians. After dismissing the macroeconomic and dependency-ratio arguments of the aging pessimists, Easterlin observes, "Perhaps too there are policy implications that have attracted some to the alarmist view of aging just as some have been attracted to the alarmist view of rapid population growth. Malthusianism has been a bulwark of opposition to reform from Malthus's *First Essay* through contemporary attacks on poverty programs. The dependency burden analysis provides rationalization for assault on yet another pillar of the welfare state—social security."[131] Easterlin's theory that fertility fluctuates with generations has often been crudely distilled as "demography is destiny." But as he suggests here, demography is not fiscal destiny.

During the 1970s, traditional population–resources questions were left unaddressed as the aging issue rose to the surface. The two developments were intimately related. The rise of pro–population growth thought, reinforced by new concerns about economic and demographic stagnation, fused with a burgeoning anti-statism to create a lasting political economy of population centered on the problem of aging. Although to this day a major overhaul of Social Security has proven impossible politically, the aging paradigm has dominated American policy makers' discussions of demography ever since.[132]

Epilogue

In 1923, John Maynard Keynes predicted that the "Problem of Population . . . is going to be not merely an economist's problem, but, in the near future, the greatest of all social questions,—a question which will arouse some of the deeper instincts and emotions of men, and about which feelings may run as passionately as in earlier struggles between religions."[1] Keynes was not incorrect. From about two billion when he wrote, the population on earth tripled to six billion by the century's end (and is projected to increase to ten billion in 2100). This tripling in about the same number of years as the average American lives has changed how humans lead their lives as profoundly as did the technological, economic, social, and environmental transformations wrought by the Industrial Revolution. And in the United States, where the population increased from 112 million when Keynes made these comments to 281 million at the century's end, fractious discussions surrounding population-related issues as diverse as eugenics, declining birthrates, the "population explosion," and the return of mass immigration roiled both culture and politics. And yet, the population question remained, at root, an economist's one—it was the great shift in prevailing economic expertise from moderate Malthusianism to veneration of population growth that determined answers to the (non-) Problem of Population most of all. Thus, a 1999 statement by the libertarian Cato Institute provides an apt bookend to Keynes's quotation. Cato declared: "In every material way, life in the United States, with a population of 270 million, is much better today than it was in 1900 when the population was 75 million people. Moreover, the American people are net resource creators, not resource depleters—protectors of the environment, not destroyers. . . . We hope and predict that millions more people will live long, healthy, happy lives in America in the 21st century."[2]

What a distance the Cato Institute had traveled from two groups that it generally lauds: the nation's founders, whose republican theory of democracy looked askance at crowded societies; and the classical economists, who believed in an iron law of eventual population growth–induced scarcity. Indeed, for much of their history, many Americans rejected bigness—big government, big business, and big numbers of people. Today, the unease with big government remains, but the critique of the nation's exceptional demographic expansion is largely submerged under a neoliberal economics that trumpets growth in all forms, an emphasis on the fiscal challenges stemming from the Baby Boom cohort, and hot-button cultural issues such as abortion.

This evolution was far from linear. Early in the twentieth century, liberal economists resisted the Malthusianism expressed by the Gilded Age's conservative theorists and by a popular culture recoiling at the so-called closing of the frontier, and yet, by the 1920s, an expert consensus emerged that the nation's optimum population would be lower than its current one. In the 1930s, population skepticism merged with consumptionist economics to form the enduring doctrine of Stable Population Keynesianism, which maintained that the state and not the stork would drive America's economic engine. In 1960, leading demographer Ansley Coale acknowledged that "a continued secular economic boom could gain partial support from a continued baby boom" yet captured Stable Population Keynesianism perfectly when he continued, "But after a century this trend would produce about a billion Americans, and after two centuries some six billion. There must be a better way to stimulate employment."[3] In the 1960s and 1970s, conservatives at the forefront of the new classical economics developed a market-knows-best demography. According to this body of ideas, America would never have six billion people because birthrates naturally and beneficently adjust to the social and economic environment, and, in the meantime, steady population growth would keep the American postwar machine humming without state demand management. In the 1970s, the ascendancy of pronatalist (and, more broadly, laissez-faire) economics, temporarily lower birthrates (which would return upwards in the 1980s), economic malaise, and the "aging crisis" eliminated the overpopulation paradigm from mainstream American political discourse. By the end of the decade, American liberalism had nearly entirely abandoned two anti–population growth principles that had animated it for the first two-thirds of the twentieth century. The first was that a smaller population would enhance macro- and microeconomic welfare. The erosion of this principle robbed opponents of population growth of the potent argument that a stable population was not something to be endured economically in the interest of ecological health but was in fact a spur to a more prosperous and equitable nation. The second idea was that a smaller population would enhance the quality of life in the United States.

To be sure, American policy makers remained mildly sympathetic to Malthusian precepts in the context of the developing world. In 1977, for example, Rep. James Scheuer (D-N.Y.) orchestrated the creation of the House Select Committee on Population. The committee was primarily charged with investigating the consequences of global growth, and Malthusian principles guided this effort. The committee also held hearings on domestic population issues. These hearings attracted experts with divergent views, from unreconstructed Malthusians to enthusiastic populationists such as Julian Simon, but on the whole they signaled the new direction of the domestic debate. Questions surrounding the aging of the population and entitlements, not the issue of aggregate growth, dominated.[4] Although some natural scientists, demographers, and economists continued to espouse limits-to-growth positions, they no longer drove policy.

During the 1980s, support for population growth in developed and less developed nations fully converged. In 1980, a group representing eleven agencies within the Carter administration was charged with predicting future environmental and population outcomes. The result was the *Global 2000 Report to the President*, which foresaw overpopulation-driven congestion, famine, deforestation, and war across the globe. It also urged domestic population stabilization. *Global 2000*, however, was the last gasp of government-sanctioned limits-to-growth thought. Although many of the report's specific projections (e.g., those regarding deforestation and species loss) have proven accurate, conservatives commonly deride it for epitomizing the Chicken Little mentality of population doomsayers as well as the general malaise of the Carter years.[5] The report did not produce any policy ripples. Ronald Reagan's optimistic and well-received declaration of "morning in America" indicated that the Malthusian epoch—much longer than a moment—was long gone. Thereafter, the US government formally renounced Malthusianism. In 1984, the Reagan administration's delegation to the UN International Population Conference in Mexico City called population growth a "neutral phenomenon."[6]

In spite of the prevailing optimistic rhetoric, few policy makers have welcomed rapid population growth in the poorest nations (especially in sub-Saharan Africa). In addition, the US government, along with a host of American-led nongovernmental organizations, continues to provide assistance for family planning in the developing world. Still, funding for family planning programs has remained relatively meager and wrapped up with the crippling politics of abortion; Republican presidents have imposed the "global gag rule," which demands that any overseas family planning organization receiving funds from the US refrain from providing information on abortion, while Democratic administrations have rescinded it.[7] Most social scientists continue to bolster population optimism, and the consolidation of conservative economic thought, which celebrates the possibilities of never-ending numerical expansion, keeps critiques of domestic and international population growth on the fringe of American political discourse. The first President Bush embodied the dramatic shift that has taken place in the past forty years. "Twenty years ago some spoke of limits to growth," he said in 1994, failing to mention that he was once one of the policy makers who did! "But today we know that growth is the engine of change. Growth is the friend of the environment."[8] Keynes's ideas, at least in the watered-down form of support for "stimulus," enjoyed a temporary comeback during the Great Recession at the end of the twenty-first century's first decade. However, anti-statist political economy survived the economic crises stronger than ever (as seen in the obsession with deficits as opposed to intractable high unemployment) and discounts the Stable Population Keynesian notion that the state can engineer economic growth.

Meanwhile, a continued emphasis on the aging of the population, however justified by spiraling deficits, has encouraged policy makers to think of babies as future taxpayers rather than as potential environmental or social externalities. The American business community, which surprisingly had few objections to population stabilization in the late 1960s, has emerged as an unabashed and vocal supporter of population growth. Business's new posture reflects the increased size and economic power of youth cohorts starting with the "Baby Boom echo" (children born during the early 1980s), which had more discretionary funds at its disposal than any other youth cohort in history. Beyond demographics, however, American companies are increasingly adopting the strategy of marketing primarily to the young, thereby welcoming more births as a quick path to greater sales.[9]

The contentious politics of contemporary America has worked against a sober conversation about population, resources, and the economy. They have also left little space for calls for beauty, calls that many intellectuals have rejected for separate reasons.[10] Today, individuals on both the Left and Right often bring up population matters only to stigmatize the other side with the taint of eugenics. Moreover, immigration politics have helped to keep the population debate frozen in place. As we have seen, during the 1970s, mainstream environmental organizations quietly backed away from their support for a smaller, stabilized population because they did not wish to be labeled anti-immigrant. As annual immigration shot past 500,000 in the 1980s and continued to climb to over one million in the 1990s—and as a variety of liberal organizations abandoned the issue—unambiguously racist anti-immigration voices have been among the loudest calling for a smaller population. The immigration debate has even become a subsidiary of the dominant aging debate, with some experts proposing that continued high levels of immigration offer a viable way of energizing the economy and shoring up Social Security.

Perhaps some combination of climate change, higher energy costs, crippling traffic in America's major cities, deteriorating national parks, and the religious right's continued effort to chip away at women's reproductive rights will awaken the population debate from its forty-year slumber. But the rightward tilt of the country suggests that neither a revival of Keynesian economics—nor a Stable Population Keynesian challenge to the sacred cow that economic growth requires a steadily rising population—is likely.

Nonetheless, population issues, including some we can not foresee today, will continue to shape the ways that Americans think about their economy, quality of life, and national identity. Historians should enrich these ongoing discussions by better integrating population dynamics into the narratives of United States history. In this process they may help forge a new, less contentious political economy of population that can confront the challenges of a vast and growing nation.

Notes

Introduction

1. Daniel Patrick Moynihan, "The Most Important Decision-Making Process," *Policy Review* 1 (Summer 1977): 89.

2. Press release, "PRB Releases 2011 World Population Data Sheet: 'World Adding Another Billion People Every 12 Years,'" available online at www.prb.org/Journalists/PressReleases/2011/2011-world-population-data-sheet.aspx?p=1.

3. For the 439 million figure, see US Census Bureau, "Projections of the Population by Selected Age Groups and Sex for the United States: 2010 to 2050," available online at www.census.gov/population/www/projections/summarytables.html. For the 570 million figure, see US Census Bureau, Population Division, "Methodology and Assumptions for the Population Projections of the United States: 1999 to 2100," Population Division Working Paper no. 38, January 2000, 24, available online at www.census.gov/population/www/documentation/twps0038.pdf. This is the "Middle Series" projection.

4. For worldwide fertility rates, see IndexMundi, "Country Comparison: Total Fertility Rate," chart compiled from CIA *World Factbook* data as of January 1, 2011, available online at www.indexmundi.com/g/r.aspx?c=ic&v=31. The rates here are "total fertility rates," which are age-adjusted; that is, the total fertility rate measures the number of babies a woman would have over her childbearing years if her fertility conformed to age-specific rates every year.

5. Ibid.

6. Samuel H. Preston and Caroline Sten Hartnett, "The Future of American Fertility," in *Demography and the Economy*, ed. John B. Shoven (Chicago: University of Chicago Press, 2011), 31.

7. John B. Shoven, "Introduction," in *Demography and the Economy*, ed. Shoven, 3.

8. Thomas Robert Malthus, *Population: The First Essay* (1798; reprint, with a foreword by Kenneth E. Boulding, Ann Arbor: University of Michigan Press,

1959), 5. The full title of Malthus's original book was *An Essay on the Principle of Population, as it Affects the Future Improvement of Society, with Remarks on the Speculations of Mr. Godwin, M. Condorcet, and Other Writers*.

9. John Stuart Mill, *Principles of Political Economy*, from the 5th London ed., vol. 2 (New York: D. Appleton and Co., 1882), 339.

10. This book, like many, tends to equate classical economics with the conservative, laissez-faire economics that have dominated Western nations for the past half century. But it is worth bearing in mind that classical economists were of various political stripes, ranging from conservatives like Malthus to left-wingers like Marx. What makes them "classical" is their commitment to the labor theory of value and their insistence that economies are best understood through the application of macroeconomic ideas—not behavioral propositions. Consult Michael A. Bernstein, "Problems in the Theory of Production and Exchange: An Essay in Classical and Marxian Themes," *Australian Economic Papers* 19 (December 1980): 248–63.

11. Gary D. Hansen and Edward C. Prescott, "Malthus to Solow," *American Economic Review* 92 (September 2002): 1205–17. Also see Julian Simon, *The Economics of Population Growth* (Princeton: Princeton University Press, 1977), introduction and chap. 3.

12. For a brief overview of the ambiguous relationship between population and economic growth, see Kingsley Davis, "Zero Population Growth: The Goal and the Means," in *The No-Growth Society*, ed. Mancur Olson and Hans H. Landsberg (New York: W. W. Norton, 1973), 18–19.

13. Marc Linder, *The Dilemmas of Laissez-Faire Population Policy in Capitalist Societies: When the Invisible Hand Controls Reproduction* (Westport, Conn.: Greenwood Press, 1997), chap. 5.

14. Gunnar Myrdal, "Population Problems and Policies," *Annals of the American Academy of Political and Social Science* 197 (May 1938): 200.

15. Linder, *Dilemmas of Laissez-Faire Population Policy*, esp. preface.

16. Thomas L. Friedman, *Hot, Flat, and Crowded: Why We Need a Green Revolution—and How It Can Renew America* (New York: Farrar, Straus and Giroux, 2008).

17. For example, see Gary S. Becker, Edward L. Glaeser, and Kevin M. Murphy, "Population and Economic Growth," *American Economic Review* 89 (May 1999): 145–49.

18. Jared Diamond, *Collapse: How Societies Choose to Fail or Succeed* (New York: Viking, 2005), explores demographically induced calamity in Rwanda (chap. 10).

19. *The Economist*, July 28–August 3, 2007.

20. "The Baby Bust," *Washington Post*, July 6, 2003.

21. Laurence J. Kotlikoff and Scott Burns, *The Coming Generational Storm: What You Need to Know about America's Economic Future* (Cambridge, Mass: MIT Press, 2004); and Ted C. Fishman, *Shock of Gray: The Aging of the World's*

Population and How it Pits Young against Old, Child against Parent, Worker against Boss, Company against Rival, and Nation against Nation (New York: Scribner, 2010).

22. For a popular press example, see Nariman Behravesh, *Spin-Free Economics: A No-Nonsense Nonpartisan Guide to Today's Global Economic Debates* (New York: McGraw-Hill, 2009), 113–18.

23. Prominent examples in the early 2010s were *Kate plus Eight* and *19 Kids and Counting*.

24. Press release from the office of Rep. Joe Pitts (R-Pa.), January 23, 2001, "Gale Norton: Carrying on for Teddy Roosevelt," available online at www.house.gov/pitts/press/commentary/012301c-norton.htm.

25. "Lawmaker: Climate Change Just Ruse to Control Population," *Salt Lake Tribune*, February 5, 2010.

26. Quoted in Bill Moyers, "Welcome to Doomsday," *New York Review of Books*, March 24, 2005, 8 and 10. The original source is Mark A. Beliles and Stephen K. McDowell, *America's Providential History, Including Biblical Principles of Education, Government, Politics, Economics, and Family Life*, 2d ed. (Charlottesville: Providence Foundation, 1991), 197.

27. US Census Bureau, "Annual Estimates of the Components of Population Change for the United States and States: July 1, 2002 to July 1, 2003," last revised May 11, 2004, available online at www.census.gov/popest/states/NST-EST2003-comp-chg.html.

28. "U.S. Population Projections: 2005–2050" (February 11, 2008), available online at www.pewhispanic.org/reports/report.php?ReportID=85.

29. T. Michael Maher, "How and Why Journalists Avoid the Population-Environment Connection," *Population and Environment* 18 (March 1997): 339–72.

30. Thomas Robertson, *The Malthusian Moment: Global Population Growth and the Birth of American Environmentalism* (New Brunswick: Rutgers University Press, 2012).

31. For example, see Elaine Tyler May, *Homeward Bound: American Families in the Cold War Era*, rev. ed. (New York: Basic Books, 1999).

32. Begin with Molly Ladd-Taylor, "Eugenics, Sterilisation and Modern Marriage in the USA: The Strange Career of Paul Popenoe," *Gender and Society* 13 (August 2001): 298–327.

33. Matthew Connelly, *Fatal Misconception: The Struggle to Control World Population* (Cambridge, Mass: The Belknap Press of Harvard University Press, 2008), esp. chap. 5.

34. See, for example, Allan Chase, *The Legacy of Malthus: The Social Costs of the New Racism* (New York: Alfred A. Knopf, 1977). For a judicious investigation of postwar Malthusianism and international family planning policy, see Donald T. Critchlow, *Intended Consequences: Birth Control, Abortion, and the Federal Government in Modern America* (New York: Oxford University Press, 1999).

35. Readers seeking a detailed demographic history of the United States may wish to consult Herbert S. Klein, *A Population History of the United States* (Cambridge: Cambridge University Press, 2004).

36. David Morris Potter, *People of Plenty: Economic Abundance and the American Character* (Chicago: University of Chicago Press, 1954).

Chapter One

1. John Locke, *Second Treatise of Government*, in *Two Treatises of Government*, ed. Peter Laslett (Cambridge: Cambridge University Press, 1988), 5.49, p. 301.

2. J. Hector St. John Crèvecoeur, *Letters from an American Farmer* (1782; reprint, New York: Dolphin Books, 1963), 50. Crèvecoeur not only placed faith in the natural bounty of the New World but also believed that America had the potential to be an ameliorative asylum for the human flotsam of Europe. See Marilyn C. Baseler, *"Asylum for Mankind": America, 1607–1800* (Ithaca: Cornell University Press, 1998), 5.

3. Crèvecoeur, *Letters from an American Farmer*, 17.

4. Ibid.

5. Edmund S. Morgan, "Don't Tread On Us," in Morgan, *The Genuine Article: An Historian Looks at Early America* (New York: W. W. Norton, 2004), 189.

6. Margo J. Anderson, *The American Census: A Social History* (New Haven: Yale University Press, 1988), 11.

7. The Indian population estimates arc from Daniel K. Richter, *Facing East from Indian Country: A Native History of Early America* (Cambridge, Mass.: Harvard University Press, 2001), 7.

8. For the interplay of liberalism and republicanism, see Isaac Kramnick, "The 'Great National Discussion': The Discourse of Politics in 1787," *William and Mary Quarterly*, 3d ser., 45 (January 1988): 3–32.

9. Patricia Cline Cohen, *A Calculating People: The Spread of Numeracy in Early America* (Chicago: University of Chicago Press, 1982), 52.

10. Susan E. Klepp, *Revolutionary Conceptions: Women, Fertility, and Family Limitation in America, 1760–1820* (Chapel Hill: University of North Carolina Press, 2009), 3–4.

11. James R. Gibson Jr., *Americans versus Malthus: The Population Debate in the Early Republic, 1790–1840* (New York: Garland, 1989), 10. For Stiles's demographic nationalism, see Theodore Draper, *A Struggle for Power: The American Revolution* (New York: Times Books, 1996), 109; and Wood, *Empire of Liberty*, 45–46.

12. On luxury, see Drew R. McCoy, *The Elusive Republic: Political Economy in Jeffersonian America* (Chapel Hill: University of North Carolina Press, 1996), 17–32.

13. Ibid., 53.

14. Ibid., 19.

15. Quoted in ibid., 51.

16. Ibid., introduction.

17. Cohen, *Calculating People*, 52–53.

18. Benjamin Franklin, "Observations Concerning the Increase of Mankind," in *The Papers of Benjamin Franklin*, ed. Leonard W. Labaree et al., vol. 4 (New Haven: Yale University Press, 1961), 228.

19. Benjamin Franklin, "Poor Richard Improved," in *The Papers of Benjamin Franklin*, ed. Labaree, 3:441.

20. A decade later, Franklin conservatively suggested that America would need "centuries" to reach 100 million people, but in this case he was trying to assuage British fears (Draper, *Struggle for Power*, 14).

21. Franklin did attribute some of England's social problems to non-demographic factors such as poor governance (McCoy, *Elusive Republic*, 52).

22. Draper, *Struggle for Power*, 103 and 112.

23. Ibid., 103.

24. Ibid., 110; and Morgan, "Don't Tread On Us," 189.

25. Draper, *Struggle for Power*, 104.

26. Edmund S. Morgan, "Secrets of Benjamin Franklin," in Morgan, *Genuine Article*, 176–77. Also see Alfred Aldridge, "Franklin as Demographer," *Journal of Economic History* 9 (May 1949): 25–44.

27. I borrow "Empire of Englishman" from Edmund S. Morgan, *Benjamin Franklin* (New Haven: Yale University Press, 2002), chap. 3.

28. Quoted in ibid., 77.

29. Ibid., 72.

30. Franklin, "Observations," 233. Compare to Thomas Robert Malthus, *Population: The First Essay* (1798; reprint, with a foreword by Kenneth E. Boulding, Ann Arbor: University of Michigan Press, 1959), 5–6 and 9–10.

31. Morgan, *Benjamin Franklin*, 78.

32. Draper, *Struggle for Power*, chap. 6. Morgan, "Don't Tread on Us," argues that Draper exaggerates rising demographic and hence economic power and slights core political, constitutional, and ideological disagreements.

33. Quoted in Draper, *Struggle for Power*, 105.

34. For an opposing view—that the Proclamation was little enforced and not a significant thorn in the colonists' side—see Esmond Wright, *Fabric of Freedom, 1763–1800*, rev. ed. (New York: Hill and Wang, 1978), 99.

35. For specific examples, see Draper, *Struggle for Power*, 105–6.

36. Gibson, *Americans versus Malthus*, 7; Anderson, *American Census*, 11; and Draper, *Struggle for Power*, 107–10.

37. Draper, *Struggle for Power*, 108–9.

38. Stanley Elkins and Eric McKitrick, *The Age of Federalism* (New York: Oxford University Press, 1993), 19.

39. Gordon S. Wood, *Empire of Liberty: A History of the Early Republic, 1789–*

1815 (New York: Oxford University Press, 2009), 14; and McCoy, *Elusive Republic*, 114.

40. McCoy, *Elusive Republic*, 114.

41. Quoted in Draper, *Struggle for Power*, 103. Elsewhere, it should be noted, Adams praised Malthus and agreed that the vast majority of humans were doomed for misery. See Edmond Cocks, "The Malthusian Theory in Pre–Civil War America: An Original Relation to the Universe," *Population Studies* 20 (March 1967): 345.

42. Wood, *Empire of Liberty*, 318.

43. Harold Hutcheson, *Tench Coxe: A Study in American Economic Development* (1938; reprint, New York: Da Capo Press, 1969), 98–101 and 199; and Jacob E. Cooke, "Tench Coxe, Alexander Hamilton, and the Encouragement of American Manufactures," *William and Mary Quarterly*, 3d ser., 32 (July 1975): 369–92.

44. McCoy, *Elusive Republic*, 60 and 146–52.

45. For Madison's demographic thinking, see Gibson, *Americans versus Malthus*, chap. 1, esp. 21–30.

46. Ibid., 30.

47. Ian Shapiro, ed., *The Federalist Papers* (New Haven: Yale University Press, 2009), 52.

48. Quoted in Jack N. Rakove, *Original Meanings: Politics and Ideas in the Making of the Constitution* (New York: Vintage Books, 1997), 184; also see Kramnick, "'Great National Discussion,'" 9.

49. Shapiro, ed., *Federalist Papers*, 52.

50. Ibid., 284.

51. Madison to Jefferson, June 19, 1786, quoted in McCoy, *Elusive Republic*, 127.

52. Gibson, *Americans versus Malthus*, 25–26.

53. Quoted in McCoy, *Elusive Republic*, 129.

54. Quoted in ibid., 130. Madison made this comment at the Virginia ratifying convention of 1788.

55. For the history of these acts, see Paul W. Gates, *History of Public Land Law Development* (1968; reprint, New York: Arno Press, 1979), esp. 64–65, 124–25, and 129–31.

56. See, for example, Nicholas Onuf and Peter Onuf, *Nations, Markets, and War: Modern History and the American Civil War* (Charlottesville: University of Virginia Press, 2006), 182.

57. Steven Stoll, *The Great Delusion: A Mad Inventor, Death in the Tropics, and the Utopian Origins of Economic Growth* (New York: Hill and Wang, 2008), 62.

58. For "passions," see Malthus, *Population: The First Essay*, 4 and 45 (quotation).

59. Ibid., 5.

60. Ibid., chap. 4.

61. Ibid., 34.

62. Thomas Robert Malthus, *An Essay on the Principle of Population*, ed. Philip Appleman, 2d ed. (New York: W. W. Norton, 2004), 125.

63. Mark Perlman, "Some Economic Growth Problems and the Part Population Policy Plays," *Quarterly Journal of Economics* 89 (May 1975): 249.

64. David Hume, "Of the Populousness of Ancient Nations," in *David Hume: Selected Essays*, ed. Stephen Copley (Oxford: Oxford University Press, 1998), 223–74; and D. P. O'Brien, *The Classical Economists Revisited* (Princeton: Princeton University Press, 2004), 66–67.

65. Smith anticipated Malthus in assuming that fertility moves in tandem with the level of subsistence, but his system was more happily self-regulating. He wrote, "It is in this manner [through market forces] that the demand for men, like that for any other commodity, necessarily regulates the production of men; quickens it when it goes on too slowly, and stops it when it advances too fast" (Adam Smith, *An Inquiry into the Nature and Causes of the Wealth of Nations* [1776; reprint, New York: P. F. Collier and Son, 1909], 84). Smith also intimated that China's large population produced its wealth (Onuf and Onuf, *Nations, Markets, and War*, 96).

66. Smith, *Wealth of Nations*, 86.

67. Bernard Semmel, "Malthus: 'Physiocracy' and the Commercial System," *Economic History Review*, n.s. 17, no. 3 (1965): 522–35.

68. Malthus, *An Essay on the Principle of Population*, ed. Appleman, 130.

69. Quoted in John Bellamy Foster, "Malthus' *Essay on Population* at Age 200: A Marxian View," *Monthly Review* 50 (December 1998): 8.

70. Quoted in John M. Sherwood, "Engels, Marx, Malthus, and the Machine," *American Historical Review* 90 (October 1985): 842.

71. I flatten a complicated and uneven process. Ricardo struggled with Malthus's theories, especially those regarding the nature of rent and surplus—and his friendly critique of them identified virtually all of the key issues in the classical theoretical tradition. See *The Works and Correspondence of David Ricardo*, ed. Piero Sraffa with the collaboration of M. H. Dobb (Cambridge: Cambridge University Press, 1951), esp. vol. 1, *On the Principles of Political Economy and Taxation* (reprint of 3d, 1821 edition), chap. 32, and vol. 2, *Notes on Malthus*. Marx—who must be regarded as a classical economist—had nothing but contempt for Malthus.

72. Ralph H. Hess, "Conservation in its Relation to Industrial Evolution" (chap. 1 of his "Conservation and Economic Theory" section), in *The Foundations of National Prosperity: Studies in the Conservation of Permanent Natural Resources*, ed. Richard T. Ely et al. (New York: Macmillan, 1917), 113.

73. Despite the obvious implications of this thesis, Malthus did not formally construct a formal theory of diminishing returns to land.

74. O'Brien, *Classical Economists*, 52–56. Also see John Stuart Mill, *Principles of Political Economy*, vol. 2 (New York: D. Appleton and Co., 1882), book 4, chap. 6.

75. See Nassau William Senior, *Two Lectures on Population* (London: John Murray, 1831). For the classical economists' criticisms of Malthus, see O'Brien, *Classical Economists*, 55 and 73–78.

76. O'Brien, *Classical Economists*, 78. Cairnes is sometimes referred to as the last classical economist.

77. Cited in ibid.

78. See esp. Gibson, *Americans versus Malthus*.

79. Laura L. Lovett, *Conceiving the Future: Pronatalism, Reproduction, and the Family in the United States, 1890–1938* (Chapel Hill: University of North Carolina Press, 2007), 80.

80. For Europe's reliance on American foodstuffs, see Joyce Appleby, *Capitalism and a New Social Order: The Republican Vision of the 1790s* (New York: New York University Press, 1984), 40–45.

81. Malthus, *Population: The First Essay*, 119–20.

82. McCoy, *Elusive Republic*, 192.

83. Quoted in Drew McCoy, "Jefferson and Madison on Malthus: Population Growth in Jeffersonian Political Economy," *Virginia Magazine of History and Biography* 88 (July 1980): 261.

84. Quoted in McCoy, *Elusive Republic*, 14.

85. Joyce Appleby, "Jefferson and His Complex Legacy," in *Jeffersonian Legacies*, ed. Peter Onuf (Charlottesville: University of Virginia Press, 1993), 8.

86. Jefferson's First Inaugural Address is available online from Princeton University's Papers of Thomas Jefferson project at www.princeton.edu/~tjpapers/inaugural/infinal.html.

87. Quoted in Appleby, *Capitalism and a New Social Order*, 98. Also see discussion of this letter in Cocks, "Malthusian Theory in Pre–Civil War America," 344–45.

88. McCoy, *Elusive Republic*, 193.

89. Gibson, *Americans versus Malthus*, chap. 2

90. Alexander H. Everett, *New Ideas on Population* (London: John Miller, 1823), 9.

91. Ralph Waldo Emerson, "Plato; Or, the Philosopher," in *The Selected Writings of Ralph Waldo Emerson*, ed. Brooks Atkinson (New York: Random House, 1950), 478.

92. Appleby, *Capitalism and a New Social Order*, 80.

93. William Diamond, "Nathaniel A. Ware, National Economist," *Journal of Southern History* 5 (November 1939): 511–12.

94. Ibid., 518.

95. Nathaniel A. Ware, *Notes on Political Economy as Applicable to the United States* (1844; reprint, New York: Augustus M. Kelly, 1967), 227.

96. Stoll, *Great Delusion*, 84–85. List is remembered primarily for his advocacy of state-sponsored economic development.

97. Ibid., 86.

98. Dorothy Ross, *The Origins of American Social Science* (Cambridge: Cambridge University Press, 1991), 44–48.

99. James L. Huston, *Securing the Fruits of Labor: The American Concept of Wealth Distribution, 1765–1900* (Baton Rouge: Louisiana State University Press, 1998), 177–82.

100. Ibid., 178.

101. Gibson, *Americans versus Malthus*, 71.

102. Ibid., 88–89.

103. Ross, *Origins of American Social Science*, 42–43.

104. Gibson, *Americans versus Malthus*, 75–81.

105. See, for example, the views of famous engineer Loammi Baldwin Jr. in ibid., 95–106.

106. Quoted in Stoll, *Great Delusion*, 64.

107. Quoted in George Johnson Cady, "The Early American Reaction to the Theory of Malthus," *Journal of Political Economy* 39 (October 1931): 608. The original is Daniel Raymond, *Thoughts on Political Economy in Two Parts* (Baltimore: Fielding Lucas, 1820), 312.

108. Stoll, *Great Delusion*, 21 and 74. Remarkably, Etzler's high estimate for the number who could live in the US "in all influence imaginable" was a mere 300 million, or roughly the population in the year 2006! (72).

109. Herbert S. Klein, *A Population History of the United States* (Cambridge: Cambridge University Press, 2004), 69; and Klepp, *Revolutionary Conceptions*, 5.

110. Klein, *Population History*, 69.

111. For the debate on the fertility transition in America, see Klepp, *Revolutionary Conceptions*, 4–7, esp. n. 6. Many other historians maintain that the Revolution produced few new opportunities for women.

112. This paragraph draws extensively from McCoy, "Jefferson and Madison on Malthus," 268–71.

113. Ibid., 270. For the early socialists' rejection of Malthus, see Cady, "Early American Reaction," 621–22.

114. For early pro-Malthusians, see ibid., 626–32; and Joseph J. Spengler, "Population Doctrines in the United States," *Journal of Political Economy* 41 (October 1933): 639–72. For McVickar, see Joseph Dorfman, *The Economic Mind in American Civilization*, vol. 2 (New York: Viking, 1946), 515–22.

115. Cocks, "Malthusian Theory in Pre–Civil War America," 352 and 358–59.

116. Huston, *Securing the Fruits of Labor*, 163–70.

117. Klein, *Population History*, 86; and Anderson, *American Census*, 24.

118. Joseph J. Spengler, "Population Theory in the Ante-bellum South," *Journal of Southern History* 2 (August 1936): 360.

119. See Paul Finkelman, "Slavery and the Constitutional Convention: Making a Covenant with Death," in *Beyond Confederation: Origins of the Constitution and American National Identity*, ed. Richard Beeman, Stephen Botein, and Edward C. Carter II (Chapel Hill: University of North Carolina Press, 1987), 188–225.

120. Drew R. McCoy, "James Madison and Visions of American Nationality in the Confederation Period: A Regional Perspective," in *Beyond Confederation*, ed. Beeman, Botein, and Carter, 230–33.

121. Ibid., 238 and 233.

122. Quoted in ibid., 228.

123. See, for example, Robert Pierce Forbes, *The Missouri Compromise and Its Aftermath* (Chapel Hill: University of North Carolina Press, 2007), 45.

124. Anderson, *American Census*, chap. 2.

125. Spengler, "Population Theory in the Ante-bellum South," 385–86.

126. The classic study is Eric Foner, *Free Soil, Free Labor, Free Men: The Ideology of the Republican Party before the Civil War* (New York: Oxford University Press, 1970).

127. Lincoln spoke these words in Baltimore on April 18, 1864, quoted in Onuf and Onuf, *Nations, Markets, and War*, 7.

128. William Sumner Jenkins, *Pro-Slavery Thought in the Old South* (Chapel Hill: University of North Carolina Press, 1935), 299.

129. Spengler, "Population Theory in the Ante-bellum South," 382 n. 72.

130. Ibid., 381.

131. Ibid., 370. See 362–63 for Tucker's early-career optimism.

132. Dew's famous "Report of the Debate of the Virginia Legislature of 1831–32 on the Abolition of Slavery" argued against taxing whites to pay for emancipation on the grounds that Malthus had shown the danger of tampering with population dynamics. The taxes would stunt the white population, and buying slaves to emancipate them would induce slaveowners to breed slaves excessively. See Cocks, "Malthusian Theory in Pre–Civil War America," 355–56; and Spengler, "Population Doctrines," 640–41.

133. "Dew on Slavery," in *The Pro-Slavery Argument* (1852; reprint, New York: Negro Universities Press, 1968). The original source was Thomas Dew, "Abolition of Negro Slavery," *American Quarterly Review* 12 (September 1832): 189–265.

134. Spengler, "Population Theory in the Ante-bellum South," 376–77.

135. Stoll, *Great Delusion*, 91.

136. Quoted in James L. Huston, "Theory's Failure: Malthusian Population Theory and the Projected Demise of Slavery," *Civil War History* 55 (September 2009): 359. Professor Huston presented an earlier version of this paper at the Mid-America Conference on History, Tulsa, September 29, 2007, where I benefited greatly from our discussion.

137. Spengler, "Population Theory in the Ante-bellum South," 369.

138. Huston, "Theory's Failure," 361.

139. I thank Professor Huston for his correspondence in developing this point.

140. Professor Huston generously helped me with the language here.

141. Huston, "Theory's Failure," 367.

142. Ibid.

143. Ibid., 374–77.

144. For examples of this dispersion argument, dating as far back as the debates surrounding Missouri's admission to the Union, see Cocks, "The Malthusian Theory in Pre–Civil War America," 347.

145. See the discussion of Sen. Robert Walker's (D–Miss.) ideas in Daniel

Walker Howe, *What Hath God Wrought: The Transformation of America, 1815–1848* (New York: Oxford University Press, 2007), 684–85.

146. Cocks, "Malthusian Theory in Pre–Civil War America," 348.

147. Quoted in Huston, "Theory's Failure," 354. See the similar argument of Missouri Territorial Delegate William Scott from 1819: "What, starve the Negroes, pen them up in the swamps and morasses, confine them to Southern latitudes, to the long scorching days of labor and fatigue, until the race becomes extinct, that the fair land of Missouri may be tenanted by that gentleman, his brothers and his sons?" Quoted in Cocks, "Malthusian Theory in Pre–Civil War America," 347.

148. Huston, "Theory's Failure," 379.

149. Conversely, some abolitionists maintained in racist terms that expansion was needed to provide an outlet for the free blacks who would inundate the North after emancipation.

150. Quoted in Reginald Horsman, *Race and Manifest Destiny: The Origins of American Racial Anglo-Saxonism* (Cambridge, Mass: Harvard University Press, 1981), 202. Jefferson and many white Americans after him believed that Native Americans were doomed to extinction if they remained in competition with European settlers; the only means to assure their survival was therefore to remove them.

151. Quoted in ibid., 219. The original source is John O'Sullivan, "Annexation," *United States Magazine and Democratic Review* 17 (July–August 1845): 5–10.

152. Quoted in Horsman, *Manifest Destiny,* 222. The original source is *Merchants' Magazine and Commercial Review* 14 (May 1846): 435–39.

153. "Senator Thomas Hart Benton on Manifest Destiny, 1846," in *Major Problems in American Environmental History: Documents and Essays*, ed. Carolyn Merchant (Lexington, Mass: D. C. Heath and Co., 1993), 250.

154. Quoted in Foner, *Free Soil, Free Labor, Free Men*, 27.

155. Thomas R. Hietala, *Manifest Design: Anxious Aggrandizement in Late Jacksonian America* (Ithaca: Cornell University Press, 1985), 100.

156. For the Whigs and immigration, see Michael F. Holt, *The Rise and Fall of the American Whig Party: Jacksonian Politics and the Onset of the Civil War* (New York: Oxford University Press, 1999), chap. 7.

157. Cited in Howe, *What Hath God Wrought*, 686.

158. Ibid., 705.

159. Hietala, *Manifest Design*, esp. chap. 4.

160. Ibid., 48.

161. Howe, *What Hath God Wrought*, 686.

162. See Polk's "Second Annual Message," December 8, 1846, available online through the American Presidency Project at www.presidency.ucsb.edu/ws/index.php?pid=29487.

163. Stoll, *Great Delusion*, 68.

164. Ibid.

165. Hietala, *Manifest Design*, 185.

166. Alexis de Tocqueville, *Democracy in America*, trans. and ed. Harvey C. Mansfield and Delba Winthrop (Chicago: University of Chicago Press, 2000), 361.

167. Drew Gilpin Faust, *This Republic of Suffering: Death and the American Civil War* (New York: Alfred A. Knopf, 2008), 266. Although the North enjoyed a substantial advantage in both total and military population, most historians attribute its victory to vast advantage in material resources rather than sheer numbers.

Chapter Two

1. See, for example, David M. Wrobel, *The End of American Exceptionalism: Frontier Anxiety from the Old West to the New Deal* (Lawrence: University Press of Kansas, 1993).

2. Quoted in ibid., 38.

3. Ibid. A decade later, Ely reiterated that the "great body of unoccupied land" in the US had mitigated the "evils" stemming from industrialization and kept wages high (Richard T. Ely, *Studies in the Evolution of Industrial Society* [New York: Macmillan, 1903], 59).

4. Frederick Jackson Turner, *The Frontier in American History* (New York: Henry Holt, 1920), 1. This volume is a compendium of Turner's essays; Turner debuted "The Significance of the Frontier in American History" as a paper at the 1893 American Historical Association meetings.

5. Joseph Spengler, "Population Doctrines in the United States," *Journal of Political Economy* 41 (October 1933): 663.

6. Thomas K. McCraw, *Prophet of Innovation: Joseph Schumpeter and Creative Destruction* (Cambridge, Mass.: Belknap Press of Harvard University Press, 2007), 44. Also see R. D. Collison Black, A. W. Coats, and Craufurd D. W. Goodwin, eds., *The Marginal Revolution in Economics: Interpretation and Evaluation* (Durham: Duke University Press, 1973).

7. For an original and accessible statement of marginalism, try John Bates Clark, *The Philosophy of Wealth: Economic Principles Newly Formulated* (1886; reprint of 2d, 1887 ed., New York: Augustus M. Kelley, 1967), chap. 5, "The Theory of Value." The marginalists used a few highly simplified assumptions about decision-making, but I do not mean to suggest that they focused on the psychology of demand or seriously engaged the new field of psychology.

8. For the classical economists and population, see D. P. O'Brien, *The Classical Economists Revisited* (Princeton: Princeton University Press, 2004), 66–78.

9. Diminishing returns to a factor of production, usually shortened to diminishing returns, refers to falling output in a theoretical world in which one factor of production is increasingly utilized while all else is held constant, for example, when the amount of labor working one constant acre of land increases. Decreas-

ing returns to scale refers to gains in production not commensurate with increases in multiple factors of production. Classical economists identified the theoretical possibility that, whereas agriculture exhibits diminishing returns, manufacturing can enjoy increasing returns. They concluded, however, that in the real economy, increasing levels of employment in manufacturing—usually the product of population growth—produce overall diminishing returns and a downward spiral toward subsistence as prices for basic necessities outpace wages, and, eventually, the terms of foreign trade turn against manufacturers. See John Toye, *Keynes on Population* (Oxford: Oxford University Press, 2000), 13–16.

10. We should distinguish between two main ideas here. Population growth may (a) generate productivity gains by promoting specialization and division of labor or (b) promote technological change by exposing bottlenecks and rapidly rising marginal costs that induce innovation, or by increasing the number of geniuses. One can also argue that technological change is unrelated to demography but that, whatever its cause, it will trump any ill effects of population growth.

11. On Jevons, see Brett Clark and John Bellamy Foster, "William Stanley Jevons and *The Coal Question*: An Introduction to Jevons's 'Of the Economy of Fuel,'" *Organization & Environment* 14 (March 2001): 93–98. For ecological economics, see chap. 6 of the present study.

12. David Owen, "The Efficiency Dilemma," *New Yorker*, December 20 and 27, 2010, 78–85, emphasizes Jevons's assertion that technologies designed to use natural resources more efficiently actually produce the opposite effect because they lower costs and increase consumption of the resource.

13. W. Stanley Jevons, *The Coal Question: An Inquiry Concerning the Progress of the Nation, and the Probable Exhaustion of our Coal-Mines* (London: Macmillan, 1865), xvi. The italics are his.

14. W. Stanley Jevons, *The Theory of Political Economy*, 2d ed. (London: Macmillan, 1879), 288.

15. Carl Menger, *Principles of Economics*, trans. and ed. James Dingwall and Bert F. Hoselitz, introduction by Frank H. Knight (1871; Glencoe, Ill.: Free Press, 1950).

16. Menger did critique the classical theory of the value of land, suggesting, "Land occupies no exceptional place among goods" (ibid., 165). But as American economist Frank Knight pointed out, Menger offered "no statement of the principle of diminishing returns, or indication that [he] recognized it" (ibid., 24–25).

17. Léon Walras, *Elements of Pure Economics, or The Theory of Social Wealth*, trans. William Jaffé (1926; reprint, Homewood, Ill.: George Allen and Unwin, 1954), 388.

18. Ibid., 387–88. According to Walras, it was "hazardous to assert that the quantity of means of subsistence increases in an arithmetical progression [as opposed to the geometric progression of population] with a constant difference of one, whether this increase results from the introduction of wheat or potatoes, the

invention of machinery, or the development of credit facilities, or whether it results from the expansion of capital.... It is much wiser, therefore to confine oneself to stating that the progression according to which means of subsistence increases in consequence of economic and technical progress is less rapid than the progression which characterizes the tendency of population to increase."

19. Ibid., 388.

20. Johannes Overbeek, "Wicksell on Population," *Economic Development and Cultural Change* 21 (January 1973): 205.

21. Monica S. Fong, "Knut Wicksell's 'The Two Population Questions,'" *History of Political Economy* 8 (Fall 1976): 314.

22. Overton H. Taylor, *A History of Economic Thought* (New York: McGraw-Hill, 1960), 338.

23. J. J. Spengler, "Marshall on the Population Question. I," *Population Studies* 8 (March 1955): 269.

24. Taylor, *History of Economic Thought*, 346–47.

25. Alfred Marshall, *Principles of Economics*, vol. 1 (London: Macmillan, 1890), 379.

26. Ibid., 378–79.

27. Ibid., 380. For Marshall on trade and population, see Spengler, "Marshall on the Population Question. I," 284–85.

28. Marshall, *Principles of Economics*, 379.

29. Ibid.

30. The continued tendency to treat political economy as a branch of moral philosophy—a majority of the AEA's founders were pastors—impeded the ascent of the mathematical and seemingly value-neutral theory of marginal utility. In addition, the reformers first overturned classical economics via the German Historical School of economics. For the diffusion of marginalism, see Emil Kauder, "The Retarded Acceptance of the Marginal Utility Theory," *Quarterly Journal of Economics* 67 (November 1953): 564–75.

31. An enduring classic is Richard Hofstadter, *Social Darwinism in American Thought*, rev. ed. (Boston: Beacon Press, 1955).

32. Dennis Hodgson, "The Ideological Origins of the Population Association of America," *Population and Development Review* 17 (March 1991): 1–34.

33. See A. Béjin, "Social Darwinists and Malthus," in *Malthus Past and Present*, ed. Jacques Dupâquier, A. Fauve-Chamoux, and E. Grebenik (London: Academic Press, 1983), 299–312.

34. William Graham Sumner, "Sociology," *Princeton Review* 57 (November 1881): 315. Also see "Earth Hunger or the Philosophy of Land Grabbing," reprinted in *Essays of William Graham Sumner*, ed. Albert Galloway Keller and Maurice R. Davie, vol. 1 (New Haven: Yale University Press, 1934), 174–207.

35. Sumner, "Sociology," 310. Also see Dorothy Ross, *The Origins of American Social Science* (Cambridge: Cambridge University Press, 1991), 85–88; Bruce Curtis, "William Graham Sumner and the Problem of Progress," *New England Quar-*

terly 51 (September 1978): 358–59; and Edith H. Parker, "William Graham Sumner and the Frontier," *Southwest Review* 41 (Autumn 1956): 357–65.

36. Hofstadter, *Social Darwinism*, 55–57. Late in life, Sumner complained, "Rights, justice, liberty, and equality are the watchwords instead of the church, faith, heaven, and hell" because the earth was temporarily "underpopulated" and thus "the struggle for existence and competition of life are not severe" (William Graham Sumner, "The Mores of the Present and Future," in *Essays of William Graham Sumner*, ed. Keller and Davie, 1:83).

37. Quoted in Harold Francis Williamson, *Edward Atkinson: The Biography of an American Liberal, 1827–1905* (Boston: Old Corner Book Store, 1934), 246.

38. Ibid.

39. Ross, *Origins of American Social Science*, 77–78; and Arthur Latham Perry, *Political Economy*, 18th ed. (New York: Charles Scribner's Sons, 1883), 238.

40. J. Laurence Laughlin, *Elements of Political Economy with Some Applications to Questions of the Day* (New York: American Book Company, 1896), 19. Laughlin did allow that the US had not "taken up all our best lands as yet" (22).

41. Ibid., 49.

42. Richard Parker, *John Kenneth Galbraith: His Life, His Politics, His Economics* (New York: Farrar, Straus and Giroux: 2005), 44.

43. F. W. Taussig, *Principles of Economics*, 2d rev. ed., vol. 2 (New York: Macmillan, 1921), 213 (quotation) and 237. However, Taussig did anticipate the modern idea of the "demographic transition" to lower fertility. See Warren C. Robinson, "F. W. Taussig's Economic Theory of Population," *Quarterly Journal of Economics* 91 (February 1977): 165–70; and "F. W. Taussig on Individualism and the Birth Rate," *Population and Development Review* 23 (March 1997): 169–76.

44. Taussig, *Principles of Economics*, 213. The italics are Taussig's.

45. Daniel T. Rodgers, *Atlantic Crossings: Social Politics in a Progressive Age* (Cambridge, Mass.: Belknap Press of Harvard University Press, 1998), 103. Also see Hadley's defense of Malthus in Arthur Twining Hadley, *Economics: An Account of the Relations between Private Property and Public Welfare* (New York: G. P. Putnam's Sons, 1896).

46. Frank A. Fetter, *Versuch einer Bevölkerungslehre ausgehen von einer Kritik des Malthus'schen Bevölkerungsprinzips* (An Essay on Population Doctrine based on a Critique of the Population Principles of Malthus) (Jena: Gustav Fischer, 1894).

47. Frank A. Fetter, "Population or Prosperity: Annual Address of the President," *American Economic Review* 3 (March 1913): 9.

48. Ibid., 11.

49. Ross, *Origins of American Social Science*, suggests that the "gentry" conservative economists of the late nineteenth century gradually incorporated Malthus into American political economy because they moved away from a stress on the exceptionalism of the American experience that had animated rejections of Malthus and the classical economists (80–81). She oversimplifies a messy trajectory.

50. Michael A. Bernstein, "American Economists and the 'Marginalist Revolu-

tion': Notes on the Intellectual and Social Contexts of Professionalization," *Journal of Historical Sociology* 16 (March 2003): 142.

51. For Clark's early fusion of socialism and evangelicalism, and subsequent move to the right, see Ross, *Origins of American Social Science*, 106–109 and 115.

52. John B. Clark, "Distribution as Determined by a Law of Rent," *Quarterly Journal of Economics* 5 (April 1891): 289–318.

53. John Bates Clark, *The Distribution of Wealth: A Theory of Wages, Interest and Profits* (New York: Macmillan, 1899), begins: "It is the purpose of this work to show that the distribution of the income of society is controlled by a natural law, and that this law, if it worked without friction, would give to every agent of production the amount of wealth which that agent creates" (v).

54. Clark, "Distribution as Determined by a Law of Rent," 304.

55. Clark, *Philosophy of Wealth*, 99. See also "Memorial to John Bates Clark, 1847–1938," *American Economic Review* 28 (June 1938): 427–29.

56. Clark, *Philosophy of Wealth*, 100 and 102–3. Also see John Bates Clark, *Essentials of Economic Theory* (New York: Macmillan, 1907), chap. 19.

57. Quoted in Joseph Dorfman, *Thorstein Veblen and his America* (1934; reprint, New York: Augustus M. Kelley, 1972), 62.

58. Amasa Walker, *The Science of Wealth*, 4th ed. (Philadelphia: J. B. Lippincott and Co., 1872), 430.

59. Francis A. Walker, *Political Economy*, 3d rev. ed. (New York: Henry Holt, 1888), 310.

60. Ross, *Origins of American Social Science*, notes Walker's "expansive version of American political economy" was tempered by recognition that the conditions necessary to lock the Malthusian devil in its chains were tenuous in modern industrial society (83–84). Spengler, "Population Doctrines," emphasizes Walker's Malthusian musings (654–59).

61. Quoted in Spengler, "Population Doctrines," 661.

62. Ibid.

63. Henry George, *Progress and Poverty*, 50th anniversary edition (New York: Robert Schalkenbach Foundation, 1942), 141.

64. Ibid., esp. bk. 2. Also see Ernest Teilhac, *Pioneers of American Economic Thought in the Nineteenth Century*, trans. E. A. J. Johnson (1936; reprint, New York: Russell and Russell, 1967), 129–31.

65. George, *Progress and Poverty*, xiv.

66. Daniel M. Fox, *The Discovery of Abundance: Simon N. Patten and the Transformation of Social Theory* (Ithaca: Cornell University Press, 1967).

67. Simon N. Patten, *The Premises of Political Economy; Being a Re-examination of Certain Fundamental Principles of Economic Science* (Philadelphia: J. B. Lippincott, 1885), chaps. 3 and 6.

68. Arthur A. Ekirch Jr., *The Decline of American Liberalism* (1955; reprint, New York: Atheneum, 1969), 187.

69. Patten, *Premises of Political Economy*, 73.

70. Ibid., 74.

71. Simon N. Patten, *The New Basis of Civilization* (New York: Macmillan, 1907), 14.

72. Hofstadter, *Social Darwinism*, 146.

73. Patten, *New Basis of Civilization*, 11.

74. Although during the 1880s and 1890s many institutionalists were removed from the theoretical and mathematic advances in economic theory, one should not exaggerate the break between them and the marginalists. Some older institutionalists such as Simon Patten did bristle at the new marginalist paradigm (see Craufurd D. W. Goodwin, "Marginalism Moves to the New World," in *Marginal Revolution*, ed. Black, Coats, and Goodwin, 299–300), but most gradually incorporated the theory into their work.

75. Edwin R. A. Seligman, *Principles of Economics, with Special Reference to American Conditions*, 8th ed., rev. (New York: Longmans, Green, and Co., 1919), 66.

76. Ibid.

77. See, for example, Richard T. Ely, part 1, "Conservation and Economic Theory," in *The Foundations of National Prosperity: Studies in the Conservation of Permanent Natural Resources*, ed. Ely et al. (New York: Macmillan, 1917), 3–91. For Ely's rightward drift, see Robert Gough, *Farming the Cutover: A Social History of Northern Wisconsin, 1900–1940* (Lawrence: University Press of Kansas, 1997), 98–111.

78. Richard T. Ely, "The Population Bugaboo," *The Country Gentleman*, May 16, 1925, 3.

79. Richard T. Ely, "The Changing Mind in the Changing World," May 5, 1931, in Richard T. Ely Papers, Wisconsin Historical Society, Madison, Wis. (hereafter Ely Papers), Mss 411, Box 2, Folder 3; and Richard T. Ely, *Ground under Our Feet: An Autobiography* (New York: Macmillan, 1938), 256–57.

80. Maurice N. Weyl, *Walter Weyl: An Appreciation* (Philadelphia: Edward Stern and Co., 1922), 142; and Wrobel, *End of American Exceptionalism*, 81–82.

81. For the market rationale behind progressive conservation, see Brian Balogh, "Scientific Forestry and the Roots of the Modern American State: Gifford Pinchot's Path to Progressive Reform," *Environmental History* 7 (April 2002): 198–225.

82. Samuel P. Hays, *Conservation and the Gospel of Efficiency: The Progressive Conservation Movement, 1890–1920* (Cambridge, Mass.: Harvard University Press, 1959), 2. I thank Tom Robertson for bringing this passage to my attention.

83. Robert W. Kelso, *Poverty* (New York: Longmans, Green and Co., 1929), 335. Kelso also identified environmental causes of poverty such as technological change.

84. See Alice O'Conner, *Poverty Knowledge: Social Science, Social Policy, and the Poor in Twentieth-Century U.S. History* (Princeton: Princeton University Press, 2001), 53–54.

85. Seligman, *Principles of Economics*, 681.

86. Amos G. Warner, *American Charities: A Study in Philanthropy and Economics* (New York: Thomas Y. Crowell, 1894), 23–24.

87. Ibid., 26.

88. For evidence that immigration kept a lid on wage growth, see Jeffrey G. Williamson, "Globalization, Labor Markets, and Policy Backlash in the Past," *Journal of Economic Perspectives* 12 (Autumn 1998): 51–72.

89. For the cowboy in America's imagination, see Wrobel, *End of American Exceptionalism*, esp. 91–93.

90. Barbara Miller Solomon, *Ancestors and Immigrants: A Changing New England Tradition* (Cambridge, Mass: Harvard University Press, 1956), provides a good entry into the history of American racial ideas, as do George Cotkin, *Reluctant Modernism: American Thought and Culture, 1880–1900* (New York: Twayne, 1992), chap. 3; and Reginald Horsman, *Race and Manifest Destiny: The Origins of American Racial Anglo-Saxonism* (Cambridge, Mass: Harvard University Press, 1981).

91. Daniel J. Kevles, *In the Name of Eugenics: Genetics and the Uses of Human Heredity* (Cambridge, Mass: Harvard University Press, 1985), 21.

92. Here I refer to August Weismann's 1890s research on germ plasm (genes), which overturned Jean-Baptiste Lamark's theory that acquired traits could be passed on, and also to the rediscovery of Gregor Mendel's 1860s research into the inheritance of traits among peas. For the switch from Lamarkian to Mendelian genetics, see Victoria Hattam, *In the Shadow of Race: Jews, Latinos, and Immigrant Politics in the United States* (Chicago: University of Chicago Press, 2007), chap. 2.

93. Kevles, *In the Name of Eugenics*, 74–76 and 98. Notably, Jews were prominent in the British movement.

94. Hodgson, "Ideological Origins," 3–6.

95. Kevles, *In the Name of Eugenics*, 9.

96. For the era's birthrates, see Herbert S. Klein, *A Population History of the United States* (Cambridge: Cambridge University Press, 2004), chap. 4.

97. Kevles, *In the Name of Eugenics*, 96–97. John Higham, *Strangers in the Land: Patterns of American Nativism, 1860–1925* (New Brunswick: Rutgers University Press, 1955) remains indispensable for the long history of anti-immigrationism. For the racial constructions behind restrictionism, see Mae M. Ngai, "The Architecture of Race in American Immigration Law: A Reexamination of the Immigration Act of 1924," *Journal of American History* 86 (June 1999): 67–92.

98. Wrobel, *End of American Exceptionalism*, 48.

99. Cited in Ngai, "Architecture of Race," 75.

100. Robert Hunter, *Poverty* (New York: Macmillan, 1904), 302.

101. John R. Commons, *Races and Immigrants in America* (1907; reprint of 2d, 1920 edition, New York: Augustus Kelley, 1967), xvii–iii.

102. Thomas C. Leonard, "Retrospectives: Eugenics and Economics in the Progressive Era," *Journal of Economic Perspectives* 19 (Autumn 2005): 212–13.

103. For the senior Osborn, see Constance Areson Clark, "Evolution for John Doe: Pictures, the Public, and the Scopes Trial Debate," *Journal of American History* 87 (March 2001): 1275–1303; the slogan is cited in Mark K. Coffey, "The American Adonis: A Natural History of the 'Average American' (Man), 1921–32," in *Popular Eugenics: National Efficiency and American Mass Culture in the 1930s*, ed. Susan Currell and Christina Cogdell (Athens: Ohio University Press, 2006), 202.

104. Madison Grant, *The Passing of the Great Race, or the Racial Basis of European History* (New York: Charles Scribner's Sons, 1916).

105. David M. Kennedy, *Birth Control in America: The Career of Margaret Sanger* (New Haven: Yale University Press, 1970), 28.

106. For example, see "Says Europe's Future Lies in Birth Control," *New York Times*, March 15, 1928.

107. Historians who dislike Sanger argue that by the 1920s her social-economic radicalism had been superseded by more narrowly eugenic arguments for birth control, in particular that broader access to it would lower birthrates among the poor and hence genetically unfit. Moreover, she supported immigration restriction, advocated for sterilization legislation, and lectured to a Klan meeting. See, for example, David Kennedy, *Birth Control in America*, esp. 121. On the other hand, Sanger's defenders, including Jean H. Baker, *Margaret Sanger: A Life of Passion* (New York: Hill and Wang, 2011), view her as a reluctant eugenicist at worst who used the eugenics movement as an important ally against the medical establishment. They contend that her stress on the degradation of women without access to contraception relied upon an environmentalist approach to social problems that was anathema to heredity-obsessed eugenicists, and that when she argued birth control would "improve the race," she mostly meant that it would enhance freedom for women. Finally, Sanger broke from eugenicists by insisting that all women wanted fewer children, which precluded her from urging higher fertility among the wealthy. See especially Carol R. McCann, *Birth Control Politics in the United States, 1916–1945* (Ithaca: Cornell University Press, 1994), chap. 4.

108. Kevles, *In the Name of Eugenics*, 58–63; and Currell and Cogdell, eds., *Popular Eugenics*.

109. The 60,000 figure comes from Edwin Black, *War against the Weak: Eugenics and America's Campaign to Create a Master Race* (New York: Four Walls Eight Windows, 2003), 7.

110. Kevles, *In the Name of Eugenics*, 118. Scholars have documented well the terrible legacies of interwar eugenics. Nonetheless, they often exaggerate the reach of an organization of scientists and conflate eugenics with garden-variety racism. See Derek S. Hoff, "The American Eugenics Movement," in *The Encyclopedia of American Social Movements*, ed. Immanuel Ness (New York: M. E. Sharpe, 2004), 899–905.

111. Michael Mezzano, "The Progressive Origins of Eugenics Critics: Raymond

Pearl, Herbert S. Jennings, and the Defense of Scientific Inquiry," *Journal of the Gilded Age and Progressive Era* 4 (January 2005): 86.

112. See, for example, Kevles, *In the Name of Eugenics*, chap. 8.

113. For the development of the demography profession and the erection of boundaries between its scientific research and nonscientific advocacy, see Edmund Ramsden, "Carving up Population Science: Eugenics, Demography and the Controversy over the 'Biological Law' of Population Growth," *Social Studies of Science* 32 (October–December 2002): 857–99.

114. A. M. Carr-Saunders, *The Population Problem: A Study in Human Evolution* (London: Clarendon Press, 1922).

115. Peter Novick, *That Noble Dream: The 'Objectivity Question' and the American Historical Profession* (Cambridge: Cambridge University Press, 1988); and Mark C. Smith, *Social Science in the Crucible: The American Debate over Objectivity and Purpose, 1918–1941* (Durham: Duke University Press, 1994).

116. Smith, *Social Science in the Crucible*, chap. 1, esp. 27–36.

117. See, for example, P. K. Whelpton, "Differentials in True Natural Increase," *Journal of the American Statistical Association* 24 (September 1929): 233–49. But historians have gone too far in emphasizing the eugenic impulse behind early demography. See, for example, Matthew Connelly, *Fatal Misconception: The Struggle to Control World Population* (Cambridge, Mass: Belknap Press of Harvard University Press, 2008), chap. 2, which pays little attention to the new stress on scientific inquiry and policy neutrality.

118. On the question of whether American demography discarded or incorporated eugenics, see Ramsden, "Carving up Population Science."

119. Dublin was a contrarian. In the 1920s, he opposed the prevailing Malthusianism and anti-immigrationism (and also argued that eugenics encouraged the Klan). Historians have emphasized Dublin's doubts about the birth control movement, but he believed in a woman's right to contraception and conducted a long and pleasant correspondence with Margaret Sanger. For this correspondence and Dublin's writings on birth control, see the Louis Dublin Papers, National Library of Medicine, National Institutes of Health, Bethesda, Md. (hereafter Dublin Papers), Boxes 8 and 9.

120. In the context of promulgating a theory of population equilibrium, Dublin was one of the first to scientifically document the declining American birthrate (Louis I. Dublin and Alfred J. Lotka, "On the True Rate of Natural Increase," *Journal of the American Statistical Association* 20 [September 1925]: 305–39).

121. This summary leans on Frank W. Notestein and Frederick W. Osborn, "Reminiscences: The Role of Foundations, the Population Association of America, Princeton University and the United Nations in Fostering American Interest in Population Problems," *Milbank Memorial Fund Quarterly* 49, no. 4, part 2, "Forty Years of Research in Human Fertility: Retrospect and Prospect. Proceedings of a Conference Honoring Clyde V. Kiser Held at the Carnegie Endowment International Center

New York City, May 5–6, 1971" (October 1971): 67–85. Also see Frank W. Notestein, "Demography in the United States: A Partial Account of the Development of the Field," *Population and Development Review* 8 (December 1982): 654.

122. Smith, *Social Science in the Crucible*, 26.

123. Ibid. Also see Ruml's correspondence with leading demographers in Records of the Laura Spelman Rockefeller Memorial, Rockefeller Archive Center, Tarrytown, N.Y. (hereafter Spelman Records), Accession 25, Series 3, Box 59, Folders "National Research Council—Population Conference 1927–28" and "National Research Council—Population Conference 1927–29."

124. These included Walter Willcox, Louis Dublin, and Raymond Pearl. Clyde Kiser, "The Role of the Milbank Memorial Fund in the Early History of the Association," *Population Index* 47 (Autumn 1981): 490–94.

125. Notestein and Osborn, "Reminiscences," 69; and interview with Frank W. Notestein, conducted by Anders Lunde at the PAA annual meeting, 1973, in Records of the Population Association of America, Silver Spring, Md. (hereafter PAA Records). Also see Cochran's correspondence in the Records of the Milbank Memorial Fund, Yale University Special Collections Library, New Haven, Conn.

126. Milbank Memorial Fund Annual Report for 1928, cited in Clyde V. Kiser et al., "The Work of the Milbank Memorial Fund in Population since 1928," *Milbank Memorial Fund Quarterly* 49 (October 1971): 18.

127. Willford I. King, "Edgar Sydenstricker," *Journal of the American Statistical Association* 31 (June 1936): 411–14.

128. For an excellent introduction to Pearl's research and population ideas, see Thomas Robertson, *The Malthusian Moment: Global Population Growth and the Birth of American Environmentalism* (New Brunswick: Rutgers University Press, 2012), chap. 1.

129. Richard Hankinson, "The U.S. Contribution to the Creation of the IUSSP," unpublished December 1984 paper in PAA Records, Box 4, Folder 62, "International Union for the Scientific Study of Population and American National Committee of IUSSP," 1–2. Also see Margaret Sanger Papers, Library of Congress, Washington, D.C., Manuscript Division, Reel 122, Folder "1927, World Population Conference, Geneva."

130. See the various documents surrounding the funding of the IUSIPP in PAA Records, Box 4, Folder 62, Folder "International Union for the Scientific Study of Population and American National Committee of IUSSP"; Spelman Records, Box 59, Folder "National Research Council—Population Conference 1927–28"; and Dublin Papers, Box 8, Folder "Population Association of America (correspondence) 1928–July 1931."

131. See Pearl's letter describing the Union in Records of the Social Science Research Council, Rockefeller Archive Center, Accession 1, Series 1, Committee Projects, Subseries 19, Miscellaneous Projects "P", Box 191, Folder "Committee on Population Reports, 1924–1942."

132. Connelly, *Fatal Misconception*, 73. For Connelly, the creation of the IUSIPP was a key moment in which eugenics seamlessly evolved into international population control.

133. *Bulletin of the International Union for the Scientific Investigation of Population Problems*, vol. 1, no. 1 (October 1929): 2.

134. Kiser et al., "The Work of the Milbank Memorial Fund," 20; and Hankinson, "U.S. Contribution to the Creation of the IUSSP," 3.

135. Hankinson, "The U.S. Contribution to the Creation of the IUSSP," 1 and 4.

136. See the recollections of Frank Lorimer for "PAA at 50" session at the 1981 annual meeting in PAA Records, Box 4a, Folder 69, "Frank Lorimer"; and Jean van der Tak, "The IUSSP and PAA People," *PAA Affairs*, Fall 1985, 1. Fairchild himself valued scientism. See Fairchild to Alfred Lotka, April 22, 1931, Dublin Papers, Box 8, Folder "Population Association of America (correspondence) 1928–July 1931."

137. Notestein and Osborn, "Reminiscences," 70.

138. "Tentative Report of Committee on Publications and Publicity," December 1932, PAA Records, Box 7, Folder 125, "Annual Meeting May 12, 1933."

139. "Minutes of the Second Annual Meeting [of the PAA,] May 12, 1933," PAA Records, Box 7, Folder 125, "Annual Meeting May 12, 1933."

140. Quoted in Connelly, *Fatal Misconception*, 78.

141. Ramsden, "Carving up Population Science," 858.

142. Quoted in Kevles, *In the Name of Eugenics*, 122. The original source was Raymond Pearl, "The Biology of Superiority," *American Mercury*, November 1927, 260.

143. Raymond Pearl, "World Overcrowding: Saturation Point for Earth's Population Soon Will Be in Sight, With the Safety Limit for United States Estimated at 200,000,000 People—How the Nations Grow," *New York Times*, October 8, 1922. Also see Mezzano, "The Progressive Origins of Eugenics Critics"; and Robertson, *Malthusian Moment*, chap. 1.

144. See Wrobel, *End of American Exceptionalism*, 116–17.

145. For early optimum theories, see Joseph Spengler, "Knut Wicksell, Father of the Optimum," *Atlantic Economic Journal* 11 (December 1983): 1–5; Knut Wicksell, *Föreläsningar i nationalekonomi: teoretisk nationalekonomi*, 2 vols. (Lund: C.W.K. Gleerups förlag, 1928–1929); and Josiah Stamp, "Eugenic Influences in Economics," *Eugenics Review* 26 (July 1934): 111.

146. Edwin Cannan, *Wealth* (London: P. S. King and Son, 1928), chap. 3; Hugh Dalton, "The Theory of Population," *Economica* 8 (1928): 28–50; and Lionel Robbins, "The Optimum Theory of Population," in *London Essays in Economics: In Honor of Edwin Cannan*, ed. T. Gregory and H. Dalton (London: George Routledge & Sons, 1927; reprint, Freeport, N.Y., 1967), 103–34.

147. Harold Wright, *Population* (New York: Harcourt, Brace and Co., 1923).

148. A. B. Wolfe, "The Optimum Size of Population," in *Population Problems*

in the United States and Canada, ed. Louis I. Dublin (Boston: Houghton Mifflin, 1926), 63–76, "Is there a Biological Law of Human Population Growth," *Quarterly Journal of Economics* 41 (August 1927): 557–94, and "The Population Problem Since the World War: A Survey of Literature and Research," three-part essay in the *Journal of Political Economy* 36 (October 1928): 529–59; 36 (December 1928): 662–85; and 37 (February 1929): 87–120. Also see H. P. Fairchild, "Optimum Population," in *Proceedings of the World Population Conference*, ed. Margaret Sanger (London: Edward Arnold, 1927), 72–85.

149. Wolfe, "Optimum Size of Population," 65.

150. Ibid., 66.

151. Ibid., 67.

152. Ibid.

153. Richard Ely, "Policy and Population," in Ely Papers, Teaching and Research Files, Box 8, Folder 6.

154. Edwin Cannan in particular was less Malthusian than most studying the optimum; see his "The Origin of the Law of Diminishing Returns, 1813–15," *Economic Journal* 2 (March 1892): 53–69. Also see the discussion of Cannan in N. S. Narasimha Aiyangar, "Some Recent Developments in the Theory of Population," *Indian Journal of Economics* 10 (1930): 422–39.

155. Manuel Gottlieb, "The Theory of the Optimum Population for a Closed Economy," *Journal of Political Economy* 53 (December 1945): 291. This was Gottlieb's summary of the criticism, not his view.

156. Edward M. East, *Mankind at the Crossroads* (New York: C. Scribner's Sons, 1923). For East's Malthusianism, see Robertson, *Malthusian Moment*, chap. 1.

157. Radhakamal Mukerjee, "On the Criterion of Optimum Population," *American Journal of Sociology* 40 (November 1934): 344–48.

158. Wrobel, *End of American Exceptionalism*, 114.

159. For the emergence of the concept of carrying capacity, see Robertson, *Malthusian Moment*, chap. 1.

160. Ralph H. Hess, "Conservation in its Relation to Industrial Evolution" (chap. 1 of his "Conservation and Economic Theory" section), in *The Foundations of National Prosperity: Studies in the Conservation of Permanent Natural Resources*, ed. Richard T. Ely et al. (New York: Macmillan, 1917), 112.

161. See Witold Krzyzanowski, "Review of the Literature of the Location of Industries," *Journal of Political Economy* 35 (April 1927): 278–91.

162. For example, see Gough, *Farming the Cutover*, esp. chap. 3.

163. Benton MacKaye, *Employment and Natural Resources: Possibilities of Making New Opportunities for Employment through the Settlement and Development of Agricultural and Forest Lands and Other Resources* (Washington, D.C.: Department of Labor, GPO, 1919).

164. José Luis Ramos Gorostiza, "Ethics and Economics: Lewis Gray and the Conservation Question," paper provided by Universidad Complutense de Madrid,

Facultad de Ciencias Económicas y Empresariales in its series Documentos de trabajo de la Facultad de Ciencias Económicas y Empresariales, number 02-06, http://ideas.repec.org/p/ucm/doctra/02-06.html. Also see L. C. Gray, "The Economics Possibilities of Conservation," *Quarterly Journal of Economics* 27 (May 1913): 497–519.

165. See, for example, O. E. Baker, "Land Utilization in the United States: Geographical Aspects of the Problem," *Geographical Review* 13 (January 1923): 1–26.

166. Hess, "Conservation in its Relation to Industrial Evolution," 112.

167. Quoted in Wrobel, *End of American Exceptionalism*, 115.

168. Wrobel, *End of American Exceptionalism*, 120. When birth rates decreased during the Depression, Baker abandoned his Malthusianism, not sharing in the widespread celebration of the expected arrival of the stable population detailed in the next chapter.

169. Ralph H. Hess, "The Possibilities of Conservation within the Different Stages of Industrial Evolution" (chap. 2 of his "Conservation and Economic Theory" section), in *Foundations of National Prosperity*, ed. Ely et al., 123–24. Italics in the original.

170. Ibid., 122.

Chapter Three

1. See John Toye, *Keynes on Population* (Oxford: Oxford University Press, 2000). For Keynes's early-career Malthusianism, see his "A Reply to Sir William Beveridge," *Economic Journal* 33 (December 1923): 476–86.

2. National Resources Committee, *The Problems of a Changing Population*, Report of the Committee on Population Problems to the National Resources Committee (Washington, D.C.: GPO, 1938).

3. On the early republic, see chap. 1 of the present study; and Herbert S. Klein, *A Population History of the United States* (Cambridge: Cambridge University Press, 2004), chap. 2.

4. Important 1920s scholarship predicting depopulation includes Louis I. Dublin and Alfred J. Lotka, "On the True Rate of Natural Increase as Exemplified by the Population of the United States, 1920," *Journal of the American Statistical Association* 20 (September 1925): 305–39; Lowell J. Reed, "Population Growth and Forecasts," in *Studies in Population: The American People*, ed. Louis I. Dublin, *Annals of the American Academy of Political and Social Science* 188 (November 1936): 159–66; and Robert R. Kuczynski, *The Balance of Births and Deaths*, vol. 1, *Western and Northern Europe* (New York: Macmillan, 1928).

5. For example, see Louis I. Dublin, "The American People: The Census Portrait," *New York Times*, October 11, 1931.

6. See the typical comments of the census director in "On Capitol Hill: U.S.

Population Will Reach 'Stability' Years Ahead of Time, Census Expert Tells House," *Washington Post*, February 18, 1938.

7. FDR's Second Inaugural Address is available online from the American Presidency Project at www.presidency.ucsb.edu/ws/index.php?pid=15349#axzz1UYVUVUcK.

8. At the National Conference of Catholic Charities, one bishop argued that more babies would reduce crop surpluses and unemployment and that a stationary, aging population would suffer from high rates of psychological depression ("Urges More Babies as an Economic Aid," *New York Times*, August 31, 1937).

9. For pre-Keynes and -Hansen assertions that prosperity required a higher birthrate, see Joseph J. Spengler, "Population Growth, Consumer Demand and Business Profits," *Harvard Business Review* 12 (January 1934): 206.

10. See, for example, Alan Brinkley, *The End of Reform: New Deal Liberalism in Recession and War* (New York: Vintage, 1996), 132–33. The best short description of the Keynes-Hansen thesis is found in Michael A. Bernstein, *The Great Depression: Delayed Recovery and Economic Change in America, 1929–1939* (1987; reprint, Cambridge: Cambridge University Press, 1997), 9–20. Also consult Theodore Rosenof, *Economics in the Long Run: New Deal Theorists and Their Legacies* (Chapel Hill: University of North Carolina Press, 1997), chaps. 4–7.

11. An early critic of Keynes at the University of Minnesota but later his leading American disciple, Hansen was the formal theorist of secular stagnation. See Paul A. Samuelson, "Alvin Hansen as a Creative Economic Theorist," *Quarterly Journal of Economics* 90 (February 1976): 24–31.

12. See note 17.

13. John Maynard Keynes, "Some Economic Consequences of a Declining Population," *Eugenics Review* 29 (April 1937): 16–17. Keynes also claimed that population growth was tangential to wage levels because society insists on a decent wage floor. See Ian Bowen, *Economics and Demography* (London: George Allen & Unwin, 1976), 18.

14. Alvin H. Hansen, "Economic Progress and Declining Population Growth," *American Economic Review* 29 (March 1939): 3. Hansen believed that the robust economic growth of the 1920s resulted from a beneficent combination of a booming urban population and the "amazing rise of the automobile," which spurred several new industries. And on the question of the disappearing frontier, he wondered, "Is there anyone who really seriously believes that should we wake up tomorrow and discover a rich new continent suddenly thrust up in the Atlantic Ocean equal to the North American Continent, and another larger and richer in the Pacific Ocean, that this great new fact would not profoundly influence business expectations and investment opportunities in the next quarter century?" Both quotations from "Comments on Terborgh's Address at the National Industrial Conference Board, November 23, 1943," Alvin Harvey Hansen Papers, Harvard University Special Collections, Cambridge, Mass. (hereafter Hansen Papers), Cor-

respondence and other Papers of Alvin H. Hansen, ca. 1918–1970s, Box 2, Folder "Articles and Manuscripts by Alvin Hansen, 2 of 3."

15. Mark Perlman, "Some Economic Growth Problems and the Part Population Policy Plays," *Quarterly Journal of Economics* 89 (May 1975): 252. As late as 1932, Hansen was not unnerved by the prospect of a stationary population, suggesting that it would spur production of consumer goods and increase per capita income. See his *Economic Stabilization in an Unbalanced World* (New York: Harcourt, Brace, and Co., 1932), 232.

16. Cited in Brinkley, *End of Reform*, 135. Hansen wrote to British economist Sir Dennis Robertson, "The decline in population growth, the recent trends in technical innovations (which seem to be of a capital-saving type), the powerful modern institutional factors, such as corporate saving, life insurance, systematic amortization of real estate and local debt, together with the tendency for a wealthy community to save a large part of its income point, it seems to me, toward the conclusion that we would do well to develop institutional arrangements which would work toward a higher consumption economy. . . . Perhaps I am getting too Keynesian" (Hansen to Robertson, September 29, 1939, Hansen Papers, Correspondence, ca. 1920–1975, L-Z, Box 2, Folder "Robertson, Sir Dennis").

17. Keynes, "Economic Consequences of a Declining Population," 14. The development of stagnationist theory can be understood only against the search for the causes of the Great Depression. See Bernstein, *Great Depression*, 4–7; and Rosenof, *Economics in the Long Run*, esp. chaps. 3 and 6. By the mid 1930s, long-run explanations of the Depression focusing on endogenous and institutional factors (e.g., excessive industrial concentration) had been superseded by analyses focused on exogenous factors of economic development. For example, Harvard economist Joseph Schumpeter, famous for theorizing capitalism's tendency toward "creative destruction," emphasized the long-term cycles or "waves" of an economy. The stagnationists stressed the exogenous factors of geography, population, and technology; they shared Schumpeter's pessimism about the pace of innovation but emphasized declining investment based on declining population growth. Keynes's *The General Theory of Employment, Interest and Money* (New York: Harcourt, Brace, 1936), did not highlight demography. Its discussion of capital investment stressed not exogenous factors such as population or land but the interest rate and the marginal efficiency of capital, which decreases as the capital stock grows. Still, Keynes linked population to his "general theory" of excess savings not converted into investment, noting that the marginal efficiency of capital and employment remained high during the nineteenth century because "the growth of population and of invention, the opening-up of new lands, the state of confidence and the frequency of war over the average of (say) each decade seem to have been sufficient" (307). In "Economic Consequences of a Declining Population," Keynes maintained, "The demand for capital depends, of course, on three factors: on population, on the standard of life, and on capital technique [e.g., its intensity relative

to labor, as well as its productivity and duration].” Keynes concluded, “Now it is necessarily the case that an increase in population increases proportionately the demand for capital.” And he offered a psychological argument in favor of higher birthrates, observing that “an era of increasing population tends to promote optimism” (all quotations appear on p. 14). For additional discussion, see Toye, *Keynes on Population*; William Petersen, “John Maynard Keynes's Theories of Population and the Concept of ‘Optimum,’” *Population Studies* 8 (March 1955): 228–46; and Vincent J. Tarascio, “Keynes on the Sources of Economic Growth,” *Journal of Economic History* 31 (June 1971): 429–44.

18. And this subtle divergence can be muddied further if one considers Keynes's hesitation! Even as Keynes wrote that the Malthusian devil had been locked up, he noted, “Unquestionably a stationary population does facilitate a rising standard of life; but on one condition only—namely that the increase in resources or in consumption . . . does actually take place” (“Economic Consequences of a Declining Population,” 16). In his view, mass unemployment—paradoxically exacerbated by diminishing birthrates—now prevented this increase from occurring.

19. Daniel J. Kevles, *In the Name of Eugenics: Genetics and the Uses of Human Heredity* (Cambridge, Mass: Harvard University Press, 1985), chap. 8 and p. 164.

20. Ibid., chap. 11.

21. Edmund Ramsden, “Social Demography and Eugenics in the Interwar United States,” *Population and Development Review* 29 (December 2003): 547–93.

22. Frank Lorimer and Frederick Osborn, *Dynamics of Population: Social and Biological Significance of Changing Birth Rates in the United States* (New York: Macmillan, 1934), 347.

23. Clyde V. Kiser, review of *Dynamics of Population*, by Lorimer and Osborn, *Social Forces* 14 (October 1935): 153.

24. The leading works were Lorimer and Osborn, *Dynamics of Population*; and Frank Lorimer, Ellen Winston, and Louise K. Kiser, *Foundations of American Population Policy* (New York: Harper & Brothers, 1940). The textbook mentioned is Warren Thompson, *Population Problems* (New York: McGraw-Hill, 1933).

25. For a list of attendees, see “Conference Members,” Rockefeller Family Archives, Rockefeller Archive Center, Tarrytown, N.Y. (hereafter RAC), Record Group 2, Medical Interests Series, Box 2, Folder “Population Association of America, 1935–36, 1940.”

26. Lorimer to Mrs. Franklin D. Roosevelt, April 5, 1935, Records of the Population Association of America, Silver Spring, Md. (hereafter PAA Records), Box 7, Folder “Annual Meeting May 2, 1935.”

27. For this committee, consult Frederick Henry Osborn Papers, American Philosophical Society, Philadelphia (hereafter Osborn Papers), Folder “Council on Population Policy.”

28. Gunnar Myrdal, *The Essential Gunnar Myrdal*, ed. Örjan Appelqvist and Stellan Andersson (New York: The New Press, 2005), xxii.

29. Gunnar Myrdal, *An American Dilemma: The Negro Problem and Modern Democracy* (New York: Harper, 1944).

30. Gunnar Myrdal, *Population: A Problem for Democracy* (Cambridge, Mass: Harvard University Press, 1940), 130.

31. Ibid., 18.

32. Alva Myrdal, *Nation and Family: The Swedish Experiment in Democratic Family and Population Policy* (1941; reprint, with a foreword by Daniel Patrick Moynihan and new preface by the author, Cambridge, Mass: MIT Press, 1968), 2.

33. Ibid. Allan Carlson, *The Swedish Experiment in Family Politics: The Myrdals and the Interwar Population Crisis* (New Brunswick: Transaction, 1990), esp. chap 3, emphasizes the Myrdals' pronatalism.

34. Walter A. Jackson, *Gunnar Myrdal and America's Conscience: Social Engineering and Racial Liberalism, 1938–1987* (Chapel Hill: University of North Carolina Press, 1990), 76.

35. A. Myrdal, *Nation and Family*, xviii. The italics are Myrdal's.

36. For eugenicists' curricular successes, see Michael A. Rembis, "'Explaining Sexual Life to Your Daughter': Gender and Eugenic Education in the United States during the 1930s," in *Popular Eugenics: National Efficiency and American Mass Culture in the 1930s*, ed. Susan Currell and Christina Cogdell (Athens: Ohio University Press, 2006), 91–119.

37. James Reed, *From Private Vice to Public Virtue: The Birth Control Movement and American Society since 1830* (New York: Basic Books, 1978), 210.

38. For European population policies, see Michael S. Teitelbaum and Jay M. Winter, *The Fear of Population Decline* (New York: Academic Press, 1985), 58–62; and A. Myrdal, *Nation and Family*, 7–15.

39. Carl Ipsen, "Population Policy in the Age of Fascism: Observations on Recent Literature," *Population and Development Review* 24 (September 1998): 579–92. For a contemporary description, see "Bonus Marriages Boon to Germany," *New York Times*, June 12, 1938.

40. A. Myrdal, *Nation and Family*, 10.

41. I ignore the fact family allowances rarely work as intended, as the social science along these lines was nascent in the 1930s.

42. Hansen, *Economic Stabilization in an Unbalanced World*, 224.

43. Here I skirt a growing and important literature on the surprising vigor of the nineteenth-century American state. Begin with Brian Balogh, *A Government Out of Sight: The Mystery of National Authority in Nineteenth-Century America* (Cambridge: Cambridge University Press, 2009).

44. Marc Linder, *The Dilemmas of Laissez-Faire Population Policy in Capitalist Societies: When the Invisible Hand Controls Reproduction* (Westport, Conn.: Greenwood Press, 1997), argues that, as a concession to the ideal of individual liberty, capitalist states mostly leave reproduction of labor up to the whims of individual families, a system Linder calls "procreational laissez-faire."

45. Donald K. Pickens, *Eugenics and the Progressives* (Nashville: Vanderbilt University Press, 1968).

46. Quoted in "Urges Birth Control to Keep World Peace," *New York Times*, January 18, 1937.

47. The continued obsession with differential fertility also helps account for the widespread indifference to proposals for direct cash payments to mothers and children. Reformers not only argued that enhancing social services was cheaper than such direct payments (and promised to build a broader political coalition) but also assumed cash payments would provide an incentive for childbirth only to those at the bottom of the socioeconomic spectrum. Many thus advocated for the family wage rather than European-style family allowances. For contemporary discussion, see "Remarks and Round Table of 'Experts,' Discussion of Eugenic Policies, 5/11/33," American Eugenics Society Records, American Philosophical Society, Philadelphia, Frederick Osborn Papers I, Folder 8.

48. The "Beveridge Report" was, more formally, Interdepartmental Committee on Social Insurance and Allied Services, *Social Insurance and Allied Services* (New York: Macmillan, 1942).

49. National Resources Planning Board, *After the War—Full Employment: Post-War Planning*, rev. ed. (Washington, D.C.: National Resources Planning Board, 1943).

50. For the decline of the planning impulse, see Brinkley, *End of Reform*, chap. 10.

51. See, for example, Matthew Connelly, *Fatal Misconception: The Struggle to Control World Population* (Cambridge, Mass: Belknap Press of Harvard University Press, 2008), 83. James Reed writes, "Rather than a cause for despair, however, the population problem provided a compelling justification for fundamental social reforms. The solution was not suppression of birth control information and enforced biological slavery but 'vast distributional reforms in the interest of families with children.' Only a state-supported system of family services from medical care to day nurseries could provide the incentives required to reinstate the four-child family norm and save the race" (*From Public Vice to Private Virtue*, 209). Reed does note some support for the stable population but places it against eugenic rather than economic concerns—he contends that those who accepted a stable population did so primarily because they worried about quality more than quantity (206–7). And he concludes—incorrectly—that 1930s America was "a world in which Malthus was still a prophet without honor" (210). Leading works on eugenics, such as Kevles, *In the Name of Eugenics*, also miss the support for a stable population.

52. For Frederick Osborn's support of a stable or even moderately declining population, see his "Social Morality in a Period of Diminishing Population," Osborn Papers, Folder "Social Morality in a Period of Diminishing Population." Also see Lorimer and Osborn, *Dynamics of Population*, 19–21.

53. Lorimer and Osborn wrote, "To a surprising degree, the most effective means of modifying present differentials in fertility, so as to decrease the fertility of handicapped groups and to increase the fertility of families with superior resources, would seem to coincide with changes which are socially desirable for other reasons" (*Dynamics of Population*, 339).

54. As Theda Skocpol, Linda Gordon, and Molly Ladd-Taylor among others have shown, the American welfare state developed along "maternalistic" lines. But while early-century state-level pensions for mothers and the Social Security Act's Aid to Families with Dependent Children program sought to address the perceived problems of single motherhood and assumed a household headed by a male breadwinner, these developments did not erect an explicitly pronatalist welfare state.

55. G. Myrdal, *Population*, 164.

56. For consumptionist thought, see Kathleen G. Donohue, *Freedom from Want: American Liberalism and the Idea of the Consumer* (Baltimore: Johns Hopkins University Press, 2003).

57. Journalist Stuart Chase, also discussed in the main text, was a crucial popularizer of consumptionist and anti-orthodox economic thought. Among his many works, see *The Economy of Abundance* (New York: Macmillan, 1934). USDA economist Mordecai Ezekiel wrote several mass-market books insisting that higher consumption and planning could usher in a new era of abundance. See *$2500 a Year: From Scarcity to Abundance* (New York: Harcourt, Brace, and Co., 1936). Also consult Paul H. Douglas, "Purchasing Power of the Masses and Business Depressions," in *Economic Essays in Honor of Wesley Clair Mitchell* (New York: Columbia University Press, 1935).

58. A well-known statement was Maurice Leven, Harold G. Moulton, and Clark Warburton, *America's Capacity to Consume* (Washington, D.C.: Brookings Institution, 1934).

59. Keynes, *General Theory*, book 3, chaps. 8–10. For the ongoing debate on the consumption function, see Karen E. Dynan, Jonathan Skinner, and Stephen P. Zeldes, "Do the Rich Save More?" National Bureau of Economic Research Working Paper 7906 (Washington, D.C.: NBER, 2000).

60. Robert M. Collins, *More: The Politics of Economic Growth in Postwar America* (New York: Oxford University Press, 2000), esp. chap. 2, and *The Business Response to Keynes, 1929–1964* (New York: Columbia University Press, 1981).

61. For the centrality of mass consumption to American liberalism, see Olivier Zunz, *Why the American Century?* (Chicago: University of Chicago Press, 1998); Brinkley, *End of Reform*; Meg Jacobs, *Pocketbook Politics: Economic Citizenship in Twentieth-Century America* (Princeton: Princeton University Press, 2005); and Liz Cohen, *A Consumer's Republic: The Politics of Mass Consumption in Postwar America* (New York: Knopf, 2003).

62. Keynes, "Economic Consequences of a Declining Population," 15.

63. Robert B. Westbrook, "Tribune of the Technostructure: The Popular Economics of Stuart Chase," *American Quarterly* 32 (Autumn 1980): 395.

64. Stuart Chase, *A New Deal* (New York: Macmillan, 1932), 71. Chase acknowledged that, during the frontier era, rapid population growth, open lands, and the laissez-faire state had combined to create the American juggernaut. But he predicted that the post-frontier era would be just as prosperous, writing, "We have left the economy of scarcity behind and entered the economy of abundance" (1).

65. Ibid., 72.

66. Ibid.

67. For a quick overview of his work, see Leonard Silk, "The Economics of Joseph J. Spengler," *Demography India* 15 (January–June 1986): 137–45.

68. Spengler's Malthus was not the coarse opponent of charitable giving, as he is often portrayed, but rather friend to the average worker. The largely unprocessed Joseph Spengler Papers, Duke University Special Collections, Durham, N.C. (hereafter Spengler Papers), include many comments to the effect that Malthus "thought the poor should be well paid."

69. Joseph J. Spengler, "Population Movements and Economic Equilibrium in the United States," *Journal of Political Economy* 48 (April 1940): 159. Also see his "Population Doctrines in the United States," *Journal of Political Economy* 41 (August 1933): 433–67.

70. Spengler, "Population Growth, Consumer Demand, and Business Profits," 217.

71. Spengler, "Population Movements and Economic Equilibrium," 173.

72. Spengler, "Population Growth, Consumer Demand, and Business Profits," 207.

73. Ibid., 221.

74. Spengler revealed his early Malthusianism and support for eugenics in unpublished essays he wrote while still a graduate student at Ohio State, circa 1928–32. See "A Eugenicist's City in the Sun" and "Is the Malthusian Devil Rechained?" both undated, in Spengler Papers, Box 1 of offsite collection. Also see J. J. Spengler, "The Birth Rate—Potential Dynamite," *Scribner's Magazine*, July 1932, 6–12. Spengler never completely abandoned eugenic assumptions. He told a North Carolina state senator in 1973, "Probably the most serious population problem confronting the United States is the relatively large number of 'born losers'—i.e. persons destined to be non-self-supporting—being brought into the world each year by women without the genetic and/or euthenic requirements of responsible motherhood and parenthood" (Spengler to Charles H. Keller, January 2, 1973, Spengler Papers, Box 7 of onsite collection). Comments such as these have led many scholars to dismiss postwar Malthusianism and campaigns for family planning programs as little more than warmed-over eugenics. As we will see, however, postwar perceptions of a population crisis were predicated much more on ecological and economic arguments than on eugenic ones.

75. P. K. Whelpton, *Population Trends in the United States* (New York: McGraw-Hill, 1933).

76. P. K. Whelpton, "Population Policy for the United States," in *Population Theory and Policy: Selected Readings*, ed. Joseph J. Spengler and Otis Dudley Duncan (Glencoe, Ill.: Free Press, 1956), 464.

77. Ibid., 467.

78. Whelpton failed to predict the great postwar surge in agricultural productivity. He was also on shaky ground predicting a constant ratio between the resource-intensive and non-resource-intensive share of national wealth, as the latter was steadily increasing.

79. "U.S. Census Errors Told at Congress," *New York Times*, July 31, 1937.

80. A leading participant in the technological unemployment debate was William Ogburn, an eminent sociologist at the University of Chicago firmly entrenched in population circles and a founding officer of the PAA.

81. Amy Sue Bix, *Inventing Ourselves Out of Jobs? America's Debate over Technological Unemployment, 1929–1981* (Baltimore: Johns Hopkins University Press, 2000).

82. Guy Irving Burch, "No Cause for Alarm: An Answer to Dr. Dublin," *Birth Control Review* 15 (December 1931): 365.

83. H. P. Fairchild, *Economics for the Millions* (New York: Modern Age Books, 1940) and "Optimum Population," in *Proceedings of the World Population Conference*, ed. Margaret Sanger (London: Arnold, 1927), 72–85.

84. Henry Pratt Fairchild, *People: The Quantity and Quality of the Population* (New York: Henry Holt, 1939), 89.

85. Henry Pratt Fairchild, "Deflating the Boom in Population," *Survey Graphic*, December 1933, 601. Also see his "Let Malthus Be Dead!" *North American Review*, March 1932, 202–8.

86. Fairchild, "Deflating the Boom," 602.

87. Don Patinkin, *Anticipations of the General Theory? And Other Essays on Keynes* (Chicago: University of Chicago Press, 1982), chap. 3 (p. 59 for Kalecki's claim).

88. Michal Kalecki, *Studies in Economic Dynamics* (London: George Allen and Unwin, 1943), 88.

89. W. B. Reddaway, *The Economics of a Declining Population* (London: George Allen & Unwin, 1939). Also see Alex Millmow, "W. Brian Reddaway—Keynes' Emissary to Australia, 1913–2002," *Economic Record* 79 (March 2003): 136–38. Keynes's inner circle, known as his "circus," also critiqued his population theory. Joan Robinson, known primarily for her theory of imperfect competition, "was less alarmed than he [Keynes] was about the possibility that a population decline would reduce the demand for investment, and thence employment" (Toye, *Keynes on Population*, 215). Indeed, Robinson maintained that population growth reduced the growth of income per head (Bowen, *Economics and Demography*,

20). Decades later, Robinson expressed her concern with the population explosion (Joan Robinson, *Freedom and Necessity* [New York: Pantheon, 1970], 62).

90. Reddaway, *Economics of a Declining Population*, 60.

91. Ibid., 172–81.

92. Ibid., 229. Reddaway also suggested that a declining population might improve a nation's international trading position; reduced demand for imports meant they could be secured on more favorable terms. Conversely, "To put it crudely, the more mouths we have to feed, the more outlets for our exports we must find and the stronger the presumption that we shall have to lower the prices we charge" (218).

93. Ibid., 229.

94. Ibid., 107.

95. For Reddaway's policy prescriptions, see ibid., 121–27.

96. Ibid., 255.

97. For example, see Rosenof, *Economics in the Long Run*, chap. 9.

98. The prologue to Collins, *More*, reviews conservative resistance to mature-economy doctrine.

99. Alexander Sachs to Alvin Hansen, February 8, 1938, in Alexander Sachs Papers, Franklin Delano Roosevelt Presidential Library, Hyde Park, N.Y. (hereafter FDR Library), Box 31, Folder "Hansen, Alvin."

100. Schumpeter did address population variables: he suggested that they and other exogenous forces were less important to investment than endogenous forces in the economy—above all, technological innovation and the entrepreneurial application of it. See Joseph A. Schumpeter, *Capitalism, Socialism, and Democracy*, 2d ed. (London: Harper & Brothers, 1947), 82–83.

101. Scholars tend to ignore the broader population discussion surrounding the stagnation debate. See, for example, Herbert Stein, *The Fiscal Revolution in America* (Chicago: University of Chicago Press, 1969), 175–76; Brinkley, *End of Reform*, 133–34; and Rosenof, *Economists in the Long Run*, chaps. 7–8.

102. See, for example, Glenn E. McLaughlin and Ralph J. Watkins, "The Problem of Industrial Growth in a Mature Economy," *American Economic Review* 29, Supplement, Papers and Proceedings of the Fifty-first Annual Meeting of the American Economic Association (March 1939): 1–14.

103. Willford I. King, *The Wealth and Income of the People of the United States* (New York: Macmillan, 1915).

104. Willford I. King, "Are We Suffering from Economic Maturity?" *Journal of Political Economy* 47 (October 1939): 612. For a rebuttal by a New Deal economist nonetheless sympathetic to stagnationist thought, see Gerhard Colm, "Comments on Willford I. King's Article in the *Journal of Political Economy*," in Richard Gilbert Papers, FDR Library, Box 4, Folder "Colm, Gerhard, 1937, June 1939–April 1940." Also consult Harold Reed, "Economists on Industrial Stagnation," *Journal of Political Economy* 48 (April 1940): 244–50.

105. King, "Are We Suffering from Economic Maturity?" 621.

106. Ibid., 614.

107. Mill wrote that the stationary state, in which capital and population are no longer growing, "implies no stationary state of human improvement. There would be [in the stationary state] as much scope as ever for all kinds of mental culture, and moral and social progress; as much room for improving the Art of Living, and much more likelihood of its being improved, when minds ceased to be engrossed by the art of getting on" (John Stuart Mill, *Principles of Political Economy*, from the 5th London ed., vol. 2 [New York: D. Appleton and Co., 1882], 339–40). At the end of the nineteenth century, Alfred Marshall worried about "such overcrowding as causes physical and moral vigour to be impaired by the want of fresh air and light and of healthy and joyous recreation to the young" (Alfred Marshall, *Principles of Economics* [London: Macmillan, 1890], 380).

108. Granted, Dublin was anxious about the implications of a steady population should the nation not undertake the reforms necessary to adjust the economy. In "Are There Too Many of Us?" *New Outlook*, March 1933, he argued, "We have for a long time lived in a fool's paradise so far as our [potentially declining] population is concerned" (28). But here he concluded: "With numbers properly adjusted to our facilities and resources, we can enjoy a well-organized society, free of such obvious maladjustments as poverty and the disordered organization of our productive machinery" (29).

109. Thompson, *Population Problems*, 446–47.

110. Hansen, "Comments on Terborgh's Address." Also see Thor Hultgren, review of *The Bogey of Economic Maturity*, by George Terborgh, *Journal of Political Economy* 55 (August 1947): 363–64.

111. President Roosevelt and Congress created the Temporary National Economic Committee in response to the "Roosevelt Recession" of 1937–38. Its primary objective was to investigate economic concentration, but hearings became a forum for debating the Keynes-Hansen thesis as much as monopolies. See Temporary National Economic Committee, *Final Report of the Executive Secretary to the Temporary National Economic Committee on the Concentration of Economic Power in the United States* (Washington, D.C.: GPO, 1941), 224, 271–73, 279–81, and 284.

112. George Terborgh, *The Bogey of Economic Maturity* (Chicago: Machinery and Allied Products Institute, 1945), 20–22 and 174.

113. George Terborgh, *The Automation Hysteria* (Washington, D.C.: Machinery and Allied Products Institute, 1965).

114. Terborgh, *Bogey of Economic Maturity*, 174.

115. Howard S. Ellis, "Monetary Policy and Investment," *American Economic Review* 30, Supplement, Papers and Proceedings of the Fifty-second Annual Meeting of the American Economic Association, September 1939 (March 1940): 37.

116. Harold Moulton et al., *Capital Expansion, Employment, and Economic Stability* (Washington, D.C.: Brookings Institution, 1940), 167–68.

117. John Kenneth Galbraith, *Economics in Perspective: A Critical History* (Boston: Houghton Mifflin, 1987), 189.

118. Paul M. Sweezy, *The Theory of Capitalist Development* (New York: Monthly Review Press, 1942), 222–26. Alan Sweezy, Paul's less radical brother, tried to split the difference between the Keynes-Hansen and SPK positions. In "Population Growth and Investment Opportunity," *Quarterly Journal of Economics* 55 (November 1940), Alan, who later became national chairman of Planned Parenthood, suggested that whether population growth "is a boon or a curse" depends largely on broader economic circumstances (76). He agreed that, during prosperous times, population growth can boost an economy, but he doubted its palliative effect during downturns (77).

119. Chester Barnard et al., "The First *Fortune* Round Table: The Effects of Government Spending upon Private Enterprise," *Fortune*, March 1939, 60 and 117.

120. Ibid., 117.

121. For example see Henry A. Wallace, *New Frontiers* (New York: Reynal and Hitchcock, 1934).

122. Quoted in David M. Wrobel, *The End of American Exceptionalism: Frontier Anxiety from the Old West to the New Deal* (Lawrence: University Press of Kansas, 1993), 139.

123. *Home Building and Loan Association v. Blaisdell*, 290 U.S. 398, 442 (1934). See John A. Fliter and Derek S. Hoff, *Fighting Foreclosure: The Blaisdell Case, the Contract Clause, and the Great Depression* (Lawrence: University Press of Kansas, 2012).

124. See Donohue, *Freedom from Want*, chap. 7.

125. Quoted in Theodore Rosenof, *Dogma, Depression, and the New Deal: The Debate of Political Leaders over Economic Recovery* (Port Washington, N.Y.: Kennikat Press, 1975), 40.

126. See Franklyn Waltman, "Roosevelt Drafts Plan to Boost U.S. Income, Help Underprivileged," *Washington Post*, June 16, 1937; and, more generally, Brinkley, *End of Reform*.

127. J. A. Hobson, *The Economics of Unemployment*, rev. ed. (London: George Allen and Unwin, 1931); William Trufant Foster and Waddill Catchings, *Progress and Plenty: Two-Minute Talks on the Economics of Prosperity* (Boston: Houghton Mifflin, 1930); Donohue, *Freedom from Want*, 213–22; and M. F. Bleaney, *Under-Consumption Theories: A History and Critical Analysis* (London: Lawrence and Wishart, 1976).

128. "New Conditions Impose New Requirements upon Government and Those Who Conduct Government," Campaign Address on Progressive Government at the Commonwealth Club, San Francisco, Calif. September 23, 1932, *The Public Papers and Addresses of Franklin D. Roosevelt*, ed. Samuel I. Rosenman, vol. 1, *The Genesis of the New Deal, 1928–32* (New York: Random House, 1938), 747–52.

129. Laughlin Currie, another of FDR's economic advisers, suggested that the American economy had reached a permanent plateau (Brinkley, *End of Reform*,

132). Rexford Tugwell was perhaps the New Deal's most ardent stagnationist. Other officials such as Mordecai Ezekiel subscribed to some tenets of mature-economy doctrine but predicted economic growth just around the corner. See Wrobel, *End of American Exceptionalism*, chap. 10; and Collins, *More*, 4–10.

130. See note 49.

131. Rexford G. Tugwell, *The Battle for Democracy* (New York: Columbia University Press, 1935), 109.

132. Frank W. Notestein and Frederick W. Osborn, "Reminiscences: The Role of Foundations, the Population Association of America, Princeton University and the United Nations in Fostering American Interest in Population Problems," *Milbank Memorial Fund Quarterly* 49, no. 4 part 2, "Forty Years of Research in Human Fertility: Retrospect and Prospect. Proceedings of a Conference Honoring Clyde V. Kiser Held at the Carnegie Endowment International Center New York City, May 5–6, 1971" (October 1971): 71.

133. Brinkley, *End of Reform*, cites the wildly erroneous population estimates in *Problems of a Changing Population* but does not review its policy prescriptions (133). Discussing the report in the context of mature-economy thought, Brinkley incorrectly conveys the impression that it articulated the Keynes-Hansen view.

134. National Resources Committee, *Problems of a Changing Population*, 7.

135. Ibid.

136. Ibid., 34.

137. Ibid., 8.

138. *Problems* joined a long list of studies bemoaning the inefficient distribution of the American population. See, for example, Rupert B. Vance, *Human Geography of the South: A Study in Regional Resources and Human Adequacy* (Chapel Hill: University of North Carolina Press, 1932).

139. Many histories of the New Deal emphasize the back-to-the-land and community-building aspects of resettlement programs and overlook the political economy of population. See Arthur M. Schlesinger Jr., *The Coming of the New Deal* (Boston: Houghton Mifflin, 1958), chap. 21; Paul K. Conkin, *Tomorrow a New World: The New Deal Community Program* (Ithaca: Cornell University Press, 1959); Joseph L. Arnold, *The New Deal in the Suburbs: A History of the Greenbelt Town Program, 1935–1954* (Columbus: Ohio State University Press, 1971); and Daniel T. Rodgers, *Atlantic Crossings: Social Politics in a Progressive Age* (Cambridge, Mass.: Belknap Press of Harvard University Press, 1998), 446–84.

140. In particular, the Southern Agrarians, a group of intellectuals centered at Vanderbilt University, championed traditionalist agrarian values and critiqued industrial capitalism. See Paul V. Murphy, *The Rebuke of History: The Southern Agrarians and American Conservative Thought* (Chapel Hill: University of North Carolina Press, 2001).

141. During the 1930s, the rural/urban distribution of the American population held steady—about 44 percent rural and 56 percent urban—reversing the long-

standing trend (Warren S. Thompson and P. K. Whelpton, "Changes in Regional and Urban Patterns of Population Growth," *American Sociological Review* 5 [December 1940]: 926). Also consult C. Warren Thornthwaite, *Internal Migration in the United States* (Philadelphia: University of Pennsylvania Press, 1934); Carter Goodrich, Bushrod W. Allin, and Marion Hayes, *Migration and Planes of Living, 1920–1934* (Philadelphia: University of Pennsylvania Press, 1935); and Carter Goodrich et al., *Migration and Economic Opportunity: The Report of the Study of Population Redistribution* (Philadelphia: University of Pennsylvania Press, 1936). All these books (and the Daniel Creamer volume cited in note 143) emerged from the Study of Population Redistribution at the Wharton School of Finance, financed by the Social Science Research Council and its Committee on Population Redistribution. One can research this committee in Records of the Social Science Research Council, RAC, Accession 1, Series 1, Committee Projects, Subseries 19, Miscellaneous Projects "P", Box 191, Folder "Committee on Population Reports, 1924–1942."

142. See Carter Goodrich's comments in "Population Redistribution: Round Table, Friday Afternoon, May 3, 1935, Conference on Population Studies in Relation to Social Planning," PAA Records, Box 7, Folder "Annual Meeting May 2, 1935."

143. On business location, see Daniel B. Creamer, *Is Industry Decentralizing? A Statistical Analysis of Locational Changes in Manufacturing Employment, 1899–1933* (Philadelphia: University of Pennsylvania Press, 1935). Creamer revealed that American industry was moving from city centers to the surrounding towns but was not, on the whole, fundamentally redrawing the economic map of the nation (even as, for example, northern textile firms migrated toward cheaper labor markets in the South).

144. T. J. Woofter Jr. and Ellen Winston, *Seven Lean Years* (Chapel Hill: University of North Carolina Press, 1939), estimated that "farm families have proportionally almost twice as many children as city families" (35).

145. Roosevelt, after all, had campaigned on the notion of increasing the purchasing power of the rural population, and his administration would declare Southern poverty the number one problem in the United States. See "The Forgotten Man," Radio Address, Albany, April 7, 1932, in *Public Papers of Franklin D. Roosevelt*, ed. Rosenman, vol. 1, 624–27.

146. For example, see Roosevelt's "Address before the American Country Life Conference on the Better Distribution of Population Away from Cities," Ithaca, N.Y., August 19, 1931, in ibid., 503–15.

147. M. L. Wilson, "Decentralization of Industry in the New Deal," *Social Forces* 13 (May 1935): 588–98. Wilson was then assistant secretary of agriculture.

148. Mordecai Ezekiel to "Mr. Secretary," May 4, 1935, in Rexford Tugwell Papers (hereafter Tugwell Papers), FDR Library, Box 7, Folder "Ezekiel, Mordecai."

149. Rexford Tugwell, "The Meaning of the Greenbelt Towns," *New Republic*, February 17, 1937, 43; and Arnold, *New Deal in the Suburbs*, 26.

150. National Industrial Recovery Act, Section 208 (Public Law 67, 73rd Cong., 1st sess. [June 16, 1933]). Uncertainty initially surrounded this congressional mandate. See Harold Ickes (Secretary of the Interior) to Colonel Louis Howe (one of FDR's most trusted advisers), October 4, 1933, in Louis Howe Papers, FDR Library, Box 52, Folder "Subsistence Homesteads, 1933." FDR's First Inaugural Address is available online from the American Presidency Project at www.presidency.ucsb.edu/ws/index.php?pid=14473#axzz1UjdfbvIE.

151. The key agencies were the Rural Rehabilitation Division of the Federal Emergency Relief Administration and the Subsistence Homesteads Division of the Department of the Interior.

152. For an optimistic early overview of these measures, see M. L. Wilson, "The Place of Subsistence Homesteads in Our National Economy," *Journal of Farm Economics* 16 (January 1934): 73–84.

153. For Tugwell's participation in the birth control movement, see Raymond Fosdick to Dunham, March 19, 1931, in Rockefeller Foundation Archives, Bureau of Social Hygiene Papers, RAC, Series 3, Box 7, Folder 166, "Birth Control 1931–32."

154. For more on this conference, see Mordecai Ezekiel Papers, FDR Library, Box 30, Folder "Pop. Redistribution Conference of Population Studies, May 1935."

155. "Population Redistribution: Round Table," 18.

156. Otis L. Graham Jr., *Toward a Planned Society: From Roosevelt to Nixon* (New York: Oxford University Press, 1976), 45.

157. Estimates from Conkin, *Tomorrow a New World*, 331. William E. Leuchtenburg, *Franklin D. Roosevelt and the New Deal, 1932–1940* (New York: Harper and Row, 1963), reports that the Resettlement Administration's original goal was to relocate 500,000 families (140).

158. For the illuminating failure to secure a Post Office equipment factory in Arthurdale, see Thomas H. Coode and Dennis E. Fabbri, "The New Deal's Arthurdale Project in West Virginia," *West Virginia History* 36 (July 1975): 291–308; and *Congressional Record*, House, February 28, 1939, 3489–3505.

159. P. Fishback, W. Horrace, and S. Kantor, "Do Federal Programs Affect Internal Migration? The Impact of New Deal Expenditures on Mobility during the Great Depression," *Explorations in Economic History* 43 (April 2006): 179–222.

160. As we will see, the zero population movement of the late 1960s argued that population distribution was a shibboleth diverting attention from the issue of aggregate population growth.

161. One example was O. E. Baker in the Department of Agriculture. See Richard S. Kirkendall, *Social Scientists and Farm Politics in the Age of Roosevelt* (Columbia: University of Missouri Press, 1966), 71–72.

162. For example, see the comments of Ellsworth Huntington, a professor of economics at Yale University, in "Population Redistribution: Round Table," 9–11.

163. Tugwell used the term "human erosion" in "The Reason for Resettlement," NBC Radio Broadcast, December 2, 1935, in Tugwell Papers, Box 57, Folder "The Reason for Resettlement." The "riotous farming" language appears in his "No More Frontiers," *Today*, June 22, 1935, 3.

164. Tugwell, "No More Frontiers," 3. Also see his "National Significance of Recent Trends in Farm Population," *Social Forces* 14 (October 1935): 1–7.

165. After the war, Tugwell dismissed the short-lived Malthusian hysteria (see chap. 4) but approved of a reduction in population—and believed that it would be engendered by economic "worldism" (globalization) and a resulting surge in production ("Beyond Malthus: Numbers and Resources," *Common Cause*, May 1949, 375–77).

166. Goodrich et al., *Migration and Economic Opportunity*, v.

167. Ibid., 61.

168. Ibid., 162.

169. Ibid., 494.

170. Ibid.

171. Ibid.

172. Eleanor Roosevelt, "Subsistence Farmsteads," *Forum*, April 1934, 199–201.

173. The demographic backdrop to economic policy making during World War II deserves a full study. Government officials continued to seek state-sponsored population redistribution, and several astute business leaders lobbied for war contracts on the grounds that ramping up production in particular locations would aid this goal. Begin by consulting Collis Stocking (Bureau of Employment Security), "Reallocation of Population and the Defense Program," Records of the National Resources Planning Board, Records of Division A (Record Group 187.4.1), Records of the Trends and Stabilization Section, 1938–43, Box 9, Folder "Papers Given at Population Meetings held at Princeton, N.J. May 17, 1941." For an overview of wartime industrial planning, see Richard Parker, *John Kenneth Galbraith: His Life, His Politics, His Economics* (New York: Farrar, Straus and Giroux, 2005), chaps. 6–7, esp. 126–29. For the rising birthrate during World War II—14 percent higher in 1941 than in 1933—see William Fielding Ogburn, "War, Babies, and the Future," Public Affairs Pamphlets no. 83 (New York: Public Affairs Committee, 1943), 1–3.

Chapter Four

1. See, for example, Joseph Spengler's forecasts in "'Standing Room Only' in the World? The Effect of Growth of Population," *U.S. News & World Report*, November 23, 1959, 84.

2. John Kenneth Galbraith, *The Affluent Society*, 50th anniversary edition, updated and with a new introduction by the author (New York: Houghton Mifflin, 1998); and David Morris Potter, *People of Plenty: Economic Abundance*

and the American Character (Chicago: University of Chicago Press, 1954). On "growthism," see Robert M. Collins, *More: The Politics of Economic Growth in Postwar America* (New York: Oxford University Press, 2000).

3. Today the terms "more developed nations" and "less developed nations" are used more than "developed" and "developing," and the term "Third World" is a relic of the Cold War. I use these weighted words because they prevailed in this era (later environmentalists would begin writing of "overdeveloped nations").

4. Thomas Robertson, *The Malthusian Moment: Global Population Growth and the Birth of American Environmentalism* (New Brunswick: Rutgers University Press, 2012), chap. 1.

5. The term "Neo-Malthusian" muddies the waters because, since the late nineteenth century, it had referred primarily to proponents of legalized birth control. I use "Malthusian" throughout this study as an umbrella term to describe an admittedly wide range of individuals who favored cessation of population growth.

6. The comparison to India's growth rate was a common trope. See, for example, Lincoln Day, "The American Fertility Cult: Our Irresponsible Birthrate," *Columbia University Forum* 3 (Summer 1960): 4.

7. For a typical summary of the population issue by an environmental historian, see Stephen Fox, *The American Conservation Movement: John Muir and His Legacy* (Madison: University of Wisconsin Press, 1981), 306–13. The most comprehensive examinations are Robertson, *Malthusian Moment*; and Björn-Ola Linnér, *The Return of Malthus: Environmentalism and Post-war Population–Resource Crises* (Isle of Harris, UK: White Horse Press, 2003).

8. For insightful discussion of the postwar population surge, consult Richard A. Easterlin, *Growth Triumphant: The Twenty-first Century in Historical Perspective* (Ann Arbor: University of Michigan Press, 1996), chaps. 6 and 7.

9. Joel E. Cohen, *How Many People Can the Earth Support?* (New York: W. W. Norton, 1995), Appendix 2, 400–401.

10. Malthusians reached this conclusion despite a prevailing underestimation of escalating expansion. For example, Joseph Spengler predicted a world population of 3.3 billion in the year 2000 ("The World's Hunger—Malthus, 1948," *Proceedings of the Academy of Political Science* 23 [January 1949]: 71).

11. Fairfield Osborn, *Our Plundered Planet* (Boston: Little, Brown & Co., 1948); and William Vogt, *Road to Survival* (New York: William Sloane Associates, 1948). Robertson, *Malthusian Moment*, devotes an entire chapter to Osborn and Vogt (chap. 2). Osborn, zoologist and president and founder of the Conservation Foundation—a postwar offshoot of the Wildlife Conservation Society with a eugenic mission to "conserve" the quality of the population as well as natural resources—was the cousin of Frederick Osborn, the leading reform eugenicist in the 1930s. Vogt, whose book was the darker, more pessimistic, and better selling of the two, was an ornithologist and conservationist and later the national director of the Planned Parenthood Federation. Fox, *American Conservation Movement*, reports

that *Road to Survival* was the "best-selling conservation book before [Rachel Carson's] *Silent Spring*" (308).

12. Demographer Paul Demeny called transition theory "the central preoccupation of modern demography" (cited in Dudley Kirk, "Demographic Transition Theory," *Population Studies* 50 [November 1996]: 361). The American demography profession further retreated into a neutral-research posture after the war as it confronted the legacy of its links to a eugenics movement now widely associated with Nazism.

13. See Michael E. Latham, *Modernization as Ideology: American Social Science and "Nation Building" in the Kennedy Era* (Chapel Hill: University of North Carolina Press, 2000); Robertson, *Malthusian Moment*, chap. 4; and Daniel Aksamit, "Precursors to Modernization Theory in United States Government Policy: A Study of the Tennessee Valley Authority, Japanese Occupation, and Point Four Program" (master's thesis, Kansas State University, 2009).

14. An excellent entry into demographic transition theory and the evolution from 1945 to 1955 of activist support for family planning programs is Dennis Hodgson, "Demography as Social Science and Policy Science," *Population and Development Review* 9 (March 1983): 1–34. Also see Robertson, *Malthusian Moment*, chap. 3. For a perspective that locates a more a consistent policy orientation among demographers and stresses the influence of the Cold War in driving the theory's evolution, see Simon Szreter, "The Idea of Demographic Transition Theory and the Study of Fertility Change: A Critical Intellectual History," *Population and Development Review* 19 (December 1993): 659–701. For a literature review, consult Susan Greenhalgh, "The Social Construction of Population Science: An Intellectual, Institutional, and Political History of Twentieth-Century Demography," *Comparative Studies in Society and History* 38 (January 1996): 26–66.

15. More technically, the idea was that high birthrates reduce the per capita supply of capital and, by lowering the capital/labor ratio, produce lower per capita incomes.

16. Ansley J. Coale and Edgar M. Hoover, *Population Growth and Economic Development in Low-Income Countries: A Case Study of India's Prospects* (Princeton: Princeton University Press, 1958).

17. Robertson, *Malthusian Moment*, chap. 4; and Linnér, *Return of Malthus*, esp. chaps. 2 and 3. Linnér argues that neo-Malthusianism was closely connected with the West's Fordist project: mass production required a global market for raw materials and hence their long-term conservation.

18. Donald Worster, foreword to Linnér, *Return of Malthus*, xii.

19. Linnér, *Return of Malthus*, chaps. 2 and 3; and Aksamit, "Precursors to Modernization Theory." Truman's Inaugural Address is available online from the American Presidency Project at www.presidency.ucsb.edu/ws/index.php?pid=13282#axzz1Ujd fbv1E.

20. Linnér, *Return of Malthus*, 47.

21. Matthew Connelly, *Fatal Misconception: The Struggle to Control World Population* (Cambridge, Mass.: Belknap Press of Harvard University Press, 2008), 142.

22. John D Rockefeller III to Dwight Eisenhower, October 4, 1966, Papers of John D. Rockefeller III, Rockefeller Archive Center, Tarrytown, N.Y., Series 1, Subseries 2, Box 27, Folder 237, "Famous People, 1946–1966."

23. For the population-related activities of foundations, consult Oscar Harkavy, *Curbing Population Growth: An Insider's Perspective on the Population Movement* (New York: Plenum Press, 1995), chaps. 1–3.

24. Connelly, *Fatal Misconception*, 157–63.

25. Harkavy, *Curbing Population Growth*, 24.

26. The total fertility rate is age-adjusted, that is, measures the number of babies a woman would have over her childbearing years if her fertility conformed to age-specific rates every year. The crude birthrate (the number of births per year per thousand people) was about 18.5 in the mid 1930s, exceeded 25 in 1956–57, and dipped below 15 by the 1970s. See Herbert S. Klein, *A Population History of the United States* (Cambridge: Cambridge University Press, 2004), 178; Michael S. Teitelbaum and Jay M. Winter, *The Fear of Population Decline* (New York: Academic Press, 1985), Appendix A, 158; *Historical Statistics of the United States: Earliest Times to the Present*, Millennial Edition, ed. Susan B. Carter et al., vol. 1, part A, *Population* (New York: Cambridge University Press, 2000), table Ab11–30, pp. 392–93; Frank D. Bean, "The Baby Boom and Its Explanations," *Sociological Quarterly* 24 (Summer 1983): 355; and Harold G. Vatter, *The U.S. Economy in the 1950s: An Economic History* (New York: W. W. Norton, 1963), 8–9.

27. Many demographers offered erroneous predictions in the late 1940s, and the Census Bureau's 1947 projections—P. K. Whelpton, *Forecasts of the Population of the United States, 1945–1975* (Bureau of the Census: Washington, D.C., 1947)—were outdated when the ink dried. A typical popular press example, from a Harvard economist, is S. H. Slichter, "How Big in 1980?" *Atlantic Monthly*, November 1949, which predicted a 1980 population of 175 million (39), whereas the eventual figure was 225 million.

28. David Riesman, in collaboration with Reuel Denney and Nathan Glazer, *The Lonely Crowd: A Study of the Changing American Character* (New Haven: Yale University Press, 1950), 7–9 and 17–19. According to Riesman, the three historical personality stages through which humans had passed—tradition-directed, inner-directed, and outer-directed—corresponded to the three historical fertility regimes—primitive societies with high birth and death rates, societies with rapid population increase due to improved sanitation, and societies undergoing the demographic transition.

29. The editors of *Fortune* in collaboration with Russell W. Davenport, *U.S.A.: The Permanent Revolution* (New York: Prentice-Hall, 1951), 170–72.

30. A few experts predicted a long-lasting Baby Boom even before the 1950 census. See Joseph S. Davis, *The Population Upsurge in the United States*, Food

Research Institute, War-Peace Pamphlets, no. 12 (Stanford: FRI, 1949); and Henry S. Shryock Jr., "Forecasts of Population in the United States," *Population Studies* 3 (March 1950): 406–12.

31. Klein, *Population History of the United States*, 178. Although average family size increased only slightly, and the percentage of families with five or more children continued to decrease, millions of American women married young, had their first child quickly, and decided to have a third child instead of stopping at two.

32. Vatter, *U.S. Economy in the 1950s*, 9.

33. Elaine Tyler May, *Homeward Bound: American Families in the Cold War Era*, 20th anniversary ed. (New York: Basic Books, 2008), 150. Scholars extending May's argument have located the roots of the Baby Boom in the family-values rhetoric of the prewar positive eugenics movement. In particular, they highlight positive eugenicists of the 1930s reborn as the marriage counselors of the 1950s. See Kristin Celello, *Making Marriage Work: A History of Marriage and Divorce in the Twentieth-Century United States* (Chapel Hill: University of North Carolina Press, 2009); Molly Ladd-Taylor, "Eugenics, Sterilisation and Modern Marriage in the USA: The Strange Career of Paul Popenoe," *Gender and Society* 13 (August 2001): 298–327; and Wendy Kline, *Building a Better Race: Gender, Sexuality, and Eugenics from the Turn of the Century to the Baby Boom* (Berkeley and Los Angeles: University of California Press, 2001).

34. Kenneth E. Boulding, *The Meaning of the Twentieth Century: The Great Transition* (New York: Harper & Row, 1964), 126.

35. For example, see James T. Patterson, *Grand Expectations: The United States, 1945–1974* (New York: Oxford University Press, 1996), 76–81.

36. Richard H. Pells, *The Liberal Mind in a Conservative Age: American Intellectuals in the 1940s and 1950s* (New York: Harper & Row, 1985), 199–200.

37. One renowned historian's textbook concludes, "The baby boom meant increased consumer demand and expanding economic growth" (Alan Brinkley, *American History: A Survey*, vol. 2, *Since 1865*, 10th ed. [Boston: McGraw Hill, 1999], 994). For a list of more such articles (and a typically exclusive focus on positive reaction to the population upsurge), see Landon Y. Jones, *Great Expectations: America and the Baby Boom Generation* (New York: Coward, McCann, and Geoghegan, 1980), 36–38.

38. Among many others, see "More People: It Means New Trade, Good Times," *U.S. News & World Report*, January 2, 1953, 77–79; and "The Why Behind the Dynamic 1950s," *Business Week*, November 10, 1956, 64–70.

39. See the widely read Samuel P. Hays, *Beauty, Health and Permanence: Environmental Politics in the United States, 1955–1985* (Cambridge: Cambridge University Press, 1987), chap. 7. Fox, *American Conservation Movement*, suggests that conservationists lost interest in the population question after the late 1940s revival, turning from eugenics to wilderness preservation, and hence writes little about population issues from the mid-1950s to the mid-1960s (306–13).

40. Alfred E. Eckes Jr., *The United States and the Global Struggle for Minerals* (Austin: University of Texas Press, 1979), chap. 4.

41. Ibid., chap. 6.

42. Ibid., 166.

43. Edward Mason, a driving force on the committee, recalls its development in "Resources in the Past and for the Future," in *Resources for an Uncertain Future*, Papers Presented at a Forum Marking the 25th Anniversary of Resources for the Future, October 13, 1977, Washington, D.C., ed. Charles J. Hitch et al. (Baltimore: Resources for the Future by the Johns Hopkins University Press, 1978), 1–22.

44. President's Materials Policy Commission, *Resources for Freedom* vols. 1 to 5 (Washington, D.C.: GPO, 1952).

45. Ibid., 1:4.

46. Ibid., 1:13.

47. The commission treated population growth as an endogenous variable; that is, it did not consider any potential influences on it.

48. For RFF's early years, see Marion Clawson, *From Sagebrush to Sage: The Making of a Natural Resource Economist* (Washington, D.C.: Ana Publications, 1987), chap. 9; and Fox, *American Conservation Movement*, 309–10. For Ford's first grant, see Harkavy, *Curbing Population Growth*, 9.

49. A widely cited optimist was Erich Zimmerman, who believed that human beings, through invention and better methods of exploitation, had long created as many resources as they destroyed. See his *World Resources and Industries*, rev. ed. (New York: Harper & Brothers, 1951), esp. chap. 50.

50. Jacob Rosin and Max Eastman, *The Road to Abundance* (New York: McGraw Hill, 1953). Arnaud Marts, who founded one of the nation's first fundraising firms, argued in *Philanthropy's Role in Civilization: Its Contribution to Human Freedom* (New York: Harper & Brothers, 1953) that the Rockefeller-sponsored Woods Hole (Mass.) Oceanographic Institute would tap the "untold wealth of protein foods" from the sea (177).

51. Joseph Davis, "Fifty Million More Americans," *Foreign Affairs* (April 1950): 425.

52. John Cassidy, "Beneath the Sand: Can a Shattered Country Be Rebuilt with Oil?" *New Yorker*, July 14 and 21, 2003, 70.

53. Henry R. Luce, "A Speculation about A.D. 1980," in *The Fabulous Future: America in 1980* (New York: E. P. Dutton & Co., 1955, 1956), 187.

54. "Editor's Introduction," in *Perspectives on Conservation: Essays on America's Natural Resources*, ed. Henry Jarrett (Baltimore: John Hopkins University Press for Resources for the Future, 1958), ix.

55. Thomas B. Nolan, "The Inexhaustible Resource of Technology," in *Perspectives on Conservation*, ed. Jarrett, 66.

56. The estimate of a million and a half pamphlets comes from Connelly, *Fatal Misconception*, 162. For Moore's early involvement in the population issue, see Robertson, *Malthusian Moment*, chap. 4.

57. See the Records of the Population Council, Rockefeller Archive Center, Tarrytown, N.Y. (hereafter, Population Council Records), esp. Box 22, Folder 344, "Moore, Hugh, 1954–1958."

58. Robert C. Cook, "Malthus' Main Thesis Still Holds," in *Perspectives on Conservation*, ed. Jarrett, 72.

59. Ibid., 75–76.

60. Ibid., 77–78.

61. Harrison Brown, "Our Productive Potential," unpublished abstract of a paper to be presented at the New York City meeting of the American Association for the Advancement of Science, 1956, Population Council Records, Box 1, Folder "A 1953–1957, I." His best-known book was *The Challenge of Man's Future* (New York: Viking, 1954).

62. Joseph J. Spengler, "Population and Per Capita Income," *Annals of the American Academy of Political and Social Science* 237 (January 1945): 182–92.

63. Joseph J. Spengler, "Population Threatens Prosperity," *Harvard Business Review* 34 (January–February 1956): 93.

64. Ironically, Malthusians ignored the specter of water scarcity in the mid-twentieth century, but currently this is one of their strongest arguments. See Bill McKibben, "Our Thirsty Future," *New York Review of Books*, September 25, 2003, 58–60.

65. Joseph J. Spengler, "The Population Problem: Dimensions, Potentialities, Limitations," *American Economic Review* 46 (May 1956): 342. Also see his "Economic Factors in Economic Development," *American Economic Review* 47 (May 1957): 42–56, and "Limitational Factors in Population Theory: A Note," *Kyklos* 7 (1954): 227–43.

66. Byron T. Shaw, "Technology on the Land," in *Perspectives on Conservation*, ed. Jarrett, 70. For additional examples of this middle-of-the-road position, see, in this volume, Harry A. Curtis, "The Barrier of Cost," and Edward S. Mason, "The Political Economy of Resource Use." For an agricultural economist's perspective, see John D. Black, "Population and Scarce Food Resources," in *Economics for Agriculture: Selected Writings of John D. Black*, ed. James Peirce Cavin (Cambridge, Mass: Harvard University Press, 1949), 453–68.

67. See, for example, Dudley Kirk, review of *The Modern Dilemma* by Robert C. Cook, *Population Studies* 7 (July 1953): 89–90. An original theorist of the demographic transition, Kirk was a State Department official and later demographic director of the Population Council.

68. Compare, for example, the dire "Population Boom: Too Many New Mouths to Feed," *Newsweek*, September 13, 1954, 72–73, with "Too Many Babies?" *Time*, August 26, 1957, 75, which suggested that more people helped the economy but noted a warning from Mellon Bank that population growth augured economic problems. Also see John R. Wilmoth and Patrick Ball, "The Population Debate in American Popular Magazines, 1946–90," *Population and Development Review* 18 (December 1992): 631–68.

69. Guy Irving Burch, "Danger! Population Explosion Ahead," *Reader's Digest*, February 1951, 44–46.

70. Kingsley Davis, "'Ideal Size' for Our Population," *New York Times Sunday Magazine*, May 1, 1955, 37.

71. Ibid., 34.

72. Ibid., 32. On housewives and inflation in the 1950s, see Meg Jacobs, "Inflation: 'The Permanent Dilemma' of the American Middle Classes," in *Social Contracts under Stress: The Middle Classes of America, Europe, and Japan at the Turn of the Century*, ed. Olivier Zunz, Leonard Schoppa, and Nobuhiro Hiwatari (New York: Russell Sage Foundation, 2002), 130–53.

73. "A Study of Mankind's Future," *New York Times*, August 17, 1953.

74. For example, Davis, "'Ideal Size,'" proposed that the US population was already sufficiently large to enjoy economies of scale (34).

75. W. W. Rostow, *Concept and Controversy: Sixty Years of Taking Ideas to Market* (Austin: University of Texas Press, 2003), 342.

76. Theodore Rosenof, *Economics in the Long Run: New Deal Theorists and Their Legacies, 1933–1993* (Chapel Hill: University of North Carolina Press, 1997), esp. chap. 9.

77. Robert M. Collins, *The Business Response to Keynes, 1929–1964* (New York: Columbia University Press, 1981).

78. I borrow "stuffed" from John H. Hotson, "The Fall of Bastard Keynesianism and the Rise of Legitimate Keynesianism," in *The Subtle Anatomy of Capitalism*, ed. Jesse Schwartz (Santa Monica, Calif.: Goodyear Publishing, 1977), 329.

79. Excavating the relationship between demography and the distribution of wealth was less urgent in these years because the high-birthrate 1950s was one of the few decades in modern American history during which the gap between the rich and poor narrowed. See Simon Kuznets, "Economic Growth and Income Inequality," *American Economic Review* 45 (March 1955): 1–28. On postwar inequality, see Derek S. Hoff, "Statistical Appendix: Historical Income Inequality in Seven Nations—France, Germany, Italy, Japan, Sweden, the United Kingdom, and the United States," in *Social Contracts under Stress*, ed. Zunz, Schoppa, and Hiwatari, 401–9.

80. R. A. Gordon, "Population Growth, Housing, and the Capital Coefficient," *American Economic Review* 46 (June 1956): 307–22; Joseph S. Davis, "The Population Upsurge and the American Economy, 1945–1980," *Journal of Political Economy* 61 (October 1953): 369–88; Everett Hagen, "Population and Economic Growth," *American Economic Review* 49 (June 1959): 310–27; and William Fellner, *Trends and Cycles in Economic Activity: An Introduction to Problems of Economic Growth* (New York: Henry Holt, 1956), esp. 239–44.

81. Rosenof, *Economics in the Long Run*, 122. In "The Stagnation Thesis," in *Readings in Fiscal Policy*, ed. Arthur Smithies and J. Keith Butters (New York: Richard D. Irwin for the American Economic Association, 1955), Hansen wrote

that "the economy cannot on its own generate enough steam to provide our full potential of growth" (553).

82. J. R. Hicks, *Value and Capital: An Inquiry into Some Fundamental Principles of Economic Theory*, 2d ed. (Oxford: Clarendon Press, 1946), 302 n. 1.

83. Davis, "Population Upsurge and the American Economy," 386.

84. Manuel Gottlieb, "The Theory of Optimum Population for a Closed Economy," *Journal of Political Economy* 53 (December 1945): 289.

85. For example, Harvey Leibenstein, *A Theory of Economic-Demographic Development* (Princeton: Princeton University Press, 1954), offered a new dynamic optimum theory incorporating a wide range of determinants and effects of population growth. Others claiming that the US had exceeded its optimal level included Clarence L. Barber, "Population Growth and the Demand for Capital," *American Economic Review* 43 (March 1953): 133–39; and Alan T. Peacock, "Theory of Population and Modern Economic Analysis, I," *Population Studies* 6 (November 1952): 114–22, and "Production Functions and Population Theory," *Population Studies* 10 (March 1957): 298–305.

86. Gottlieb, "Theory of Optimum Population," 306.

87. Horace Belshaw, *Population Growth and Levels of Consumption, With Special Reference to Countries in Asia* (New York: Institute of Pacific Relations, 1956), 70.

88. Ibid., 70–71.

89. Josef Steindl, *Maturity and Stagnation in American Capitalism*, Oxford University Institute of Statistics, Monograph no. 4 (Oxford: Basil Blackwell, 1952), esp. 168.

90. Harrod's theory of economic growth assumed that the "natural rate of growth" was determined by the rate of technical change and the labor supply's rate of growth, of which population was obviously the leading determinant. See R. F. Harrod, *Towards Dynamic Economics: Some Recent Developments of Economic Theory and Their Application to Policy* (London: Macmillan, 1948), and *The Trade Cycle: An Essay* (Oxford: Clarendon Press, 1936), esp. 106–8. In "Modern Population Trends," *Manchester School of Economics and Social Studies* 10 (April 1939): 1–20, Harrod fretted about the declining birthrates of the 1930s. Also see "The Population Problem," in his *Economic Essays* (New York: Harcourt, Brace, 1952), originally a memo Harrod wrote in 1944 to the Royal Commission on Population. Finally, consult Larry Neal, "Is Secular Stagnation Just around the Corner? A Survey of the Influences of Slowing Population Growth upon Investment Demand," in *The Economic Consequences of Slowing Population Growth*, ed. Thomas J. Espenshade and William J. Serow (New York: Academic Press, 1978), 108–9.

91. A classic statement is Evsey D. Domar, "Capital Expansion, Rate of Growth, and Employment," *Econometrica* 14 (April 1946): 137–47.

92. The Coale-Hoover and Harrod-Domar models are very similar, except the former assumes a rising and the latter a constant population growth rate.

93. Hagen, "Population and Economic Growth," 324.

94. See Joseph J. Spengler, "Theories in Socio-economic Growth," in Universities-National Bureau Committee on Economic Research, *Problems in the Study of Economic Growth* (New York: National Bureau of Economic Research, 1949), 45–114.

95. Joseph J. Spengler, "The Population Obstacle to Economic Betterment," *American Economic Review* 41 (May 1951): 354. According to Spengler, the main problem in the developing world was an age pyramid bottom-heavy with children; he predicted that the productivity of poor nations would increase 20–30 percent if their age distribution and healthcare became "westernized" (344).

96. Ibid., 352–53.

97. Spengler, "'Standing Room Only' in the World?" 84.

98. Ibid., 87.

99. Earle L. Rauber, "Population and Economic Growth," *Population Bulletin* 13 (February 1957): 4. Also see his "Industrial Growth in the Twentieth Century," in *Our Crowded Planet: Essays on the Pressures of Population*, ed. Fairfield Osborn (New York: Doubleday, 1962), 93–100.

100. Rauber, "Population and Economic Growth," 7, and "The Realm of the Red Queen," *Monthly Review* (newsletter of the Federal Reserve Bank of Atlanta), January 31, 1956, 3–4. Rauber's apprehension of population trends was part of his broader heterodox skepticism of what he considered to be false claims of large per capita gains in production.

101. Rauber, "Population and Economic Growth," 7.

102. United States Department of Labor, Bureau of Labor Statistics, "Summaries of Studies and Reports," *Monthly Labor Review* 82 (February 1959): 25.

103. For the place of population in modern growth theory, see Simon Kuznets, *Postwar Economic Growth: Four Lectures* (Cambridge, Mass.: Belknap Press of Harvard University Press, 1964), esp. lecture 1; Moses Abramovitz, *Thinking about Growth and other Essays on Economic Growth Welfare* (Cambridge: Cambridge University Press, 1989); and Robert M. Solow, *Growth Theory: An Exposition*, 2d ed. (New York: Oxford University Press, 2000). For most of the twentieth century, economists tended to treat population as an endogenous variable. During the past forty years, they have constructed more interactive models of demographic and economic change. These models assume that population growth waxes and wanes with the economy and thus tend to be less fearful of it.

104. Ian Bowen, *Economics and Demography* (London: George Allen and Unwin, 1976), 95–96.

105. Julian L. Simon, *A Life Against the Grain: The Autobiography of an Unconventional Economist* (New Brunswick: Transaction, 2003), 252. Also see similar discussion about neoclassical theory in Paul A. Samuelson, "The Optimum Growth Rate for Population: Agreement and Evaluations," *International Economic Review* 17 (June 1976): 519.

106. Nicholas Kaldor, "A Model of Economic Growth," *Economic Journal* 67 (December 1957): esp. 614–18.

107. Abramovitz, *Thinking about Growth*, xvi.

108. W. A. Lewis, *The Theory of Economic Growth* (London: George Allen and Unwin, 1955), 330. In his autobiography on the Nobel Prize's website, Lewis discusses the role of "population pressure" in depressing wages (www.nobelprize.org/economics/laureates/1979/lewis-autobio.html).

109. See Robert Solow, "A Contribution to the Theory of Economic Growth," *Quarterly Journal of Economics* 70 (February 1956): 65–94.

110. Committee meetings centered on the developing world and reflected the shift in demographic transition theory from the assumption that modernization and economic development were sufficient to lower population growth to the stress on direct family planning programs.

111. "Minutes to Ad Hoc Committee May 11, 1955," in Population Council Records, Box 1, Folder "Ad Hoc Philosophy Committee, Kirk, Dudley, 1955."

112. Author unknown, "Addenda to Report on Ad Hoc meeting of April 11, 1956," Population Council Records, Box 1, Folder "Ad Hoc Philosophy Committee, Kirk, Dudley, 1956–1957."

113. Notestein to Osborn, Dec. 14, 1956, Population Council Records, Box 1, Folder "Ad Hoc Philosophy Committee, Kirk, Dudley, 1956–1957."

114. After calling for a meeting on the economics of population growth, Osborn's first version of the agenda had "Depression" under the heading "some effects of [population] growth considered bad!" Dudley Kirk, director of the council's Demographic Division, deleted "Depression" and softened it to "lower per capita income." The various outlines of the meeting are in Population Council Records, Box 1, Folder "Ad Hoc Philosophy Committee, Kirk, Dudley, 1956–1957."

115. Frederick Osborn, "Summary of VII Ad Hoc Meeting, April 4, 1957," Population Council Records, Box 2, Folder 12, "Ad Hoc Philosophy Committee, Meeting 7, Correspondence and Discussion Papers, 1956–1957," 5.

116. Ibid., 2.

117. Ibid., 3.

118. Kuznets spent his career quantifying capital formation and national income. In the 1930s, he postulated the presence of what came to be called "Kuznets cycles"—15- to 25-year movements of business conditions that operate independently of shorter business cycles. In *Postwar Economic Growth*, Kuznets connected sustained historical increases in national per capita income with population growth (39). Yet in *Population, Capital, and Growth: Selected Essays* (New York: W. W. Norton, 1973), he wrote, "That modern economic growth meant a strikingly accelerated rise not only in product per capita but also in population does not imply that the latter was a necessary condition for the former" (2).

119. Simon Kuznets, *Six Lectures on Economic Growth* (New York: Free Press of Glencoe, 1959), 37. The next year, Kuznets suggested that larger populations

happily produce more geniuses ("Population Change and Aggregate Output," in *Demographic and Economic Change in Developed Countries* [Princeton: Princeton University Press, 1960], 324–39).

120. Simon Kuznets, "Toward a Theory of Economic Growth," in *National Economic Welfare at Home and Abroad*, ed. Robert Lekachman (Garden City, N.Y.: Doubleday, 1955; New York: Russell & Russell, 1961), 23.

121. Osborn, "Summary of VII Ad Hoc Meeting," 6. For Kuznets's ambivalence, see Kuznets to Osborn, April 6, 1957, Population Council Records, Box 2, Folder 12, "Ad Hoc Philosophy Committee, Meeting 7, Correspondence and Discussion Papers, 1956–1957." Kuznets was relatively optimistic about population growth. Osborn, "Summary of VII Ad Hoc Meeting, April 4, 1957," paraphrased him as saying, "Given all we know now about technological progress, continuation of present population growth does not mean reduction of capital growth" (7). In a separate letter to Osborn, however, Kuznets said that it was "not improbable that a lower rate of growth in numbers ... might permit a higher rate of growth of product per capita" (Kuznets to Osborn, Oct. 7, 1957, Population Council Records, Box 2, Folder "Meetings 1–8 Summary and Comments on Summary, A–N, 1957").

122. Fredrick Osborn, "Summary of the Proceedings of the Ad Hoc Committee, May 1, 1955 thru May 16, 1957," 64–65, Population Council Records, Box 1, Folder "Ad Hoc Philosophy Committee, Kirk, Dudley, 1956–1957."

123. Summing up the burgeoning literature on economic growth at the end of the decade, Kuznets described a consensus that "the enormous increase in per capita product, which characterizes modern economic growth, is largely the result of a rise in efficiency" (*Postwar Economic Growth*, 41).

124. This is not to deny that postwar policy makers connected natural resources to economic growth. See Council of Economic Advisers, "The American Economy in 1961: Problems and Policies," Statement of the Council of Economic Advisers before the Joint Economic Committee, March 6, 1961, Papers of President John F. Kennedy, John F. Kennedy Presidential Library, Boston, President's Office Files, Departments and Agencies, Box 73, Folder "Council of Economic Advisers Testimony, 3/6/61"; and Paul Charles Milazzo, *Unlikely Environmentalists: Congress and Clean Water, 1945–1972* (Lawrence: University Press of Kansas, 2006).

125. See, for example, John Maurice Clark, "Common and Disparate Elements in National Growth and Decline," in Universities-National Bureau Committee on Economic Research, *Problems in the Study of Economic Growth*, 30–32.

126. Potter, *People of Plenty*, 59.

127. Belshaw, *Population Growth and Levels of Consumption*, 71.

128. See especially Galbraith, *The Affluent Society*.

129. Vogt, *Road to Survival*, 133.

130. Linnér, *Return of Malthus*, 89.

131. Jeffrey C. Ellis, "On the Search for a Root Cause: Essentialist Tendencies

in Environmental Discourse," in *Uncommon Ground: Toward Reinventing Nature*, ed. William Cronon (New York: W. W. Norton, 1995), 256–68.

132. Wilmoth and Ball, "The Population Debate in American Popular Magazines."

133. For postwar Keynesianism, see the later chapters in Richard Parker, *John Kenneth Galbraith: His Life, His Politics, His Economics* (New York: Farrar, Straus and Giroux, 2005).

134. See Pells, *Liberal Mind in a Conservative Age*, esp. the discussion of the "problems of prosperity" beginning on 188.

135. Arthur Schlesinger Jr., "The Challenge of Abundance," *The Reporter*, May 3, 1956, 8.

136. For a summary of *The Affluent Society*, see Parker, *John Kenneth Galbraith*, chap. 13.

137. John Kenneth Galbraith, "Economics and Environment," *AIA Journal*, September 1966, 57.

138. Lewis Mumford, "The Natural History of Urbanization," in *Man's Role in Changing the Face of the Earth*, ed. William L. Thomas Jr. (Chicago: University of Chicago Press, 1956), 395.

139. Samuel Hays introduces this line of inquiry in *Beauty, Health, and Permanence*, noting that the environmental movement's new concern with "amenities" in the 1960s emerged from and reinforced the postwar rise of postmaterialist values (266). Also see Adam Rome, *The Bulldozer in the Countryside: Suburban Sprawl and the Rise of American Environmentalism* (Cambridge: Cambridge University Press, 2001).

140. Adam Rome, "'Give Earth a Chance': The Environmental Movement and the Sixties," *Journal of American History* 90 (September 2003): 525–54.

141. Writing in the 1970s, Hays noted, "The concern for the limits of growth emerges from this 'amenity' sector of the environmental conservation movement" (Samuel P. Hays, "The Limits-to-Growth Issue: A Historical Perspective," in *Explorations in Environmental History: Essays by Samuel P. Hays* [Pittsburgh: University of Pittsburgh Press, 1998], 8). Yet he provided no further discussion and ignored pre-1960s origins.

142. Galbraith, *The Affluent Society*, 187–88.

143. John Kenneth Galbraith, "How Much Should a Country Consume?" in *Perspectives on Conservation*, ed. Jarrett, 92. Just a year earlier, in *The Affluent Society*, Galbraith had urged Americans to abandon the politics of scarcity!

144. Galbraith, "How Much Should a Country Consume?" 98.

145. Adam Rome comes closest. In *Bulldozer in the Countryside*, he confines his discussion of population to the two well-known Malthusian books published in 1948, as well as the intersection between demographic concerns and the 1960s "urban crisis." Rome does note that, in the interim years, population concerns informed the campaign to protect suburban "open space" (142). As I will describe,

however, environmental organizations were anxious about the US domestic population surge even before the open-space issue picked up steam. Rome may have the causal relationship backwards when he writes, "The open-space issue also intensified concern about population growth" (141).

146. See chap. 6 for the rise of environmental and ecological economics.

147. "The Aesthetics of Population," in *Population Economics: Selected Essays of Joseph J. Spengler*, comp. Robert S. Smith, Frank T. de Vyver, and William R. Allen (Durham: Duke University Press, 1972), 311.

148. Ibid., 301–3.

149. Ibid., 300.

150. Philip M. Hauser, "The Crucial Value Problems," in *Perspectives on Conservation*, ed. Jarrett, 100–105.

151. Ibid., 104.

152. Kenneth E. Boulding, "The Economics of the Coming Spaceship Earth," in *Environmental Quality in a Growing Economy: Essays from the Sixth RFF Forum*, ed. Henry Jarrett (Baltimore: Johns Hopkins University Press for Resources for the Future, 1966), 3–14.

153. Robert C. Cook, "It's Going to be a Crowded Planet," *Parents' Magazine and Home Guide*, October 1957, 131.

154. Joseph J. Spengler, review of *The Road to Serfdom*, by Friedrich A. Hayek, *Southern Economic Journal* 12 (July 1945): 48–55.

155. Spengler, "'Standing Room Only' in the World?" 87.

156. "Ad Hoc Meeting—April 4, 1957, Concluding Statement by the Chairman [Frederick Osborn]," Population Council Records, Box 2, Folder 12, "Ad Hoc Philosophy Committee, Meeting 7, Correspondence and Discussion Papers, 1956–1957," 2.

157. Dudley Kirk, "Cultural Implications of Population Growth in the United States," unpublished manuscript, Population Council Records, Box 2, Folder 13, "Ad Hoc Philosophy Committee, Meeting 8 Correspondence and Discussion Papers, 1958" [should read 1957], 4–5.

158. John D. Rockefeller III, "A Citizen's Perspective on Population," seventh draft (April 28, 1960) of a talk given at "A New Look at the Population Crisis," a conference sponsored by the Dallas Council on World Affairs and *Newsweek*, May 17–19, 1961, Population Council Records, Box 8, Folder 90, "Dallas Council of World Affairs, 1960–1961." Robertson, *Malthusian Moment*, notes that Rockefeller made these arguments as far back as the 1952 Williamsburg, Virginia, conference (chap. 3).

159. Many January 1960 editorials previewing the decade ahead identified looming population problems. See, for example, "Population Boom," *Washington Post*, January 3, 1960; and "Population Rise: What It Implies," *New York Times*, January 11, 1960.

Chapter Five

1. Joel E. Cohen, *How Many People Can the Earth Support?* (New York: W. W. Norton, 1995), 13.

2. Donald J. Bogue, "Population Growth in the United States," in *The Population Dilemma*, ed. Philip M. Hauser (Englewood Cliffs, N.J.: Prentice-Hall, 1963), 70–75.

3. "Remarks of the President to a Group from New Haven," press release, October 18, 1963, Papers of President John F. Kennedy (hereafter JFK Papers), John F. Kennedy Presidential Library, Boston (hereafter JFKL), President's Office Files, Speech Files, Box 47, Folder "Statement Announcing a Grant for a Youth Training Demonstration Project in New Haven, 10/18/63."

4. W. W. Rostow, *The Stages of Economic Growth: A Non-Communist Manifesto* (New York: Cambridge University Press, 1960), esp. chap. 6.

5. Ibid., 141–44. Jack Parsons, *Population Fallacies* (London: Elek/Pemberton, 1977), concluded, "In none of [Rostow's five] stages is any potency attributed to population pressure as a factor inducing economic development or growth" (139). For more on Ansley J. Coale and Edgar M. Hoover, *Population Growth and Economic Development in Low-Income Countries: A Case Study of India's Prospects* (Princeton: Princeton University Press, 1958), see chap. 4 of the present study.

6. Rostow, *Stages of Economic Growth*, 156.

7. LBJ's address launching the Great Society included quintessential statements of the quality-of-life perspective: "Remarks at the University of Michigan, May 22, 1964," *Public Papers of the Presidents of the United States: Lyndon B. Johnson, 1963–64*, book 1 (Washington, D.C.: GPO, 1965), 704–7.

8. 1965 brought no sharp break in fertility, and generations are as much cultural as empirical constructs. But 1964 was the last year until 1989 in which total births in the US exceeded four million (*Historical Statistics of the United States: Earliest Times to the Present*, Millennial Edition, ed. Susan B Carter et al., vol. 1, part A, *Population* [New York: Cambridge University Press, 2000], table Ab11–30, pp. 392–93).

9. For the drifting-upwards unemployment of the 1950s, see Council of Economic Advisers (hereafter CEA), "Dramatic Facts on Unemployment and Labor Force," JFK Papers, President's Office Files, Staff Memoranda, Box 63A, Folder "Heller, Walter W. Briefing Book on Economic Matters, 12/20/62."

10. *National Party Platforms*, vol. 2, *1960–1976*, comp. Donald Bruce Johnson (Urbana: University of Illinois, 1978), 582.

11. Oral History Interview with Walter Heller, Kermit Gordon, James Tobin, Gardner Ackley, and Paul Samuelson, by Joseph Pechman, August 1, 1964, John F. Kennedy Library Oral History Program.

12. CEA, "Dramatic Facts."

13. John Kenneth Galbraith to JFK, June 12, 1961, Papers of John Kenneth Galbraith, JKFL, Box 76, Folder "Correspondence with JFK, 1/6/61–11/15/63."

14. James L. Sundquist, *Politics and Policy: The Eisenhower, Kennedy, and Johnson Years* (Washington, D.C.: Brookings Institution, 1968), 73.

15. CEA, "Dramatic Facts."

16. Ibid.

17. See Margaret Weir, "The Federal Government and Unemployment," in *The Politics of Social Policy in the United States*, ed. Margaret Weir, Ann Schola Orloff, and Theda Skocpol (Princeton: Princeton University Press, 1988), 149–90.

18. See Martin's comments quoted in Robert Solow to Messrs. Heller, Gordon, and Tobin, March 14, 1961, Kermit Gordon Papers, JFKL (hereafter Gordon Papers), Box 30, Folder "Employment and Unemployment," 3. CEA members held Martin in low esteem. Gardner Ackley said that he was "absolutely zero as an economist" (Gardner Ackley Oral History, Interview II, by Joe B. Frantz, March 7, 1974, Lyndon Baines Johnson Presidential Library, Austin, Tex., 6).

19. Walter Heller labeled the GOP's tendency to identify structural unemployment a cop-out—another way of saying Americans should simply accept high unemployment (CEA, "A Second Look at Economic Policy in 1961," March 17, 1961, JFK Papers, President's Office Files, Staff Memoranda, Box 63A, Folder "Heller, Walter W., 1961").

20. See Amy Sue Bix, *Inventing Ourselves Out of Jobs? America's Debate over Technological Unemployment, 1929–1981* (Baltimore: Johns Hopkins University Press, 2000), esp. chap. 8; and Henry J. Aaron, *Politics and the Professors: The Great Society in Perspective* (Washington, D.C.: Brookings Institution, 1978), chap. 4.

21. Bix, *Inventing Ourselves Out of Jobs*, 255.

22. Ibid., 250–54.

23. For the manpower issue in the 1950s, see Henry David, *Manpower Policies for a Democratic Society: The Final Statement of the Council* (New York: Columbia University Press for the National Manpower Council, 1965).

24. For the impression West Virginian poverty made on Kennedy, see Theodore H. White, *The Making of the President, 1960* (New York: Atheneum, 1961), 106.

25. Historians have not ignored youth unemployment. For example, Irving Bernstein notes the Labor Department's apprehension about youth employment and cites Secretary of Labor Wirtz's concern that "the baby boom is just now rolling into the workforce" (*Guns or Butter: The Presidency of Lyndon Johnson* [New York: Oxford University Press, 1996], 103). But these occasional references do not capture the widespread trepidation that the Baby Boom posed a serious macroeconomic challenge. Historians primarily discuss the youth unemployment issue in terms of anxiety about the juvenile delinquent (Sundquist, *Politics and Policy*, 73); the ghetto (Carl Solberg, *Hubert Humphrey: A Biography* [1984; reprint, St. Paul: Borealis Books, 2003], 216); a "culture of poverty" argument then in vogue (Gareth Davies, *From Opportunity to Entitlement: The Transformation and Decline of Great Society Liberalism* [Lawrence: University of Press of Kansas, 1996], chap. 2); or the development of human capital theory (Alice O'Connor, *Pov-*

erty Knowledge: Social Science, Social Policy, and the Poor in Twentieth-Century U.S. History [Princeton: Princeton University Press, 2001], 141–42).

26. David, *Manpower Policies*, 6.

27. Senate Committee on Labor and Public Welfare, Subcommittee on Employment and Manpower, *Nation's Manpower Revolution*, 88th Cong., 1st sess., part 1, May 20, 21, 22, and 23, 1963, 292–93.

28. Gunnar Myrdal, *Challenge to Affluence* (New York: Pantheon, 1963), 5.

29. Ibid., 16–17; and "Economic Stagnation Chief Problem for America, Swedish Expert Says," *Washington Post*, June 9, 1962.

30. For example, see "The U.S. Labor Force: 1950–1960: 'Islands of Obsolete Capacity and Unwanted Skills,'" *Population Bulletin* 20 (May 1964): 57–87; and Helen Hill Miller, ed., "A Report on the Economy—Time for a Keynes: An Inquiry into What New Economic Thinking Is Required for the U.S. in the Sixties," *New Republic*, October 20, 1962, 9–10.

31. Public Law 27, 87th Cong., 1st sess. (May 1, 1961) emerged from Senate bill number 1.

32. Sar A. Levitan, *Federal Aid to Depressed Areas: An Evaluation of the Area Redevelopment Administration* (Baltimore: Johns Hopkins University Press, 1964), 152.

33. Public Law 415, 87th Cong., 2d sess. (March 15, 1962).

34. For these policy initiatives, see Christopher P. Loss, *Between Citizens and the State: The Politics of American Higher Education in the Twentieth Century* (Princeton: Princeton University Press, 2012), chaps. 6–7.

35. Solberg, *Hubert Humphrey*, 209 and 216.

36. See Christopher Weeks, *Job Corps: Dollars and Dropouts* (Boston: Little, Brown and Company, 1967), 33–37; House Committee on Education and Labor, General Subcommittee on Labor, *Youth Conservation Corps*, 87th Cong., 1st sess., February 18–25, 1963; and House Committee on Education and Labor, General Subcommittee on Labor, *Youth Employment Opportunities Act of 1961*, 87th Cong., 1st sess., June 14–July 6, 1961.

37. "Statement of the President," JFK Papers, President's Office Files, Speech Files, Box 36, Folder "Statement by the President upon Establishing the President's Committee on Youth Employment."

38. See Wirtz's speech "National Trends and Goals for Youth," Papers of Willard Wirtz, JFKL, Box 131, Folder "Youth Employment Conference June 5, 1963, Chicago, Illinois."

39. House Committee on Education and Labor, *Youth Conservation Corps*, 1.

40. President's Committee on Youth Unemployment, *The Challenge of Jobless Youth* (Washington, D.C.: GPO, 1963).

41. "Annual Message to the Congress: The Economic Report of the President," *Public Papers of Lyndon B. Johnson, 1963–64*, book 1, 155–67.

42. Public Law 452, 88th Cong., 2d sess. (August 20, 1964).

43. Irwin Unger, *The Best of Intentions: The Triumphs and Failures of the Great Society Under Kennedy, Johnson, and Nixon* (New York: Doubleday, 1996), 83. This is not to overlook the myriad causes of the War on Poverty, which include the development of human capital theory, the fear of juvenile delinquency, the peaking of activist liberalism, the "rediscovery of poverty" by social scientists, the burgeoning civil rights movement, the climate created by the assassination of JFK, and the landslide victory for Johnson and the Democrats in the 1964 elections. Still, the literature should allow a larger place for macroeconomic anxiety about the demographic bubble.

44. The process cut both ways: according to Okun's Law (named after Arthur Okun, a CEA staffer and, later, LBJ's final CEA chair), lower unemployment generates economic growth.

45. Critics on the Left would have disagreed with my assessment; they derided the new economics with terms such as "watered-down Keynesianism."

46. Walter Heller, "Article on the Recession for *Life*" (draft), March 2, 1961, JFK Papers, President's Office Files, Staff Memoranda, Box 63A, Folder "Heller, Walter W., 1961." CEA economists never denied the presence of structural unemployment, but they held that it represented nothing new and that economic growth was more effective in spurring full employment than worker-retraining and area-redevelopment policies (which they did support). See CEA, "The Problem of Full Recovery," May 24, 1961, JFK Papers, White House Central Subject Files, Business-Economics, Box 17, Folder "BE 5 National Economy, April 1, 1961–September 30, 1961"; and Heller to JFK, "Structural Unemployment Once Again," June 8, 1963, JFK Papers, President's Office Files, Departments and Agencies, Box 76, Folder "Council of Economic Advisers, 6/1/63–6/13/63." Kennedy, too, often split the difference between the two camps, and even as the administration primarily tried to reduce unemployment though macroeconomic growth, new social spending targeted structural problems such as automation and an excess of youth. "I do not see that there is a basic clash between these two views," Kennedy stated at a press conference ("The President's News Conference of March 15, 1961," *Public Papers of the Presidents of the United States: John F. Kennedy, 1961* [Washington, D.C.: GPO, 1962], 187). Kennedy's dabbling with structuralism drew the CEA's ire. See Kermit Gordon to Walter Heller, March 16, 1961, Gordon Papers, Box 30, Folder "Employment and Unemployment."

47. *Economic Report of the President Transmitted to the Congress January 1962* (Washington, D.C.: GPO, 1962), esp. 66–67; and James Tobin and Murray Weidenbaum, "Preface," in *Two Revolutions in Economic Theory: The First Economic Reports of Presidents Kennedy and Reagan*, ed. Tobin and Weidenbaum (Cambridge, Mass.: MIT Press, 1988), vii.

48. The CEA summarized its position in "The American Economy in 1961: Problems and Policies," JFK Papers, President's Office Files, Departments and Agencies, Box 73, Folder "Council of Economic Advisers testimony, 3/6/61," 15.

49. Gardner Ackley, *Macroeconomic Theory* (New York: Macmillan, 1961), 511–12. Ackley argued that Hansen failed to recognize that an expansion of income was just as efficient as population increase in creating effective demand. Hansen praised the economic effects of the Baby Boom in a letter to Ackley (Hansen to Ackley, April 23, 1963, in Alvin Harvey Hansen Papers, Harvard University Special Collections, Cambridge, Mass., Correspondence, 1920–1975, Box 2, Folder "*New York Times, New Republic*—Commentaries").

50. Gardner Ackley, *Macroeconomics: Theory and Policy* (New York: Macmillan, 1978), 555–56.

51. John Kenneth Galbraith, "Poverty and the Way People Behave," in *A Contemporary Guide to Economics, Peace, and Laughter* (Boston: Houghton Mifflin, 1971), 214. This lecture was originally delivered as a 1965 Massey Lecture on Canadian Broadcasting Corporation radio.

52. Ibid., 216.

53. Peter L. Bernstein, "The Trojan Horse of Population Growth," *Harvard Business Review* 39 (March–April 1961): 78.

54. Ansley J. Coale, "Population Change and Demand, Prices, and the Level of Employment," in National Bureau of Economic Research, *Demographic and Economic Change in Developed Countries: A Conference of the Universities-National Bureau Committee for Economic Research* (Princeton: Princeton University Press, 1960), 352–71, esp. 370.

55. For this concept, see Nathaniel H. Leff, "Dependency Rates and Savings Rates," *American Economic Review* 59 (December 1969): 886–96.

56. Foundation grants for population activities increased thirtyfold from 1962 to 1970 (Oscar Harkavy, *Curbing Population Growth: An Insider's Perspective on the Population Movement* [New York: Plenum Press, 1995], 41).

57. Quoted in *News Views* (newsletter of the National Association of Counties), vol. 1, no. 9, copy in Senator Joseph Tydings Papers, University of Maryland Special Collections, College Park, Md. (hereafter Tydings Papers), Series 1, Subseries 1, Box 1, Folder "Population Articles, 1969–1970."

58. For a recent statement, see Matthew Connelly, *Fatal Misconception: The Struggle to Control World Population* (Cambridge, Mass.: Belknap Press of Harvard University Press, 2008), chap. 7.

59. See Donald T. Critchlow, *Intended Consequences: Birth Control, Abortion, and the Federal Government in Modern America* (New York: Oxford University Press, 1999); Otis L. Graham Jr., *Toward a Planned Society: From Roosevelt to Nixon* (New York: Oxford University Press, 1976), chap. 4; Phyllis Tilson Piotrow, *World Population Crisis: The United States Response* (New York: Praeger, 1973); and Harkavy, *Curbing Population Growth*.

60. Connelly, *Fatal Misconception*, 187.

61. "The President's News Conference of December 2, 1959," *Public Papers of the Presidents of the United States: Dwight D. Eisenhower, 1959* (Washington, D.C.: GPO, 1960), 787.

62. The President's Committee to Study the United States Military Assistance Program, *Composite Report*, 2 vols. (Washington, D.C.: GPO, 1959).

63. For more on Draper, see Thomas Robertson, *The Malthusian Moment: Global Population Growth and the Birth of American Environmentalism* (New Brunswick: Rutgers University Press, 2012), chap. 4.

64. Pope John XXIII wrote in *Mater et Magistra* (1961), "Truth to tell, we do not seem to be faced with any immediate or imminent world problem arising from the disproportion between the increase of population and the supply of food" (cited in Parsons, *Population Fallacies*, 22).

65. Alan Petigny, "Illegitimacy, Postwar Psychology, and the Reperiodization of the Sexual Revolution," *Journal of Social History* 38 (Fall 2004): 63–79.

66. See Dr. E. W. Gutkind to Mrs. Franklin D. Roosevelt, March 4, 1961; Kenneth O'Donnell (special assistant to the president) to Dr. Gutkind, March 29, 1961; and O'Donnell to Mrs. Roosevelt, March 29, 1961, all in JFK Papers, Central Subject Files, Business-Economics, Box 17, Folder "BE 5 National Economy, Jan 1, 1961–March 31, 1961." For White House skittishness, see Richard N. Gardner (Deputy Assistant Secretary for International Organization Affairs, Department of State) to Ralph [no last name], JFK Papers, Central Subject Files, Business-Economics, Box 17, Folder "BE 5, 6/1/63."

67. "The President's News Conference of April 24, 1963," *Public Papers of the Presidents of the United States: John F. Kennedy, 1963* (Washington, D.C.: GPO, 1964), 344–45.

68. "Remarks to Members of the World Food Congress, 6/4/63," JFK Papers, President's Office Files, Speech Files, Box 44, Folder "Remarks to Members of the World Food Congress, 6/4/63."

69. In 1962, Deputy Assistant Secretary of State Richard Gardner issued a circular, "A Population Policy for the United States," which advocated moving forward on a limited scale. In May 1963, according to the Population Reference Bureau, "Secretary of State Dean Rusk sent a memo to all missions of the Agency for International Development stating that the United States Government is now receptive to requests for certain kinds of assistance in population planning" ("The Population Problem: Toward a Solution," *Population Bulletin* 19 [July 1963]: 83–84). Sen. Tydings testified that Kennedy "quietly authorized AID to consider requests for family planning information from foreign countries and encouraged research in this area by establishing the National Institute of Child Health and Human Development" (Senate Committee on Labor and Public Welfare, Subcommittee on Employment, Manpower, and Poverty, *Family Planning Program*, 89th Cong., 2d sess., May 10, 1966, 32).

70. "Extract from an Address by Ambassadeur Adlai E. Stevenson at the Annual Banquet of Planned Parenthood-World Population, Tuesday evening, October 15, 1963, The Plaza Hotel, New York City," in *The Population Crisis and the Use of World Resources*, ed. Stuart Mudd, World Academy of Art and Science, no. 2 (The Hague: W. Junk, 1964), xiv.

71. Critchlow, *Intended Consequences*, 50.

72. *Congressional Record*, Senate, August 15, 1963, 15237–39.

73. The *Life* reference comes from Robert David Johnson, *Ernest Gruening and the American Dissenting Tradition* (Cambridge, Mass.: Harvard University Press, 1998), 267. For Gruening's first Senate address on population, see *Congressional Record*, Senate, October 10, 1963, 19196–215.

74. Critchlow, *Intended Consequences*, 48. Harkavy, *Curbing Population Growth*, reports that the Federal Government provided its first (tiny) direct allocations for family planning in 1964 (165).

75. Harkavy, *Curbing Population Growth*, 46.

76. *Public Papers of the Presidents of the United States: Lyndon B. Johnson, 1965*, book 1 (Washington, D.C.: GPO, 1966), 4.

77. "Address in San Francisco at the 20th Anniversary Commemorative Session of the United Nations," June 25, 1965, *Public Papers of the Presidents of the United States: Lyndon B. Johnson, 1965*, book 2 (Washington, D.C.: GPO, 1966), 705.

78. LBJ to JDR III, January 24, 1966, in Rockefeller Family Archives, Papers of John D. Rockefeller III, Rockefeller Archive Center, Tarrytown, N.Y., Series 3, Subseries 2, Box 30, Folder "Famous People, 1966–1971."

79. Johnson, *Ernest Gruening*, 268–69.

80. *Griswold v. Connecticut*, 381 US 479 (1965).

81. *Many Battles: The Autobiography of Ernest Gruening* (New York: Liveright, 1973), chap. 28. For the hearings, begin with the multiple volumes of the Senate Committee on Government Operations, Subcommittee on Foreign Aid Expenditures, *Population Crisis*, 89th Cong.

82. Quoted in Johnson, *Ernest Gruening*, 270.

83. "Remarks prepared for delivery by Senator Tydings on the Floor of the United States Senate" (press release from the Office of Sen. Joseph Tydings), August 16, 1965, Tydings Papers, Series 6, Box 12, Folder "Press Releases—Obscenity; Population; Post Office; Public Works (1965–1970)."

84. For the food aid–population tie-in, see Connelly, *Fatal Misconception*, 221–28. Johnson told his Special Assistant, Joseph Califano Jr., "I'm not going to piss away foreign aid in nations where they refuse to deal with their own population problems" (quoted on 221).

85. Tydings estimated that in 1966, "funds made available for family planning programs under maternal and child health programs amounted to approximately $3 million with an additional $2.4 million spent by community action agencies under the anti-poverty program" (press release from the Office of Sen. Joseph Tydings, April 12, 1967, Tydings Papers, Series 6, Box 12, Folder "Press Releases—Obscenity; Population; Post Office; Public Works [1965–1970]").

86. Gruening, *Many Battles*, 490.

87. *Public Papers of the Presidents of the United States: Lyndon B. Johnson, 1967*, book 1 (Washington, D.C.: GPO, 1968), 11.

88. Harkavy, *Curbing Population Growth*, 46–47 and 50.

89. Critchlow, *Intended Consequences*, 79.

90. Ibid.

91. Ibid., 50.

92. Several nations greatly expanded overseas population aid in the 1960s, and the United Nations, which had done little more in the field than sponsor research through its Population Commission (born in 1947), became a much more active supporter of family planning programs through the creation, in 1969, of the United Nations Fund for Population Activities. See Harkavy, *Curbing Population Growth*, chap. 2.

93. For African-American critiques, see Robertson, *Malthusian Moment*, chaps. 6 and 8.

94. The literature has largely omitted the perspective of black women. A corrective is Johanna Schoen, "Fighting for Child Health: Race, Birth Control, and the State in the Jim Crow South," *Social Politics* 4 (Spring 1997): 90–113. King received one of Planned Parenthood's inaugural Margaret Sanger Awards in 1966. For King's comments on family planning—"Like all poor, Negro and white, they [African Americans] have many unwanted children. This is a cruel evil they urgently need to control"—see *Congressional Record*, Senate, May 10, 1966, 10164–65.

95. President's Committee on Population and Family Planning, *Population and Family Planning — The Transition from Concern to Action* (Washington, D.C.: GPO, 1968).

96. Critchlow, *Intended Consequences*, 51.

97. Ibid.

98. Connelly, *Fatal Misconception*, esp. chaps. 5 and 6.

99. Linda Gordon, *Woman's Body, Woman's Right: A Social History of Birth Control in America* (New York: Penguin, 1977), 397.

100. Ibid.

101. Ibid., 398. Rickie Solinger updates the Gordon thesis in *Wake Up Little Susie: Single Pregnancy before Roe v. Wade*, 2d ed. (New York: Routledge, 2000). According to Solinger, the "population bomb" was not a Malthusian image of generalized overpopulation and resource exhaustion; it and the "sexual revolution" were "racially specific metaphors of destruction" that referenced the alleged danger of African-American birthrates spiraling out of control, especially among the unmarried (206).

102. A classic statement is Gordon, *Woman's Body, Woman's Right*, chap. 13. Solinger, for example, misrepresents LBJ's statement at the United Nations' twentieth anniversary celebration "that less than five dollars invested in population control is worth $100 invested in economic growth" (quoted in *Wake Up Little Susie*, 209). Solinger writes, "These cost-accounting arguments extended the grounds for accusing poor unwed mothers, often black, of consumer violations: an unmarried girl or woman who failed to buy into the contraceptive bargain was

forcing society to pay full price for an unwanted item." But LBJ's comment was directed at an international audience, referred to population growth in the developing world, not unwed mothers in the US, and reflected the prevailing Coale-Hoover model. Indeed, the $100 figure was the one frequently used by economist Stephen Enke, deputy assistant secretary of defense in 1965 and 1966, in the context of the developing world. For a thoughtful critique of the economic ideas of Enke and others sympathetic to population control, albeit a critique that unfortunately detaches 1960s population activists from the broader historic economic-demographic discussion that guided them, see Connelly, *Fatal Misconception*, chap. 6, esp. 207–13.

103. Dorothy Roberts, *Killing the Black Body: Race, Reproduction, and the Meaning of Liberty* (New York: Vintage, 1999), 9.

104. See, for example, Johanna Schoen, *Choice and Coercion: Birth Control, Sterilization, and Abortion in Public Health and Welfare* (Chapel Hill: University of North Carolina Press, 2005).

105. Solinger, *Wake Up Little Susie*, 208 and 292–93 n. 9.

106. Scholars frequently manufacture population experts' racism. For instance, Solinger, ibid., 208, suggests that anti-Black animus motivated demographer Philip Hauser, when in fact Hauser was a racial liberal who served on an advisory panel guiding the desegregation of Chicago's public schools.

107. For his early liberalism, see Gruening, *Many Battles*, 57.

108. Catholic opposition squelched the fourteen maternal health clinics funded by the New Deal, but most continued with private funding, and a new law permitted the distribution of information about birth control. See ibid., 200–202. It is worth noting that many midcentury observers, Puerto Rican and American alike, believed that the small island was headed for a serious overpopulation problem.

109. Ibid., 55–60.

110. Ibid., 65.

111. Ibid., 181.

112. For example, see Gruening's account of his opposition to Senate filibusters against civil rights legislation (ibid., 406 and 461–62). His was also one of the two "no" votes on the 1964 Tonkin Gulf Resolution.

113. Clark asked, "So, your conclusion, based on your experience would be that there is nothing fundamentally inferior about the Negro child as compared to a white child given equal opportunity as assuming that the home background in many instances is inferior?" (Senate Committee on Labor and Public Welfare, Subcommittee on Employment and Manpower, *Nation's Manpower Revolution*, part 6, October 16, 17, 18, 22, 23, 24, and 25, 1963, 1913).

114. See Tydings Papers, Series 6, Box 10, Folder "Press Releases—1964 Election Campaign."

115. Norman B. Ryder, "Recent Trends and Group Differences in Fertility," in *Toward the End of Growth: Population in America*, ed. Charles Westoff (Engle-

wood Cliffs, N.J.: Prentice-Hall, 1973), reported (from the National Fertility Study of 1965) that from 1961 to 1965, "Blacks had approximately three times as many unwanted births per capita as whites" (62). This gap narrowed significantly between 1965 and 1970.

116. "Testimony of Senator Tydings before a Government Operations Subcommittee Hearing on Federal Aid for Family Planning Programs" (press release from the Office of Sen. Joseph Tydings, November 2, 1967), Tydings Papers, Series 6, Box 12, Folder "Press Releases—Obscenity; Population; Post Office; Public Works (1965–1970)."

117. For the history of the poverty–procreation link, see Marc Linder, *The Dilemmas of Laissez-Faire Population Policy in Capitalist Societies: When the Invisible Hand Controls Reproduction* (Westport, Conn.: Greenwood Press, 1997), chaps. 1 and 8.

118. It is worth noting that most social programs in the United States must be sold with reassurances of fiscal responsibility. This was particularly true during the Great Society, when liberals battled conservatives' claims that a significant expansion of social programs would break the bank.

119. Myron Lefcowitz and Kent Earnhardt, "Poverty and Family Planning," Office of Economic Opportunity, Office of Research, Plans, Programs, and Evaluation, copy in Records of the Population Council, Rockefeller Archive Center, Tarrytown, N.Y., Box 116, Folder 2133, "U.S. Office of Economic Opportunity."

120. Mollie Orshanksky, "The Shape of Poverty in 1966," *Social Security Bulletin* 31 (March 1968): 3–32.

121. For the emphasis on the "deserving" poor, see Davies, *Opportunity to Entitlement*, chap. 2. For Tydings' assertion that birth control was a human right and his desire to "give all segments of our society the opportunity to exercise birth control," see "Statement of Senator Joseph D. Tydings before the Subcommittee on Foreign Aid Expenditures," June 23, 1965, Tydings Papers, Series 6, Box 23, Folder "Testimony—Population (1965–1970)." In "Testimony of Senator Joseph D. Tydings Prepared for Delivery before the Senate Finance Committee Regarding H.R. 12080, the Social Security Amendments," September 22, 1967, Tydings Papers, Series 6, Box 23, Folder "Testimony—Social Security (1967)," Tydings noted Department of Health, Education, and Welfare estimates that of the 5 million Americans who could not afford family planning in 1967, about 700,000 received some form of it through governmental and third-sector programs.

122. "What are the Solutions?" *Newsweek*, January 25, 1965, 78.

123. Gordon acknowledged as much in *Woman's Body, Woman's Right*, 400.

124. Untitled press release from the Office of Senator Joseph Tydings, November 25, 1969, Tydings Papers, Series 6, Box 12, Folder "Press Releases—Obscenity; Population; Post Office; Public Works (1965–1970)."

125. Radio interview on the program "Washington Window," June 4, 1970, transcript in Tydings Papers, Series 5, Box 4, Folder "Tydings for Senate '70—Population Control and Statistics."

126. Linder, *Dilemmas of Laissez-Faire Population Policy*, 24–25.

127. Lee Rainwater and Karol Kane Weinstein, *And the Poor Get Children: Sex, Contraception, and Family Planning in the Working Class* (Chicago: Quadrangle Books, 1960). Also see Kathryn Edin, *Promises I Can Keep: Why Poor Women Put Motherhood before Marriage* (Berkeley and Los Angeles: University of California Press, 2005).

128. "Statement of Joseph D. Tydings announcing his intention to introduce legislation to aid voluntary family planning programs at home and abroad," February 28, 1966, Tydings Papers, Series 6, Box 12, Folder "Press Releases—Obscenity; Population; Post Office; Public Works (1965–1970)."

129. See Tydings's prepared statement in Senate Committee on Finance, *Social Security Amendments of 1967: Hearings on H.R. 12080*, 90th Cong., 1st sess., part 3, September 20, 21, 22, and 26, 1967, 1807–10.

130. Solinger's curious evidence of an insistence on "duty," for example, includes testimony by Rep. John Conyers (D-Mich.)—an African American—suggesting that Blacks should have fewer babies to "stabilize and improve the Negro family structure" hurt by "the tragedy of unwanted children" (quoted in *Wake Up Little Susie*, 210).

131. According to Johnson, *Ernest Gruening*, "Gruening's support for birth control derived from both his own medical school experience and the commitment to upholding individual rights which he inherited from his father" (16). In *Many Battles*, Gruening reports that he first saw the need for birth control after visiting the poor areas of South Boston (28). Gruening was also a suffragist prior to the Nineteenth Amendment.

132. *Congressional Record*, Senate, August 15, 1963, 15239.

133. Ibid.

134. Draft of "The Rediscovery of Excellence," JFK Papers, President's Office Files, Special Correspondence, Box 30, Folder "Jackson, Henry M. 12/6/60–6/4/62." Historians have largely missed the automation/population connection. Bix, *Inventing Ourselves Out of Jobs?*, incorrectly dismisses it as the ancillary purview of radicals (269).

135. *Congressional Record*, Senate, August 15, 1963, 15239.

136. Ibid.

137. *Congressional Record*, Senate, February 28, 1966, 4276.

138. Ibid.

139. Ibid., 4278. By the end of the 1960s, Tydings' moderate views on natural resource scarcity would give way to a dire ecological Malthusianism.

140. Ibid.

141. Untitled press release from the Office of Sen. Joseph Tydings, February 22 [most likely 1969], Tydings Papers, Series 6, Box 12, Folder "Press Releases—Obscenity; Population; Post Office; Public Works (1965–1970)."

142. For example, see "Our Burgeoning Birth Rate," Tydings Papers, Series 6, Box 20, Folder "Speeches—Population 2 (1967–1969)."

143. John Kenneth Galbraith, "Economics and the Quality of Life," in *A Contemporary Guide to Economics, Peace, and Laughter*, 20. A version of this essay was originally delivered as a lecture to the American Association for the Advancement of Science in 1963.

144. US Department of Labor, Office of Policy Planning and Research, *The Negro Family: The Case for National Action* (Washington, D.C.: GPO, 1965).

145. For the Moynihan Report, see Davies, *Opportunity to Entitlement*, chaps. 3 and 4; and Godfrey Hodgson, *The Gentleman from New York: Daniel Patrick Moynihan: A Biography* (New York: Houghton Mifflin, 2000), chaps. 4 and 5.

146. Daryl Michael Scott, *Contempt and Pity: Social Policy and the Image of the Damaged Black Psyche, 1880–1996* (Chapel Hill: University of North Carolina Press, 1997), 150–56.

147. Congress had severely curtailed immigration from Asia in the late nineteenth century.

148. The most readable summary of the 1965 Immigration Act is Steven M. Gillon, "*That's Not What We Meant to Do": Reform and Its Unintended Consequences in Twentieth-Century America* (New York: W. W. Norton, 2000), chap. 4. Also see David M. Reimers, *Still the Golden Door: The Third World Comes to America*, 2d ed. (New York: Columbia University Press, 1992), chap. 3; and Hugh Davis Graham, *Collision Course: The Strange Convergence of Affirmative Action and Immigration Policy in America* (New York: Oxford University Press, 2002), chap. 3.

149. Carl Bon Tempo, *Americans at the Gate: The United States and Refugees during the Cold War* (Princeton: Princeton University Press, 2008).

150. For example, a recent summation by a leading immigration scholar—Roger Daniels, *Guarding the Golden Door: American Immigration Policy and Immigrants since 1882* (New York: Hill and Wang, 2004)—includes nary a mention of overpopulation concerns.

151. Consult Edward Prince Hutchinson, *Legislative History of American Immigration Policy, 1798–1965* (Philadelphia: University of Pennsylvania Press, 1981).

152. I borrow the phrase from the title of chap. 1 of Reimers, *Still the Golden Door*.

153. John F. Kennedy, *A Nation of Immigrants* (New York: Anti-Defamation League of B'nai B'rith, 1959).

154. "The President's News Conference of January 24, 1963," *Public Papers of John F. Kennedy, 1963*, 95–96.

155. "Letter to the President of the Senate and to the Speaker of the House on Revision of the Immigration Laws," July 23, 1963, ibid., 594–97.

156. Daniels, *Guarding the Golden Door*, 131–32.

157. *Public Papers of Lyndon B. Johnson, 1963–64*, 116.

158. For Feighan's role, see Bernstein, *Guns or Butter*, 253–55. For the feud between Feighan and Celler, see Reimers, *Still the Golden Door*, 65.

159. For Gallup polls, see Graham, *Collision Course*, 60.

160. Daniels, *Guarding the Golden Door*, 133.

161. Reimers, *Still the Golden Door*, 69–71.

162. Quoted in Bernstein, *Guns or Butter*, 257.

163. For example, Graham, *Collision Course*, mentions the population issue only once, when discussing Sen. Ervin (62).

164. Bon Tempo, *Americans at the Gate*, 89.

165. *Congressional Record*, Senate, September 17, 1965, 24236.

166. *Congressional Record*, Senate, March 4, 1965, 4144. When the handwriting was on the wall, Ervin decided to work for a bill with numerical limits rather than endure passage of an even more liberal bill.

167. *Congressional Record*, House, April 6, 1965, 7195, cited in Betty K. Koed, "The Politics of Reform: Policymakers and the Immigration Act of 1965" (Ph.D. diss., University of California, Santa Barbara, 1999), 187.

168. Koed, "Politics of Reform," 188.

169. "Statement of the Military Order of the World Wars," House Committee on the Judiciary, Subcommittee No. 1, *Immigration*, 88th Cong, 2d sess., part 3, August 5, 6, 7, 10, 11, 14, 20, 21; September 2, 3, 11, 17, 1964, 674.

170. Ibid., 675–76.

171. Several demographers told Congress that immigration from Western Hemisphere nations would skyrocket if reform passed and argued that the US should not serve as the "escape hatch" for global population growth. These hearings were compiled as House Committee on the Judiciary, Subcommittee No. 1, *Study of Population and Immigration Problems*, 12 vols., 1962–1963 (Washington, D.C.: GPO, 1962–63).

172. Koed, "Politics of Reform," 158.

173. Quoted in ibid., 188–89.

174. Gillon, "*That's Not What We Meant to Do*," 173.

175. House Committee on the Judiciary, Subcommittee No. 1, *Immigration*, part 1, June 11, 18, 19, 22, 23, 25, 26, 29, 30, 1964, p. 6. One finds hundreds of such statements during the various 1964 and 1965 hearings. For Labor Department assurances that reform would not flood labor markets, see Graham, *Collision Course*, 59.

176. Cited in Gillon, "*That's Not What We Meant to Do*," 172.

177. "For Release after the Senate passes the Immigration Reform Bill HR 258" (undated press release from the Office of Sen. Joseph Tydings), Tydings Papers, Series 6, Box 10, Folder "Press Releases—Immigration (1964–1970)."

178. House Committee on the Judiciary, Subcommittee No. 1, *Immigration*, part 1, 117.

179. Ibid., 52.

180. House Committee on the Judiciary, Subcommittee No. 1, *Immigration*, part 3, 676.

181. House Committee on the Judiciary, Subcommittee on Immigration and Naturalization, 89th Cong., 1st sess., *Immigration: Hearings on S. 500*, part 2,

March 8, 12, 15, 16, 17, 22; June 3, 4, 8, 9, 15, 16, 23, 24, 25; July 15, 21, 22, 28, 29; and August 3, 1965, 676. This organization should not be confused with the executive agency created during the Clinton administration.

Chapter Six

1. For postwar Malthusianism, see Thomas Robertson, *The Malthusian Moment: Global Population Growth and the Birth of American Environmentalism* (New Brunswick: Rutgers University Press, 2012); Donald T. Critchlow, *Intended Consequences: Birth Control, Abortion, and the Federal Government in Modern America* (New York: Oxford University Press, 1999); and Björn-Ola Linnér, *The Return of Malthus: Environmentalism and Post-war Population-Resource Crises* (Isle of Harris, UK: White Horse Press, 2003).

2. For example, see Kenneth E. Boulding, *The Meaning of the Twentieth Century: The Great Transition* (New York: Harper & Row, 1964), 121–25.

3. Paul R. Ehrlich, *The Population Bomb* (New York: Ballantine Books, 1968).

4. Thomas G. Smith, "John Kennedy, Stewart Udall, and New Frontier Conservation," *Pacific Historical Review* 64 (August 1995): 329–62.

5. Cited in ibid., 334.

6. The two most important pieces of legislation were the 1964 Land and Water Conservation Fund Act, which created a system through which outdoor recreation revenue would support federal land purchases, and the Wilderness Act.

7. See "Special Message to the Congress on Natural Resources," February 23, 1961, and "Remarks at the Dedication of the National Wildlife Federation Building," March 3, 1961, in *Public Papers of the Presidents of the United States: John F. Kennedy, 1961* (Washington, D.C.: GPO, 1962), 114–21 and 147–48; and "Special Message to the Congress on Conservation," March 1, 1962, *Public Papers of the Presidents of the United States: John F. Kennedy, 1962* (Washington, D.C.: GPO, 1963), 176–84.

8. See chap. 4 of the present study; and Samuel P. Hays, *Beauty, Health, and Permanence: Environmental Politics in the United States, 1955–1985* (Cambridge: Cambridge University Press, 1987), esp. chap. 1.

9. Donald J. Bogue, "Population Growth in the United States," in *The Population Dilemma*, ed. Philip M. Hauser (Englewood Cliffs, N.J.: Prentice-Hall, 1963), 92.

10. This was the language from the White House press release, May 25, 1962, "Remarks of the President to the White House Conference on Conservation," Papers of President John F. Kennedy (hereafter JFK Papers), John F. Kennedy Presidential Library, Boston (hereafter JFKL), President's Office Files, Speech Files, Box 38A, Folder "Remarks to the White House Conference on Conservation—5/22/62." For a slightly different version, see "Remarks to the White House on Conservation," *Public Papers of John F. Kennedy, 1962*, 441–43.

11. See Walter Heller to JFK, "Present and Prospective Measures to Accelerate Economic Growth," July 14, 1961, JFK Papers, White House Central Subject Files, Business-Economics, Box 17, Folder "BE 5 National Economy, April 1, 1961–September 30, 1961."

12. Paul Charles Milazzo, *Unlikely Environmentalists: Congress and Clean Water, 1945–1972* (Lawrence: University Press of Kansas, 2006).

13. It was one thing for Kennedy to pepper his speeches with romantic comments about the need for "scenic beauty," quite another for the CEA to devote a section of its *Economic Report of the President to the Congress, 1966* (Washington, D.C.: GPO, 1966) to "Rubbish, Garbage, and Junk Automobiles" (96–109).

14. Press release, Sept. 25, 1963, "Remarks of the President, University of North Dakota Field House, Grand Forks, North Dakota," JFK Papers, White House Central Subject Files, Speeches, Box 927, Folder "SP 3-100/ST, Conservation Trip Speeches." Also see "Text of a Letter from The President to the President of Senate and the Speaker of the House Transmitting a Development Program for the National Forests," Sept. 21, 1961, JFK Papers, President's Office Files, Box 36, Folder "Remarks at Big Cedar, Oklahoma on the Opening of the Ouachite National Forest Road, 10/29/62."

15. Rachel Carson, *Silent Spring* (Boston: Houghton Mifflin, 1962); and Stewart L. Udall, *The Quiet Crisis and the Next Generation* (Salt Lake City: Peregrine Smith Books, 1988), 195 and 197.

16. Kennedy publicly promised action after reading "Miss Carson's book" serialized in the *New Yorker* ("The President's News Conference of August 29, 1962," *Public Papers of John F. Kennedy, 1962*, 648–55).

17. Cited in Robert Rienow and Leona Train Rienow, *Moment in the Sun: A Report on the Deteriorating Quality of the American Environment* (New York: Dial Press, 1967), 29.

18. For Udall's efforts to reconcile aesthetic environmentalism and wise-use doctrine, see *Quiet Crisis*, chap. 13.

19. Ibid., 185–86.

20. Ibid., 187.

21. Ibid.

22. Stewart Udall, "The Conservation Challenge of the Sixties," speech given at the University of California, Berkeley, April 19, 1963, JFK Papers, President's Office Files, Departments and Agencies, Box 80, Folder "Interior: 'The Conservation Challenge of the Sixties,'" 2 and 33.

23. Until the fine treatment in Robertson, *Malthusian Moment*, chap. 5, scholars have downplayed the extent to which population concerns informed the wilderness discussion, stressing instead increased leisure time, the diffusion of the automobile, the rise of ecological science, and the desire for therapeutic recess from modern, urban living. And in accounting for passage of the Wilderness Act they have emphasized parliamentary machinations, especially by pro–resource

development Congressman Wayne Aspinall (D-Colo.). A seminal work, Roderick Nash, *Wilderness and the American Mind*, 3d ed. (New Haven: Yale University Press, 1982), considers population growth only in the epilogue (380–81). Other works minimizing the population–wilderness connection include Michael Frome, *Battle for the Wilderness*, rev. ed. (Salt Lake City: University of Utah Press, 1997); Steven C. Schulte, *Wayne Aspinall and the Shaping of the American West* (Boulder: University Press of Colorado, 2002); Michael P. Cohen, *The History of the Sierra Club: 1892–1970* (San Francisco: Sierra Club Books, 1988); and Hays, *Beauty, Health, and Permanence*.

24. Paul S. Sutter, *Driven Wild: How the Fight against Automobiles Launched the Modern Wilderness Movement* (Seattle: University of Washington Press, 2002), 230–34 and 248–55.

25. Outdoor Recreation Resources Review Commission, *Outdoor Recreation for America: A Report to the President and to the Congress* (Washington, D.C.: GPO, 1962). President Kennedy's 1962 special message on conservation advocated implementing ORRRC recommendations ("Special Message to the Congress on Conservation," March 1, 1962, *Public Papers of John F. Kennedy, 1962*, 176–84).

26. Quoted in *The Living Wilderness* (the bulletin of the Wilderness Society), no. 44 (Spring 1953): 30, citing the editorial "Stop, Look, and Listen!" from *Planning and Civic Comment* (the bulletin of the American Planning and Civic Association), March 1953. Even relatively agnostic voices took it for granted that a growing population necessitated a wilderness system. See the statement of the National Association of Soil Conservation Districts in House Committee on Interior and Insular Affairs, Subcommittee on Public Lands, *Wilderness Preservation System*, Serial no. 12, part 1, October 30 and 31, 1961, 288.

27. Eisenhower to William Magie, Executive Director of Friends of the Wilderness (a Minnesota organization), responding to a request to speak in Duluth, reprinted in *The Living Wilderness*, no. 58 (Fall–Winter 1956–57), 53.

28. *Congressional Record*, Senate, June 7, 1956, 9772. Sen. Clinton Anderson (D-N.Mex.) was another leading wilderness proponent who had long articulated Malthusian themes. See the various folders on population in the Sen. Clinton Anderson Papers, Library of Congress Manuscript Room, Washington, D.C. The legislative campaign for wilderness, spearheaded by Wilderness Society president Howard Zahniser, took off after environmentalists' 1956 victory in a multiyear campaign to prevent construction of Echo Park Dam in Dinosaur National Monument.

29. This claim is admittedly not based on rigorous statistical analysis, but a quick comparison of congressional discussion of wilderness in 1956 and 1963 provides ample evidence of growing salience.

30. For detailed description of mainstream organizations and the postwar quest for wilderness, see Robertson, *Malthusian Moment*, chap. 5.

31. Charlotte Lauk, "The Paradox of the Pioneer Spirit," *The Living Wilderness*, no. 65 (Summer–Fall 1958): 5.

32. *The Living Wilderness*, no. 68 (Spring 1959): 24.

33. At the 1959 Wilderness Conference, zoologist Raymond Cowles introduced a resolution stating, to borrow Michael Cohen's paraphrase, "that there was no point in talking about wilderness, which would only be an incidental victim of the coming malignant population explosion" (Cohen, *History of the Sierra Club*, 232).

34. "The Wilderness and the Future," *San Francisco Chronicle*, April 15, 1957.

35. "One Hundred Million Arguments," *San Francisco Chronicle*, November 12, 1958.

36. "Preserving a Refuge," *Washington Post*, July 20, 1959.

37. "Fencing the Wilderness," *Boston Sunday Globe*, July 12, 1959.

38. Religious Americans emphasized that wilderness provides opportunities for spiritual reflection. Others echoed the turn-of-the-twentieth-century cult of masculinity and claimed that wilderness promotes physical strength. Economists assured critics that the economic effects of preserving mostly mountainous and remote areas would be minimal. Still others more attuned to administrative nuance argued natural lands had to be protected from the future whims of any particular presidency or Forest Service.

39. House Committee on Interior and Insular Affairs, Subcommittee on Public Lands, *Wilderness Preservation System*, 22.

40. Ibid., 379.

41. Ibid., 302.

42. For example, see the statement of California Institute of Technology biologist James Bonner in ibid., 161–64.

43. Ibid., 212.

44. Ibid., 213.

45. Public Law 517, 86th Cong., 2d sess. (June 12, 1960).

46. Public Law 577, 88th Cong., 2d sess. (September 3, 1964).

47. "Special Message to the Congress on Conservation and Restoration of Natural Beauty," February 8, 1965, *Public Papers of the Presidents of the United States: Lyndon B. Johnson, 1965*, book 1 (Washington, D.C.: GPO, 1966), 155.

48. *Scenic Hudson Preservation Conference v. Federal Power Commission*, 354 F.2d 608 (1965), 88. In *Sierra Club v. Morton*, 405 U.S. 734 (1971), the Supreme Court contended, "Aesthetic and environmental well-being, like economic well-being, are important ingredients in the quality of life in our society, and the fact that particular environmental interests are shared by the many rather than the few does not make them less deserving of legal protection through the judicial process."

49. For example, see Rienow and Rienow, *Moment in the Sun*.

50. These estimates assumed continuation of the era's immigration levels, when in fact immigration was about to soar. For the different anticipated scenarios through which zero population growth might have been achieved, see Ansley J. Coale, "Man and His Environment: Economic Factors are More Important than Population Growth in Threatening the Quality of Life," *Science* 170 (October 9,

1970): 132–36; and Nathan Keyfitz, "On the Momentum of Population Growth," *Demography* 8 (February 1971): 71–80.

51. For example, Philip Appleman, *The Silent Explosion* (Boston: Beacon Press, 1965), argued that the US had its own population explosion but ignored pollution and ecology. Also see Paul Paddock and William Paddock, *Famine—1975! America's Decision: Who Will Survive?* (Boston: Little, Brown and Company, 1967); and Arthur Hopcraft, *Born to Hunger* (Boston: Houghton Mifflin, 1968).

52. Roy Beck and Leon Kolankiewicz, "The Environmental Movement's Retreat from Advocating U.S. Population Stabilization (1970–1998): A First Draft of History," *Journal of Policy History* 12 (January 2000), 152 n. 4, lists leading ecologists.

53. For environmental economics, see Peter Hay, *Main Currents in Western Environmental Thought* (Bloomington: Indiana University Press, 2002), chap. 8. For a quick overview, see Paul Krugman, "Green Economics," *New York Times Magazine*, April 11, 2010.

54. Herman E. Daly, "Introduction," in *Economics, Ecology, Ethics: Essays Toward a Steady-State Economy*, ed. Daly (San Francisco: W. H. Freeman and Company, 1973), 19.

55. Aaron B. Wildavsky, "Aesthetic Power or the Triumph of the Sensitive Minority over the Vulgar Masses: A Political Analysis of the New Economics," *Daedalus* 96 (Fall 1967): 1115–28.

56. For a collection of contemporary essays edited by one of the leading ecological economics, see *Economics, Ecology, Ethics*, ed. Daly.

57. Nicholas Georgescu-Roegen, "Matter Matters, Too," in *Prospects for Growth: Changing Expectations for the Future*, ed. K. D. Wilson (New York: Praeger, 1977), 293–313. His leading work was *The Entropy Law and the Economic Process* (Cambridge, Mass.: Harvard University Press, 1971). Also see his "Measure, Quality, and Optimal Scale," in *Essays on Econometrics and Planning Presented to Professor P. C. Mahalanobis on the Occasion of His 70th Birthday*, ed. C. R. Rao (Oxford: Pergamon, 1963), 231–56.

58. Thomas Robert Malthus, *Population: The First Essay* (1798; reprint, with a foreword by Kenneth E. Boulding, Ann Arbor: University of Michigan Press, 1959).

59. Kenneth E. Boulding, "The Economics of the Coming Spaceship Earth," in *Environmental Quality in a Growing Economy: Essays from the Sixth RFF Forum*, ed. Henry Jarrett (Baltimore: Johns Hopkins University Press for Resources for the Future, 1966), 9.

60. Ibid. Also see Boulding, *Meaning of the Twentieth Century*, chap. 7, "The Entropy Trap."

61. Boulding, *Meaning of the Twentieth Century*, 135–36. Boulding later wrote that this proposal was "a little tongue in cheek" ("The Shadow of the Stationary State," in *The No-Growth Society*, ed. Mancur Olson and Hans H. Landsberg [New York: W. W. Norton, 1973], 93).

62. Georg Borgström, *The Hungry Planet: The Modern World at the Edge of Famine* (London: Macmillan, 1965), chap. 9.

63. Kingsley Davis, "Population Policy: Will Current Programs Succeed?" *Science* 158 (November 10, 1967): 730–39.

64. Kingsley Davis, "Zero Population Growth: The Goal and the Means," in *No-Growth Society*, ed. Olson and Landsberg, esp. 21. Also see Davis, "Population Policy"; Ansley J. Coale, "Should the United States Start a Campaign for Fewer Births?" *Population Index* 34 (October–December 1968): 467–74 (his presidential speech to the Population Association of America of April 19, 1968); and Thomas Frejka, "Reflections on the Demographic Conditions Needed to Establish a U.S. Stationary Population Growth," *Population Studies* 22 (November 1968): 379–97.

65. Davis, "Zero Population Growth."

66. Rienow and Rienow, *Moment in the Sun*, 211–12.

67. Garrett Hardin, "The Tragedy of the Commons," *Science* 162 (December 13, 1968): 1243–48.

68. Ibid., 1246.

69. Ibid., 1247.

70. Garrett Hardin, "Living on a Lifeboat," *BioScience* 24 (October 1974): 561–68.

71. Hardin wrote that "those who are biologically more fit to be the custodians of property and power should legally inherit more" ("Tragedy of the Commons," 1247). Still, he rejected the notion that genetics should guide such transfers and never suggested that members of various ethnic groups have different innate abilities. Hardin continued to skirt the eugenic line until his recent death. In a 1992 interview, he complained that "ZPG's entire attraction has been among the college population. So, in effect, ZPG is encouraging college-educated people to have fewer children instead of encouraging reduced fertility among the less intelligent" (Cathy Spencer, "Interview: Garrett Hardin," *Omni*, June 1992, 59).

72. For an excellent and detailed discussion of Ehrlich, see Robertson, *Malthusian Moment*, chap. 6.

73. Ehrlich, *Population Bomb*, xi.

74. Cited in Martin Lasden, "Paul Ehrlich: Apocalypse Then and Now," *Stanford*, September 1990, 56.

75. Ehrlich, *Population Bomb*, chap. 1.

76. Ibid., chap. 4.

77. See in particular Paul R. Ehrlich and Anne H. Ehrlich, *Population, Resources, Environment: Issues in Human Ecology* (San Francisco: W. H. Freeman, 1970).

78. Ehrlich, *Population Bomb*, chap. 4.

79. Cited in Udall, *Quiet Crisis*, 239.

80. *Population Bomb* was published under the auspices of the Sierra Club and introduced by Brower.

81. Critchlow, *Intended Consequences*, 56.

82. For more on Ehrlich and the counterculture, see Robertson, *Malthusian Moment*, chap. 6. Law professor Larry Barnett, president of ZPG in 1970–71, suggested that *Population Bomb*'s warnings of widespread disease touched the rawest nerve: "Americans are more concerned with the health effects of a problem than they are with the social and economic effects. Ehrlich was thus able to strike a more responsive chord with Americans than were demographers, who had been the only organized group studying human population growth as a problem" (Larry Barnett, "A History of Zero Population Growth," unpublished manuscript, Records of Zero Population Growth, Washington, D.C. [hereafter ZPG Records], Folder "History of ZPG").

83. "Thirty Years of ZPG—A Brief History" (unpublished manuscript, ZPG Records, Folder "History of ZPG").

84. Critchlow, *Intended Consequences*, 56; and Larry D. Barnett, "Political Affiliation and Attitudes Toward Population Limitation," *Social Biology* 17 (June 1970): 124–31. Barnett reported that 49 percent of Republicans favored population control versus 40 percent of Democrats, but he did not control for the higher incomes of Republicans (which corresponded with higher levels of education and more liberal views on these matters).

85. Some editions of *Population Bomb* included a coupon to join ZPG (Suzanne Staggenborg, *The Pro-Choice Movement: Organization and Activism in the Abortion Conflict* [New York: Oxford University Press, 1991], 162).

86. Also at the original meeting was Lincoln Day, who headed the UN's demographic division.

87. For the activities of the local branches, see *ZPG National Reporter*, esp. September 1970. The organization's bulletin was initially called the *ZPG Communicator*, became the *ZPG Newsletter* in September 1969, and was finally renamed the *ZPG National Reporter* (hereafter *ZPG Reporter*) in February 1970. I read most issues in the ZPG Records.

88. Environmental historians sometimes briefly note the creation of ZPG, but as Donald Critchlow observes, the group "need[s] further scholarly attention" (*Intended Consequences*, 275 n. 25).

89. This brief history is based largely on "ZPG: Why Does it Exist? A Planning Document for Discussion at ZPG's 1975 Annual Meeting, April 11–14, 1975 S[an]F[ranciso]"; "Thirty Years of ZPG—A Brief History"; and Richard Bowers, "Memorandum on the Founding of Zero Population Growth," all in ZPG Records, Folder "History of ZPG." Also see Wade Greene, "The Militant Malthusians," *Saturday Review*, March 11, 1972, 40–49. Membership in ZPG was concentrated in the liberal outposts of the Northeast and California; in 1974, it had twelve members in Mississippi (see "ZPG Membership and Charter Map, 4/1/74," ZPG Records, Folder "History of ZPG"). According to the *ZPG Reporter*, membership peaked in July–August 1971. In 1976, the vice president of ZPG suggested to the new incom-

ing director that membership counts had been exaggerated by computer error and may have peaked at fewer than 25,000 (Judith Kunofsky to Roy Morgan, November 18, 1976, in ZPG Records, Folder "History of ZPG"). ZPG members were better educated, younger, and slightly less Catholic than the general population. However, social attitudes, not demographic characteristics, were the largest determinants of membership. In particular, ZPG members rejected traditional religious institutions and were oriented toward the future. I thank Larry Barnett for the original source of the translation of his "Zero Population Growth, Inc.: A Study of a Population Interest Group in the United States," which appeared in L. D. Barnett and F. L. Leeuw, *Bevolking als vraagstuk: Dimensies van bevolkingsbeleid in Nederland en de Verenigde Staten* (The Hague: Vuga-Uitgeverij, 1981). For analysis of the organization a bit later, in the 1970s, see Larry D. Barnett, "Population Growth, Population Organization Participants, and the Right of Privacy," *Family Law Quarterly* 12 (Spring 1978): 37–60.

90. The environmental movement itself embraced the overpopulation critique, a "central theme" of the first Earth Day in 1970 (Beck and Kolankiewicz, "Environmental Movement's Retreat," 124). In 1969, the Sierra Club's Board of Directors urged "the people of the United States to abandon population growth as a pattern and goal; to commit themselves to limit the total population of the United States in order to achieve a balance between population and resources; and to achieve a stable population no later than the year 1990" (125). The Audubon Society also supported the goal of replacement-level fertility rates (Alexandra Minna Stern, *Eugenic Nation: Faults and Frontiers of Better Breeding in Modern America* [Berkeley and Los Angeles: University of California Press, 2005], 127).

91. Carl Pope, "Population," in *Nixon and the Environment: The Politics of Devastation*, ed. James Rathlesberger (New York: Village Voice, 1972), 164.

92. The moderate population establishment, in contrast, emphasized the minority of unwanted births; contraception could prevent these without a fundamental shift in values.

93. For example, see "Myth of the Month," *ZPG Reporter*, May 1971.

94. A letter to the editor in the September 1971 *ZPG Reporter*, in response to Carl Pope's suggestion in a previous issue that the group adopt an immigration policy, claimed that Pope's was the first mention of immigration in the *Reporter*'s two-plus years.

95. Judith Kunofsky to Roy Morgan, November 18, 1976.

96. "Myth of the Month," *ZPG Reporter*, May 1971.

97. Greene, "Militant Malthusians," 43. The National Council on Population Policy was formed by former senator Joseph Tydings (D-Md.) and Milton Eisenhower, the former president's brother.

98. Quoted in "Legal Analysis and Population Control: The Problem of Coercion," *Harvard Law Review* 84 (June 1971): 1863.

99. The September 1969 *ZPG Newsletter* was devoted entirely to women's rights

issues. In the November 1969 issue, Executive Director Shirley Radl responded to charges that the group was sexist.

100. For example, see Critchlow, *Intended Consequences*, 132–37.

101. Ibid., 133.

102. Population activists participated at the February 1969 conference in Chicago that led to the creation of NARAL. See *ZPG Communicator*, July 1969.

103. Staggenborg, *Pro-Choice Movement*, 15–16, 57–58, and 151–52. Citing Staggenborg, Critchlow writes, "In some areas ZPG activists were the only organized representatives of the nascent abortion movement" (*Intended Consequences*, 135).

104. One political scientist concluded that "abortion is not perceived by the general public as a population issue. Nor, for the most part, has it been fought as one" (John M. Ostheimer, "Abortion and American Population Politics," in *Population Policy Analysis*, ed. Michael E. Kraft and Mark Schneider [Lexington, Mass.: D.C. Heath and Co., 1978], 93).

105. The leading work on abortion reform at the state level—David J. Garrow's nearly 1,000-page *Liberty and Sexuality: The Right to Privacy and the Making of Roe v. Wade* (New York: Macmillan, 1994)—mentions the organization ZPG just once, in the context of a lawsuit it initiated in Vermont to liberalize abortion (487). Garrow discusses Garrett Hardin's support for abortion in the context of feminist goals without mentioning his famous calls to arrest overpopulation (293–94) and, similarly, reviews the abortion activism of Colorado state representative Richard Lamm without noting he was later a ZPG official (323–27). Kristin Luker, *Abortion and the Politics of Motherhood* (Berkeley and Los Angeles: University of California Press, 1984), only briefly mentions ZPG's support for abortion (142–43) and incorrectly estimates the group's peak membership at 300,000—about 265,000 too high!

106. On the first count, see James Weber, "Let's Hear It for Population Growth!" *Human Life Review* 31 (Winter 2005): 5–16. Linda Gordon, *Woman's Body, Woman's Right: A Social History of Birth Control in America* (New York: Penguin, 1977), argued, "Population controllers support the legalization of contraception and sterilization, but not necessarily of abortion or any forms of birth control that let women make their own choices exclusively.... Birth-rate reduction always comes first" (416). For the argument that population activists' interest in abortion was racially motivated, see Leslie J. Reagan, *When Abortion Was a Crime: Women, Medicine, and Law in the United States, 1867–1973* (Berkeley and Los Angeles: University of California Press, 1997), 230–31; and Rosalind Pollack Petchesky, *Abortion and Woman's Choice: The State, Sexuality, and Reproductive Freedom*, rev. ed. (Boston: Northeastern University Press, 1990), 130. These scholars ignore not only the support for abortion rights from population-centric groups such as ZPG but also the efforts in the early 1970s by John D. Rockefeller III and Joan Dunlop of the Population Council to inject into the mainstream population movement a greater emphasis on enhancing women's rights and opportunities.

107. I expanded on these state-level efforts in "Was *Roe v. Wade* Population Policy? Rethinking the Connections between the Abortion and Population Movements" (paper presented at the annual meeting of the Social Science History Association, Portland, Oregon, November 2004).

108. See Richard Lamm, "The Reproductive Revolution," *American Bar Association Journal* 56 (January 1970): 41–44, and "The Legislative Process in Changing Therapeutic Abortion Laws: The Colorado Experience," *American Journal of Orthopsychiatry* 39 (July 1969): 684–90. I thank Governor Lamm for sending me copies of these articles.

109. *ZPG Reporter*, February 1971, 38.

110. *Roe v. Wade*, 410 U.S. 116 (1973). An investigation of the Harry Blackmun Papers in the Library of Congress Manuscript Room did not reveal the justice's thoughts on population. Several citizens who sent letters praising the *Roe v. Wade* decision mentioned the need to rein in population growth, but Blackmun did not address the issue in his responses.

111. An important example was National Research Council, Committee on Resources and Man, *Resources and Man: A Study and Recommendations* (San Francisco: W. H. Freeman, 1969).

112. For Malthusian fiction, see Critchlow, *Intended Consequences*, 55.

113. For Bowie's environmental thinking, see Craig Copetas, "Beat Godfather Meets Glitter Mainman," *Rolling Stone*, February 28, 1974, 24–27.

114. French demographer Alfred Sauvy said that "the real take-off point for [the limits-to-growth] movement was the exploration of the moon" (Alfred Sauvy, *Zero Growth?* trans. A. Maguire [Oxford: Basil Blackwell, 1975], x).

115. Office of Population (United States Agency for International Development, Bureau for Technical Assistance), *Program Assistance: Aid to Developing Countries by the United States, Other Nations, and International and Private Agencies* (Washington, D.C.: GPO, 1971), iii.

116. According to Ian Bowen, *Economics and Demography* (London: George Allen & Unwin, 1976), a majority of participants at a 1968 conference on population at Princeton believed that "the world was capable of increasing food supplies to sustain [population growth], and that while it might impose severe strains on the world's capacity to organise jobs and amenities the task was not insuperable" (22).

117. "Population Heads for a Zero Growth Rate," *Business Week*, October 24, 1970, 103.

118. See, for example, Harold L. Votey Jr., "The Optimum Population and Growth: A New Look: A Modification to include a Preference for Children in the Welfare Function," *Journal of Economic Theory* 1 (October 1969): 273–90.

119. Muskie vacillated about whether to cosponsor a proposed 1971 congressional resolution (discussed in the next chapter) that would have declared the goal of zero population growth to be official state policy. According to the *ZPG Reporter*, July–August 1971, "Senator Edmund Muskie of Maine considered co-sponsoring [the legislation] but apparently decided it's still too soon to legisla-

tively endorse the principle that infinite growth is neither possible nor desirable in a finite world" (12).

120. Bill Christofferson, *The Man from Clear Lake: Earth Day Founder Senator Gaylord Nelson* (Madison: University of Wisconsin Press, 2004), 261.

121. Gaylord Nelson, *America's Last Chance* (Waukesha, Wis.: Country Beautiful Corporation, 1970), 93.

122. Beck and Kolankiewicz, "Environmental Movement's Retreat," claims, "Business groups always have defined one end of the growth issue spectrum as they pushed for ever more population growth" (126). Neo-Marxists sometimes argue that business groups sometimes support population policies because they seek to regulate the future labor supply, hold back the mob, and cut welfare spending. Yet the business community never organized in any meaningful way to reverse the Malthusian craze, perhaps because, for a time, it did not wish to be seen as anti-environmental. Still, it is true, as Critchlow concludes, that "big business's assumption that expanding population was equated with economic growth was seen [by population activists] as a serious obstacle to population control" (*Intended Consequences*, 18).

123. Charles F. Westoff, "Recent Developments in Population Growth Policy in the United States," in Westoff et al., *Toward the End of Growth: Population in America* (Englewood Cliffs, N.J.: Prentice-Hall, 1973), 168.

124. See "Birth Control: Businessmen Back It," *Business Week*, May 15, 1965, 34.

125. Quoted in Stephen Viederman and Sharmon Sollitto, "Economic Groups: Business, Labor, Welfare," in *Population Policy and Ethics: The American Experience*, ed. Robert M. Veatch (New York: Irvington, 1977), 330.

126. Unspecified testimony by Carl Madden, Chief Economist, Chamber of Commerce of the US, April 15, 1971, Richard Nixon Presidential Materials, National Archives II, College Park, Md., White House Central Files, Subject Files, FG 275, Commission on Population Growth and the American Future, Box 2, Folder "FG 275 Commission on Population Growth and the American Future 1/1/71 (1 of 2)."

127. This statement appeared on page 2 of the June 1970 issue of *Fortune*, previewing Lawrence A. Mayer, "U.S. Population Growth: Will Slower Be Better?"

128. Stephen D. Mumford, *The Life and Death of NSSM 200: How the Destruction of Political Will Doomed a U.S. Population Policy* (Research Triangle Park, N.C.: Center for Research on Population and Security, 1996), 19. Also see Beck and Kolankiewicz, "Environmental Movement's Retreat," 124; and Arthur J. Dyck, "Religious Views," in *Population Policy and Ethics*, ed. Veatch, 277–323.

129. Howard D. Samuel, "Population and the American Future," *American Federationist* 79 (May 1972): 17.

130. House Committee on Government Operations, Conservation and Natural Resources Subcommittee, *Effects of Population Growth on Natural Resources and the Environment*, 91st Cong., 1st sess., September 15 and 16, 1969.

131. See Bush's prepared statement in House Committee on Government Operations, Executive and Legislative Reorganization Subcommittee, *Establishing a Commission on Population Growth, and Related Matters*, 91st Cong., 1st sess., November 19 and 20, 1969, 58.

132. *Congressional Record*, House, July 21, 1969, 20137. Also see *Congressional Record*, House, February 24, 1969, 4207.

133. Public Law 190, 91st Cong., 1st sess. (January 1, 1970), sec. 101. Jackson's comment appears in *Congressional Record*, Senate, December 20, 1969, 40416. Also see Matthew J. Lindstrom and Zachary A. Smith, *The National Environmental Policy Act: Judicial Misconstruction, Legislative Indifference, and Executive Neglect* (College Station: Texas A&M University Press, 2001).

134. Senate Committee on Interior and Insular Affairs, and House Committee on Science and Astronautics, *Joint House-Senate Colloquium to Discuss a National Policy for the Environment*, 90th Cong., 2d sess., July 17, 1968.

135. Ibid., 55.

136. Ibid., 15.

137. Senate Committee on Interior and Insular Affairs, "Preamble," in *Special Report to the Senate Committee on Interior and Insular Affairs*, 90th Cong., 2d sess., July 11, 1968, reprinted in Senate Committee on Interior and Insular Affairs, and House Committee on Science and Astronautics, *Joint House-Senate Colloquium*, 93. The resulting white paper was *Congressional White Paper on a National Policy for the Environment* (Washington, D.C.: GPO, 1968). Senator Jackson wrote John D. Rockefeller III, March 24, 1972, "I am convinced that we must play a more active role in dealing with the problem of population growth" (Papers of John D. Rockefeller III, Rockefeller Archive Center, Tarrytown, N.Y. [hereafter JDR III Papers], Series 3, Subseries 2, Box 30, Folder 138, "Famous People, 1972–1977").

138. Public Law 190, 91st Cong., 1st sess. (January 1, 1970).

139. The language on population was drafted in the spring of 1969 by the staff of Henry Jackson's Interior Committee. See Appendix 2, "Statement by Senator Jackson," in Senate Committee on Interior and Insular Affairs, *National Environmental Policy: Hearing on S. 1075, S. 237, and S. 1752*, 91st Cong., 1st sess., April 16, 1969, 207.

140. Justice William Rehnquist wrote in *Vermont Yankee Nuclear Power Corp. v. Natural Resources Defense Council*, 435 U.S. 558 (1978), "NEPA does set forth significant substantive goals for the Nation, but its mandate to the agencies is essentially procedural." Also see *Kleppe v. Sierra Club*, 427 U.S. 390 (1975).

141. *ZPG Reporter*, July–August 1971, 12.

142. Public Law 516, 91st Cong., 2d sess. (October 30, 1970).

143. Senate Committee on Labor and Public Welfare, Subcommittee on Education, *Environmental Quality Act*, 91st Cong., 2d sess., May 19 and 20, 1970, 39. Representatives John Brademas (D-Ind.) and John Tunney (D-Calif.) introduced similar House bills.

144. Amendment No. 614 to S. 3151, reprinted in ibid., 16. Also see "Statement of Garrett De Bell, Washington Representative, Zero Population Growth," in ibid., 336–43.

145. *ZPG Reporter*, September 1970.

146. Further research might investigate the extent to which population education made its way into America's schools.

147. For these divisions, see Critchlow, *Intended Consequences*, 150–60. For the radical perspective, consult Davis, "Zero Population Growth."

148. Ronald M. Baker, "Population Control in the Year 2000: The Constitutionality of Placing Anti-Fertility Agents in the Water Supply," *Ohio State Law Journal* 32 (Winter 1971): 108–18.

149. Quoted in Critchlow, *Intended Consequences*, 156.

150. Ibid., 157.

151. Ibid.

152. "Selection of the name Zero Population Growth by Dick Bowers," ZPG Records, Folder "History of ZPG."

153. JDR III to Willard Johnson (ZPG board member), June 15, 1972, JDR III Papers, Series 3, Subseries 2, Box 34, Folder 187, "Correspondence Chronological File June 1972."

154. Ralph Hollow, "The Blacks Cry Genocide," *The Nation*, April 28, 1969, 535–37.

155. Critchlow, *Intended Consequences*, 151.

156. Ibid.

157. For example, see Edward G. Stockwell, *Population and People* (Chicago: Quadrangle Books, 1968), 11.

158. 1971 data showed that one-half of African Americans considered population growth to be a serious problem as opposed to two-thirds of whites (Westoff, "Recent Developments in Population Growth Policy," 171). See also Larry D. Barnett, "Demographic Factors in Attitudes towards Population Growth and Control," *Journal of Biosocial Science* 4 (January 1972): 9–23. Lynn E. McCutcheon and Marc Vick, "Racial Differences in Attitudes toward Population Control and Overpopulation as an Abstract Problem," *Virginia Journal of Science* 27 (Spring 1976): 10–14, found more skepticism among African Americans toward the idea of population control but not toward the ideal of smaller families.

159. McCutcheon and Vick, "Racial Differences in Attitudes toward Population Control," 10.

160. See Judith Blake, "Population Policy for America: Is the Government Being Misled?" *Science* 164 (May 2, 1969): 522–29. Also see her "Are Babies Consumer Durables? A Critique of the Economic Theory of Reproductive Motivation," *Population Studies* 22 (March 1968): 5–25, and "Coercive Pronatalism and American Population Policy," in Commission on Population Growth and the American Future, *Aspects of Population Growth Policy*, ed. Robert Parke Jr. and

Charles F. Westoff, vol. 6 of *Commission Research Reports* (Washington, D.C.: GPO, 1972): 81–109.

161. For a summary of Blake's thesis and reaction to it (which depicts a more intractable divide between Blake and the population movement than do I), see Critchlow, *Intended Consequences*, 159–60. Also see Oscar Harkavy, Frederick S. Jaffe, and Samuel M. Wishik, "Family Planning and Public Policy: Who Is Misleading Whom?" *Science* 165 (July 25, 1969): 367–73.

162. Hardin, "Tragedy of the Commons," 1245.

163. This camp also held that a fairer distribution of resources would ameliorate many of the problems incorrectly attributed to population growth, even though a more even distribution of resources would in fact increase consumption and pollution.

164. For the chasm between environmentalists and the New Left, see Beck and Kolankiewicz, "Environmental Movement's Retreat," 136–38. Also see Mark Dowie, *Losing Ground: American Environmentalism at the Close of the Twentieth Century* (Cambridge, Mass: MIT Press, 1995), 127.

165. Greene, "Militant Malthusians," 43.

166. See David Dickson, *The Politics of Alternative Technology* (New York: Universe Books, 1975).

167. Coale, "Man and His Environment," 132.

168. Quoted in Christofferson, *Man from Clear Lake*, 309.

169. Cited in Michael Egan, "'A Copout of the Worst Kind': Population Control as a Political Position" (paper presented at the annual meeting of the American Society for Environmental History, Victoria, British Columbia, April 2004), in possession of the author. Also see Michael Egan, *Barry Commoner and the Science of Survival: The Remaking of American Environmentalism* (Cambridge, Mass: MIT Press, 2009). The original source is "A Clash of Gloomy Prophets," *Time*, January 11, 1971, 56–57. Also see Robertson, *Malthusian Moment*, chap. 8.

170. Barry Commoner, *The Closing Circle: Nature, Man, and Technology* (New York: Knopf, 1971), esp. 237–49. Commoner argued that prior to the second half of the twentieth century colonialism had robbed the developing world of its wealth without improving standards of living and thus blocked the demographic transition.

171. Ibid., chap. 8 and 233–35.

172. Quoted in Jeffrey C. Ellis, "On the Search for a Root Cause: Essentialist Tendencies in Environmental Discourse," in *Uncommon Ground: Toward Reinventing Nature*, ed. William Cronon (New York: W. W. Norton, 1995), 260.

173. In particular, see Paul R. Ehrlich and John P. Holdren, "Impact of Population Growth," *Science* 171 (March 26, 1971): 1212–17. Here the authors offered a formula for environmental impact of I = PAT, in which environmental impact (I) equals population size (P) times affluence, or per capita consumption (A), times technology, or damage per unit of consumption (T).

174. One of the few articles during the heyday of the zero population growth movement to argue that high fertility exacerbated inequality was Herman E. Daly, "A Marxian-Malthusian View of Population and Development," *Population Studies* 25 (March 1971): 25–37. Environmental economists increasingly insisted upon the necessity of economic redistribution—especially from the developed to the developing nations—in contrast to the new classical economics' stress on aggregate GDP growth.

175. See National Research Council, *Resources and Man*, 38, which suggested that the market unsatisfactorily arbitrates the development of technologies.

176. E. F. Schumacher, *Small Is Beautiful: Economics as if People Mattered* (New York: Harper & Row, 1973), 138 and 147. Also see his "Buddhist Economics," in *Economics, Ecology, Ethics*, ed. Daly, 138–45, which originally appeared in 1968 in the underground journal *Resurgence*.

177. Senate Committee on Interior and Insular Affairs, and House Committee on Science and Astronautics, *Joint House-Senate Colloquium*, 40. Hearings were held on the matter, but the committee did not materialize.

178. In *Sustainable America: A New Consensus for Prosperity, Opportunity, and a Healthy Environment* (Washington, D.C.: GPO, 1996), the President's Council on Sustainable Development, established by President Clinton after the 1996 "Earth Summit" in Rio de Janeiro, concluded that "clearly, human impact on the environment is a function of both population and consumption patterns" (142).

179. "Myth of the Month," *ZPG Reporter*, April 1971.

180. See "Economy Doesn't Need More People," *ZPG Reporter*, April 1970.

181. See *ZPG Reporter*, October 1971, 8.

182. Greene, "Militant Malthusians," 44.

183. For example, see Warren C. Robinson, "Population Growth and Economic Welfare," *Reports on Population/Family Planning* 6 (February 1971): 1–39. This was a Population Council newsletter.

184. Commoner, *Closing Circle*, chap. 9.

185. In addition, reconciling a stationary population with economic growth would have alleviated the concerns of social scientists who predicted an entirely new set of problems with the end of economic growth. As chap. 8 discusses, concerns about the distributional outcomes of a zero-growth economy contributed to liberals' retreat from anti-growth thought.

186. For example, see H. C. Coombs, *The Return of Scarcity: Strategies for an Economic Future* (Cambridge: Cambridge University Press, 1990).

187. Judith Kunofsky to Roy Morgan, November 18, 1976.

Chapter Seven

1. Late in its tenure, in lieu of a formal commission proposed by John D. Rockefeller III, the Johnson administration convened an internal task force on these

matters. Its report, *Population and Family Planning: The Transition from Concern to Action: Report of the President's Committee on Population and Family Planning* (Department of Health, Education, and Welfare: Washington, D.C., 1968), called for the expansion of family planning and population-research programs. Records of this committee are located in Lyndon Baines Johnson Presidential Library, Austin, Tex. (hereafter LBJ Library), White House Central Files (hereafter WHCF), Federal Government Operations, Box 382, Folder "FG 659 Committee on Population and Family Planning (I)." Johnson's interest in the population movement grew as his administration waned. See USAID administrator William Gaud to Johnson, February 1, 1968, LBJ Library, WHCF, Welfare, Box 2, Folder "1/1/68–2/29/68." Johnson signed the UN's "World Leader's Statement Declaration on Population" (1967) and asked Secretary of State Dean Rusk to urge the Soviets to sign (Dean Rusk to LBJ, October 9, 1967, LBJ Library, National Security Files, Subject Files, Box 38, Folder "Population"). Yet the administration was reluctant to take additional action. See Phillip Hughes, Deputy Director Bureau of the Budget, to Harry McPherson, Special Counsel to the President, February 1, 1967, LBJ Library, WHCF, Legislation, Box 164, Folder "LE/WE." Also see LBJ Library, WHCF, Office Files of White House Aids, Files of Ervin Duggan, Box 12, Folder "John D. Rockefeller 3rd Proposal on Population Comm."

2. See Matthew Connelly, *Fatal Misconception: The Struggle to Control World Population* (Cambridge, Mass: Belknap Press of Harvard University Press, 2008), chap. 7; and Bernard Berelson, "Beyond Family Planning," *Studies in Family Planning* 1 (February 1969): 1–16. Berelson was president of the Population Council.

3. "Special Message to the Congress on Problems of Population Growth," July 18, 1969, *Public Papers of the Presidents of the United States: Richard Nixon, 1969* (Washington, D.C.: GPO, 1971), 529.

4. Commission on Population Growth and the American Future, *Population and the American Future* (Washington, D.C.: GPO, 1972).

5. See T. Michael Maher, "How and Why Journalists Avoid the Population-Environment Connection," *Population and Environment* 18 (March 1997): 339–72. Appetite for enhanced overseas efforts waned, too. In 1975, President Ford approved National Security Study Memorandum 200, which maintained that global population growth was "a current danger of the highest magnitude calling for urgent measures." But little action came of its directives. See Stephen D. Mumford, *The Life and Death of NSSM 200: How the Destruction of Political Will Doomed a U.S. Population Policy* (Research Triangle Park, N.C.: Center for Research on Population and Security, 1996), 24.

6. Donald T. Critchlow, *Intended Consequences: Birth Control, Abortion, and the Federal Government in Modern America* (New York: Oxford University Press, 1999), asserts, "The continuing decline in the American birthrate belied the urgency of the [Rockefeller] commission" (148).

7. See, for example, Roy Howard Beck and Leon J. Kolankiewicz, "The Environmental Movement's Retreat from Advocating U.S. Population Stabilization

(1970–1998): A First Draft of History," *Journal of Policy History* 12 (January 2000): 123–56.

8. Among many others, Connelly, *Fatal Misconception*, argues that a resilient eugenic mindset eroded the population movement's political capital. Eugenic ideas did survive as a motivating force on the modern population movement, but as I have argued throughout this study, they were less important than other impulses, such as a genuine concern with ecological crisis and a philanthropic desire to lessen poverty and hasten development in the Third World.

9. For example, during hearings on the population commission legislation, Lewis Butler, an assistant secretary at HEW, said that "we are on the threshold of another period of rapid growth" ("Testimony by the Honorable Lewis H. Butler, Assistant Secretary for Planning and Evaluation, before the Executive and Legislative Reorganization Subcommittee of the House Committee on Government Operations, Nov. 19, 1969," Richard Nixon Presidential Materials, National Archives II, College Park, Md. [hereafter Nixon Papers], WHCF, Subject Files, FG 275, Commission on Population Growth and the American Future [hereafter Nixon Commission Papers], Box 1, Folder "FG 275 4/1/70–8/31/70 Oversize Attachment 2973 November 1969"). Also see Conrad Tauber, Associate Director, Bureau of the Census, to Daniel Patrick Moynihan, July 1, 1969, Daniel Patrick Moynihan Papers, Library of Congress Manuscript Room, Washington, D.C. (hereafter DPM Papers), Box 295, Folder "Population: General 1969 3." Predictions of imminent growth were off the mark, but only by a few years. The birthrate would bottom out in 1976, at 1.7, before turning back upwards. See Michael S. Teitelbaum and Jay M. Winter, *The Fear of Population Decline* (New York: Academic Press, 1985), 159.

10. For the widespread assumption that "the population of the United States will undoubtedly have to stop growing," see the comments of Herman Miller, head of the population division of the US Census Bureau, in H. Erich Heinemann, "Babies vs. the GNP," *New York Times*, June 3, 1970.

11. For example, see the discussion of the New Right and population in Thomas Robertson, *The Malthusian Moment: Global Population Growth and the Birth of American Environmentalism* (New Brunswick: Rutgers University Press, 2012), chap. 9. When examining the rise of today's populationist consensus, many scholars are content to focus on Julian Simon, the leading pro–population growth economist of the 1980s and 1990s. For example, see Otis Graham Jr., "Epilogue: A Look Ahead," *Journal of Policy History* 12 (January 2000): 159. Scholars have traced the development of demographic "revisionism"—a new optimism about enlargement—but generally ignore the links between revisionism and broader economic debates. Moreover, they tend to incorrectly date the intellectual transformation to the 1970s or the 1980s rather than the 1960s. See, example, Susan Greenhalgh, "The Social Construction of Population Science: An Intellectual, Institutional, and Political History of Twentieth-Century Demography," *Comparative Studies in Society and History* 38 (January 1996): esp. 52–55.

12. The 1968 GOP platform is available from the American Presidency Project at www.presidency.ucsb.edu/ws/index.php?pid=25841.

13. "Special Message to the Congress on Problems of Population Growth," 524.

14. Nixon appointed as the US representative to the UN Population Fund Gen. William Draper, the Malthusian whose 1959 report on military preparedness and foreign aid planted an important seed for federal action on family planning (see chap. 5). Draper seems to have had Nixon's ear. John R. Brown III, White House staff assistant, told Moynihan on February 3, 1970: "The President noted that he feels Draper has been right on this issue for years" (Nixon Commission Papers, Box 2, Folder "FG 275 4/1/70–8/31/70 Oversize Attachment 2973 February 1970").

15. James Reston, "Washington: Who Said 'Love Makes the World Go Round'?" *New York Times*, January 21, 1970, observed that "it is interesting that the population question is being faced more directly by a conservative administration than by any before it."

16. In addition to Senators Joseph Clark (D-Pa.), Ernest Gruening (D-Alaska), and Joseph Tydings (D-Md.), who all lost reelection bids in 1968 or 1970, the issue leaders in Congress included: Sen. Ralph Yarborough (D-Tex.), the liberal chairman of the Senate Committee on Labor and Public Welfare and its Health Subcommittee; Sen. Jacob Javits (R-N.Y.), the ranking minority member of the Senate Committee on Labor and Public Welfare; Sen. Alan Cranston (D-Wyo.); Rep. James Scheuer (D-N.Y.), who would emerge as the primary leader in Congress on population during the 1970s; and Rep. Morris Udall (D-Ariz.).

17. Chester Finn to Moynihan, July 14, 1969, DPM Papers, Box 294, Folder "Population: Family Planning 1969 3": "One reason for the reorganization and expanded family planning services promised in our population Message is because we need to seize the initiative from Senator Tydings."

18. These included Lee DuBridge, Nixon's scientific adviser, Robert Finch, secretary of the Department of Health, Education, and Welfare until 1970, and Arthur Burns, a counselor to Nixon who was chair of the Council of Economic Advisers under Eisenhower and later chairman of the Federal Reserve. DuBridge told *U.S. News and World Report*, "It would be very desirable as a goal in this country to reduce population growth-rate to zero" ("How to Control Population: Interview with President's Science Adviser," January 19, 1970, 49). Finch testified in 1971 to the Commission on Population Growth that in order to reduce the average number of children per family to two, a "sustained Federal effort is essential; occasional actions are no longer sufficient" (Jerry Lipson and Diane Wolman to Commissioners, September 14, 1971, "The Commission's National Public Opinion Survey, and the New York Hearing," Records of the Commission on Population Growth and the American Future, 1970–1972, National Archives II, College Park, Md., RG 220, Records of Temporary Committees, Commissions, and Boards, [hereafter Commission on Population Growth Records], Box 5, Folder "September," 2). Burns called for a population commission early in Nixon's presidency and was charged with studying the merits of it. See Alexander Butterfield to Burns, April 2, 1969, in

Nixon Papers, WHCF, Subject Files, FG 96, 97, 98, and 99, Box 1, Folder 22, "FG 99 Committee on Population and Family Planning."

19. Lipson and Wolman, "The Commission's National Public Opinion Survey," 6.

20. "Family-Planning Breakthrough," *New York Times*, January 11, 1971. The Family Planning Services and Population Research Act, Public Law 572, 91st Cong., 2d Sess. (December 24, 1970), followed through on most of the requests in Nixon's special message. See "Statement on Signing the Family Planning Services and Population Research Act of 1970," December 26, 1970, *Public Papers of the Presidents of the United States: Richard Nixon, 1970* (Washington, D.C.: GPO, 1971), 1156–57. The act consolidated and expanded a scattered array of family planning programs and created a new Office for Population Affairs in the Department of Health, Education, and Welfare. It provided for increased family planning services through direct federal grants to providers, increased research and manpower training in the population field, and enhanced population education. Congress consistently underfunded it.

21. Untitled press release from the Office of Senator Joseph D. Tydings, June 18, 1970, Senator Joseph Tydings Papers, University of Maryland Special Collections, College Park, Md. (hereafter Tydings Papers), Series 6, Box 12, Folder "Press Releases—Obscenity; Population; Post Office; Public Works (1965–1970)." Many lawmakers were avowed Malthusians. In *Look* magazine, for example, Senator George McGovern (D-S.Dak.) wrote, "The world is running out of food. That is a fact of life, and of death" ("We Are Losing the Race Against Hunger," March 7, 1967).

22. For descriptions of the various population-related bills that Congress debated in 1970, see *ZPG Reporter* (newsletter of the organization Zero Population Growth), April and May 1970. (I read the April issue in the Records of Zero Population Growth, Washington, D.C., and the May issue in Records of the Wilderness Society, Conservation Collection, Denver Public Library [hereafter, Wilderness Society Records], Box 43, Folder 18).

23. The idea of a national population commission had been floating around for some time, and to some degree Nixon's group extended President Johnson's Committee on Population and Family Planning. Early in Nixon's presidency, the White House debated creating a commission and concluded that such a body would give the president the upper hand on the population issue while, as one staffer put it, "absorbing much of the political animosity that 'population' creates" (Chester Finn Jr. to Daniel Patrick Moynihan, April 1, 1969, Nixon Papers, WHCF, Subject Files, FG 96, 97, 98, and 99, Box 1, Folder 22, "FG 99 Committee on Population and Family Planning").

24. Moynihan claimed authorship in his "The Most Important Decision-Making Process," *Policy Review* 1 (Summer 1977): 92. Robert Finch also helped draft the special message. See Charles Westoff to Finch, March 30, 1971, Commission on Population Growth Records, Box 1, Folder "1971 Meeting."

25. The hearings were House Committee on Government Operations, Executive and Legislative Reorganization Subcommittee, *Establishing a Commission on Population Growth, and Related Matters: Hearings on S. 2701 to Establish a Commission on Population Growth and the American Future and Related House Bills*, 91st Cong., 1st sess., November 19 and 20, 1969.

26. The *New Republic* noted that "the problem as it is officially defined is essentially one of accommodating the growth by intelligent planning and use of available resources, and of curbing only the addition of 'unwanted children' to the domestic population" ("Unwanted People," August 2, 1969, 7).

27. Moynihan to Nixon, March 12, 1970, DPM Papers, Box 294, Folder "Population: Commission on Population Growth and the American Future 1970 2."

28. "The White House Press Conference of Dr. Daniel P. Moynihan," June 4, 1970, DPM Papers, Box 295, Folder "Population: Commission on Population Growth and the American Future 1970 5."

29. Senator Bob Packwood (D-Ore.) feared that the commission would be merely technocratic. He wrote to Moynihan on April 28, 1970, "It is my sincere hope that those concerned over the population problem will be as well represented as those merely interested in aspects of the population growth" (DPM Papers, Box 294, Folder "Population: Commission on Population Growth and the American Future 1970 3").

30. House Committee on Government Operations, *Establishing a Commission on Population Growth*, 33.

31. Udall to Stewart Brandborg, Executive Director of the Wilderness Society, July 31, 1969, Wilderness Society Records, Box 43, Folder 14.

32. The text of Udall's bill appears in House Committee on Government Operations, *Establishing a Commission on Population Growth*, 24–29. Because the Senate had already passed commission legislation, Udall did not fight for his bill (46).

33. William H. Timmons to Rep. John McCormack (Speaker of the House), March 9, 1970, DPM Papers, Box 294, Folder "Population: Commission on Population Growth and the American Future 1970 2."

34. Moynihan to John D. Ehrlichman, June 1, 1970, DPM Papers, Box 294, Folder "Population: Commission on Population Growth and the American Future 1970 4." Recommendations and requests to serve from members of the population community, academia, the federal family planning bureaucracy, and politicians deluged the White House. See "Single Political Recommendations," Nixon Commission Papers, Box 2, Folder "FG 275 4/1/70–8/31/70 Oversize Attachment 2973 March 1970"; and Moynihan to Nixon, March 5, 1970, in DPM Papers, Box 294, Folder "Population: Commission on Population Growth and the American Future 1970 2." Moynihan complained to the president, "It is just one awful struggle to get anyone approved who is not a solid no-nonsense Republican" (Moynihan to Nixon, May 8, 1970, Nixon Commission Papers, Box 1, Folder "FG 275 4/1/70–8/31/70"). *Washington Star* reporter Carl Rowan accused the White House of

stalling and playing it safe despite the clear mandate for "more than a tea-and-crumpets commission" (Carl Rowan, "What Has Become of the Population Commission?" *Sunday Evening Star*, May 24, 1970). Rowan reported that "the foot-dragging comes about because Daniel P. Moynihan, the presidential counselor in charge of this matter, reportedly is having potential commission members investigated and checked out the way Supreme Court nominees ought to be." Rowan also accused the White House of turning the selection of members into a patronage machine for GOP donors. Historian Gareth Davies told me Rowan's charges were likely inaccurate—it was Harry Flemming who would have insisted on the investigation of potential members.

35. After his defeat in 1970, Tydings was replaced by Sen. Alan Cranston (D-Wyo.). The other congressional members on the commission were Sen. Packwood, Rep. John Blatnik (D-Minn.), who was replaced a year later by Rep. James Scheuer (R-N.Y.), and Rep. John Erlenborn (R-Ill.).

36. The members included businesspersons (one of them Puerto Rican), a labor leader, an Hispanic lawyer and activist, a Ford Foundation economist who oversaw the foundation's overseas population work, several additional social scientists, an African-American college president, a housewife, a Catholic scholar, a social worker, and two college students.

37. Charles F. Westoff, "The Commission on Population Growth and the American Future: Its Origins, Operations, and Aftermath," in *Sociology and Public Policy: The Case of Presidential Commissions*, ed. Mirra Komarovsky (New York: Elsevier, 1975), 47–48. According to Moynihan, the "public" members, as opposed to the academics, were mostly Republican (Moynihan to Harry Fleming, April 20, 1970, DPM Papers, Box 294, Folder "Population: Commission on Population Growth and the American Future 1970 2").

38. On Scranton, see Moynihan to Nixon, February 12, 1970, DPM Papers, Box 294, Folder "Population: Commission on Population Growth and the American Future 1970 4." For Moynihan's thoughts on Rockefeller, see Moynihan to Nixon, March 5, 1970, in DPM Papers, Box 294, Folder "Population: Commission on Population Growth and the American Future 1970 2."

39. Commission on Population Growth and the American Future, *An Interim Report to the President and the Congress* (Washington, D.C.: GPO, 1971), 24.

40. Critchlow, *Intended Consequences*, chap. 4; and John T. McGreevy, *Catholicism and American Freedom: A History* (New York: W. W. Norton, 2003), chap. 9. We have already seen the Catholic Church push back against family planning policy. Widespread optimism regarding a possible change in the Church's position on birth control dissipated abruptly with Pope Paul VI's 1968 encyclical *Humanae Vitae*, which defended the traditionally defined nuclear family and reaffirmed the church's longstanding opposition to birth control. See Garry Wills, "Is Our Civilization Oversubscribed?" *National Review*, June 16, 1970, 631–32.

41. See chap. 6 for the abortion-rights activism of the zero population growth movement.

42. "Statement about Policy on Abortions at Military Base Hospitals in the United States," April 3, 1971, *Public Papers of the Presidents of the United States: Richard Nixon, 1971* (Washington, D.C.: GPO, 1972), 500.

43. A few African-American leaders implied that federal family planning programs were genocidal. Moderate leaders shied away from such incendiary language—and the implication that population policy was the eugenic ghost in the closet—but nonetheless worried family planning programs targeted minorities. See the comments of the president of the New York Urban Coalition in Eugene Callender, draft of "Population Control and Black Survival," September 28, 1971, Rockefeller Family Archives, John D. Rockefeller III Papers, Rockefeller Archive Center, Tarrytown, N.Y. (hereafter JDR III Papers), Series 3, Subseries 4, Box 67, Folder 443, "Population Interests, Background Materials, 1969, 1970–1971."

44. Ehrlichman's handwritten note in Nixon Papers, White House Special Files, White House Central Files, Confidential 1969–1974, Box 1, Folder 9. I thank Professor Shelley Hurt for bringing this document to my attention.

45. See Bruce J. Schulman, *The Seventies: The Great Shift in American Culture, Society, and Politics* (New York: Free Press, 2001), chap. 1.

46. Federal population-redistribution initiatives had begun during the New Deal, and calls for new policies to shape internal migration returned to the fore during the Johnson administration, primarily due to Agriculture Secretary Orville Freeman's efforts to highlight rural depopulation—a phenomenon many saw as the equally destructive flipside of the urban crisis.

47. From the end of World War II through the late 1960s, the total US population grew 50 percent, while the coastal population grew 80 percent (John Brooks Flippen, "Containing the Urban Sprawl: The Nixon Administration's Land Use Policy," *Presidential Studies Quarterly* 26 [Winter 1996]: 198).

48. A plethora of organizations, from the National League of Cities to the National Governors' Conference, supported new migration policies to address both concentration in the nation's major urban areas and the depopulation of rural America. See Duane Elgin to the commissioners, July 1, 1971, "Past Precedents for Population Distribution Policies," Commission on Population Growth Records, Box 4, Folder "July."

49. Moynihan to Dr. Martin Anderson, July 18, 1969, DPM Papers, Box 228, Folder "[Correspondence] May–Dec. 1969 A." Also see in this folder Moynihan's letter to Rep. John B. Anderson (R-Ill.), July 16, 1969.

50. Daniel P. Moynihan, "Toward a National Urban Policy," *Public Interest* 17 (Fall 1969): 14.

51. "Annual Message to the Congress on the State of the Union," January 22, 1970, *Public Papers of Richard Nixon, 1970*, 14. Of course, the suburbs were growing much faster than the central cities. National Goals Research Staff, *Toward Balanced Growth: Quantity with Quality* (Washington, D.C.: GPO, 1970), estimated that since 1960, the former had grown 28 percent and the latter just 1 percent (43).

52. The drive for national growth policy also succumbed to bureaucratic turf

battles and tensions between rural and urban interests. See Flippen, "Containing the Urban Sprawl"; James L. Sundquist, *Dispersing Population: What America Can Learn from Europe* (Washington, D.C.: Brookings Institution, 1975), 12–16, and "A Comparison of Policy-Making Capacity in the United States and Five European Countries: The Case of Population Distribution," in *Population Policy Analysis*, ed. Michael E. Kraft and Mark Schneider (Lexington, Mass.: D.C. Heath and Co., 1978), 67–80; and Adam Rome, *The Bulldozer in the Countryside: Suburban Sprawl and the Rise of American Environmentalism* (Cambridge: Cambridge University Press, 2001), 236–53.

53. J. Brooks Flippen, *Nixon and the Environment* (Albuquerque: University of New Mexico Press, 2000), 102.

54. In 1967, Moynihan revealed his fear of urban population growth when he told an interviewer that a system of family allowances (paying benefits per baby)—which would primarily help the urban poor—would not affect the birthrate. See "The Case for a Family Allowance," *New York Times Magazine*, February 5, 1967, 71.

55. For the meeting, see Flippen, *Nixon and the Environment*, 102.

56. Moynihan to Phillip Berry, July 2, 1970, DPM Papers, Box 294, Folder "Population: Commission on Population Growth and the American Future 1970 4." Also see Berry's letter to Nixon, April 9, 1970, in which Berry complains that "the solutions discussed in [Nixon's population] message aim toward accommodating expected growth" but "fall far short of a real antidote for such growth."

57. Conversation 700-10, April 3, 1972, Nixon Presidential Materials, The White House Communications Agency Sound Recordings Collection (hereafter Nixon Tapes). I also listened to the tapes on Nixontapes.org.

58. Ibid.

59. Paul Ehrlich and John R. Holdren, "Impact of Population Growth," JDR III Papers, Series 3, Subseries 4, Box 69, Folder 460, "National Commission on Population Growth and the American Future, Environmental Issues, 1971." Also see Ehrlich's letter to John D Rockefeller III urging that the commission emphasize "aggregate size" rather than "maldistribution" in Folder 456, "National Commission on Population Growth and the American Future, 1970–1971."

60. "Annual Message to the Congress on the State of the Union," January 22, 1970, 9.

61. Flippen, *Nixon and the Environment*, 102.

62. Quoted in ibid. Nixon tended to think in terms of a trade-off between a cleaner environment and jobs. In 1971, with the election drawing nearer and the economy muddling through a sluggish recovery, jobs increasing won out. See Allen J. Matusow, *Nixon's Economy: Booms, Busts, Dollars, and Votes* (Lawrence: University Press of Kansas, 1998), chap. 7.

63. For example, Nixon argued in 1971, "This concentration of population growth in already crowded areas is not a trend that we wish to perpetuate. This administration would prefer a more balanced growth pattern—and we are tak-

ing a number of steps to encourage more development and settlement in the less densely populated areas of our country" ("Special Message to the Congress on Special Revenue Sharing for Urban Community Development," March 5, 1971, *Public Papers of Richard Nixon, 1971*, 396).

64. "Toward National Growth Policy: Population Distribution Effects," Progress Report of the National Goals Research Staff, March 23, 1970, Population Commission Records, Box 4, Folder "March Meeting," 4; also see 12–13. Nixon had formed this group within the White House and instructed it to report on "what kind of a nation we want to be as we begin our third century." See "Statement by the President upon Announcing the Establishment of the Staff within the White House," July 13, 1969, reprinted in National Goals Research Staff, *Toward Balanced Growth*, 219–23.

65. National Goals Research Staff, *Toward Balanced Growth*, 60.

66. Ibid.

67. Ibid.

68. Ibid.

69. I encountered the phrase "market-knows-best demography" in Marc Linder, *The Dilemmas of Laissez-Faire Population Policy in Capitalist Societies: When the Invisible Hand Controls Reproduction* (Westport, Conn.: Greenwood Press, 1997), 16. Linder uses it to refer specifically to the new household microeconomics, which treats children as consumer durables. I apply it more broadly to a whole constellation of overlapping pro-market and pro–population growth positions. A crucial discussion—and rejection—of these ideas was Paul Demeny's 1986 Population Association of America presidential address (Paul Demeny, "Population and the Invisible Hand," *Demography* 23 [November 1986]: 473–87).

70. Demeny, "Population and the Invisible Hand," 479.

71. See Albert O. Hirschman, *The Strategy of Economic Development* (New Haven: Yale University Press, 1958); and Ester Boserup, *The Conditions of Agricultural Growth: The Economics of Agrarian Change under Population Pressure* (New York: Aldine, 1965). Several development theorists located historical links between population and economic growth. Economic historians Douglass North and Robert Thomas concluded in a famous essay on the economic history of the Western world, "In capsule form our explanation is that changes in relative product and factor prices, initially induced by Malthusian population pressure, and changes in the size of markets induced a set of fundamental institutional changes which channeled incentives towards productivity-raising types of economic activity" (Douglass C. North and Robert Paul Thomas, "An Economic Theory of the Growth of the Western World," *Economic History Review*, n.s., 23 [April 1970]: 1).

72. Friedrich Hayek, *The Constitution of Liberty* (Chicago: University of Chicago Press, 1960), chaps. 2 and 23. Population social scientists sustained Hayek's position. A 1960 conference, "Natural Resources and Economic Growth," convened by Resources for the Future and the Committee on Economic Growth of the Social Science Research Council, signaled a new consensus downplaying

the economic importance of natural resources. Stanford's Moses Abramovitz, a pioneer of modern growth theory, summarized the proceedings when he noted, "An important theme that recurs in the papers before the Conference is that, in the course of economic development, natural resources have become of smaller importance than they used to be" (Moses Abramovitz, "Comment," in *Natural Resources and Economic Growth: Papers Presented at a Conference Held at Ann Arbor, Michigan, April 7–9, 1960*, ed. Joseph J. Spengler [Washington, D.C.: Resources for the Future, 1961], 9).

73. Harold J. Barnett and Chandler Morse, *Scarcity and Growth: The Economics of Natural Resource Availability* (Baltimore: Johns Hopkins University Press for Resources for the Future, 1963), 11.

74. For the human capital debate, see the supplement "Investment in Human Beings," *Journal of Political Economy* 70 (October 1962).

75. Schultz's links to the population community are detailed in the Records of the Population Council, Rockefeller Archive Center, Tarrytown, N.Y., Box 39, Folder 560, "Schultz, Theodore W., 1956–1966."

76. For example, Simon Kuznets believed that the ability of societies to invest in human capital upset traditional assumptions about the effects of population growth on capital formation. See his "Population and Economic Growth," *Proceedings of American Philosophical Society* 111 (June 1967): 178–84.

77. The original human capital theorists were conservative labor economists associated with the "Chicago School," but their findings ironically provided theoretical support for the Great Society's social investment. See Alice O'Connor, *Poverty Knowledge: Social Science, Social Policy, and the Poor in Twentieth-Century U.S. History* (Princeton: Princeton University Press, 2001), 140–43. Less well known is that human capital theory was closely connected to population debates. The link stretched back to prewar demography, when the eugenic emphasis on population "quality" spurred interest in measuring the economic value of investment in population "improvement." See Louis I. Dublin and Alfred J. Lotka, *The Money Value of a Man*, rev. ed. (New York: Ronald Press, 1946).

78. Demeny, "Population and the Invisible Hand."

79. Gary Becker offered a crucial early statement in "An Economic Analysis of Fertility," in National Bureau of Economic Research, *Demographic and Economic Change in Developed Countries* (Princeton: Princeton University Press, 1960), 209–31. Also see Theodore W. Schultz, "The Value of Children: An Economic Perspective," *Journal of Political Economy* 81 (March–April 1973): S2–S13. For a critique of the new microeconomics of fertility, which suggests that it "must engage in considerable conceptual contortion to convert children into commodities," see Linder, *Dilemmas of Laissez-Faire Population Policy*, 15–26 (quotation, 19). Also see Judith Blake, "Are Babies Consumer Durables? A Critique of the Economic Theory of Reproductive Motivation," *Population Studies* 22 (March 1968): 5–25, which stresses women's psychological and situational motives for childbirth.

80. For a recent example of Gary Becker's population optimism, see his blog post from May 8, 2011, "Yes, the Earth Will Have Ample Resources for 10 Billion People," available at www.becker-posner-blog.com/2011/05/yes-the-earth-will-have-ample-resources-for-10-billion-people-becker.html.

81. More specifically, Easterlin attempted to reconcile the anomalous 1950s Baby Boom with the longer story of American fertility. In his view, the Baby Boom resulted from the children of the Depression years growing up poor but then, after World War II, doing better in young adulthood than their parents had. This "relative affluence" compared to their parents translated into optimism about the future and lots of babies. Writing during the 1960s, when fertility rates fell from their Baby Boom highs, Easterlin's economic-demographic feedback model predicted further declines: the large crop of children born in the 1950s would face hard economic times and reduce their fertility. See Richard Easterlin, *The American Baby Boom in Historical Perspective*, National Bureau of Economic Research, Occasional Paper No. 79 (New York: NBER, 1962), reprinted from the December 1961 *American Economic Review*, and "Does Human Fertility Adjust to the Environment?" *American Economic Review* 61 (May 1971): 399–407.

82. For the differences between, and gradual convergence of, the Becker and Easterlin theories, see Warren C. Sanderson, "On Two Schools of the Economics of Fertility," *Population and Development Review* 2 (September–December 1976): 469–77. For a critical view of Easterlin's theories, see Alan Sweezy, "The Economic Explanations of Fertility Changes in the United States," *Population Studies* 25 (July 1971): 255–67.

83. Easterlin also saw historical links between population and economic growth in both the developing and developed words, although he suggested that economic booms are rarely driven by demographic trends. See Richard A. Easterlin, Michael L. Wachter, and Susan M. Wachter, "Demographic Influences on Economic Stability: The United States Experience," *Population and Development Review* 4 (March 1978): 5. For Easterlin's doubts on the "population explosion" paradigm, see his *Growth Triumphant: The Twenty-first Century in Historical Perspective* (Ann Arbor: University of Michigan Press, 1996), 9–10.

84. The stress on the individual also critiqued the state-centered thrust of the family planning movement. Market-knows-best demographers not only assumed that government family planning programs at home and abroad were inefficient and ineffective. They also noted that nations pursuing vigorous population-control programs tended to be those with high levels of state economic planning. Hence they suggested that instead of concentrating on family planning programs, nations worried about population growth should concentrate on freeing the market.

85. For a typical statement, see Göran Ohlin, *Population Control and Economic Development* (Paris: OECD, 1967). Thereafter, Ohlin moved into the anti-Malthusian camp.

86. Commenting on a series of papers in the May 1971 *American Economic*

Review, Paul Demeny wrote, "It is wholly unsatisfactory to argue that 'people' behave rationally in the interest of their children. They obviously do so only as individuals, and there exists no mechanism that would ensure that individual decisions somehow add up to a social optimum" (T. Paul Schultz and Paul Demeny, "Discussion," *American Economic Review* 61 [May 1971]: 421). Notably, all three papers in the series downplayed population problems.

87. "A Population Policy?" *Wall Street Journal*, March 23, 1971. Also see John G. Welles, "The Economy Doesn't Need More People," *Wall Street Journal*, April 22, 1970.

88. William F. Buckley, "The Birth Rate," *National Review*, March 23, 1965, 231.

89. Editorial blurb accompanying Theodore Sturgeon, "The Avalanche," *National Review*, July 27, 1965, 634. The supplement also included Alan F. Guttmacher's "How Births Can Be Controlled."

90. Sturgeon, "The Avalanche," 636.

91. Ibid.

92. Pyrrho, "What Exit for Asia?" *National Review*, July 27, 1965, 640.

93. For Clark's populationism, see his *Population Growth and Land Use* (London: Macmillan, 1967). Clark served on the Vatican's Commission on Population (1964–66), which resulted in *Humanae Vitae*.

94. Colin Clark, "World Power and Population," *National Review*, May 20, 1969, 481–84.

95. Clark, *Population Growth and Land Use*, 274.

96. Milton Friedman, "The Market v. the Bureaucrat," *National Review*, May 19, 1970, 507.

97. Robert Moses, "Bomb Shelters, Arks, and Ecology," *National Review*, September 8, 1970, 939.

98. For example, the *Population Bulletin* argued in February 1970, "The larger, the more complex and the more crowded a society is—and the more its resource base is subjected to intensely competing demands—the more numerous and restrictive are the laws and regulations required for its governance" (quoted in National Goals Research Staff, *Toward Balanced Growth*, 42).

99. In *Newsweek*, for example, Henry Wallich, a Yale economist who served on Eisenhower's Council of Economic Advisers (and whom Nixon would later appoint to be a Federal Reserve Governor), wrote: "Everybody has his pet prescription for curing society's ills. A peculiarly misguided one has surfaced recently—zero population growth. If this wholesale misanthropy prevails, we are in trouble. . . . If large parts of our country are polluted, it is not because we are too numerous, but because we pollute. The way to stop that disgrace is not to stop having children, but to start cleaning up" ("Henry C. Wallich on Population Growth," June 29, 1970, 70).

100. Moynihan's comments on television quoted in "The Drive to Stop Population Growth," *U.S. News and World Report*, March 2, 1970, 38.

101. S.J. Res. 108, with twenty-six co-sponsors, was introduced on June 2, 1971, by Senators Alan Cranston (D-Calif.) and Robert Taft (R-Ohio); H.J. Res. 789 was introduced in the House on July 19, 1971. I found discussion of these resolutions in Coalition for a National Population Policy, untitled October 1971 report, Wilderness Society Records, Box 43, Folder 19.

102. *ZPG Reporter*, April 1971, 8.

103. The *National Journal* wrote that due to fear of upsetting Catholics, "Government efforts to set an official goal of stabilizing the United States population ground to a halt Nov. 23 when the Senate Labor and Public Welfare Committee decided not to consider the issue this year" ("Cranston Defers Action on Resolution Setting Population Stabilization Goals," December 4, 1971, 2401). Also see Senate Committee on Labor and Public Welfare, Subcommittee on Human Resources, *Declaration of U.S. Policy of Population Stabilization by Voluntary Means*, 92d Cong., 1st sess., August 5, October 5, 8, 14, and November 3, 1971; and JDR III Papers, Series 3, Subseries 4, Box 67, Folder 447, "Population Interests, Cranston Resolution (S.J. 108) 1971."

104. Commission on Population Growth and the American Future, *Population and the American Future*, chap. 4 ("The Economy") and 5 ("Resources and the Environment").

105. Importantly, the commission maintained that a reduction in "unwanted" children would be nearly sufficient to bring about population stabilization. This posture disappointed the radicals, who believed that Americans' desire for too many "wanted" children was the core problem.

106. Commission on Population Growth and the American Future, *Population and the American Future*, 141–47 ("Compilation of Recommendations"). Internal debate on immigration produced a stalemate that precluded significant proposals. See Critchlow, *Intended Consequences*, 164. Westoff, "The Commission on Population Growth and the American Future," reports that the commission discovered that if the birthrate averaged 2.0, zero population growth could be reached with no changes to immigration at almost the same speed as with a birthrate of 2.1 and a reduction in immigration (55).

107. Commission on Population Growth and the American Future, *Population and the American Future*, chap. 3.

108. John D. Rockefeller III wanted to release the final report in three separate sections so that no one issue or finding dominated public discussion. Anti-abortion members of the commission, led by Rep. John Erlenborn, were amenable to this three-section strategy but insisted on issuing a dissenting statement on abortion. In February 1972, however, White House staff met with commission members to "emphasize the President's desire for a single report" but "met with resistance" (Ray Waldmann, Staff Assistant to President Nixon, to Ken Cole, February 22, 1972, and Waldmann to Cole, February 23, 1972, Nixon Commission Papers, Box 2, Folder "FG 275 Commission on Population Growth and the American Future 1/1/71 [1 of 2]").

109. The White House put off meeting with commission members. See John D. Rockefeller III to Ehrlichman, March 2 and 17, 1972, in Nixon Commission Papers, Box 2, Folder "FG 275 Commission on Population Growth and the American Future 1/1/71 (2 of 2); and John D. Rockefeller III to Nixon, April 7 and March 19, 1972, JDR III Papers, Box 30, Series 3, Subseries 2, Folder 138, "Famous People, 1972–1977."

110. Abortion already had been a contentious issue within the commission, which at one point tabled its discussion of abortion for fear of splintering. White House records include letters from Americans excoriating the commission's pro-abortion stance and newspaper clippings about Catholic leaders with similar concerns. For example, see the exchange between Waldmann and the County Attorney from Nobles County, Minnesota, Nixon Commission Papers, Box 2, Folder "FG 275 Commission on Population Growth and the American Future 1/1/71 (1 of 2)," and the clippings about James McHugh, director of the Family Life Bureau of the US Catholic Conference, in Folder 2. Critchlow, *Intended Consequences*, 164–73, excellently summarizes the commission's entanglement with the ascendant abortion politics of the early 1970s.

111. See the unsigned memo reviewing five options and several drafts of the president's comments in Nixon Commission Papers, Box 2, Folder "FG 275 Commission on Population Growth and the American Future 1/1/71 (1 of 2)."

112. Waldmann and Gergen, "Statement on Report of Commission on Population Growth and the American Future," March 24, 1972, Nixon Commission Papers, Box 2, Folder "FG 275 Commission on Population Growth and the American Future 1/1/71 (2 of 2)."

113. "Draft Statement on Population Commission: Draft: Buchanan, 3/29/72," Nixon Commission Papers, Box 2, Folder "FG 275 Commission on Population Growth and the American Future 1/1/71 (2 of 2)."

114. Ibid.

115. Ibid.

116. Ibid.

117. Ibid.

118. Ibid.

119. Ibid.

120. Ibid.

121. Internal White House memos discussed Nixon "moving away" from the commission. See, for example, Agnes Waldron (director of the White House research office) to Neal Ball (Deputy Press Secretary), Nixon Commission Papers, Box 2, Folder "FG 275 Commission on Population Growth and the American Future 1/1/71 (2 of 2)."

122. Nixon Tapes, Conversation 697-29, March 30, 1972.

123. Ibid.

124. Ibid.

125. Critchlow, *Intended Consequences*, 167.

126. Ibid., 167–70.

127. Nixon Tapes, Conversation 699-1, March 31, 1972.

128. Ibid. Kissinger's response was hilarious and emblematic of conservatives' antipathy to the academic establishment. He explained to the president that academic life is fraught with insecurity and that college professors become like the teenagers they teach. He suggested that intellectuals are easily manipulated (the Kennedys successfully flattered them) and that in the second Nixon administration, the president should mollify them by giving "them the illusion that they're participating in something . . . not because they can contribute a goddamn thing" but because it would be dangerous to have all the writers criticizing the nation. The MIT study, discussed in the next chapter, is Donella H. Meadows, et al., *The Limits to Growth: A Report for the Club of Rome's Project on the Predicament of Mankind* (New York: Universe Books, 1972).

129. Edwin L. Dale Jr., "A Nixon Economic Adviser Doubts Overpopulation," *New York Times*, March 29, 1970.

130. Ibid.

131. For the meetings between Friedman and Nixon, see Lanny Ebenstein, *Milton Friedman: A Biography* (New York: Palgrave MacMillan, 2007), 186.

132. Nixon Tapes, Conversation 700-10, April 3, 1972.

133. Ibid.

134. Ibid.

135. Ibid.

136. See John D. Rockefeller III to Nixon, April 7, 1972, Nixon Commission Papers, Box 2, Folder "FG 275 Commission on Population Growth and the American Future 1/1/71 (2 of 2)."

137. "Statement about the Report of the Commission on Population Growth and the American Future," May 5, 1972, *Public Papers of the Presidents of the United States: Richard Nixon, 1972* (Washington, D.C.: GPO, 1974), 576–77.

138. Peter Collier and David Horowitz, *The Rockefellers: An American Dynasty* (New York: Holt, Rinehart and Winston, 1976), 376.

139. Nixon Tapes, Conversation 720-12, May 5, 1972.

140. This task force included representatives from Nixon's Domestic Council, the Council of Environmental Quality, the Council of Economic Advisers, and the Office of Science and Technology. It is not clear from the archival record how often this group met.

141. Documents surrounding these films are in Nixon Commission Papers, Box 3, Folder "Gen FG 275 Commission on Population Growth and the American Future 1/1/73." For the ABC special, see "Population: Problem for the Populace," *The Nation*, January 15, 1973, 71.

142. Leonard Laster, Office of Science and Technology, to Edward E. David Jr., Nixon Commission Papers, Box 3, Folder "Commission on Population Growth Oversize Attachment 14264."

143. Commission on Population Growth and the American Future, *Popula-*

tion, Resources, and the Environment, ed. Ronald G. Ridker, vol. 3 of *Commission Research Reports* (Washington, D.C.: GPO, 1972), esp. 13 and 37.

144. Richard Easterlin, "Comment," in *Economic Aspects of Population Change*, ed. Elliott R. Morss and Ritchie H. Reed, vol. 2 of *Commission Research Reports*, 46.

145. See the first four essays in *Economic Aspects of Population Change*. One of these essays, by Joseph Spengler (then entering his sixth decade as a published participant in the population debate), espoused the now-residual Stable Population Keynesian position that a smaller population would yield significant economic and environmental benefits ("Declining Population Growth: Economic Effects," 91–133). The other three papers, however, ranged from neutral to supportive of population growth and cut against the "overpopulation" paradigm that had launched the commission. Harvey Leibenstein wrote, "the economies of scale and employment stimulation advantages of population growth more or less counterbalance the loss due to the dilution of difficult to substitute natural resources. Another advantageous factor is that a younger population contains more 'human capital' per person" ("The Impact of Population Growth on the American Economy," 51). In the spirit of Barry Commoner, Edmund C. Phelps, "Some Macroeconomics of Population Leveling," maintained that technology, not population, was primarily responsible for pollution. Allen C. Kelley, "Demographic Changes and American Economic Development: Past, Present and Future," held that "a population policy justified noticeably by its favorable impact on pollution reduction may not only be unjustified, but also undesirable. The most appropriate 'economic' policy in the area of population is a neutral position regarding an economically desirable family size" (11). For internal commission discussion of these papers, see JDR III Papers, Series 3, Subseries 4, Box 69, Folder 459, "National Commission on Population Growth and the American Future, Economic Issues, 1971."

146. Kelley, "Demographic Changes," 31. Kelley also stated, "Neither economic theory, nor the empirical studies in the area of economic demography, as yet provide a sufficiently firm basis for concluding that a reduction in the average American family size will have a quantitatively significant effect on the pace of material advancement" (15).

147. Allen C. Kelley, "Population Growth and Historical Rates of American Economic Progress: A Summary," JDR III Papers, Series 3, Subseries 4, Box 69, Folder 459, "National Commission on Population Growth and the American Future, Economic Issues, 1971."

148. Easterlin, "Comment," 45.

149. Commission on Population Growth and the American Future, *Population and the American Future*, 38–39.

150. Ibid., 40–41.

151. Ibid., 12.

152. C. F. Westoff, "Further Reflections on Population Policy," September 17, 1971, JDR III Papers, Series 3, Subseries 4, Box 67, Folder 443, "Population Interests, Background Materials, 1969, 1970–1971."

153. John D. Rockefeller III to the President and Congress of the United States, March 27, 1972, reprinted in Commission on Population Growth and the American Future, *Population and the American Future*, 4.

154. "Extended Outline for Chapter 1," JDR III Papers, Series 3, Subseries 4, Box 71, Folder 471, "National Commission on Population Growth and the American Future, Population Distribution, 1971," 3.

155. For example, Howard Samuel wrote Westoff, August 10, 1971: "I don't think sufficient recognition has been given to the fact that in a stabilized population we will have an older population" (Records of the Commission on Population Growth, Box 4, Folder "July").

156. Ansley J. Coale, "Should the United States Start a Campaign for Fewer Births?" *Population Index* 34 (October 1968): 471.

Chapter Eight

1. For recent analyses of the fiscal implications of America's aging, consult Social Security and Medicare Boards of Trustees, "A Summary of the 2011 Annual Social Security and Medicare Trust Fund Reports," available online at www.ssa.gov/oact/tr/; and National Commission on Fiscal Responsibility and Reform (Bowles-Simpson Commission), "The Moment of Truth," December 2010, available online at www.fiscalcommission.gov/sites/fiscalcommission.gov/files/documents/TheMomentofTruth12_1_2010.pdf.

2. For the common misconception that increased longevity primarily drives population aging, see Phil Mullan, *The Imaginary Time Bomb: Why an Ageing Population Is Not a Social Problem* (London: I. B. Tauris, 2000), 31–35. Demographers' projections of the path toward zero population growth did not necessarily assume a bulging cohort of older Americans. See Norman B. Ryder, "Two Cheers for ZPG," in *The No-Growth Society*, ed. Mancur Olson and Hans H. Landsberg (New York: W. W. Norton, 1973), 48–51.

3. Robert L. Clark and Joseph J. Spengler, *The Economics of Individual and Population Aging* (Cambridge: Cambridge University Press, 1980), 16 and 25.

4. U.S. Census Bureau, "State and County QuickFacts," available online at www.quickfacts.census.gov/qfd/states/00000.html.

5. Larry Neal, "Is Secular Stagnation Just around the Corner? A Survey of the Influences of Slowing Population Growth upon Investment Demand," in *The Economic Consequences of Slowing Population Growth*, ed. Thomas J. Espenshade and William J. Serow (New York: Academic Press, 1978), 102.

6. The total fertility rate bottomed out in 1976 at about 1.7. See Michael S. Teit-

elbaum and Jay M. Winter, *The Fear of Population Decline* (New York: Academic Press, 1985), Appendix A, 158–59.

7. Population Reference Bureau, "America's Aging Population" (February 2011), available online at www.prb.org/Publications/PopulationBulletins/2011/americas-aging-population.aspx. Also see Laurence J. Kotlikoff and Scott Burns, *The Coming Generational Storm: What You Need to Know about America's Economic Future* (Cambridge, Mass: MIT Press, 2004), 4; and Peter G. Peterson, *Gray Dawn: How the Coming Age Wave Will Transform America—and the World* (New York: Random House, 1999), 214.

8. Paul Krugman, "America's Senior Moment," review of *Coming Generational Storm*, by Kotlikoff and Burns, *New York Review of Books*, March 10, 2005, 6–11.

9. The concern in the 1970s with the old-age dependency ratio ironically came close on the heels of Malthusians' insistence that the young imposed the biggest burden on society.

10. Although apprehension of overseas population growth remained the norm within the American population community in the 1970s, the emphasis on birth control as the primary means of fertility reduction gave way to a broader "developmental" approach that stressed the need for societal reforms, such as enhanced women's rights. This switch was captured famously by John D. Rockefeller III at the 1974 World Population Conference in Bucharest. Here Rockefeller said, "Population planning must be placed within the context of economic and social development" (cited in Donald T. Critchlow, *Intended Consequences: Birth Control, Abortion, and the Federal Government in Modern America* [New York: Oxford University Press, 1999], 181). For the rise of "revisionism" among American demographers, see Dennis Hodgson, "Orthodoxy and Revisionism in American Demography," *Population and Development Review* 14 (September 1988): 541–69.

11. W. W. Rostow, *The Great Population Spike and After: Reflections on the 21st Century* (New York: Oxford University Press, 1998), 87.

12. See, for example, the Population Crisis Committee's "Declaration on Food and Population," reprinted in House Committee on Merchant Marine and Fisheries, Subcommittee on Fisheries and Wildlife Conservation and the Environment, *Growth and Its Implications for the Future*, part 4, 93rd Cong., 2d sess., June 11, 12, and 13 and November 25, 1974, 85–87. For US consumption of raw materials and energy, see Johannes Overbeek, *The Population Challenge: A Handbook for Nonspecialists* (Westport, Conn.: Greenwood Press, 1976), chap. 11. Also consult John P. Holdren, "Population and the American Predicament: The Case against Complacency," in *No-Growth Society*, ed. Olson and Landsberg, 31–43.

13. The US articulated this position at the 1974 World Population Conference. See Jyoti Shankar Singh, *Creating a New Consensus on Population: The International Conference on Population and Development* (London: Earthscan, 1998), 4–12.

14. Donella H. Meadows et al., *The Limits to Growth: A Report for the Club of Rome's Project on the Predicament of Mankind* (New York: Universe Books,

1972). Also see Joel E. Cohen, *How Many People Can the Earth Support?* (New York: W. W. Norton, 1995), 120–29; Paul Neurath, *From Malthus to the Club of Rome and Back: Problems of Limits to Growth, Population Control, and Migrations* (Armonk, N.Y.: M. E. Sharpe, 1994), 58–64; and Robert M. Collins, *More: The Politics of Economic Growth in Postwar America* (New York: Oxford University Press, 2000), 139–40.

15. Meadows et al., *Limits to Growth*, 23.

16. Ibid.

17. Ibid.

18. The sale figures come from the October 21, 2009, entry to the "Environmental 360" blog, by environmentalist Bill McKibben: www.e360.yale.edu /content/feature.msp?id=2195. For the debate surrounding *Limits to Growth*, see Francis Sandbach, "The Rise and Fall of the Limits to Growth Debate," *Social Studies of Science* 8 (November 1978): 495–520; and Neurath, *From Malthus to the Club of Rome*, chap. 3. For a prominent critique, see H. S. D. Cole et al., eds., *Models of Doom: A Critique of the Limits to Growth* (New York: Universe Books, 1973).

19. Ezra J. Mishan, *The Costs of Economic Growth* (New York: Praeger, 1967). Also see his "Growth and Antigrowth: What Are the Issues?" in *The Economic Growth Controversy*, ed. Andrew Weintraub, Eli Schwartz, and J. Richard Aronson (White Plains, N.Y.: International Arts and Sciences, 1973), 3–38.

20. "A Dialogue on the Issues," in *Economic Growth Controversy*, ed. Weintraub, Schwartz, and Aronson, 216.

21. E. J. Mishan, "The Wages of Growth," in *No-Growth Society*, ed. Olson and Landsberg, 85. This argument was indebted to Richard Easterlin's observation that rising expectations may reduce happiness.

22. E. F. Schumacher, *Small is Beautiful: Economics as if People Mattered* (New York: Harper & Row, 1973).

23. A representative defense of the zero-growth society is Lincoln H. Day, "Social Consequences of Zero Economic Growth," in *Economic Growth Controversy*, ed. Weintraub, Schwartz, and Aronson, 116–40.

24. See Collins, *More*, 132–39; and Eva S. Moskowitz, *In Therapy We Trust: America's Obsession with Self Fulfillment* (Baltimore: Johns Hopkins University Press, 2001).

25. House Committee on Merchant Marine and Fisheries, Subcommittee on Fisheries and Wildlife Conservation and the Environment, *Growth and Its Implications for the Future*, 4 parts, 93rd Cong., 1st and 2d sessions.

26. Collins, *More*, 134.

27. The concept of zero economic growth usually connoted zero population growth as well, but the theoretical and proscriptive relationship between the two phenomena was often left vague, and the population side of the equation fell by the wayside during the 1970s.

28. See T. Michael Maher, "How and Why Journalists Avoid the Population-Environment Connection," *Population and Environment* 18 (March 1997): 339–72.

29. Since the 1965 Immigration Act, the number of legal immigrants to the US per annum has grown from 400,000 (the number envisioned by policy makers in 1965) to over one million. Immigrants have also accounted for a steadily increasing percentage of America's total population growth. During the 1970s, immigrants had higher birthrates than non-immigrants, African Americans had higher rates than whites, and Hispanic whites had higher rates than non-Hispanic whites (the last being the only group that dipped below the replacement level). See Roy Howard Beck and Leon J. Kolankiewicz, "The Environmental Movement's Retreat from Advocating U.S. Population Stabilization (1970–1998): A First Draft of History," *Journal of Policy History* 12 (January 2000)," 153 n. 22; pp. 131 and 140 for the growing avoidance of the population issue, especially by liberal interest groups.

30. During the 1970s, American women delayed marriage longer and had fewer total children than previous cohorts. See Teitelbaum and Winter, *Fear of Population Decline*, 82. In addition, the percentages of women who never married and of childless couples rose, in part because the zero population growth movement changed attitudes. See Elaine Tyler May, *Barren in the Promised Land: Childless Americans and the Pursuit of Happiness* (New York: Basic Books, 1995), esp. 201. Continued diffusion of the pill, the legalization of abortion, improvements in vasectomy technology, and growth in female sterilizations also reinforced lower birthrates. But many demographers accurately predicted that the US birthrate was poised for a recovery. For example, see June Sklar and Beth Berkov, "The American Birth Rate: Evidences of a Coming Rise," *Science* 189 (August 29, 1975): 693–700; and Ronald Demos Lee, "Demographic Forecasting and the Easterlin Thesis," *Population and Development Review* 2 (September–December 1976): 467. Richard Easterlin and other economists predicted fertility increase beginning in the 1980s, when children born during the relatively low-birthrate lull in the late 1960s would enjoy good employment prospects and higher incomes. See Richard A. Easterlin, "The Conflict between Aspirations and Resources," *Population and Development Review* 2 (September–December 1976): 417–25; and William P. Butz and Michael P. Ward, "The Emergence of Countercyclical U.S. Fertility," *American Economic Review* 69 (June 1979): 318–28.

31. See Bureau of the Census, "Illustrative Population Projections for the United States: The Demographic Effects of Alternate Paths to Zero Growth," *Current Population Reports*, series P-25, no. 480 (1972). For a less technical treatment of demographic trends in the 1970s, see the two chapters by Norman B. Ryder in Charles F. Westoff et al., *Toward the End of Growth: Population in America* (Englewood Cliffs, N.J.: Prentice-Hall, 1973): chap. 6, "Recent Trends and Group Differences in Fertility," and chap. 8, "The Future Growth of the American Population."

32. Cited in Mauricio Schoijet, "Limits to Growth and the Rise of Catastrophism," *Environmental History* 4 (October 1999): 520.

33. William D. Nordhaus, "Resources as a Constraint on Growth," *American Economic Review* 64 (May 1974): 22.

34. Conversation with Samuelson in Willem L. Oltmans, ed., *On Growth* (New York: Capricorn, 1974), 50. For a defense by the Club of Rome's founder, see the conversation with Aurelio Peccei in this volume, 470–83.

35. Robert Solow, "Is the End of the World at Hand?" in *Economic Growth Controversy*, ed. Weintraub, Schwartz, and Aronson, 47. In "The Economics of Resources or the Resources of Economics," *American Economic Review* 64 (May 1974), Solow noted that "like everyone else," he had been "suckered into reading *The Limits to Growth*" (1).

36. See, for example, Marc J. Roberts, "On Reforming Economic Growth," in *No-Growth Society*, ed. Olson and Landsberg, 119–37.

37. For example, see William D. Nordhaus and James Tobin, "Is Growth Obsolete?" in *Pollution, Resources, and the Environment*, ed. Alain C. Enthoven and A. Myrick Freeman III (New York: W. W. Norton, 1973), 205–11.

38. Richard A. Easterlin, "[Comments on] Thurow and Singer Papers," in *Economic Growth Controversy*, ed. Weintraub, Schwartz, and Aronson, 203.

39. Wilfred Beckerman, *In Defence of Economic Growth* (London: Jonathan Cape, 1974).

40. For example, see Melvin Kranzberg, "Can Technological Progress Continue to Provide for the Future?" in *Economic Growth Controversy*, ed. Weintraub, Schwartz, and Aronson, 74–75.

41. Richard Zeckhauser, "The Risks of Growth," in *No-Growth Society*, ed. Olson and Landsberg, 103–18, quotation on 109.

42. Cited in Garrett Hardin, *The Ostrich Factor: Our Population Myopia* (New York: Oxford University Press, 1999), 14. See Wilfred Beckerman, *Small Is Stupid: Blowing the Whistle on the Greens* (London: Duckworth, 1995).

43. Gerald Feinberg, *Consequences of Growth: The Prospects for a Limitless Future* (New York: Seabury Press, 1977).

44. Julian L. Simon, *A Life Against the Grain: The Autobiography of an Unconventional Economist* (New Brunswick: Transaction, 2003), 237.

45. Julian L. Simon, "Some 'Marketing Correct' Recommendations for Family Planning Campaigns," *Demography* 5, no. 1 (1968): 504–7.

46. Simon, *A Life Against the Grain*, 242–43.

47. For revisionism, see Hodgson, "Orthodoxy and Revisionism in American Demography."

48. His pathbreaking work was Julian L. Simon, *The Economics of Population Growth* (Princeton: Princeton University Press, 1977).

49. See the summary on the Center for Conservation Biology's web page: www.stanford.edu/group/CCB/Pubs/Ecofablesdocs/thebet.htm. Short-term price trends, regardless of direction, hardly prove or disprove the presence of population problems. As the Russian economist N. D. Kondratieff demonstrated early in

the twentieth century (and as Simon conceded), raw material prices follow long-term cycles. Interestingly, the waxing and waning of Malthusian ideas seem to roughly follow these Kondratieff swings. See Rostow, *Great Population Spike*, chap. 4.

50. Simon, *A Life Against the Grain*, 249. It is true the population movement tended to think only about the short-term consequences of population growth in the developing world (and reacted to a burst of high birthrates that likely will never be repeated). However, population optimists are guilty of the same myopia. Today, they worry about the fiscal consequences of the Baby Boomers' retirement in the next generation but rarely pause to consider the significant additional growth expected in the American population in the next century.

51. Julian L. Simon, *The Ultimate Resource* (Princeton: Princeton University Press, 1981).

52. The letter from Hayek to Simon, March 22, 1981, is reprinted in Simon, *A Life Against the Grain*, 268.

53. For Reagan and population, see Robertson, *Malthusian Moment*, chap. 9.

54. Julian L. Simon and Herman Kahn, eds., *The Resourceful Earth: A Response to Global 2000* (New York: Basil Blackwell, 1984).

55. George Gilder, *Wealth and Poverty* (New York: Basic Books, 1981), 268.

56. Central Intelligence Agency, Directorate of Intelligence, Office of Political Research, "Potential Implications of Trends in World Population, Food Production, and Climate," August 1974, chap. 4. Also see Jack Parsons, *Population Fallacies* (London: Elek/Pemberton, 1977), 35.

57. Simon and Kahn, *Resourceful Earth*, includes a chapter on global climate change addressing the then-nascent science (chap. 10, "Global Climate Trends," by H. E. Landsberg).

58. For more on the idea of ZNED, see Barry R. Chiswisk, "[Comments on] Thurow and Singer Papers," in *Economic Growth Controversy*, ed. Weintraub, Schwartz, and Aronson, 194–99. Even John Holdren, one of Paul Ehrlich's co-authors, suggested, "Economic growth itself can be channeled into sectors in which resource consumption and environmental impact per dollar of GNP are minimized" (Holdren, "Population and the American Predicament," 38).

59. The progress of market-knows-best demography was evident in Joseph Spengler's friendly foreword to Simon, *Economics of Population Growth*. The life-long Malthusian neither agreed nor disagreed with Simon's extreme populationism in suggesting the book "advances what may be treated as a new paradigm in the Kuhnian sense" (xxix).

60. For example, see Allen C. Kelley, "The Role of Population in Models of Economic Growth," *American Economic Review* 64 (May 1974): 40. When population growth is endogenous, the logic proceeds, it is likely to decline in response to the poor economic conditions it helps create. See also the discussion of postwar growth theory in chap. 4 of the present study.

61. Norman Ryder, "Two Cheers for ZPG," 52–53. Also see Norman Ryder, "Notes on Stationary Populations," *Population Index* 41 (January 1975): 3–28.

62. For the decline of Keynesianism, see Michael A. Bernstein, *A Perilous Progress: Economists and Public Purpose in Twentieth-Century America* (Princeton: Princeton University Press, 2001), chap. 6.

63. See Jay W. Forrester, "An Alternate Approach to Economic Policy: Macrobehavior from Microstructure," in *Economic Issues of the Eighties*, ed. Nake M. Kamrany and Richard H. Day (Baltimore: Johns Hopkins University Press, 1979), 103.

64. Collins, *More*, 152. For a quick contemporary overview of the new skepticism, see Leonard Silk, "The 'Secular Slowdown' Thesis," *New York Times*, October 21, 1976.

65. Consult William J. Serow and Thomas J. Espenshade, "The Economics of Declining Population Growth: An Assessment of the Current Literature," in *Economic Consequences of Slowing Population Growth*, ed. Espenshade and Serow, 13–40. As in the 1930s, the birthrate was just one of many perceived causes of the new stagnation. The perceived lack of new lands to develop was no longer a major issue, but anxiety about the waning of technological advances remained in the form of a contentious discussion about slowing productivity growth and scientific discovery. See Mark Perlman, "One Man's Baedeker to Productivity Growth Discussion," in *Contemporary Economic Problems, 1979*, ed. William Fellner (Washington, D.C.: American Enterprise Institute, 1979), 79–113.

66. Clarence L. Barber, "On the Origins of the Great Depression," *Southern Economic Journal* 44 (January 1978): 432–56. Also see Serow and Espenshade, "Economics of Declining Population Growth," 19.

67. Neal, "Is Secular Stagnation Just around the Corner?" 102.

68. Ibid., 104.

69. This position was richly ironic, given that Keynes's first conservative opponents had scoffed at the assertion that demographic trends helped cause the Great Depression.

70. James A. Weber, *Grow or Die!* (New Rochelle, N.Y.: Arlington House Publishers, 1977), 35–36.

71. Weber updated these views in "Let's Hear It for Population Growth!" *Human Life Review* 31 (Winter 2005): 5–16.

72. A good place to gauge conservative views on population and the economy in the late 1970s is John Kendrick, "Productivity Trends and the Recent Slowdown," in *Contemporary Economic Problems, 1979*, ed. Fellner, 48–51.

73. Joseph J. Spengler, *Declining Population Growth Revisited* (Chapel Hill: Carolina Population Center, 1971).

74. Joseph Spengler, "Introduction," in *Zero Population Growth: Implications* (Chapel Hill: Carolina Population Center, 1975), 15. As in the 1930s, Spengler admitted that adjusting to a zero-growth society would prove a challenge. In "Prospective Population Change and Price Level Tendencies," *Southern Economic*

Journal 38 (April 1972): 459–67, he suggested that a stationary population might induce inflation.

75. See, for example, Robert W. Resek and Frederick Siegel, "Population Growth Rates and Consumption Demand," *Eastern Economic Journal* 1 (October 1974): 282–90.

76. Ryder, "Two Cheers for ZPG," 53.

77. See Alan R. Sweezy and Aaron Owens, "The Impact of Population Growth on Employment," *American Economic Review* 64 (May 1974): 45–50. Michael L. Wachter and Susan M. Wachter, "The Fiscal Policy Dilemma: Cyclical Swings Dominated by Supply-Side Constraints," in *Economic Consequences of Slowing Population Growth*, ed. Espenshade and Serow, 75, declared: "Regardless of the percentage of the population that is in the labor force, the economy can fluctuate around the equilibrium unemployment rate." See also Ronald G. Ridker, "The Effects of Slowing Population Growth on Long-Run Economic Growth in the United States during the Next Half Century," in *Economic Consequences of Slowing Population Growth*, ed. Espenshade and Serow, 155.

78. Richard A. Easterlin, *Growth Triumphant: The Twenty-first Century in Historical Perspective* (Ann Arbor: University of Michigan Press, 1996), 117.

79. See Peter H. Lindert, *Fertility and Scarcity in America* (Princeton: Princeton University Press, 1978). For the real estate argument, see Overbeek, *Population Challenge*, 74.

80. There was little empirical research into the distributional implications of zero population growth, though one study predicted that it would not significantly affect income inequality. See Serow and Espenshade, "Economics of Declining Population Growth," 34–35.

81. Cited in Zeckhauser, "Risks of Growth," 109.

82. Lester Thurow, "Zero Economic Growth and the Distribution of Income," in *Economic Growth Controversy*, ed. Weintraub, Schwartz, and Aronson, 141–53. This phrase anticipated Thurow's best-known work: *The Zero-Sum Society: Distribution and the Possibilities for Economic Change* (New York: Basic Books, 1980). Similarly, Anthony Crosland, a well-known British socialist, complained that the wealthy proponents of the no-growth scenario wanted to "kick the ladder down behind them" (cited in Willard R. Johnson, "Should the Poor Buy No Growth?" in *No-Growth Society*, ed. Olson and Landsberg, 165).

83. Mancur Olson, "Introduction," in *No-Growth Society*, ed. Olson and Landsberg, 7.

84. Johnson, "Should the Poor Buy No Growth?"

85. Quoted in "A Dialog on the Issues," in *Economic Growth Controversy*, ed. Weintraub, Schwartz, and Aronson, 217.

86. Kenneth E. Boulding, "The Shadow of the Stationary State," in *No-Growth Society*, ed. Olson and Landsberg, 95.

87. Roberts, "On Reforming Economic Growth," 132.

88. See Sauvy's comments in Teitelbaum and Winter, *Fear of Population Decline*, 121. Sauvy was a founding member of the (French) Association for a Demographic Renaissance, created in 1976 to promote population growth.

89. Paul Samuelson, "An Exact Consumption Loan Model of Interest with or without the Social Contrivance of Money," *Journal of Political Economy* 66 (December 1958): 467–82.

90. Henry Aaron, "The Social Insurance Paradox," *Canadian Journal of Economics and Political Science* 32 (August 1966): 371–74.

91. For intergenerational conflict, see Anne Foner, "Age Stratification and Age Conflict in Political Life," *American Sociological Review* 39 (April 1974): 187–96; and Leonard D. Cain, "The Young and the Old: Coalition or Conflict Ahead?" *American Behavioral Scientist* 19 (November–December 1975): 166–75.

92. See Alfred M. Pitts, "Social Security and Aging Populations," in *Economic Consequences of Slowing Population Growth*, ed. Espenshade and Serow, 187. Also see Joseph Pechman, Henry Aaron, and Michael Taussig, "The Objectives of Social Security," in *Old Age Income Assistance* (Washington, D.C.: Joint Economic Committee, 1967); and Philip Cagan, *The Effect of Pension Plans on Aggregate Saving: Evidence from a Sample Survey* (New York: National Bureau of Economic Research, 1965).

93. National Commission on Fiscal Responsibility and Reform, "Moment of Truth," 48.

94. For the growing political power of the elderly in twentieth-century America, see Henry J. Pratt, "National Interest Groups among the Elderly: Consolidation and Constraint," in *Aging and Public Policy: The Politics of Growing Old in America*, ed. William P. Browne and Laura Katz Olson (Westport, Conn.: Greenwood, 1983). The retirement age steadily decreased in the twentieth century, and, according to most accounts, Baby Boomers feel entitled to retirements of unprecedented length.

95. One study suggests that even after the Great Recession threw the federal budget into disarray—and after forty years of conservative ascendancy—young Americans remain committed to sustaining a public retirement system (Andrea Louise Campbell, "Is the Economic Crisis Driving Wedges between Young and Old? Rich and Poor? *Generations* 33 [Fall 2009]: 47–53).

96. For the macroeconomic debates surrounding population aging, see Clark and Spengler, *Economics of Individual and Population Aging*.

97. Mullan, *Imaginary Time Bomb*, 208.

98. Whereas many demographers worried about the aggregate effects of an aging population on productivity and innovation, labor economists tended to focus on the skills of the individual worker and thus see elderly workers in a more positive light. For more recent statements, see Peter Cappelli and Bill Novelli, *Managing the Older Worker: How to Prepare for the New Organizational Order* (Cambridge, Mass: Harvard Business Press, 2010); and Richard Disney, *Can We Afford to Grow Older? A Perspective on the Economics of Aging* (Cambridge, Mass: MIT

Press, 1996), chap. 6. For optimistic discussions of the health of the elderly, see "The Planet is Ever Greyer; But as Longevity Rises Faster than Forecast, the Elderly are also Becoming Healthier," *Financial Times*, January 19, 2004; and Thomas T. Perls, "The Oldest Old," *Scientific American*, January 1995, 70–75.

99. Mullan, *Imaginary Time Bomb*, 120. Optimists also claim that the dependency ratio is a crude measure that lumps the unemployed, early retirees, and students in with productive workers.

100. Harold L. Sheppard and Sarah E. Rix, *The Graying of Working America: The Coming Crisis in Retirement-Age Policy* (New York: Free Press, 1977), cite economist Robert Clark's estimate that elderly dependents were three times as expensive for society as young ones (24). Kotlikoff and Burns, *Coming Generational Storm*, estimate that, in 1995, the federal government spent $1,693 per child under 18 and $15,636 per person over 65 (12). For a dismissal of the "'total dependency' fallacy," see Peterson, *Gray Dawn*, 106–11.

101. The best overview of the no-crisis position is Mullan, *Imaginary Time Bomb*. Kotlikoff and Burns, *Coming Generational Storm*, identify—and reject—several "popular tonics" and "snake oils" through which the aging crisis can allegedly be averted, including technological progress, inheritances from the Baby Boomers, and foreign investment (chap. 4).

102. Martha Derthick, *Policymaking for Social Security* (Washington, D.C.: Brookings Institution, 1979), 383–84.

103. According to many sources, Rep. Wilbur Mills (D-Ark.), the long-time chair of the House Ways and Means Committee, came up with the idea for a substantial increase in benefits because he planned to run for president. See, for example, Edward D. Berkowitz, *America's Welfare State: From Roosevelt to Reagan* (Baltimore: Johns Hopkins University Press, 1991), 70.

104. Pitts, "Social Security and Aging Populations," 163; and Mullan, *Imaginary Time Bomb*, 96. For the effects of the 1970s recession on Social Security's finances, see Carroll L. Estes, "Social Security: The Social Construction of a Crisis," *Milbank Memorial Fund Quarterly* 61 (Summer 1983): 445–61.

105. Derthick, *Policymaking for Social Security*, overviews the social science (387–91).

106. Krugman, "America's Senior Moment." Today the debate centers on the Social Security "trust fund," which President Obama's recent National Commission on Fiscal Responsibility and Reform predicted would be "fully exhausted" in 2037 without reform ("Moment of Truth," 48).

107. Robert Clark, "Increasing Income Transfers to the Elderly Implied by Zero Population Growth," *Review of Social Economy* 35 (April 1977): 53.

108. Nathan Keyfitz, "How Do We Know the Facts of Demography?" *Population and Development Review* 1 (December 1975): 267–88.

109. Nathan Keyfitz, "Individual Mobility in a Stationary Population," *Population Studies* 27 (July 1973): 348.

110. For example, see Timothy D. Hogan, "The Implications of Population Stationarity for the Social Security System," *Social Science Quarterly* 55 (June 1974): 151–58.

111. W. B. Reddaway, "The Economic Consequences of Zero Population Growth," *Lloyds Bank Review*, no. 124 (April 1977): 14–29.

112. Martin Feldstein, "Toward a Reform of Social Security," *Public Interest* 40 (Summer 1975): 75–95, and "Facing the Social Security Crisis," *Public Interest* 47 (Spring 1977): 88–100.

113. See Martin Feldstein, "Social Security, Induced Retirement, and Aggregate Capital Accumulation," *Journal of Political Economy* 82 (September–October 1974): 905–26.

114. For Social Security policy in the 1970s and 1980s, see Berkowitz, *America's Welfare State*, chap. 4.

115. The amendments, Public Law 21, 98th Cong., 1st sess. (April 20, 1983), decoupled Social Security benefits from the Consumer Price Index, in part to correct an overindexing effect stemming from the 1972 Social Security Act.

116. Mullan, *Imaginary Time Bomb*, 96.

117. Keyfitz made this comment at the 1980 meeting of the Population Association of America. For the abstract of his paper, "Demographic Effects on Large-Scale Organizations," see "The 1980 Meeting of the Population Association of America," *Population Index* 46 (Autumn 1980): 437–38.

118. Mullan, *Imaginary Time Bomb*, 96.

119. National Commission on Social Security Reform, *Report of the National Commission on Social Security Reform* (Washington, D.C.: GPO, 1983).

120. For the commission's compromises, see Berkowitz, *America's Welfare State*, 77–80.

121. "The Greenspan View of Social Security, Taxes, Deficits, Recovery," *Christian Science Monitor*, October 3, 1983.

122. Mullan, *Imaginary Time Bomb*, 93.

123. Samuel H. Preston, "Children and the Elderly: Divergent Paths for America's Dependents," *Demography* 21 (November 1984): 435–57.

124. For the debates about savings and consumption over the life cycle, see Karen E. Dynan, Jonathan Skinner, and Stephen P. Zeldes, "Do the Rich Save More?" NBER Working Paper no. 7906 (September 2000). Distinguished economist Franco Modigliani's life-cycle analysis postulated that the elderly dis-saved, but he was frustrated by the ways in which conservatives used his theories. See David Warsh, "Nobel for MIT Economist," *Boston Globe*, October 16, 1985.

125. Conversely, it was no coincidence that some of the last surviving Stable Population Keynesians were among the few who maintained that an aging population is not a serious macroeconomic problem. For example, see Sweezy and Owens, "Impact of Population Growth on Employment."

126. Frank Furedi, "Foreword," in Mullan, *Imaginary Time Bomb*, xi.

127. Julian L. Simon, "More Immigration Can Cut the Deficit," *New York Times*, May 10, 1990.

128. William Petersen, "Population Policy and Age Structure," in *Population Policy Analysis*, ed. Michael E. Kraft and Mark Schneider (Lexington, Mass.: D.C. Heath and Co., 1978), 15. Such comments ignore the possibility that the zero population growth movement contributed to the decline in the birthrate.

129. For example, see Mullan, *Imaginary Time Bomb*, 122–23.

130. Typical examples include Ben J. Wattenberg, *The Birth Dearth* (New York: Pharos, 1987), esp. 97–98; and Patrick J. Buchanan, *The Death of the West: How Dying Populations and Immigrant Invasions Imperil our Country and Civilization* (New York: Thomas Dunne, 2002).

131. Easterlin, *Growth Triumphant*, 127.

132. President Clinton tried to educate the American public about what he saw as the danger of population aging to the future viability of Social Security, and, in the 1990s, calls to privatize Social Security were more prevalent than calls to raise taxes. George W. Bush described Social Security as a ticking demographic time bomb, but his administration's failures, the Great Recession, and the resultant modest uptick in Americans' acceptance of state capacity likely will shelve privatization proposals until Republicans control both Congress and the presidency.

Epilogue

1. John Maynard Keynes, "Preface," in Harold Wright, *Population* (New York: Harcourt, Brace, and Co., 1923), vi–vii.

2. Stephen Moore and Julian L. Simon, "The Greatest Century That Ever Was: 25 Miraculous Trends of the Past 100 Years," *Cato Institute Policy Analysis* no. 364, December 15, 1999, 32.

3. Ansley J. Coale, "Population Change and Demand, Prices, and the Level of Employment," in National Bureau of Economic Research, *Demographic and Economic Change in Developed Countries: A Conference of the Universities-National Bureau Committee for Economic Research* (Princeton: Princeton University Press, 1960), 371.

4. See especially House Select Committee on Population and House Select Committee on Aging, *Consequences of Changing U.S. Population,* 95th Cong., 2d sess., vol. 1, *Demographics of Aging* May 24, 1978, and vol. 2, *Baby Boom and Bust*, May 23 and 25 and June 1 and 2, 1978.

5. Council of Environmental Quality and the Department of State, *The Global 2000 Report of the President* (New York: Penguin, 1982).

6. See Deirdre Wulf and Michael Klitsch, "Population Growth and Economic Development: Two New U.S. Perspectives," *International Family Planning Perspectives* 12 (June 1986): 62.

7. For a discussion of family planning policy during the 1980s and 1990s, see Donald T. Critchlow, *Intended Consequences: Birth Control, Abortion, and the Federal Government in Modern America* (New York: Oxford University Press, 1999), chap. 6.

8. Quoted in *The Reporter* (formerly *ZPG Reporter*), Winter 2005, 6.

9. Ellen Seiter, *Sold Separately: Children and Parents in Consumer Culture* (New Brunswick: Rutgers University Press, 1993).

10. For a defense of beauty, see Elaine Scarry, *On Beauty and Being Just* (Princeton: Princeton University Press, 1999).

Index